AMERICAN LIBRARY ASSOCIATION

BEST OF THE BEST
FOR CHILDREN

AMERICAN·LIBRARY·ASSOCIATION · 1876

AMERICAN LIBRARY ASSOCIATION

BEST OF THE BEST FOR CHILDREN

BOOKS · MAGAZINES · VIDEOS · AUDIO · SOFTWARE
· TOYS · TRAVEL

DENISE PERRY DONAVIN

Editor

RANDOM HOUSE   NEW YORK

Copyright © 1992 by the American Library Association

All rights reserved under International and Pan-American Copyright Conventions. Published in the United States by Random House, Inc., New York, and simultaneously in Canada by Random House of Canada Limited, Toronto.

Library of Congress Cataloging-in-Publication Data

American Library Association best of the best for children: books, software, magazines, videos, audio, toys, travel / Denise Perry Donavin, editor.
    p. cm.
    Includes index.
    ISBN 0-679-40450-3.—ISBN 0-679-74250-6 (pbk.)
    1. Bibliography—Best books—Children's literature. 2. Children's literature—Bibliography. 3. Audio-visual materials—Catalogs. 4. Children—Books and reading. I. Donavin, Denise Perry. II. American Library Association. III. Title: Best of the best for children.
Z1037.A496   1992
[PN1009.A1]
011.62—dc20   92-24234

Designed by M 'N O Production Services, Inc.

Manufactured in the United States of America

First Edition

Products and organizations appear in this guide for informational purposes. Inclusion itself does not imply American Library Association endorsement, nor does omission indicate disapproval.

New York   Toronto   London   Sydney   Auckland

ADVISERS

Julie A. Cummins, Coordinator of Children's Services, New York Public Library

Steven L. Herb, Education Librarian, Pennsylvania State University, University Park, Pennsylvania

Eleanor R. Kulleseid, Director, Bank Street College of Education Library, New York

Mildred C. Lee, Librarian/Consultant, Sonoma County Office of Education, Santa Rosa, California

Isabel Schon, Director, Center for the Study of the Book in Spanish for Children and Adolescents, California State University, San Marcos, California

Jeanette M. Smith, Media Services Director, Forsyth County Day School, Louisville, North Carolina

Deborah D. Taylor, Young Adult Services Specialist, Enoch Pratt Free Library, Baltimore, Maryland

American Library Association Staff Advisers

Barbara Elleman, Editor, *Book Links;* Sally Estes, Books for Youth Editor, *Booklist;* Susan Roman, Executive Director, Association for Library Service to Children; Ann C. Weeks, Executive Director, American Association of School Librarians and Young Adult Library Services Association; Irene Wood, Audiovisual Media Editor, *Booklist*

CONTRIBUTORS

Elizabeth Herbert (infants, preschool); Kathryn Broderick (early grades); Candace Smith (middle grades); Sandy Whitely (reference); Irene Wood (video); Stephanie Zvirin (young adults)

CONSULTANTS

Jan Keller (software); Hazel Rochman (young adult literature); Patty Toht (toys); Joy L. Wilcox (storytelling)

PROJECT EDITORIAL STAFF
(AMERICAN LIBRARY ASSOCIATION)

Edgar S. McLarin, ALA Associate Executive Director, Publishing

Arthur Plotnik, Project Publisher

Denise Perry Donavin, Editor

Kathryn Broderick and **Gerri Taylor,** Editorial Assistants

Martin Brady, Copy Editor

ACKNOWLEDGMENTS

In addition to the advisers, consultants, and contributors named elsewhere, these are some of the "best of the best" people who helped make this projet happen: Sue-Ellen Beauregard, Mary Frances Concepcion, Ilene Cooper, Jill George, Laurie Hartshorn, Ellen Mandel, Nancy McCray, Diane Osmundsen, Carolyn Phelan, Annie Smith, Frances Wallace, staff members of the Elgin, Glen Ellyn, Glenview, Naperville, Villa Park, and Wheaton public libraries in Illinois; staff (especially Sandra Monahu and Gail Posegay) and children of the First Care child center in Glen Ellyn; and the family Donavin: Paul, Daniel, and Craig. Our thanks to all.

BOOKS

MAGAZINES

KidSports: The Official Sports Magazine for Kids. Copyright © 1992 by ProServe Publishing Corporation. Cover photo by Bruce L. Schwartzman.

VIDEOS

Concerto Grosso Modo. Illustration courtesy of the National Film Board of Canada.

Don't Say Yes When You Really Mean No! Copyright © 1990 by Louie Stevens/Magic Music Productions.

Fancy That! Copyright © 1990 by Gemini and Better Communication, Inc.

Frog and Toad Are Friends/Frog and Toad Together. Illustrations courtesy of Churchill Media.

Joe's First Video. Copyright © 1989 by Educational Graphics Press, Inc.

Kids Get Cooking. Courtesy of KIDVIDZ.

Kids' Kitchen. Copyright © 1990 by Lee H. Hascall.

Let's Be Friends. Copyright © 1989 by Tickle Tune Typhoon Productions.

Mufaro's Beautiful Daughters. Illustration copyright © 1987 by John Steptoe. Courtesy of Weston Woods Studios.

The Story of the Dancing Frog. Illustrations courtesy of Italtoons Corporation.

The Teddy Bears' Picnic. Copyright © 1986, 1991 by Rosenshontz, Inc. and WCVB-TV.

The Tender Tale of Cinderella Penguin and Other Stories. Copyright © 1990 by Smarty Pants Audio and Video, Inc.

Turn on the Music. Copyright © 1988 by Heron Communications, Inc.

AUDIO

Can a Cherry Pie Wave Goodbye? Copyright © 1991 by Hap-Pal Music, Inc. Photo of Hap Palmer courtesy of Michael LeRoy.

A Car Full of Songs. Copyright © 1989 by Pax Music.

Cherokee Legends I. Courtesy of Cherokee Publications.

Ghostly Tales from Japan. Photograph of Rafe Martin courtesy of Sam Campanaro.

Jump Tales. Photograph of Jackie Torrence courtesy of Irene Young.

Mozart's Magic Fantasy. Courtesy of The Children's Group, Inc.

Mr. Bach Comes to Call. Courtesy of The Children's Group, Inc.

Peter and the Wolf. Copyright © 1990 by Alacazam!

Stories from the Other Side. Photograph of Dan Keding courtesy of Tandy Lacy.

Traffic Jams. Copyright © 1985 by Education Graphics Press, Inc.

Vivaldi's Ring of Mystery. Courtesy of The Children's Group, Inc.

You'll Sing a Song and I'll Sing a Song. Photograph of Ella Jenkins courtesy of Bernadelle Richter.

SOFTWARE

Children's Writing and Publishing Center. Courtesy of the Learning Company.

Kid Pix. Copyright © 1991 by Broderbund Software, Inc..

Mickey's Jigsaw Puzzles. Copyright © Disney. Courtesy of Walt Disney Computer Software, Inc.

The New Print Shop. Copyright © 1990 by Broderbund Software, Inc.

Where in the World is Carmen Sandiego. Copyright © 1990 by Broderbund Software, Inc.

TOYS AND DOLLS

Clifford. Courtesy of Scholastic, Inc.

Curious George. Courtesy of Gund, Inc., Copyright © 1941, 1990 by Margaret Rey.

Felicity Merriman. Courtesy of Pleasant Company Publications, Inc.

Linnea. Courtesy of Determined Productions, Inc.

Max. Courtesy of Determined Productions, Inc. and Weston Woods.

Madeline. Courtesy of Gund, Inc.

Ramona. Courtesy of Determined Productions.

Snowman. Courtesy of Eden Toys, Inc.

CONTENTS

BEST OF THE BEST FOR CHILDREN

PREFACE

Call it stimulation, development, or even empowerment; we want it for our children and we know it doesn't come from passive diversion. The most stimulating children's "media"—materials to read, see, hear, and interact with—are those that stretch young minds, sharpen senses, and reveal possibilities beyond the child's small world. But how to sort out the best children's media from the multitude of offerings today?

In simpler times, media for children were less a mystery; parents and educators could rely on established brand names, trusted book dealers, and a few major awards to inform their choices. But the vast numbers of baby boomers and their offspring have triggered an avalanche of products for children—and of guides to the "best" of them.

With literally hundreds of guides and "best" lists representing an overwhelming number of items, the consumer now needs another level of advice, one that recommends with care and authority the best of the best for today's children. And that means children of all backgrounds, children of divergent tastes, children who jump from toys to storytelling to books to video to software faster than Mr. Toad "devoured the street and leapt forth on the high road."

The *American Library Association Best of the Best for Children* offers that selection, discerning, yet covering every readiness level from infancy to early teens and reflecting the richness of cultural diversity. It is a guide to some fifteen hundred adventures away from commercial television's worst stupefactions; a guide to fifteen hundred new and wonderful books, magazines, videos, music and story cassettes, computer software programs, toys, and even travel adventures. It is a guide that connects themes and authors across various formats to help children (with their parents, caregivers, and educators) follow paths of interest.

If anyone can identify so exceptional yet varied an assortment of new materials, it's assuredly the children's and media experts of the American Library Association, the world's oldest library organization and, with some 54,000 members, the largest. Each year, to bring learning and delight to the millions of children who use libraries, ALA members and staff handpick the very best items from the tens of thousands produced. They do so based on their training in children's media, everyday experience with kids and parents from all walks of life, exposure to new products, and exchange of views with colleagues on evaluation committees and panels.

These and other activities in children's development are channeled through ALA's three youth organizations. The ALA groups issue their own media lists, many of which are cited in this guide and which form the wellspring, though not the entire range, of our *Best of the Best* offerings. Here's a quick look at the ALA organizations dedicated to youngsters:

- The *Association for Library Service to Children* has long encouraged high-quality materials in all media. Each year it selects winners of the nation's two most prestigious children's book awards: the Newbery Medal for literature (since 1922) and the Caldecott Medal for picture-book art (since 1938). Its annual lists of Notable Children's Books and Notable Children's Films/Videos, Filmstrips, Computer Software, and Recordings are further evaluations involving scores of professional librarians working with children and children's materials.

- The *Young Adult Library Services Association* focuses on youngsters in those difficult "between" and teen years, advocating the right of every "YA" to resources for enrichment and enlightenment. "We're a family," says one association member, "connected by our love of kids and libraries." Selection of materials that click with YAs is one of the group's major programs, resulting in such valued lists as the annual Best Books for Young Adults and Outstanding Books for the College Bound.

- The *American Association of School Librarians* serves the interests of the nearly 50 million students using school libraries in the United States. By providing leadership for school library media specialists and guidelines for the collections and facilities, by integrating the library with the curriculum, the association has helped foster literacy and literature-based learning at all levels of education. Several of the association's members lent expertise to our *Best of the Best* collection.

Numerous other ALA groups, working with these organizations, touch on the interests of children and their media. An annual Coretta Scott King Award recognizes outstanding children's books by black illustrators and authors. ALA's Library Bill of Rights supports every child's freedom to explore the widest range of learning and recreational media. All these interests have guided the selection of materials before you.

Two other key resources at ALA enabled *Best of the Best* to gather up-to-date, expert evaluations of all children's media: ALA's *Booklist,* the library field's most comprehensive reviewing magazine, and *Book Links,* ALA's popular bimonthly guide to literature supporting classroom teaching. The professional librarians who staff both magazines contributed invaluable information, advice, and background for hundreds of selected items.

BEYOND ALA

Though ALA resources give *Best of the Best* a unique advantage, editor Denise Perry Donavin also looked beyond the association's award winners, as she explains in the introduction that follows. Naturally, one could not encompass every group's "best" choices, any more than one could represent unanimity among librarians. There are several centers of expertise in children's books—the Children's Book Council and the Library of Congress among them—and they issue fine materials of their own. ALA's guide has a particular focus, and it pioneers in presenting the widest range of selected new media—including software, toys, and travel ideas.

ALA has its own spirit as well, a belief—call it a missionary zeal—expressed in one former president's theme: "Kids who read succeed." Reading can take many forms; children throughout the nation are reading electronic pages of mixed-media "hypertext." Although printed books have unique values, we know that format can be secondary to content; success grows from the passion to know, a passion stimulated and satisfied by the special content of quality media. We believe you'll find that content in the *Best of the Best for Children*.

—Arthur Plotnik
Project Publisher for the American Library Association

EDITOR'S INTRODUCTION

Look through the children's collections in libraries and bookstores these days and you'll see a great deal more than books. This new guide from the American Library Association reflects the amazing breadth of today's quality offerings for young minds. In selecting, describing, and linking thousands of items, the editors have called upon a network of authorities in books, magazines, videos, music, storytelling, software, science materials, toys, games, and travel experiences for kids from infancy through age 14.

In every section except Travel, the items are divided by age levels: Infants and Toddlers (birth to age 2), Preschoolers (ages 3–5), Early Graders (ages 6–8), Middle Graders (ages 9–11), and Teenagers (ages 12–14). In many cases, the materials can be used well beyond (or below) the designated age levels. For example, a book may appear under Early Graders, yet be fine for readers 6–10. So within each general age category, we have given a suggested age range for each individual item. In two chapters—Magazines and Audio—the Middle Graders and Teenagers material overlapped to such a degree that the two levels were combined.

Selections for this guide have been made by active professionals in children's media. Sound advice and criticism came from librarians, storytellers, computer instructors, day care professionals, schoolteachers, moms and dads, reviewers, travel writers, toymakers, and toy store owners. Books and other resources that have proved helpful are cited at the end of the chapters.

In making our selections, we scrutinized award winners from the past five years in every category. We also evaluated popular titles and productions that might not have won honors but have clearly found a place in children's hearts and minds.

In covering nonprint materials, we are not getting away from the value of reading. Though we value all quality media, we also seek to anchor books more firmly in modern life by linking them to other important learning and recreational experiences. Through the highlighted "Connections" we've provided for video, toys, and travel, users will be drawn back to books—the original source of many of the listed items.

Perhaps the most important connection our guide can help build is the one that families enjoy as they play, read, view, listen, and travel together.

Denise Perry Donavin

Denise Perry Donavin is a writer, reviewer, and parent with a background in librarianship and journalism. In addition to evaluating new publications and interviewing authors for the American Library Association's *Booklist* magazine, she has written for the Chicago *Sun-Times, FamilyStyle* magazine, National Public Radio and Television, and numerous other media. Author of *Aging with Style and Savvy* (ALA), a guide to resources for seniors, she has contributed to *Books, Babies, and Libraries* (ALA) and *From Page to Screen: Children's and Young Adult Books on Film and Video* (Gale). A member of ALA's Association for Library Service to Children, she is a leader in her community (Glen Ellyn, Illinois) of such children's activities as the Junior Great Books Program.

KEY TO AMERICAN LIBRARY ASSOCIATION AWARDS, HONORS, AND LISTS

Among the awards and honors cited for materials in this guide are the following, given by units of the American Library Association. Information on the latest listings, brochures, and other publications for each award may be obtained from the appropriate unit at the American Library Association, 50 E. Huron Street, Chicago, IL 60611; telephone (312) 280-2153.

BBYA (BEST BOOKS FOR YOUNG ADULTS)
Annual selection of books with proven appeal and value to readers from ages 12 to 18. Young Adult Library Services Association (YALSA).

(RANDOLPH) CALDECOTT HONOR BOOK
Exceptional picture books of the year. Association for Library Service to Children (ALSC).

(RANDOLPH) CALDECOTT MEDAL
Best picture book of the year. ALSC.

(ANDREW) CARNEGIE MEDAL
The year's outstanding video production (released in the United States) for children. ALSC.

CORETTA SCOTT KING AWARD
Yearly recognition of a black illustrator and a black author for outstanding inspirational or educational contributions. Social Responsibilities Round Table.

MILDRED L. BATCHELDER AWARD
The year's most outstanding children's book originally published in a foreign language in a foreign country. ALSC.

(JOHN) NEWBERY HONOR BOOK
One of the year's exceptional works of literature for children published in the United States. ALSC.

(JOHN) NEWBERY MEDAL
>The year's most distinguished work of literature for children published in the United States. ALSC.

NOTABLE CHILDREN'S BOOKS, FILMS, VIDEOS, COMPUTER SOFTWARE, AND RECORDINGS
>Yearly selections of outstanding materials in these formats. ALSC.

NOTHIN' BUT THE BEST
>Selected titles of 1968–88 for young adults. YALSA.

AMERICAN LIBRARY ASSOCIATION

BEST OF THE BEST
FOR CHILDREN

1

Books

INTRODUCTION

Maurice Sendak, author of *Where the Wild Things Are,* once posed and answered a pertinent question: "Why would any one book be good for all children? That's silly. No grown-up book is good for all people."

With Sendak's advice in mind, the compilers of this guide have cast their nets widely in search of books that will touch many children. The primary factor here is quality, of course; but we have definitely valued "kid appeal." Kid appeal is measured every day by front-line librarians. They can tell you (and did tell us) which books kids return to again and again.

Because the classics of children's literature are recorded in other excellent resources (cited at the end of this chapter), the emphasis here is on the newest treasures in children's literature.* The editors have drawn on librarians' and parents' judgments in selecting recent books that will last and have that return-to quality.

If, as Sendak says, no one book will suit every child, how should you isolate the appropriate books for your own young readers from this rich treasury? Our advice: "read" the children first—their interests, reading ability, sense of humor, stage of growth. Go straight to the designated age level. The divisions are basic: Infants and Toddlers (birth to age 2), Preschoolers (ages 3–5), Early Graders (ages 6–8), Middle Graders (ages 9–11), and Teenagers (ages 12–14).

We know adolescence does not end at age 14 (and many of the selections are appropriate

---

* The older book classics, however, are not lost in this guide; a great many are described in other chapters, such as Videos, because they form the basis for new media productions. So that none of these book classics are overlooked, we've identified each one in this chapter, but without the descriptive matter. Instead, we cross-reference to the page where the description may be found. Some classics are now "out of print" (o.p.), meaning that the title is more likely to be found in a library than a bookstore. The author and title indexes in this guide will also lead to new versions of favorite classics.

DON'T MISS THE OLDER CLASSICS

Because numerous guides describe older classics for children, this chapter limits itself to the best of the new and recent books. However, many older favorites are treated in other chapters, such as Videos, when the books have formed the basis for a new production. To locate such treatments, just follow the "see" references after the book titles in this chapter. You'll find scores of new ways to return children to the enduring classics or to lead them there for the first time.

---

through ages 16 and 17), but at this stage, many young adults are caught up in teen-appealing adult literature. We have kept our focus on material published for youth.

We encourage you to move freely among these sections, since many books transcend age and reading levels. Starting in Middle Grades, we separate fiction from nonfiction. Frequently, we present a group of books on a special topic (Sex Education) or genres (Fractured Fairy Tales) to help match materials to interests, needs, moods, and special programs.

There are so many series in today's publishing world that once a child is hooked on an idea or style of book, it is easy to find more of the same. That's fine. Still, keep "reading" the child and scouting for new books. This can be an adventure in itself, like panning for gold. When you hit a lode, the rewards are immeasurable. For advice on how to select books, try Betsy Hearne's *Choosing Books for Children* (cited in Resources section at the end of this chapter).

Parents will gain as much as their kids by reading through these entertaining, intriguing stories and works of nonfiction. For special insight and pleasure, read them as a family.

HOW TO USE THIS CHAPTER

The books in this section are either annotated with descriptions of plot and style, or they are simply listed with an "imprint" citing publisher and price. The books with no annotations are usually older classics and are described elsewhere, for example, as the plot of a video based on the book (see footnote.) Everything is cross-referenced.

Each imprint lists the title, author and/or illustrator, date of initial publication, publisher of available edition, and price as of late 1991. Price information, though subject to change, is given to indicate the general affordability of each item and for comparing costs. If a paperback is available as well as a hardcover, the paperback publisher and price are also mentioned. Many of the hardcover-only titles mentioned here will be in paperback when you read this. Check your library or bookstore for paperback availability.

Once more, because it's so important, we remind you to consider age-level categories as a first rough sort in finding the best materials for your children. Kids continue to defy categorization—and amen to that!

INFANTS AND TODDLERS

All Fall Down
Clap Hands
Say Goodnight
Tickle, Tickle
by Helen Oxenbury
(Ages Infant–2)
1987. Aladdin, $4.95 each.

If you are familiar with the author's many other board books, these more recent works will please and surprise you. Their large format is a change from the earlier size. Another change is in the art. Don't worry, Oxenbury's signature pie-faced babies are still present. This time these infants appear in a rainbow of ethnic backgrounds as they sing, run, bounce, and finally tumble in *All Fall Down*. The titles serve as springboards to a jolly riot of activity that will be fun to share with enthusiastic toddlers. Also be sure to take a look at Oxenbury's storybooks, like *Eating Out* (1983), and her Pippo series starring a toddler named Tom and his toy monkey. These tales are a regular item in *Ladybug* magazine (see p. 133).

Awards: Notable Children's Book 1987

Baby around the Clock
by Guusje Slegers
(Ages Infant–18 months)
1987. Barron's, $1.95.

A wordless concertina-style book guaranteed to sit nicely in a crib or on a highchair and entertain a very young audience. The plump, blond-tufted infant seen on each of the 12 panel-pages goes through a day's routines: eating, sleeping, bathing, counting toes, playing blocks, and dozing off. Simplicity itself, this book is just right anytime of the day.

The Baby's Good Morning Book
by Kay Chorao
(Ages 2–5)
1986. Dutton, $11.95.

Soft-toned illustrations of kissable children set the mood for the poems, songs, and rhymes in this collection. Verses by Robert Louis Stevenson, A. A. Milne, and Emily Dickinson as well as familiar Mother Goose rhymes make for an irresistible compilation perfect for before bed or greeting the day. Along with *The Baby's Bedtime Book* and *The Baby's Lap Book,* this title has been adapted into a charming video (see p. 149). Chorao's *The Baby's Christmas Treasury* is also highly recommended.

Baby's World: A First Catalog
by Stephen Shott
(Ages 1–3)
1990. Dutton, $13.95.

Crisp photographs invite toddlers to pore over them and point out with delight the many items of their world that they recognize. Organized under headings, such as "My Clothes," "Eating and Drinking," "Pets," and "In the Bath," the depicted objects are usually set into artful arrangements on a blank background. Other stills show items being used by one or more contented toddlers. A one-of-a-kind book for little ones.

Bear and Mrs. Duck
by Elizabeth Winthrop
(Ages 2–5)
Illustrated by Patience Brewster.
1988. Holiday House, $13.95.

A common childhood fear is put to rest in this story about little Bear and his first time left alone with Mrs. Duck, the babysitter. Slow to welcome the caregiver at first, Bear soon warms to her amusing activities. Yet when the bear's owner Nora returns, Bear greets her with open arms. Bright primary colors accent the delicate watercolors.

Becca Backward, Becca Frontward: A Book of Concept Pairs
by Bruce McMillan
(Ages 2–4)
1986. Lothrop, $11.75.

In crisp photographs, blond Becca poses to illustrate opposites. With cartons of glistening red raspberries and one of blackberries, she demonstrates *same* and *different.* Or Becca fills, then drinks a glass of milk to define the words *full* and *empty.* Preschoolers will catch on quickly and soon will be devising lots of concept pairs on their own.

Bend and Stretch
Making Friends
Mom's Home
This Little Nose
by Jan Ormerod
(Ages 1–2)
1987. Lothrop, $5.95 each.

Slices of everyday life for a little one, his pregnant mother, and his black cat are examined in these picture books. Imitating mom's prenatal exercises, creating a handmade doll, exploring the shopping basket are some of the familiar activities depicted here that youngsters will relate to, while adults will chuckle at these all-too-true snapshots of life at home.

Awards: Notable Children's Book 1987

Color Farm
by Lois Ehlert
(Ages 1–5)
1990. HarperCollins/Lippincott, $12.95.

As she did in her *Color Zoo,* Ehlert ingeniously uses bold-colored art and geometric cutouts to create stylized animal faces. Every fourth page reviews the basic shapes, and the entire barnyard goes on parade in the final visual.

Subtly, Ehlert offers lessons on drawing as well as on shapes.

Awards: Caldecott Honor Book 1990

Corduroy

by Donald Freeman
(See Videos.)
1968. Viking, $13.95; Puffin, paper, $3.95.

Fast-Slow, High-Low:
A Book of Opposites

by Peter Spier
(Ages 1–5)
1972 (1988, rev. ed.). Doubleday, $5.95.

A smorgasbord of items to compare and contrast served up by well-known author/illustrator Speir, acclaimed for his version of Noah's Ark (see Videos). This board book features headlined pages—for example, "Big-Small"—decorated with toy boat and ocean liner, pup tent and circus big top, small town and metropolis, and so on. Kids will love studying the detailed, lighthearted visuals that contain many references to their everyday lives.

The First Snowfall

by Anne and Harlow Rockwell
(Ages 2–4)
1987. Macmillan, $12.95.

After a big snowfall, a little girl describes the clothing she dons to play outside. As she introduces the shovel she uses to clear a path, the snowball she makes to start a snowman, the sled she takes to the park, and the cocoa she drinks to warm her, we see her antics in the snow in easy-to-view visuals that match the eloquent narrative. The Rockwells have created many other excellent books for children, such as, *My Dentist* and *In Our House.*

Flying

by Donald Crews
(Ages 1–3)
1986. Greenwillow, $11.75.

Bold blocks of color form airplanes in the futuristic airbrushed paintings of this picture book, while brief captions outline the story of an airplane ride. Text and illustrations are quite similar to those in Crews's well-known books, *Freight Train* and *Truck.* Look for the author's other books on visual subjects guaranteed to fascinate toddlers.

I Hear
I See
I Touch

by Rachel Isadora
(Ages 6 months–3)
1985 (1991, rev. ed.). Greenwillow, $6.95.

The familiar sounds of birds chirping outside and of Mommy's and Daddy's footsteps are some of the everyday noises that the first of these three picture books explores. In soft, impressionistic paintings, the daily activities of a small child are depicted and then verbalized with appropriate early language. In like fashion, *I See* captures the teddy bear, stroller, and other important objects in a toddler's life. *I Touch* focuses on tactile sensations: the soft teddy bear, a hot coffee cup ("Don't touch!"), and a sticky lollipop. Perfect first books for sharing at bedtime or exploring alone in the crib at dawn.

Jesse Bear, What Will You Wear?
by Nancy White Carlstrom
(Ages 2–4)

Illustrated by Bruce Degen.
1986. Macmillan, $11.95.

He happens to be an adorable, cuddly bear, but otherwise Jesse is a normal active preschooler. Rhymes about the cub's daily routine—dressing, lunchtime, and bedtime—spotlight the cub's activities. Complementing the warm mood are colorful pictures that take a bemused look at family life. Look for other books about Jesse by this author.

Mary Had a Little Lamb
by Sarah Josepha Hale
(Ages 1–6)

Illustrated by Bruce McMillan.
1990. Scholastic, $12.95.

McMillan's large color photographs transform this old verse into something new. His "Mary" is a black schoolgirl with eyeglasses and bright yellow overalls; her lamb is a frolicsome creature who does indeed follow her to school. Mary is seen caring for and playing with her favorite pet throughout. McMillan closes with a note about the nineteenth-century author of this verse and a lesson from an 1857 McGuffey's reader.

Max's Christmas
by Rosemary Wells
(Ages 3–7)
1986. Dutton, $7.95.

Full-color washes are added to line drawings to form the illustrations of mischievous rabbit Max and his older sister Ruby, already well known from hits like *Max's Breakfast* and *Max's Birthday*. Here, the younger bunny stays up to see Santa and actually encounters the jolly old elf, much to his sister's dismay. Not just a holiday book, this tale will be a good choice for new readers anytime.

Awards: Notable Children's Book 1986

Moo, Baa, La La La
by Sandra Boynton
(Ages 1–3)
1982. Simon & Schuster, $3.50.

The animal sounds set to silly rhymes will have toddlers in stitches. Funny pigs who say "la la la" plus googly-eyed beasts make a winning board book. Don't stop here either; Boynton has authored several other board books. Some teach concepts such as opposites, while others have jaunty verses that beg to be recited again and again.

"More More More" Said the Baby:
3 Love Stories
by Vera B. Williams
(Ages 2–4)
1991. Greenwillow, $12.95.

Captured here in disarming, spare descriptions and playful pictures are the ecstatic moments that parents and grandparents share with babies. From games of toss-and-catch to toe-kissing tickles, the little ones respond with cries of, "More. More. More." An endearing reminder of the joy babies bring.

Awards: Caldecott Honor Book 1991; Notable Children's Book 1991

Mouse Paint
by Ellen Stoll Walsh
(Ages 2–6)
1989. HBJ, $10.95.

Three white mice live safely on a piece of white paper where the cat can't find them. One day they find some blue, yellow, and red paint and start experimenting. Their antics provide just the means to introduce ideas about primary colors and color mixing. A delightful art lesson. Don't overlook *Mouse Count* (a 1992 Notable) by the same author.

My Five Senses
by Aliki
(Ages 2–5)
1989. Crowell, $12.89.

Part of the terrific Let's-Read-and-Find-Out-Science series, this book introduces the five senses by portraying a wide-eyed boy interacting with his environment. Aliki's description of how the child uses a combination of his senses to play with his puppy and bounce a ball will fascinate kids. Aliki has created many other nonfiction books as well as numerous picture books.

The Owl and the Pussycat
by Edward Lear
(See Poems in Picture Books, p. 28.)

Play Day: A Book of Terse Verse
by Bruce McMillan
(Ages 2–5)
1991. Holiday House, $14.95.

Combine two one-syllable words that rhyme, like *blue/shoe* or *duck/truck,* and you have a "terse verse." This phenomenon, first seen in McMillan's *One Sun,* in which kids explore the seashore, is engagingly reprised here. This time, five two-year-olds are photographed playing in a yard. Their antics, revolving around gear well known to the preschool set, will intrigue young poets-to-be and establish

terse-versing as a popular impromptu pastime in many households.

Pumpkin, Pumpkin
by Jeanne Titherington
(Ages 2–6)
1986. Greenwillow, $11.75.

The cyclical nature of life has never been so eloquently or lovingly expressed as in this look at a boy's cultivation of a pumpkin plant, from sowing to storing seeds for next spring. The misty color-pencil illustrations capture details of a garden throughout the summer growing season. The young hero's obvious joy in his tasks will inspire novice gardeners to ask, "Can we do that, too?"

Awards: Notable Children's Book 1991

Tail Toes Eyes Ears Nose
by Marilee Robin Burton
(Ages 2–5)
1989. HarperCollins, $15.95.

A child sees the items of the title in the correct position on a yellow page, but the body is invisible; so the reader must guess which animal belongs in the picture. Burton's bright drawings lend personality to every feature of every mouse, elephant, horse, and other depicted animal. Most fun of all are the mixed-up pages at the end, full of all tails or toes.

Tomie dePaola's Mother Goose
(Ages 2–6)
1985. Putnam, $17.95.

Going back to classic versions of more than 200 nursery rhymes collected by scholars Iona and Peter Opie, artist-author Tomie dePaola has compiled a Mother Goose volume that both children and adults will enjoy. Accompanying the rhymes are colorful paintings done in the inimitable dePaola style. Look for *Strega Nona* (see p. 26 or Videos) and other dePaola books.

The Very Busy Spider
by Eric Carle
(Ages 2–5)
1985. Philomel, $18.95; miniature version, $5.95.

Charming pictures of an industrious spider and the barnyard animals that try to distract her from weaving her web. This simple story, by the creator of *The Very Hungry Caterpillar*, features attractive, textured artwork that begs to be touched. Available in two book sizes.

What Game Shall We Play?
by Pat Hutchins
(Ages 2–4)
1990. Greenwillow, $12.95.

Frog and Duck can't decide what game to play, so they search out their friends to gather ideas. After the pair looks high and low for each animal, the wise owl advises them that "Hide and Seek" would be the best game of all. Vivid watercolors that create the texture of fur and feathers are outlined in bold black ink, making the pictures of the characters, first seen in Hutchin's *Surprise Party*, come to life. Hutchins is also the author of *Happy Birthday, Sam* and many other books.

Who Said Red?
by Mary Serfozo
(Ages 2–5)
Illustrated by Keiko Narahashi.
1988. McElderry, $12.95.

Exuberant double-page spreads depict a small boy's search for his lost red kite, aided by his big sister. As older siblings will, she teases her brother as she points out the colors along their path. Refreshing illustrations make this a distinctive picture book about colors. The siblings share an equally entertaining exchange in a book about numbers, *Who Wants One?*

Yellow Ball
by Molly Bang
(Ages 2–6)
1991. Morrow, $12.95.

Told with a minimum of text, this unusual book follows a beach ball forgotten by a small boy. The toy drifts away with the ocean tide and ultimately washes up on a distant shore where another boy happily finds it. Enticing pastels and tempera in well-crafted compositions create riveting scenes of the marine landscape. Bang is the author of many splendid books for the young, including the Caldecott Honor Book, *Ten, Nine, Eight*.

You Push, I Ride
by Abby Levine
(Ages 2–4)
Illustrated by Margot Apple.
1989. Whitman, $12.95.

An adorable baby pig and his loving parents star in this litany of a preschooler's day at home. Such charming touches as corncob-decorated bedposts and the pig's wizard cap highlight the ebullient pictures, while clever singsong rhymes serve as captions.

PRESCHOOLERS

Aardvarks, Disembark
by Ann Jonas
(See ABCs, p. 12.)

Alexander and the Terrible, Horrible, No Good, Very Bad Day
by Judith Viorst
(See *Alexander, Who Used to Be Rich Last Sunday* in Videos.)
Illustrated by Ray Cruz.
1972. Atheneum, $12.95; Aladdin, paper, $3.95.

All Night, All Day: A Child's First Book of African-American Spirituals
Edited and illustrated by Ashley Bryan
(Ages 3–8)
Music arranged by David M. Thomas.
1991. Atheneum, $14.95.

Glorious double-page paintings illuminate the verses and musical notations of 20 spirituals with themes such as angels, stars, bells, trains, heaven, and earth. Seven of the songs are drawn from Bryan's earlier books, including *What a Morning!,* but the art is more stylized here, with a flatness suggestive of stained-glass windows.

Awards: Coretta Scott King Honor Book 1992

The Amazing Bone
by William Steig
(See Videos.)
1976. Farrar, Straus & Giroux, $14.95; paper, $3.95.

Awards: Caldecott Honor Book 1977; Reading Rainbow selection

Angus Lost
by Marjorie Flack
(See Videos.)
1932. Doubleday, $12.95.

Annabelle Swift, Kindergartner
by Amy Schwartz
(Ages 4–7)
1988. Orchard Books, $12.95.

When Annabelle puts big sister Lucy's lessons on school etiquette into practice the first day of kindergarten, her classmates ridicule her for labeling the color red "Raving Scarlet" (as her sister taught her) and for announcing her name as "Annabelle Swift, Kindergartner." But even Annabelle's displeased teacher is impressed when she can count way past 100 at milk-money time. Annabelle is duly appointed milk monitor and sent to deliver the

ABCs

Aardvarks, Disembark by Ann Jonas   (Ages 3–8)   1990. Greenwillow, $14.95.

When the rains finally stop and the water recedes, Noah opens the door to the ark and says, "Aardvarks, disembark!" Thus begins a parade of animals whose unusual names make an alphabetical catalog of endangered and extinct beasts. At first trudging through mountaintop snow very far away, the animal pairs march right up to readers in dramatic closeup. A list of creatures concludes this unique and purposeful selection. Jonas has done other equally distinctive books, *Holes and Peeks* and *Reflections,* to name but two.

Alphabatics by Suse MacDonald   (Ages 6–8)   1986. Bradbury, $15.95.

On one page, in a strip of three or four boxes, MacDonald presents a letter of the alphabet, manipulating it into a different position, and adding color and detail to place it in a larger context. On the opposite page she offers a full picture of the object the letter has become or become a part of, in full color, completing her concept: an *A* becomes an ark, and *M* becomes a mustache. This fascinating look at letter forms in primary colors will have children predicting what the letter will turn into, before they search for its shape in the final picture.
Awards: Caldecott Honor Book 1987; Notable Children's Book 1986

Chicka Chicka Boom Boom by Bill Martin and John Archambault   (Ages 4–6)
Illustrated by Lois Ehlert.   1989. Simon & Schuster, $13.95.

Brightly colored, geometric-style figures sizzle with the rhythmic verse in this standout alphabet book. Read this aloud once and kids will be endlessly reciting the catchy rhymes, such as:

> A told B
> and B told C,
> I'll meet you at the top
> of the coconut tree.

What a great way to learn the ABCs. A cassette version read by Ray Charles is also available from Simon & Schuster.
Awards: Notable Children's Book 1990

Eating the Alphabet: Fruits and Vegetables from A to Z by Lois Ehlert   (Ages 3–6)   1989. HBJ, $13.95.

Eating fruits and vegetables to learn the alphabet? If these illustrations of scrumptious foods are any incentive, kids will be doing both by the last page. The fruits and vegetables, ranging from apple to zucchini, are pictured in colorful, eye-catching arrangements—alphabetically, of course. The last few pages list the foods with pronunciations and descriptions that include original growing regions, adding a bit of geography to this appetizing alphabet book.

The Handmade Alphabet by Laura Rankin   (Ages 5–Adult)   1991. Dial, $13.95.

Spelling out the American Sign Language, Rankin's color drawings show a hand performing each sign along with a hand-related pictorial clue to the letter—a gloved hand for G, nail polish for N, and so on. Rankin draws realistic hands representing young and old, white and persons of color. The featured letters appear at page top. High quality and imaginative elements extend its use to art classes and general alphabet learning.

I Can Be the Alphabet by Marinella Bonini   (Ages 4–8)   1986. Viking, $6.95.

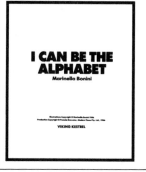

Bonini's unusual, physical approach to learning the ABCs features colorful drawings of leotard-clad children making each letter's shape with their bodies. The book can be strung out as a poster, so it's great for classrooms, bedroom walls, and even birthday parties. A great concertina of a book that will draw immediate reactions from kids.

If There Were Dreams to Sell by Barbara Laliki   (Ages 4–7)   Illustrated by Margot Tomes. 1984. Lothrop, $11.50.

A medley of literature, language, and art enliven the letters of the alphabet. This singular collection draws from works by such giants as Tennyson, Longfellow, Coleridge, and Pope. Dreamy original artwork makes this a perfect poetry volume to share with preschool and primary-grade children.

Pigs from A to Z by Arthur Geisert   (Ages 6–10)   1986. Houghton Mifflin, $15.95.

This ABC puzzle book features Geisert's intricate pen-and-ink drawings of seven piglets on a mission to build a tree house. Each letter of the alphabet receives its own treatment in the context of the tree-house project. But the reader must look carefully because the artist has included in each picture all seven piglets and five formations of the featured letter. He has also tucked into each picture one image of the previous letter and one image of the next letter in the alphabet. The book includes an answer key at the end of the book. The drawings are fantastical and full of interesting perspectives, and all show the ingenious architectural feats of the piglets. The story, told in short sentences on the pages facing the illustrations, uses vocabulary words beginning with the letter in question ("L is for lunchtime. Lower the ladder!").

vast sum of $1.08 to the cafeteria. Children about to cross into the realm of "real school" will be delighted with this lighthearted look at the rites of passage.

Awards: Notable Children's Book 1988

At the Crossroads
by Rachel Isadora
(Ages 3–7)
1991. Greenwillow, $13.95.

The excitement a child feels waiting for an absent parent is ingeniously conveyed in this South African setting. Isadora's intense, full-page watercolors show joyous children who live in tin shacks in a segregated township. A group of these children scrub and dress, wiggle through a day of school, and gather at the crossroads where the bus will drop off their fathers: "For ten months they have been away working in the mines." While they wait, the children start an impromptu band with pebbles in a can and a drum as a welcoming committee. Soon it seems the whole town is dancing and singing at the crossroads: "Our fathers are coming home."

Awards: Notable Children's Book 1992

Beach Ball
by Peter Sis
(Ages 3–8)
1990. Greenwillow, $12.95.

When Mary's beach ball is blown across the beach by the wind, it rushes along the sand in a linear chase sequence that provides page after page of new games. From leading Mary through a maze to locating objects for each letter of the alphabet, the activities in this

mostly wordless picture book will fascinate the *Where's Waldo* crowd.

Awards: Notable Children's Book 1988

The Big Alfie and Annie Rose Storybook
by Shirley Hughes
(Ages 3–6)
1988. Lothrop, $15.

Alfie is a force to be reckoned with—a preschooler with vim and vigor. He enjoys stomping about in new boots, racing home first, playing with his grandma, and teaching his baby sister Annie Rose all sorts of things. From the opening drawing in this oversized book—showing Alfie at the bottom step in his pj's and Annie Rose not far behind climbing down backwards—it's evident that where Alfie goes, Annie Rose follows. (Even down the aisle at a wedding in which Alfie is the ring bearer—and Annie Rose an uninvited participant.) Alfie handles his sister with an aplomb that will warm parents' hearts and cheer on older siblings.

Awards: Notable Children's Book 1990

Bigmama's
by Donald Crews
(Ages 4–7)
1991. Greenwillow, $13.95.

Crews's picture-book memoir of childhood visits to his grandmother's (Bigmama's) house in the country is magically evocative. With watercolor and ink illustrations, Crews conveys the excitement he felt as a child on the long train ride to the annual summertime family reunion.

Block City
by Robert Louis Stevenson
(See Poems in Picture Books, p. 27.)

Blueberries for Sal
by Robert McCloskey
(See *Corduroy* and *The Robert McCloskey Library* in Videos.)
1948. Viking, $13.95; Puffin, paper, $3.95.

Awards: Caldecott Honor Book 1949

A Boy, a Dog, and a Frog
by Mercer Mayer
(See *Frog Goes to Dinner* in Videos.)
1967. Dial, $9.95; paper, $2.95

Burt Dow: Deep Water Man
by Robert McCloskey
(See *The Robert McCloskey Library* in Videos.)
1963. Viking, $15.95.

Bye Bye Baby: A Sad Story with a Happy Ending
by Janet Ahlberg and Allan Ahlberg
(Ages 3–6)
1990. Little, Brown, $12.95.

Though he lives in a little house all by himself—and can even change his own diaper—the sad baby in this absurd and endearing tale sets out to find a mommy. A cat, teddy bear, windup hen, and elderly uncle all decline to fill the post, but they aid his search until, at last, he finds a mom in need of a baby. Only one thing missing now—a daddy, who is located straightaway. This tongue-in-cheek tale adds to the Ahlbergs' popular array of preschool literature: *Each Peach Pear and Plum: An I Spy Story, The Jolly Postman,* and *Peek-A-Boo!* are other winners for tots.

The Caterpillar and the Polliwog
by Jack Kent
(See *Owl Moon and Other Stories* in Videos.)
1982. Simon & Schuster, $12.95; paper, $5.95.

The Chalk Doll
by Charlotte Pomerantz
(Ages 4–8)
Illustrated by Frané Lessac.
1989. Lippincott, $12.95.

Two-dimensional paintings reminiscent of folk art depict Rose with her mother as they talk about the mother's upbringing in Jamaica. Mother recalls how a store-bought doll with white skin seemed unattainable until her aunt brought her one thrown out by the family that employed her. After hearing about her mother's impoverished childhood and the many ways they found inexpensive amusement, Rose longs for similar small pleasures. In the end, daughter and mother set about fashioning a homemade Jamaican rag doll.

Chicka Chicka Boom Boom
by Bill Martin and John Archambault
(See ABCs, p. 13.)

Chicken Little
by Steven Kellogg
(Ages 4–7)
1985. Morrow, $13.00.

A contemporary retelling of the favorite tale features a shady Foxy Loxy wanted by the law. This fox is somewhat of a gourmet, eagerly anticipating the dishes he can prepare from Chicken Little and her cronies, who are heading to the police station to announce that the sky is falling. Foxy tries to outwit the crew with a disguise, but this time luck is on the fowls' side, and the police drop in just in time.

Kellogg's visuals are replete with humorous touches.

Christina Katerina and the Time She Quit the Family
by Patricia Lee Gauch
(Ages 3–8)
Illustrated by Elise Primavera.
1987. Putnam, $12.95.

On a perfectly good Saturday morning, Christina Katerina quits her family and becomes Agnes. She and her mother divide the house and Agnes sets out to do whatever she pleases. For seven days, she eats exactly what she likes and no one says, "Please don't lick your fingers, dear." Just as Agnes is getting a little lonely—but too proud to admit it—Mother comes to the rescue and the girl decides to become Christina again. With droll paintings in rich hues, this story is the stuff of many a child's daydream.

Circles, Triangles and Squares
by Tana Hoban
(See *Colors and Shapes* in Videos.)
1974. Macmillan, $12.95.

Cornelius
by Leo Lionni
(See *Five Lionni Classics* in Videos.)
1983. Pantheon, $13.99.

Counting Wildflowers
by Bruce McMillan
(Ages 2–6)
1986. Lothrop, $11.75.

Luminescent photographs of wildflowers distinguish this counting book. Common American flowers represent the numbers 1 to 20. Below each photograph are shaded-in circles that reinforce the quantity. Flower names are tucked into the corners, and an appended list gives scientific names, growing seasons, and the flowers' typical locales. Here is a beautiful and practical approach to learning numbers.

Awards: Notable Children's Book 1986

A Country Far Away
by Nigel Gray
(See Multicultural Fare, p. 35.)

Creatures of the Desert World
Strange Animals of the Sea
by Barbara Gibson and Jerry Pinkney
(Ages 4–10)
1987. National Geographic, $17.95 (set of two books).

These National Geographic Action Books and other titles in this series feature animal and nature drawings that spring to life every time you turn a page, slide a rock, pull a tab, or turn a wheel. As pop-up books go, these are fairly sturdy, but they should be kept away from reckless hands or the magic will quickly disintegrate. Every page is covered in scenic detail, with no wasted space. In the desert world, a Saguaro cactus rises off the page capped by birds and with snakes, gila monsters, deer, and fox kits resting or wrestling below. In *Strange Animals of the Sea*, full-page kelp plants, movable hammerhead sharks, and shimmery coral gardens spring forth. Scenes in the desert book move naturally from daylight to dusk, while in the sea book progression is from sunny, shallow water to murky depths. Perusing these books over and over is like a treasure hunt; readers are bound to find a creature or plant previously unnoticed.

Curious George Rides a Bike
by H. A. Rey
(See *Doctor Desoto* in Videos.)
1952. Houghton Mifflin, $12.95; paper, $3.95.

Doctor Desoto
by William Steig
(See Videos.)
1982. Farrar, Straus & Giroux, $13.95; paper, $4.95.

Awards: Newbery Honor Book 1983

Dollars and Cents for Harriet
by Betsy Maestro
(Ages 3–6)
Illustrated by Giulio Maestro.
1988. Crown, $12.95.

Neon colors sizzle in this concept book about money. Harriet, the roller-skating elephant, finds she does not have enough pennies to purchase a toy. So she sets about working for her friends, never once asking her unseen parents for the balance. For each task she earns a dollar, delivered first in nickels, then in dimes, quarters, and lastly half dollars. At the bank she changes her coins into paper bills, which like the coins are drawn realistically enough so that preschoolers can recognize the denominations. Then Harriet buys her kite and heads for the park. Other Harriet books—*Harriet Reads Signs and More Signs, Harriet Goes to the Circus,* and *Where Is My Friend?*—cover street signs, ordinal numbers, and spatial relationships.

Do Not Open
by Brinton Turkle
(Ages 4–8)
1981. Dutton, $12.95.

Glorious dark hues enshroud the windswept New England coastal home of the eccentric Miss Moody and her cat, Captain Kidd. After a violent storm, Miss Moody finds a small bottle on the beach that seems to speak to her. When she opens it, a demon appears that can transform itself into horrible creatures. Unafraid of what she does not believe in, Miss Moody cleverly rids herself of the pesky monster and gets her heartfelt wish at the same time. A satisfying fantasy tale for youngsters who believe they have seen a monster or two.

Eating the Alphabet: Fruits and Vegetables from A to Z
by Louis Ehlert
(See ABCs, p. 13.)

Emma's Vacation
by David McPhail
(Ages 2–4)
1987. Dutton, paper, $7.95.

A family of three bears starts off on vacation to relax, but drive too far and do too much. It is only when Emma says "enough" that the family slows down and learns to luxuriate in their time together. Cheery, low-key visuals combine with the book's small, "holdable" size that's perfect for little ones. Emma's fans will be happy to know they can rejoin her in *Fix-it.* When the family's TV breaks, Emma's caring parents try all sorts of distractions, but it is only when Mama Bear reads a book that the little bear is enthralled. By the time Dad fixes the popular appliance, Emma is caught up in her book and is too busy for television. Mc-Phail is the author of many other books, including the Pig Pig series.

Exactly the Opposite
by Tana Hoban
(Ages 3–6)
1990. Greenwillow, $13.95.

Engaging photographs that teach the concept of opposites create a book that will intrigue children on several levels. Like other works by Hoban, this book encourages kids to look at photographs as art. The turquoise hightop sneakers on the jacket draw young readers right into a series of photographs that demonstrate "up" and "down," "open" and "closed," and much more. Each page seems to hold a story of its own, and older readers could use these scenes to develop creative-writing and storytelling skills.

Fish Is Fish
by Leo Lionni
(See *Five Lionni Classics* in Videos.)
1970. Pantheon, $12.99; Knopf, paper, $2.95.

The Five Chinese Brothers
by Claire Bishop
(See *The Mysterious Tadpole* in Videos.)
Illustrated by Kurt Weise.
1938. Coward-McCann, $7.95; paper, $5.95.

Frederick
by Leo Lionni
(See Videos.)
1967. Knopf, $14.95; paper, $2.95.

Awards: Caldecott Honor Book 1968

Frog and Toad Are Friends
by Arnold Lobel
(See Videos.)
1970. HarperCollins, $10.95; paper, $3.50.

Awards: Caldecott Honor Book 1971

Frog and Toad Together
by Arnold Lobel
(See Videos.)
1972. HarperCollins, $10.95; paper, $3.50.

Awards: Newbery Honor Book 1973; Reading Rainbow selection

Frog Goes to Dinner
by Mercer Mayer
(See Videos.)
1974. Dial, $8.95; paper, $2.95.

Frog on his Own
by Mercer Mayer
(See *Frog Goes to Dinner* in Videos.)
1973. Dial, $9.95; paper, $2.95.

Georgie
by Robert Bright
(See *What's under My Bed and Other Creepy Stories* in Videos.)
1944. Doubleday, $7.95; Scholastic, paper, $1.50

Ghost's Hour, Spook's Hour
by Eve Bunting
(Ages 4–7)
Illustrated by Donald Carrick.
1987. Clarion, $12.95.

What if you woke up in the middle of the night and Mom and Dad weren't in their bed? This is what befalls the young hero of this tale, who overcomes his fear of the howling wind, creaking house noises, and a horrifying white blob in the mirror (himself and his pet dog) to locate his reassuring parents. Carrick, who has collaborated with a variety of other authors (see *What Happened to Patrick's Dinosaurs?*, p. 31), capitalizes on unusual perspectives and gloomy colors to evoke the mood of a dark house.

The Gingerbread Boy
Retold and illustrated by Scott Cook
(Ages 3–6)
1987. Knopf, $7.99.

Glowing autumn colors, textured by a dappled effect, infuse this sprightly version of the classic tale. Cook's humor-laced visuals are populated by a bonneted cow, bridled horse, farm folk, and, of course, the suave fox and mischievous Gingerbread Boy. Ready to be read aloud, this book will win children over with its much-loved story and lively art. Also, don't miss Jan Brett's classic version of this title and many other folk and fairy tales.

Goggles
by Ezra Jack Keats
(See Videos.)
1969. Aladdin, paper, $4.50.

Awards: Caldecott Honor Book 1970

Goldilocks and the Three Bears
Retold and illustrated by Jan Brett
(Ages 3–6)
1987. Dodd, $13.95.

In Brett's version of this fairy tale, the home of the three bears is an elaborately embellished cottage. The decorative bric-a-brac and the characters' Nordic costumes add lushness to the distinctive scenes, as do the page borders, which appear to be carved out of wood. Brett's

retelling matches her original visuals in detail well. This delightful book will stand up to repeated scrutiny by inquisitive little eyes. Don't miss *The Mitten* (see p. 23).

Hand Rhymes
by Marc Brown
(See Videos.)
1985. Dutton, $12.95.

Happy Birthday Moon
by Frank Asch
(See Videos.)
1981. Simon & Schuster, $12.95; paper, $4.95.

The Happy Lion
by Louise Fatio
(See Videos.)
Illustrated by Roger Duvoisin.
1954. Scholastic, paper, $3.95.

Hattie and the Fox
by Mem Fox
(Ages 3–5)
Illustrated by Patricia Mullins.
1987. Bradbury, $12.95.

Intriguing collages resembling watercolor paintings depict the story of Hattie, the big black hen. While the goose, pig, and other farm animals are complacent, it is Hattie who sees the eyes, legs, ears, and body of what she suddenly realizes is a fox. When she sounds the alarm, the other creatures finally act to oust the unwelcome intruder. Kids will love the plot and action in this animal tale.

Horton Hears a Who
by Dr. Seuss
(See Videos.)
1954. Random House, $9.95.

Hot Hippo

by Mwenyee Hadithi

(See Videos.)

Illustrated by Adrienne Kennaway.
1986. Little, Brown, $12.95.

House on East Eighty-Eighth Street

by Bernard Waber

(See Videos.)

1973. Houghton Mifflin, $13.95; Sandpiper, paper,
$4.95.

How the Grinch Stole Christmas

by Dr. Seuss

(See Videos.)

1957. Random House, $6.95.

I Can Be the Alphabet

by Marinella Bonini

(See ABCs, p. 13.)

If There Were Dreams to Sell

by Barbara Laliki

(See ABCs, p. 14.)

I Have a Friend

by Keiko Narahashi

(Ages 3–6)

1987. McElderry, $12.95.

What child has not been fascinated by his or
her shadow? This distinctive book celebrates
the shadow's mystery, the elusive quality that
makes it so timeless. Soft watercolor paintings
freeze moments with that ever-changing figure, which the author labels "yesterday's night,
left behind for day." Robert Louis Stevenson's
poem "My Shadow," from *A Child's Garden of
Verses,* is the perfect companion to this dreamy
selection (see Poems in Picture Books, p. 27).

In the Night Kitchen

by Maurice Sendak

(See *The Maurice Sendak Library* in Videos.)

1970. HarperCollins, $14.95; paper, $4.95.

Awards: Caldecott Honor Book 1971

Ira Says Goodbye

by Bernard Waber

(Ages 4–8)

1988. Houghton Mifflin, $13.95.

Ira is devastated because his best friend is
moving away. As he thinks about all the good
times the two have shared, he feels worse. But
Reggie doesn't feel the same; all he can talk
about is how wonderful his new home will be.
Appealing watercolor pictures outlined in
black ink depict a troubled Ira, who tries to
cancel his grief by recalling all the unpleasant
habits his friend has. The book captures an
anxious time for youngsters and brings it to a
satisfying conclusion. Ira can also be seen in
Ira Sleeps Over.

It's Mine

by Leo Lionni

(See *Five Lionni Classics* in Videos.)

1986. Knopf, $14.95.

I Want to Be An Astronaut

by Byron Barton

(Ages 3–5)

1988. Crowell/HarperCollins, $7.95.

Barton's mission is to share a space shuttle
expedition with young dreamers. The bright
colors captivate. The bold, simple drawings do
most of the telling in this book, which has only
five short sentences.

Awards: Notable Children's Book 1988

Jake Baked the Cake
by B. G. Hennessy
(Ages 2–6)
Illustrated by Mary Morgan.
1990. Viking, $12.95.

An upbeat rhyme about the bustling preparations for a wedding repeats the refrain about
Jake and the cake, while brightly colored
paintings depict the shiny-cheeked baker and
busy wedding party all decked out in turn-of-
the-century finery. In this wedding, the baker
and his towering cake are the couple who take
center stage. Another treat is Hennessy's *The
Missing Tarts,* an uproarious retelling of a
traditional nursery rhyme.

John Brown, Rose, and the Midnight Cat
by Jenny Wagner
(See *The Amazing Bone* in Videos.)
Illustrated by Ron Brooks.
1978. Puffin, paper, $3.95.

Jonah and the Great Fish
by Warwick Hutton
(See *The Mysterious Tadpole* in Videos.)
1984. McElderry, $13.95.

Keeping House
by Margaret Mahy
(Ages 3–7)
Illustrated by Wendy Smith.
1981. McElderry, $13.95.

Lizzie Firkin's home is such a mess that she
has to hire a cleaning man to bail herself out.
But in order for him to work, she tidies up for
hours until the place shines. Kids will love the
role reversal and the joke about Lizzie's cleaning, brought to life in sprightly pastel watercolors. They will also welcome the eccentric
Lizzie, who will win them over with her
vitality.

King Bidgood's in the Bathtub
by Audrey Wood
(See Videos.)
Illustrated by Don Wood.
1985. HBJ, $14.95.

Awards: Caldecott Honor Book 1986

Koko's Kitten
by Francine Patterson
(See Videos.)
1985. Scholastic, $9.95; paper, $3.95.

Lentil
by Robert McCloskey
(See Videos.)
1940. Viking, $14.95.

A Letter to Amy
by Ezra Jack Keats
(See *The Pigs' Wedding* in Videos.)
1968. HarperCollins, $13.95; paper, $4.95.

Little Bear's Trousers
by Jane Hissey
(Ages 3–5)
1987. Philomel, $13.95.

Little Bear's mysteriously missing trousers are
finally returned, but not before Camel tries
them as hump warmers, Sailor uses them for
sails, Rabbit dons them as a ski hat, and Bram-
well Brown turns them into an icing bag to
decorate a cake. When the trousers are washed
and returned, the crowd enjoys the cake in
celebration. Vibrant color-pencil and crayon
artwork is seen here and in all of the books
starring Old Bear and his protégé Little Bear

(both of which are actual toys owned by the author).

Madeline
by Ludwig Bemelmans
(See *Madeline's Rescue* in Videos.)
1939. Viking, $13.95; Puffin, paper, $3.95.

Awards: Caldecott Honor Book 1949

Madeline and the Bad Hat
by Ludwig Bemelmans
(See *Madeline's Rescue* in Videos.)
1957. Viking, $13.95; Puffin, paper, $3.95.

Madeline and the Gypsies
by Ludwig Bemelmans
(See *Madeline's Rescue* in Videos.)
1959. Viking, $13.95; Puffin, paper, $3.95.

Madeline's Rescue
by Ludwig Bemelmans
(See Videos.)
1953. Viking, $13.95; Puffin, paper, $3.95.

Awards: Caldecott Medal 1954

Make Way for Ducklings
by Robert McCloskey
(See *The Robert McCloskey Library* in Videos.)
1941. Viking, $12.95; Puffin, paper, $3.95.

Awards: Caldecott Medal 1942

Mama Don't Allow: Starring Miles and the Swamp Band
by Thacher Hurd
(Ages 3–6)
1984. HarperCollins, $11.49.

A bird, lizard, mole, and opossum form the Swamp Band and perform enthusiastically for the home crowd, which recommends the dis-tant swamp as a better stage for the itinerant group. Undaunted, the band moves on to play for the swamp alligators, who love the music and the performers (they look like lunch!). All turns out well in this just-for-fun story, illustrated in broad strokes of color that match its broad humor.

Awards: Reading Rainbow selection

Midnight Farm
by Reeve Lindbergh
(Ages 4–6)
Illustrated by Susan Jeffers.
1987. Dial, $13.95.

In this gentle story, a child's fear of the dark inspires the mother to take her little one on a sunset tour of the house and barnyard. Balancing the evocative counting poem are dramatic scenes in dark evening tones and screenlike crosshatching that depict mother and child viewing the transformation from day to night. Preschoolers harboring similar fears will be soothed by the tender presentation.

The Mitten
by Jan Brett
(Ages 3–6)
1989. Putnam, $14.95.

A boy's lost mitten is transformed into a home for an unbelievable collection of forest animals. In this charming Ukrainian folk tale, birch-bark frames surround the center illustration of each double-page spread. In a border, mitten-shaped windows foreshadow the story line. The crisp snow-white nature scenes meet a lovely contrast in the lush colors of the Ukrainian costumes. Brett's memorable artwork here is reminiscent of her work in *The Wild Christmas Reindeer, Goldilocks and the*

Three Bears, and *Annie and the Wild Animals.* Kids will clamor for Brett's eye-catching books and parents will find pleasure in reading them over and over again.

Morris Goes to School
by Bernard Wiseman
(See Videos.)
1970. HarperCollins, $10.89; paper, $3.50.

My Shadow
by Robert Louis Stevenson
(See Poems in Picture Books, p. 27.)

The Mysterious Tadpole
by Steven Kellogg
(See Videos.)
1977. Dial, $13.95; paper, $3.95.

The Napping House
By Audrey Wood
(See *Happy Birthday Moon* in Videos.)
Illustrated by Don Wood.
1984. HBJ, $14.95.

Noah's Ark
by Peter Spier
(See Videos.)
1977. Doubleday, $12.95; paper, $5.95.

Of Colors and Things
by Tana Hoban
(See *Colors and Shapes* in Videos.)
1989. Greenwillow, $12.95.

Old Henry
by Joan W. Blos
(Ages 4–6)
Illustrated by Stephen Gammell.
1987. Morrow, $13.

In this moralistic tale with a sense of humor, the neighbors nag Henry so much about the slovenly state of his property that he eventually moves. But Henry misses his tumble-down place, and, strangely enough, the neighbors find they miss Henry. Thus begin the negotiations to bring Henry home and make everyone happy. This winning story in rhyme is complemented by vibrant color-pencil illustrations that depict a loveable cast of frumpy characters.

Over, Under, and Through
by Tana Hoban
(See *Colors and Shapes* in Videos.)
1973. Macmillan, $12.95; Aladdin, paper, $3.95.

Owl Moon
by Jane Yolen
(See Videos.)
Illustrated by John Schoenherr.
1987. Philomel, $13.95.

Awards: Caldecott Medal 1988; Notable Children's Book 1987; Reading Rainbow selection

Paper John
by David Small
(Ages 4–7)
1987. Farrar, Straus & Giroux, $13.95.

When Paper John arrives in a candy-colored town, he befriends all through his kindness and his marvelous folded-paper origami. Soon he rescues a dingy, gray-colored man, who turns out to be a devil. This demon steals the villagers' money and escapes on John's splendid kite. How John uses the wind to blow the devil back to his home brings this story to a happy conclusion. The fable is enhanced by quaint art that children will want to study at length.

Party Rhymes
by Marc Brown
(Ages 3–5)
1988. Dutton, $13.95.

Twelve old-fashioned verses that preschoolers will love are put into action by a master of rhyme-motion choreography. Each double-page spread contains the rhyme and its hand movements, shown in small boxes next to each line, as well as a full-color illustration that brings the poem to life. Perfect for parties, playtime, and as lap books for parent-child sharing. Two videos are available of this author's work: *Marc Brown Does Hand Rhymes* and *Marc Brown Does Play Rhymes* (see Videos). Brown also did the pictures for *Read-Aloud Rhymes for the Very Young* (see p.000), and he is the author of the popular Arthur series.

Peter's Chair
by Ezra Jack Keats
(See *Happy Birthday Moon* in Videos.)
1967. HarperCollins, $13.95; paper, $4.95.

Awards: Reading Rainbow selection

A Picture for Harold's Room
by Crockett Johnson
(See *The Amazing Bone* in Videos.)
1960. HarperCollins, $10.89; paper, $3.50.

The Pigs' Wedding
by Helme Heine
(See Videos.)
1979. McElderry, $12.95; Aladdin, paper, $4.95.

Play Rhymes
by Marc Brown
(See *Marc Brown Does Play Rhymes* in Videos.)
1985. Dutton, $10.95.

The Polar Express
by Chris Van Allsburg
(Ages 4–Adult)
1985. Houghton Mifflin, $16.95.

Paintings that rivet the eye and stop one's breath with their tender moments and striking perspectives illustrate this timeless story. Adults may appreciate the narrative even more than children, as Van Allsburg gently tells of a boy's visit to the North Pole and his precious gift from Santa Claus. Sure to bring a tear to true believers' eyes, this, like the author's other works, is a beautifully crafted and enduring book. The video adaptation, available from Random House, is faithful to the original. The author's story, *Ben's Dream,* is also in video (see *Fun in a Box #1,* p. 173).

Awards: Caldecott Medal 1986; Reading Rainbow selection

Random House Book of Mother Goose
Retold and illustrated by Arnold Lobel
(Ages 2–6)
1986. Random House, $14.95.

A winning collection of nursery rhymes bedecked with merry pictures by Arnold Lobel, who has inspired children with his many wonderful books. This treasury includes familiar as well as other more unusual verses. A varied compilation that will provide years of enjoyment. Also, take a look at *Whiskers & Rhymes* by Lobel on p. 31.

Read-Aloud Rhymes for the Very Young
Selected by Jack Prelutsky
(Ages 3–6)
Illustrated by Marc Brown.
1986. Knopf, $13.95.

Familiar verses get added punch from Marc Brown's lively artwork. On one page, a swirling chubby-cheeked wind takes a bite out of a cookie moon to visualize Vachel Lindsay's "The Moon's the North Wind's Cookie." Elsewhere, slimy-fingered children accompany an apropos poem called "Table Manners." Cheery illustrations enliven this treasury for readers of all ages.

The Selkie Girl
by Susan Cooper
(See *The Pigs' Wedding* in Videos.)
Illustrated by Warwick Hutton.
1986. McElderry, $13.95; Aladdin, paper, $4.95.

17 Kings and 42 Elephants
by Margaret Mahey
(See Poems in Picture Books, p. 28.)

Shake It to the One That You Love the Best: Play Songs and Lullabies from Black Musical Traditions
(See Audio.)
Edited by Cheryl Warren Mattox
Illustrated by Varnette P. Honeywood.
1990. Warren-Mattox Productions, paper, $5.95.

Sheep in a Shop
by Nancy Shaw
(Ages 4–6)
Illustrated by Margot Apple.
1991. Houghton Mifflin, $12.95.

Return to the woolly world of *Sheep in a Jeep* with this winner done in the same mode. This time the five sheep need a birthday gift and manage to make chaos out of a simple errand. The ruminants climb and grumble, they reach and fumble in Shaw's adroit, rhyming phrases that are accompanied by Apple's color-pencil illustrations. Good for more than a chuckle or two from preschoolers and beginning readers.

The Snowman
by Raymond Briggs
(See Videos.)
1978. Random House, $12.95; paper, $4.95; miniature edition, $4.95.

A Story—A Story: An African Tale
by Gail E. Haley
(See Videos.)
1970. Atheneum, $14.95; Aladdin, paper, $4.95.

Awards: Caldecott Medal 1971

The Story of the Dancing Frog
by Quentin Blake
(See Videos.)
1985. Knopf, $9.99; McKay, paper, $4.95.

Strega Nona
by Tomie de Paola
(See Videos.)
1975. Simon & Schuster, $13.95.

Awards: Caldecott Honor Book 1976

The Stupids Take Off
by Harry Allard and James Marshall
(Ages 4–8)
1989. Houghton Mifflin, $13.95.

The good-natured but incredibly backward Stupid family sets off on a day of adventure to avoid the arrival of dreaded Uncle Carbuncle. Along the way they greet relatives everywhere who, of course, are as ridiculous as they are.

POEMS IN PICTURE BOOKS

Block City by Robert Louis Stevenson   (Ages 3–6)   Illustrated by Ashley Wolff.   1988. Dutton, $12.95.

Dramatic artwork captures the imaginary world in Stevenson's six-stanza poem from *A Child's Garden of Verses*. When a young boy falls asleep next to the castles he has just made out of building blocks, his turrets and towers transform into a medieval town bustling with knights and peasants. Wolff's visuals remain true to the poet's tone while conjuring up enthralling images from the past.

My Shadow by Robert Louis Stevenson   (Ages 3–6)   Illustrated by Ted Rand.   1990. Putnam, $14.95.

"I have a little shadow that goes in and out with me" is the familiar opening of Stevenson's poem. Matched with Ted Rand's radiant watercolors, the verse, drawn from the classic *A Child's Garden of Verses,* becomes an exhilarating international tour. Shadows of children playing in Italy, England, Africa, the Orient, and the United States offer an agreeable intercultural message.

The Owl and the Pussycat by Edward Lear   (Ages 2–8)   Illustrated by Jan Brett.
1991. Putnam,
$14.95.

The Owl and the Pussycat went to sea
In a beautiful pea-green boat

opens this much-loved poem, for which Brett has created a verdant tropical world. Elaborate, colorful artwork not only depicts the "elegant fowl" and "beautiful pussy," but also adds slapstick humor when the boat overturns and the lovers encounter the pig with a ring—who here appears as a sleazy beachcomber. Other artists—Paul Galdone, Hilary Knight, and Lorinda Bryan Cauley— have created memorable versions of Lear's nonsense verse; Barbara Cooney's is available on video (see *Happy Birthday Moon and Other Stories* in Video.). This interpretation is guaranteed to keep kids giggling.
Awards: Notable Children's Book 1992

17 Kings and 42 Elephants by Margaret Mahy   (Ages 4–8)   Illustrated by Patricia MacCarthy.
1987. Dial, $10.95.

Jewel-like colors dazzle the eyes in this book's batik paintings. These unusual visuals give perfect life to a nonsense poem about the 17 kings and their many pachyderms. This is one book that has to be read aloud to be appreciated. A marvelous jungle journey includes jungle wildlife never found in any zoo.

The Walrus and the Carpenter by Lewis Carroll   (Ages 4–Adult)   Illustrated by Jan Breskin Zalben.   1986. Holt, $13.95.

Intended as a companion to Zalben's interpretation of Lewis Carroll's "Jabberwocky," this entrancing picture book parallels the classic poem from Carroll's *Through the Looking Glass* with wonderfully nonsensical illustrations. Blue oceanic tones predominate, with the scenes adroitly capturing the purposeful Walrus and the carpenter as they lure innocent young oysters out for a stroll. Done in watercolor and colored pencil, these richly embellished pictures bring out the humor in Carroll's much-loved verse to even the very young.

The pictures continue the joke, adding more zaniness to the already ludicrous happenings. Kids will love it. Be sure to look for more on the family. (As Buster says, "The Stupids are everywhere.")

Swimmy
by Leo Lionni
(See *Five Lionni Classics* in Videos.)
1963. Knopf, paper, $2.95.

Awards: Caldecott Honor Book 1964

The Tailor of Gloucester
by Beatrix Potter
(See Audio.)
Illustrated by David Jorgensen.
1988. Picture Book Studio, $14.95.

Tar Beach
by Faith Ringgold
(Ages 4–7)
1991. Crown, $14.95.

Cassie spends summer nights on "Tar Beach," the rooftop of her 1939 New York City apartment building. Nearby the grownups play cards and decry the racism in the construction workers' unions. Cassie wishes she could magically cure such worries. In her dreams, she takes flight over the city, eventually teaching her little brother her magical skills. Based on Ringgold's quilt called *Tar Beach* that hangs in the Guggenheim Museum in New York City, this picture book carries quilt-patch patterns along the bottom of each page and shows the complete artwork at the book's conclusion.

Awards: Caldecott Honor Book 1992; Coretta Scott King Illustrator Award 1992

The Three Robbers
by Tomi Ungerer
(See *What's Under My Bed* in Videos.)
1962. Atheneum, $14.95; Aladdin, paper, $4.95.

Thunder Cake
by Patricia Polacco
(Ages 4–8)
1990. Philomel, $14.95.

Instead of cowering from a thunderstorm, a little girl's Russian-American grandmother teaches her how to make thunder cake. The recipe includes not only standard ingredients but also careful timing; the cake must be ready for the oven before the raindrops fall. It is only when the cake is baking that the child understands how brave she really is. This true-to-life incident from the author's childhood is portrayed through her vivid text and sweeping though painstakingly composed art. The author's *Uncle Vova's Tree* and *Rechenka's Eggs* are also based on family lore.

Tikki Tikki Tembo
by Arlene Mosel
(See *Strega Nona* in Videos.)
Illustrated by Blair Lent.
1968. Holt, $14.95; paper, $5.95.

Time of Wonder
by Robert McCloskey
(See *Owl Moon* and *The Robert McCloskey Library* in Videos.)
1957. Viking, $15.95; Puffin, paper, $4.95.

Awards: Caldecott Honor Book 1958

The Trip
by Ezra Jack Keats
(See *The Amazing Bone* in Videos.)
1978. Greenwillow, $12.88; Mulberry, paper, $3.95.

Tucking Mommy In
by Morag Loh
(Ages 3–6)
Illustrated by Donna Rawlins.
1988. Orchard Books, $12.95; paper, $4.95.

Mommy expresses her fatigue while getting Sue and Jenny ready for bed, so Sue volunteers to tell the bedtime story. Then Mommy falls sound asleep during the tale and in a reversal of roles, the two children tuck her in. First, they gently wake her up, get her into pajamas, kiss her, and tell the story again. When Daddy comes home from work, the two girls retell the events of the evening as he carries them to bed in a tandem piggyback ride. Rawlins's double-page spreads in watercolor and colored pencil capture family love, the effect of a long day on a mother of two, and the spontaneous generosity of children and their disheveled world.

Awards: Notable Children's Book 1988

Uncle Elephant
by Arnold Lobel
(See Videos.)
1981. HarperCollins, $10.95; paper, $3.50.

The Village of Round and Square Houses
by Ann Grifalconi
(Ages 4–7)
1986. Little, Brown, $14.95.

A real village in West Africa is described with nostalgia from the point of view of a woman who grew up there. Bold chalk artwork captures life in a faraway place where the men live in square houses and the women and children in round ones. The tale of how the villagers arrived at this unique living arrangement after the eruption of a nearby volcano will give pause to preschoolers, and start them thinking about the customs of their own and other cultures.

Awards: Caldecott Honor Book 1987

A Visit to Grandma's
by Nancy Carlson
(Ages 3–8)
1991. Viking, $13.95.

Grandma has moved from the farm to a Florida condo, so Tina and her family fly down for Thanksgiving. But Grandma has changed. She no longer spends her time cooking; instead, she takes aerobics classes and plans to take the whole family to a restaurant for the holiday meal. At first, these changes in Grandma do not please Tina and her father. Eventually, the two begin to accept Grandma's new lifestyle. Vivacious, colorful artwork helps deliver a candid story about family changes. Be sure to look for *The Perfect Family* about being an only child, as well as Carlson's other books.

We're Going on a Bear Hunt
by Michael Rosen
(Ages 3–6)
Illustrated by Helen Oxenbury.
1989. McElderry, $14.95.

The call-and-answer story that kids have loved for years is presented in book format by two renowned talents in the children's field. Rosen has added word equivalents for the hand claps, taps, and other sound effects usually created by listening children. Otherwise the tale remains happily the same. Oxenbury infuses her pencil drawings and paintings—alternating throughout this book—with insightful details and humor. Don't miss seeing who else ends up under the covers with the children in the last illustration.

What Happened to Patrick's Dinosaurs?

by Carol Carrick

(Ages 4–8)

Illustrated by Donald Carrick.
1986. Clarion, $12.95; paper and audiocassette, $7.95.

Patrick has dinosaurs on the brain. In *Patrick's Dinosaurs,* his big brother Hank shows off his factual knowledge of the extinct beasts, but that doesn't stop Patrick from imagining them everywhere. In this book, Patrick tells Hank his theory about the dinosaurs' disappearance. Preschoolers and even primary graders will really take off on Patrick's world, in which dinosaurs invent cars and airplanes and put on shows for people until one day they pile into a spaceship for a final exit. Full-color paintings depict the absurd happenings with just enough verisimilitude to make this tall tale a hit.

Awards: Notable Children's Book 1986

What's under My Bed?

by James Stevenson
(See Videos.)
1983. Greenwillow, $13.95; paper, $3.95.

Where the Wild Things Are

by Maurice Sendak
(See *The Maurice Sendak Library* in Videos.)
1962. HarperCollins, $12.95; paper, $4.95.

Awards: Caldecott Medal 1964

Whiskers & Rhymes

by Arnold Lobel
(Ages 3–8)
1985. Greenwillow, $13.

Silly characters and tender emotions are a successful mix in this collection of all-new nursery rhymes. George, who brushes his teeth with pickle paste, and loose and limber Beanbag Jim sit alongside a poem about an old woman who stitches the sun to a hill (to stop the day from ending). Paralleling these rhymes that children will demand again and again are muted illustrations by Lobel, who is well known for the series about Frog and Toad. *The Faber Book of Nursery Verse* edited by Barbara Ireson is a fine un-spoofed version of the classic childhood verses.

The Wizard

by Jack Kent
(See *The Mysterious Tadpole* in Videos.)
Four Winds, paper, $5.95.

A Year of Beasts

by Ashley Wolff
(Ages 3–5)
1986. Dutton, $10.95.

In January, Ellie and Peter see two deer while making a snowman. Wolff provides a look at animal and family activities and interactions throughout the year. In December, squirrels, deer, and rabbits watch the family cut their Christmas tree. Both people and animals are pictured in hand-tinted, linoleum-block prints. Wolff's *A Year of the Birds* offers a similar look at the seasons and birds.

EARLY GRADERS

Abuela
by Arthur Dorros
(Ages 5–8)
Illustrated by Elisa Kleven.
1991. Dutton, $13.95.

Rosalba visits the park with her abuela (grandmother in Spanish) and dreams of flying like the birds they are feeding. In her imagination, and in Kleven's detailed, colorful collages, they do. Soaring over the sights of New York City, the pair see ethnic neighborhoods, the Statue of Liberty (where the grandmother recalls her first visit), the coastal area, and the airport. The clever placement of Spanish words and phrases within the text makes the appended glossary almost unnecessary.

Awards: Notable Children's Book 1992

Alexander, Who Used to Be Rich Last Sunday
by Judith Viorst
(See Videos.)
Illustrated by Ray Cruz.
1978. Macmillan, $13.95; paper, $3.95.

Alphabatics
by Suse MacDonald
(See ABCs, p. 12.)

And Sunday Makes Seven
by Robert Baden
(See Multicultural Fare, p. 35.)

Arthur Meets the President
by Marc Brown
(Ages 6–8)
1991. Little, Brown, $14.95.

Bespectacled Arthur the mouse was only doing a homework assignment, issued by Mr. Ratburn, when he wrote his essay, "How I Can Help Make America Great." Now, clad in a suit and a red bow tie, he must, in the words of a TV news announcer, "recite his winning essay to the President of the United States while all of America looks on." Arthur is worried sick. "Not as sick as you're going to feel . . . " says his pesty little sister who literally turns upside down to save the day. A tour of the most famous sites of Washington, D.C., narrated by Arthur's classmates, adds an extra plus to this amusing tale. Author-illustrator Brown has guided Arthur through many adventures, including lost teeth and new glasses.

The Art Lesson
by Tomie dePaola
(Ages 5–8)
1989. Putnam, $13.95.

Tommy, who furiously desires to be an artist when he grows up, is discouraged when he starts school and learns that he has to wait until first grade for real art lessons. Then, when Mrs. Bowers the art teacher tells him he must *copy* her drawing, he's indignant. Not until Mrs. Bowers proves herself to be the true teacher that Tommy hoped she would be—and allows him to use his creativity and imagination—does he learn a valuable lesson. The well-known and prolific dePaola draws on his own childhood experiences in this delightful picture book.

Beauty and the Beast

by Mordicai Gerstein
(See Videos.)
1989. Dutton, $12.95.

Beezus and Ramona

by Beverly Cleary
(See *Ramona Stories* in Videos.)
1955. Morrow, $13.95; paper, Dell, $3.25.

Ben's Dream

by Chris Van Allsburg
(See *Fun in a Box #1* in Videos.)
1982. Houghton Mifflin, $14.95.

Ben's Trumpet

by Rachel Isadora
(Ages 5–10)
1979. Greenwillow, $13; Mulberry, paper, $4.95.

Playing on an imaginary trumpet, "Ben sits on the fire escape and listens to the music of the Zig Zag Jazz Club," until some neighborhood kids mock him and destroy his fantasy. A trumpeter from the club notices Ben's silent fingers and brings his dream to life. There is minimal text here, yet the tale emerges through the black, white, and gray drawings, especially the "zig-zaggedy" lines that vivify the hot jazz and Ben's yearnings.

Awards: Caldecott Honor Book 1979; Reading Rainbow selection

The Black Snowman

by Phil Mendez
(Ages 5–9)
Illustrated by Carole Byard.
1989. Scholastic, $13.95.

Jacob Miller and his younger brother, Pee Wee, are two black children living in the inner city with their mother. It's Christmas time, but that doesn't help Jacob: "I hate being black . . . Everything black is bad." Pee Wee, however, is not bitter, and he begs Jacob to help build a black snowman. Looking for a shawl to throw over the snowman's shoulders, the boys find a magic *kente* that brings their creation to life, conjuring past ancestral heroes and forever altering Jacob's attitude toward himself and his situation. The *kente* cloth, explained in a prologue, makes a fantastical but legitimate connection between modern city life and tribal Africa. Byard's full-color paintings stretch across the pages, reflecting the changing moods of the story.

The Boy of the Three-Year Nap

by Dianne Snyder
(Ages 5–8)
Illustrated by Allen Say.
1988. Houghton Mifflin, $14.95.

In this adaptation of a Japanese folktale, a widow slaves at sewing silk kimonos, while her lazy son, Taro, naps the day away. When a rich merchant moves to town, Taro comes up with a plan to "get it all" without working. Donning a black kimono and painting his face, the boy appears in front of the merchant as the *ujigami*—the village patron god—demanding that his daughter marry "that fine young man called Taro." Together the merchant and the widow thwart Taro's scheme. Say's rich, Japanese-style illustrations depict the architecture, costume, and politics of Japanese village life.

Awards: Caldecott Honor Book 1989; Notable Children's Book 1988

Brave Irene
by William Steig
(Ages 5–8)
1986. Farrar, Straus & Giroux, $13.95; paper, $3.95.

Brave Irene is the daughter of a dressmaker who falls ill just as she is putting the finishing touches on the duchess's ball gown. Irene tucks her mother into bed and sets off into a fierce snowstorm to deliver the dress. "The wind wrestled her for the package—walloped, twisted it, shook it, snatched at it." Steig's descriptions and drawings of the vulnerable little messenger are almost heartbreaking . . . until Irene is seen in triumph dancing at the ball.

Bugs
by Nancy Winslow Parker and Joan Richards Wright
(Ages 5–8)
Illustrated by Nancy Winslow Parker.
1987. Greenwillow, $11.75.

Insects and "their cousins, such as spiders, ticks, and centipedes" hold an endless facina-

tion for kids. This book on the subject manages to be both informative and fun. Each bug receives a double-page spread. On the right is a large-scale picture with all body parts identified; on the left is a ministory with full-color illustrations that reveal the critter interacting with children and pets.

Awards: Reading Rainbow selection

Captain Snap and the Children of Vinegar Lane
by Roni Schotter
(Ages 5–8)
Illustrated by Marcia Sewall.
1989. Orchard Books, $14.95.

Spunky Emily Ann Crocker leads Myrna, Moe, Maxie, and Curly Jess to the doorstep of the neighborhood curmudgeon, Captain Snap. "He was thin and mean and bent and bitter. His skin was as cracked and as dry as a slice of stale bread." But one day the old captain lies ailing, and the partners in crime give blankets and soup as a peace offering. Captain Snap pulls through, revealing his hidden artistic side and befriending everyone on Vinegar Lane. Schotter's rhythmic text is brought to life by the award-winning Sewall's bright blues and yellows.

Cherries and Cherry Pits
by Vera Williams
(Ages 5–7)
1986. Greenwillow, $13.95; Mulberry, paper, $3.95.

Bidemmi, a young black girl, has her color markers and her paper and her friend and her imagination. Drawing one picture after another, she narrates the stories behind them. All involve cherries and cherry pits, and the

MULTICULTURAL FARE

Here is a sampling of the many fine stories that can introduce children to life in other lands and cultures. Some are historical, some are modern-day scenarios. There is a mix of folklore, picture books, biography, and fiction. For more multicultural fare, see *Skipping Stones: A Multi-Ethnic Children's Forum* in Magazines, p. 136.

And Sunday Makes Seven by Robert Baden   (Ages 5–8)   Illustrated by Michelle Edwards. 1990. Whitman, $12.95.

In this rhythmic folktale set in a village in Costa Rica, Baden teaches the days of the week in Spanish, and much more. Edwards's colorful prints depict the contrast between the lives of the wealthy Ricardo and the poor couple, Ana and Carlos, who live across the street. Baden's story contains elements of magic, including witches and warts, and a satisfying victory of good over evil. A Spanish edition, *Y Dominga, Siete,* is also available.

A Country Far Away by Nigel Gray   (Ages 3–6)   Illustrated by Philippe Dupasquier. 1988. Orchard Books, $12.95; paper, $4.95.

One single line of text separates top and bottom illustrations in running panels. The top set shows a boy from an African village; the bottom features a blond-haired boy from a suburb in a Western nation. The text is basic, with such lines as, "I helped my mom and dad." Dupasquier's bright color drawings tell the story, with one lad carrying water from a well and milking a goat, while the other boy runs a vacuum cleaner and helps mow the lawn. The boys each play soccer, go swimming, have family celebrations, and look at a book with pictures of each other's homeland. The story closes with each dreaming of making a friend just like the one in the accompanying panel.

The Day of Ahmed's Secret by Florence Parry Heide   (Ages 5–8)   Illustrated by Ted Lewin. 1990. Lothrop, $13.95.

On an average day in historic, downtown Cairo, a little boy drives a cart holding large bottles of water, stopping to talk to some of his clients. All the while he appreciates the sights, sounds, and feel of his hometown. But he is also anticipating the evening with his family when he will share a wonderful secret—that he has learned to write his name. Lewin's watercolors evoke the shadows, diverse people, and energy that is Cairo.
Awards: Notable Children's Book 1991

A Hand Full of Stars by Rafik Schami   (Ages 12–15)   Translated from German by Rika Lesser.   1990. Dutton, $14.95.

Contemporary Damascus provides a rich, multicultural backdrop for this moving, sometimes funny novel, written in the form of a journal. Crisscrossing four years of an Arab teenager's life, the journal entries focus both on the people who live on the young man's poor and narrow street as well as on his courageous resistance to government injustices, aspirations to become a journalist, relationships with family and friends, and love for a neighborhood girl.
Awards: BBYA 1991; Mildred L. Batchelder Award 1991

In the Beginning: Creation Stories from around the World by Virginia Hamilton   (Ages 11–14)   Illustrated by Barry Moser.   1988. HBJ, $18.95.

Award-winning author Virginia Hamilton has gathered five myths of creation, stories that "go back beyond anything that ever was and begin before anything has happened." Some of the tales, based on biblical lore or Greek and Roman legends, are familiar. Others, coming from African, Native American, or aborigine tribes, may not be as recognizable. But each, illustrated by rich, full-page oil paintings, evokes the mystery of human origins. Hamilton adds brief sources of information following each myth.
Awards: Newbery Honor Book 1989; Notable Children's Book 1988

The Last Princess: The Story of Princess Ka'iulani of Hawai'i by Fay Stanley   (Ages 8–12)
Illustrated by Diane Stanley.   1991. Four Winds, $14.95.

The Hawaiian Islands, annexed to the United States in 1898 (and granted statehood in 1959), now seem a natural, if exotic, part of this country. This stunningly illustrated biography of Princess

Ka'iulani tells another side of the story. The princess, raised to become queen of the islands and educated in England, personally contested the annexation to President Grover Cleveland. Her arguments and those of others were discounted. Stanley's full-color portraits and scenic paintings add depth to this authentic account.
Awards: Notable Children's Book 1992

On the Pampas by María Cristina Brusca (Ages 5–8) 1991. Holt, $14.95.

An Argentine ranch is the perfect setting for the antics of two young cousins, both girls, who ride horses, help round up cattle, and locate an ostrich egg for a birthday cake. The cousins listen to the gauchos' tales, dance at their grandmother's birthday party, and relish the work and play to be found all summer long on their grandparents' *estancia* (ranch). In addition to the author's bright watercolors, this picture book features definitions of the Spanish words used in the story and end papers with a map of South America.

Shabanu: Daughter of the Wind by Suzanne Fisher Staples (Ages 11–15) 1989. Knopf, $13.95.

Shabanu lives with her nomadic family in present-day Pakistan's Cholistan Desert, and although she's only 12, her future is already planned. In one year she is to marry her cousin Murad. After Murad's brother is killed, however, Shabanu finds herself betrothed instead to a much older man, who already has three wives. It's a match she doesn't like, but it's one that can bring prestige, even wealth, to her family. To enter into the arrangement may bring Shabanu unhappiness; to refuse may bring her family dishonor.
Awards: Notable Children's Book 1990; BBYA 1990; Newbery Honor Book 1990

Two Short and One Long by Nina Ring Aamundsen (Ages 9–12) 1990. Houghton Mifflin, $13.95.

The friendship of two Norwegian lads, Jonas and Einar, is threatened when Jonas befriends a new boy, an Afghan refugee. Quiet scenes in this novel give way to intense, even violent, action. An antiracist message is developed on many levels as both parents and children reassess their behavior. A thought-provoking tale, with lighter moments and an inside look at European social patterns.

A Wave in Her Pocket by Lynn Joseph (Ages 7–10) Illustrated by Brian Pinkney. 1991. Clarion, $13.95.

A young girl named Amber recounts the mystical, magical, exuberant adventures and stories of her Tantie (grandaunt). Tantie is a woman of remarkable qualities who can settle the ghostly "jumbies," tame a *soucouyant* (a fiery vampire), or throw a magnificent party. Joseph brings the island folklore straight to children in sparkling, distinctive language, while Pinkney's drawings, with dark backgrounds, lend an aura of mystery. An irresistible set of tales.
Awards: Notable Children's Book 1992

last one expresses Bidemmi's dream of planting a cherry "forest" on her street. Williams's language is respectful of children, and her artwork—effervescent in color and content—reveals the element of fun in giving and loving.

Awards: Notable Children's Book 1986

The Children We Remember
by Chana Byers Abells
(Ages 7–12)
1986. Greenwillow, $9.95.

These black-and-white photographs from the Holocaust are organized in a chronological fashion. The collection moves from scenes depicting a typical pre–World War II town, synagogue, and school to photos of children wearing yellow stars and, finally, in concentration camps. The harsh realities of the Nazi regime are brought into sharp, painful focus.

Chita's Christmas Tree
by Elizabeth Fitzgerald Howard
(Ages 5–8)
Illustrated by Floyd Cooper.
1989. Bradbury, $13.95.

A special Christmas Eve for a black family is depicted in short chapters. Papa and Chita go in a sleigh to the forest to pick out the best tree for Santa to deliver. Chita finds the special one and Papa carves her name on its trunk (so that Santa knows which one to bring). Then they go home to 20 dozen sugar cookies, Smithfield ham, music, and dancing. Christmas morning, Chita runs downstairs and sees the tree delivered and decorated. Cooper's fuzzy watercolors set the scene in Baltimore, and his blotches of bright pinks and greens bring to life the hopes of the holiday.

Awards: Notable Children's Book 1990

Come a Tide
by George Ella Lyon
(Ages 5–7)
Illustrated by Stephen Gammell.
1990. Orchard Books, $14.95.

After a four-day downpour, Grandma predicts, "It'll come a tide," and as the waters rise, the reader sees that she is right. The characters who live in the hollows pictured in the book start packing belongings, and the narrator's family hightails it up the hill to Grandma's house and safety. The next day, everyone checks out the damage and begins the cleaning-up process. Gammell's rainbow watercolors reflect the disruption of a flood, but do so with an eye for the lighter side of things.

Cowboy Dreams
by Dayal Kaur Khalsa
(Ages 4–7)
1990. Clarkson N. Potter, $13.95.

The author-illustrator's own childhood passion to be a cowgirl is relived through vibrant artwork and a touching autobiographical tale. Khalsa reveals how, since she had no horse, she nicknamed her bike "Old Paint" and rode the basement banister, instead of her bike, when it was too cold for outdoor excursions. Cowboy movies, western music, and other inspiring touches are acknowledged in a wistful, elegantly illustrated fashion.

The Day of Ahmed's Secret
by Florence Parry Heide
(See Multicultural Fare, p. 35.)

A Day with Wilbur Robinson
by William Joyce
(Ages 5–7)
1990. HarperCollins, $13.95.

In this tale, set in a kind of 1950s "grade B" science fiction atmosphere, the narrator goes to see his best friend, Wilbur Robinson, whose house "is the *greatest* place to visit." They encounter an octopus, giant train set, human cannonballs, tigers, robots, mummies, as they search for Grandfather Robinson's false teeth. An understated text coupled with wild illustrations make this an outstanding read from the author of *Dinosaur Bob and His Adventures with the Family Lazardo* (a Reading Rainbow selection).

The Doorbell Rang
by Pat Hutchins
(Ages 5–7)
1986. Greenwillow, $11.75.

A dozen freshly baked cookies tempt Victoria and Sam. They thoughtfully determine that equal shares would bring six treats each. But the doorbell rings and rings again—bringing new friends and lowering the cookie-per-kid ratio. Hutchins's picture book presents a lively assortment of children of varied races in a homey kitchen full of bright colors and designs. Best of all, when the bell rings for the last time, Grandma arrives with a new batch of cookies—and the mathematical considerations begin anew.

Awards: Notable Children's Book 1986

Eric Carle's Animals, Animals
Compiled by Laura Whipple
(Ages 6–10)
1989. Philomel, $18.95.

The works of a popular children's illustrator— the creator of *The Very Hungry Caterpillar*—are now collected in a thick book filled with many of his beasts, birds, and fish. To accompany Carle's artwork, anthologist Whipple has matched short poems from the likes of Ogden Nash, Lewis Carroll, and Judith Viorst, as well as other verses reflecting various ethnic origins: the Japanese haiku, Pawnee Indian chants, and African lore. Carle's colorful collages on white backgrounds show a variety of animals in their own milieus. An exceptionally well-designed book that will please parents as much as children.

Awards: Notable Children's Book 1990

Feelings
by Aliki
(Ages 4–8)
1984. Greenwillow, $13.95; Mulberry, paper, $3.95.

Aliki's drawings clarify emotions by picturing kids sharing candy, grieving over a pet, fretting over friendships, sulking in boredom, feeling lost, or just being quiet. The illustrations are terrific, ranging from strip format to full-page spreads. The natural-sounding dialogue gets the point across without preaching or overexplaining. On a sad day—or any day—there are lessons here for parents and children. Aliki has created a similar book on manners.

Awards: Reading Rainbow selection

The Fir Tree

by Hans Christian Andersen

(See Videos.)

Illustrated by Nancy Eckholm Burkert.
1986. HarperCollins, $13.95; paper, $3.95.

Follow the Drinking Gourd

by Jeanette Winter

(See Videos.)

1988. Knopf, $14.95.

A Frog Prince

by Alix Berenzy

(See Fractured Fairy Tales, p. 53.)

Funnybones

by Allan Ahlberg

(Ages 6–8)

Illustrated by André Amstutz.
1981. Greenwillow, $12.88; Mulberry, paper, $3.95.

A big skeleton, little skeleton, and dog skeleton make up the trio called Funnybones. Here, the threesome set out one night in search of fun—that is, someone or something to scare. After a trip to the zoo (full of skeleton animals) and some silly mishaps, they scare one another all the way home. More funny bones are tickled in this ongoing series, which also includes *Dinosaur Dreams* and *Mystery Tour*.

The Furry News: How to Make a Newspaper

by Loreen Leedy

(Ages 5–8)

1990. Holiday House, $13.95.

Big Bear, fed up with the city paper's lack of coverage of his neighborhood, tells his animal friends that they must make their own newspaper. Raccoon is the mystery diner who writes restaurant critiques, Fox is the features editor, and Beaver composes crossword puzzles. Then the papers are delivered by fleet-footed Pig. Keeping young readers in mind, Leedy summarizes the basics of publishing a newspaper, including the ins and outs of writing, editing, and printing it. In a similar book, *The Bunny Play*, Leedy covers theater production.

Goldilocks and the Three Bears

by James Marshall

(See Fractured Fairy Tales, p. 53.)

Grandpa's Face

by Eloise Greenfield

(Ages 5–8)

Illustrated by Floyd Cooper.
1988. Philomel, $13.95.

A story featuring a close-knit black family. Young Tamika takes comfort in the smooth, kind lines of her grandfather's face. But one day she sees a very different, very angry face in grandfather's mirror, as she watches him prepare for an acting part. Fearing that the day will come when he will look at her with that same cruelty is enough to frighten the young girl into withdrawing from the family. Cooper's sunlit, double-page spreads capture the delicate balance between the generations.

Awards: Notable Children's Book 1988

The Great Wall of China

by Leonard Everett Fisher

(Ages 6–9)

1986. Macmillan, $11.95.

The uniting of Chinese provinces 2,200 years ago by King Chen of Ch'in, the First Supreme Emperor of China, is explained in minimal text and striking black-and-white drawings. Unification of monetary, measuring, and writing systems is addressed, but the book's main focus is on the construction of the Great Wall—designed to keep out the marauding Mongols. The Chinese characters that run along the margins are actually chapter summaries, which are translated in a closing note.

A Guide Dog Puppy Grows Up
by Caroline Arnold
(Ages 6–9)
Photographs by Richard Hewitt.
1991. HBJ, $16.95.

Arnold's practical and engaging book leads readers through the process of a golden retriever's training as a guide dog. The full-page color photographs and text focus on the dog Honey, but also give a thorough behind-the-scenes look at the Guide Dogs for the Blind campus in San Rafael, California.

Harald and the Great Stag
by Donald Carrick
(Ages 5–8)
1988. Clarion, $14.95; paper, $4.95.

The baron sends young Harald in search of the Great Stag, but Harald, who has met the noble beast eye to eye, deliberately throws the dogs off the stag's path. Alas, Harald has the stag's scent upon him and becomes himself the hunted. Carrick's watercolors and the Middle Ages atmosphere deliver the terror of the hunt and the true courage of a boy in a man's world.

Harry and the Lady Next Door
by Gene Zion
(See *Harry Comes Home* in Videos.)
Illustrated by Margaret Bloy Graham.
1960. HarperCollins, $11.95; paper, $3.50.

Harry the Dirty Dog
by Gene Zion
(See *Harry Comes Home* in Videos.)
Illustrated by Margaret Bloy Graham.
1956. HarperCollins, $12.95; paper, $3.95.

Heckedy Peg
by Audrey Wood
(Ages 4–7)
Illustrated by Don Wood.
1987. HBJ, $14.95.

A tale about a mother and her seven children, all named after the days of the week. Their obedience is rewarded with gifts from the market. But then wicked old Heckedy Peg steals the children away and transforms them into various morsels. Only by identifying the children by name can the mother seal the witch's fate. Wood's oil paintings depict the warm glow from the family fire, the sunny English countryside, and the dark environs of the witch's cave. This talented wife-and-husband team is also responsible for the 1992 Notable Children's Book *Piggies*.

Henry and Mudge Take the Big Test
by Cynthia Rylant
(Ages 6–8)
Illustrated by Sucie Stevenson.
1991. Bradbury, $11.95.

Mudge is a drooling, overgrown bulldog and a dear friend to Henry. Both have appeared in nine previous stories, including the 1987 Notable Children's Book, *Henry and Mudge under the Yellow Moon*. Here, Henry and his mom decide that it's time to take Mudge to school. Mudge has a loving teacher who actually dances with the overly affectionate pooch. Rylant's text has plenty of repetition for the new reader and a funny, involving plot.

Kids will love to study the bright, action-packed watercolors.

Hershel and the Hanukkah Goblins
by Eric Kimmel
(Ages 5–8)
Illustrated by Trina Schart Hyman.
1989. Holiday House, $14.95.

Hershel thinks his trek through the snow is about to end as he approaches a village where Hanukkah should soon be celebrated. But when he arrives, there are no candles, and the villagers are frightened of goblins who have taken over the synagogue. Armed with some hard-boiled eggs, pickles, and his own courage and wit, Hershel saves the day in an exciting conclusion. Hyman's illustrations move from a snowy village to the forbidding interior of the haunted synagogue upon the hill. Her goblins are the kind that children will love to hate and her hero is the embodiment of strength.

Awards: Caldecott Honor Book 1990; Notable Children's Book 1990

The Hoboken Chicken Emergency
by Daniel Manus Pinkwater
(See Videos.)
1977. Simon & Schuster, $10.95; paper, $4.95.

If You Made a Million
by David M. Schwartz
(Ages 7–10)
Illustrated by Steven Kellogg.
1989. Lothrop, $14.95.

Marvelosissimo the Mathematical Magician leads the Cheerful and Willing kids on a tour of earning money, saving it, and spending it. The book begins with an introduction to pennies, nickels, dimes, and quarters and how many of them are in a dollar. Later, borrowing is introduced, as are earning and paying interest. Kellogg's zany watercolors of ogres and castles feature his typical sense of humor. This is the companion volume to *How Much Is a Million?*, recommended for slightly older readers.

Awards: Notable Children's Book 1990

Iktomi and the Buffalo Skull: A Plains Indian Story
by Paul Goble
(Ages 6–9)
1991. Orchard Books, $14.95.

Iktomi is a character drawn from Plains Indian lore—part buffoon, part prankster—whose narcissism lands him in such impossible situations as inside a buffalo skull or in the path of a huge, crashing boulder, as in *Iktomi and the Boulder* (a Notable Children's Book in 1988). Goble uses visual and verbal tricks to tell an amusing tale and share essential points of Native American culture. The bright illustrations feature captions that define the Indian's colorful attire and accoutrements. Comments uttered with simplistic vanity by Iktomi are set in small print against Goble's straightforward narration. Also, italicized notes are designed to spur specific responses from young readers and listeners. A great read-aloud book.

In Coal Country
by Judith Hendershot
(Ages 6–8)
Illustrated by Thomas B. Allen.
1987. Knopf, $14.95.

Growing up in a 1930s coal-mining town had its pleasures, according to this memoir brimming with coal dust and nostalgia. Allen's charcoal drawings depict the gritty life that encircles the busy children as they swim, collect flowers, sled, and play happily throughout the seasons.

Awards: Notable Children's Book 1987

Insect Metamorphosis: From Egg to Adult
by Ron and Nancy Goor
(Ages 7–10)
1990. Atheneum, $13.95.

Sharp, closeup photographs and a well-organized text explain and illustrate each stage of both complete and incomplete insect metamorphosis. The royal walnut moth, for example, is shown progressing from egg to larva to pupa to moth. Along the way terms, such as *exoskeleton* and *molting,* are discussed. Both familiar insects (butterflies, wasps, mosquitoes, grasshoppers) and the not-so-familiar (praying mantises, dragonflies, and cicadas) are revealed along their passage to maturity.

Awards: Notable Children's Book 1990

Island Boy
by Barbara Cooney
(Ages 4–9)
1988. Viking, $14.95.

An ambitious and evocative record of the life of Matthias Tibbetts, this picture book sets its scene on a rugged island off the coast of Maine during the nineteenth century. Watercolors portray the shipbuilding, farming, and seagoing lifestyle of Matthias, who runs off to sea at age 10 but returns to the island to raise his children and grandchildren. The detailed illustrations call to mind the flat dimensions of American Primitive paintings. An imagina-tion-stretching exercise and a great history lesson for young readers.

Jim and the Beanstalk
by Raymond Briggs
(See Fractured Fairy Tales, p. 53.)

Jimmy's Boa and the Big Splash Birthday Bash
by Trinka Hakes Noble
(Ages 5–8)
Illustrated by Steven Kellogg.
1989. Dial, $12.95.

This year Jimmy's birthday party is at SeaLand. When his pet goldfish and boa get involved, everyone ends up in the tank despite his mom's efforts to control the chaotic events. Kellogg's pictures are typically wild, funny, and bursting out of their frames. A romp of a book that children will read and listen to again and again. It's told in flashback by Maggie to her mother, just like Noble's earlier Boa stories, including *The Day Jimmy's Boa Ate the Wash* (a Reading Rainbow selection) and *Jimmy's Boa Bounces Back.*

The Josefina Story Quilt
by Eleanor Coerr
(Ages 5–8)
Illustrated by Bruce Degen.
1986. HarperCollins, $9.98.

Westward travel in a covered wagon, seen through the eyes of a young girl. Faith pleads with her father to allow her pet hen, Josefina, to accompany them. "She is too old to lay eggs and too tough to eat," says Faith's father; but he relents and allows his daughter her wish. Along the way, Josefina starts a stampede, nearly drowns Faith's brother, and rescues the wagon train from robbers. This simple introduction to the westward expansion ends with a historical note about the quilt Faith created to remember the journey's high and low points.

Julius: The Baby of the World
by Kevin Henkes
(Ages 5–8)
1990. Greenwillow, $12.95.

Lily the mouse, who debuted in *Chester's Way,* faces some stiff competition in this story. She discovers that the "bump" in her mother's dress is going to be a baby. After Julius arrives, Lily warns pregnant strangers, "You will live to regret that bump in your dress." Then, when a cousin, imitating Lily, disparages the new baby, Lily pounces, making a sudden staunch defense of her brother. Family loyalty wins out over sibling rivalry in Henkes's delightfully illustrated story. Another great story on this theme is *The Very Worst Monster* by Pat Hutchins.

Awards: Notable Children's Book 1991

Jump! The Adventures of Brer Rabbit
Retold by Van Dyke Parks and Malcolm Jones
(Ages 7–10)
Illustrated by Barry Moser.
1986. HBJ, $14.95.

The original folktales set down by Joel Chandler Harris retain their spunk in these newer versions. The broad dialect has been exchanged for a rolling storytelling style loyal to the era and the characters. Moser alternates bright color and graywash illustrations featuring Brer Rabbit, Brer Fox, Brer Weasel, and their compatriots in fancy nineteenth-century attire. The starring hare outwits his fellow creatures most of the time, but he also meets his match on occasion. The famous Tar Baby story is in the equally enthralling sequel, *Jump Again! More Adventures of Brer Rabbit.*

Awards: Notable Children's Book 1986

The Kid's Guide to Social Action: How to Solve the Social Problems You Choose—And Turn Creative Thinking into Positive Action
by Barbara A. Lewis
(Ages 8–12)
1991. Free Spirit (400 First Avenue, North Suite 616, Minneapolis, MN 55401), paper, $14.95.

Lewis's book teaches kids that they have the power to make things change. The successful work of their peers is displayed, while techniques are explained for writing letters and news releases, performing interviews, forming action groups, and keeping oneself inspired and informed. Plenty of addresses for government agencies, organizations, and awards are included along with sample forms for contacting the right people. Good advice is offered on handling media attention: "What to do after you send the release and the reporters arrive." And arrive they will, if kids follow these guidelines.

Knots on a Counting Rope
by Bill Martin and John Archambault
(Ages 4–10)
Illustrated by Ted Rand.
1987. Holt, $14.95.

A blind Native American boy listens to his grandfather tell the story of the boy's short life. The boy, named Strength-of-Blue-Horses, participates in the storytelling, as in the oral tradition. After each recounting of the tale, the grandfather ties another knot in a rope, and this tradition gives the boy confidence to overcome his handicap. The values of faith, family, and love are beautifully enhanced by Rand's illustrations.

Awards: Reading Rainbow selection

The Legend of the Indian Paintbrush
by Tomie dePaola
(Ages 7–10)
1988. Putnam, $13.95; paper, $5.95.

A gorgeous retelling of a Native American folktale about the origin of Wyoming's state flower. Little Gopher wishes to capture the colors of the sunset on his canvas of white buckskin. Though he envies the other boys who ride out on great hunts, Little Gopher stays home painting the events. But soon he is celebrated as "He-Who-Brought-the-Sunset-to-the-Earth." DePaola's peaceful watercolors make a strong visual impact on even a casual reader.

Awards: Reading Rainbow selection

Lon Po Po: A Red Riding Hood Story from China
by Ed Young
(Ages 6–9)
1989. Philomel, $14.95.

In a different setting, a familiar story is imbued with just enough suspense for those who have heard it before. Three sisters—Shang, Tao, and Paotze—all alone, are visited by the wolf, who pretends to be their Po-Po (grandmother). Young's soft pastels depict the wolf in twisted positions as he tries to attack his prey. The fruit of the gingko tree woos the wolf away; its branches shield the children.

Awards: Caldecott Medal 1990; Notable Children's Book 1989; Reading Rainbow selection

The Magic Schoolbus inside the Human Body
by Joanna Cole
(Ages 6–9)
Illustrated by Bruce Degen.
1989. Scholastic, $13.95.

Ms. Frizzle is a dream (or a nightmare) of a science teacher. Her outfits always reflect the day's study program, her classroom is packed with relevant displays, and her field trips are out of this world. Really. The magic school bus has traveled into space and to the center of the earth in previous stories. In this tale, the school bus sets out for the science museum, but winds up inside one student's body. Traveling through the stomach, heart, and brain, the kids on board issue their usual wisecracks, learn quite a bit, and arrive back at school very relieved. Every book in this series is stuffed with practical facts taught in an unusual, outrageous fashion. *The Magic Schoolbus inside the Earth* is a Reading Rainbow selection.

Marguerite, Go Wash Your Feet
Compiled and illustrated by Wallace Tripp
(Ages 5–10)
1985. Houghton Mifflin, $14.95; paper, $5.95.

Irreverence is too mild a term for the cartoons and drawings Tripp matches to the droll and funny poems pulled together for this collection. Presented are jokes, rhymes, linguistic

BEST OF THE BEST FOR CHILDREN

puns, and, in general, lots of fun for readers of all ages. Younger readers will also enjoy *Granfa' Grig Had a Pig: And Other Rhymes without Reason from Mother Goose.*

The Microscope
by Maxine Kumin
(Ages 6–10)
Illustrated by Arnold Lobel.
1984. HarperCollins, $11.95; paper, $2.95.

Within this slim book, Kumin tells the story of Anton van Leeuwenhoek, the inventor of the microscope. Lobel's black-and-white portraits of the seventeenth-century Dutch and the creatures under the lens of the microscope are perfectly paired with Kumin's whimsical verse.

Awards: Reading Rainbow selection

Mirandy and Brother Wind
by Patricia McKissack
(Ages 8–11)
Illustrated by Jerry Pinkney.
1988. Knopf, $12.95.

Mirandy wants, with all her heart, to win the junior cakewalk, and Ezel the young neighbor boy wants to be her partner. But Mirandy has her mother's words on her mind, "There's an old saying that whoever can catch the Wind can make him do their bidding," Mirandy sets out to do just that—catch Brother Wind. Miss Poinsettia, the local conjure woman, helps Mirandy with her quest and Mirandy and Ezel win the competition. Pinkney's double-page spreads, done in watercolors, capture the tender side of teenage behavior and the richness of early-nineteenth-century, African-American tradition.

Awards: Caldecott Honor Book 1989; Notable Children's Book 1988; Coretta Scott King Award 1989

The Mouse and the Motorcycle
by Beverly Cleary
(See *Ralph S. Mouse* in Videos.)
1965. Morrow, $12.95; Dell, paper, $3.25.

Mrs. Pig Gets Cross and Other Stories
by Mary Rayner
(Ages 5–8)
1987. Dutton, $11.95.

Seven short stories featuring Mr. and Mrs. Pig and their 10 piglets. The first story introduces the spunky family as Mrs. Pig refuses to clean up. Other stories relate the antics of "Wicked William," who ironically rescues his little brother from a locked bathroom; stubborn Benjamin Pig, who decides to have his own way for once; feminist Sorrel Pig, who challenges the boys in sports competition; and Garth, who innocently captures the wolf in the last story of the book. Rayner's storytelling is neat, understated, and funny. Her watercolor illustrations perfectly complement this fourth book about the Pig family.

Mufaro's Beautiful Daughters:
An African Tale
by John Steptoe
(See Videos.)
1987. Lothrop, $13.95.

Awards: Caldecott Honor Book 1988; Coretta Scott King Award 1988; Notable Children's Book 1987; Reading Rainbow selection

My Father Always Embarrasses Me

by Meir Shalev

(Ages 4–8)

Translated from the Hebrew by Dagmar Herrmann.
Illustrated by Yossi Abolafia.
1990. Wellington Publishing, $13.95.

With a father who stays at home and "does nothing—only hammers away at his typewriter and embarrasses his son," Mortimer Dunne is not a happy kid (though he is proud of his mother—a successful television reporter). Dunne is embarrassed enough when his dad snores at PTA meetings, but when his father volunteers for the school baking contest, Mortimer is beyond the moon. His dad's entry turns out to be a surprise to all, and brings the father and son closer together. Originally written in Hebrew, this tale is a universal one, wittily told and enlivened by piquant watercolors.

My Friend Jacob

by Lucille Clifton

(Ages 6–10)

Illustrated by Thomas DiGrazia.
1980. Dutton, $7.95.

Eight-year-old Sam's friend Jacob is 16 and mentally retarded, but nowhere in this book does it actually state that the boy is disabled. Instead the story focuses on Jacob's particular talents—perfect aim with a basketball and astounding recognition of car makes and models. Sam tries to teach Jacob some practical life skills, such as knocking on doors, but the story and its accompanying soft, black-and-white drawings home in on the interaction between the two boys. A warm and understated examination of human individuality.

My Prairie Year: Based on the Diary of Elenore Paisted

by Brett Harvey

(Ages 7–10)

1986. Holiday House, $11.95.

Author Harvey's family left Maine in 1889 to homestead in the Dakota Territory. Using her grandmother's diary, Harvey re-creates daily life on the prairie. Monday was washday, Tuesday was ironing and mending, Wednesday was gardening, Thursday was shopping, Friday was cleaning, and Saturday was baking. Only on Sunday, after lessons, could the children run freely through the prairie grass or ride on horseback. Each season also had its tasks and dangers, from planting and harvest to tornadoes and prairie fires. Charcoal drawings enhance the descriptive text.

Awards: Notable Children's Book 1986

The Nativity

by Julie Vivas

(Ages 10–Adult)

1988. HBJ, $13.95.

At first glance, some readers may be offended by this decidedly unglorified version of the Christmas story. For example, Vivas's watercolors show the angel Gabriel with tattered iridescent wings and combat boots, while Mary's breasts and stomach swell obviously. But the down-to-earth images loom powerful next to the language of the King James Bible. This thought-provoking treatment effectively underscores the mystery of Christ's birth.

Awards: Notable Children's Book 1988

Nebulae: The Birth & Death of Stars

by Necia H. Apfel

(Ages 7–10)

1988. Lothrop, $13.95.

Spectacular photographs of exploding stars are accompanied by Apfel's lucid explanations of these clouds of interstellar gases and particles lit by other stars. Nebulae make fantastic shows in the sky and provide information on star aging and star formation. Both light show and science are well conveyed here.

Nellie, A Cat on Her Own

by Natalie Babbitt

(Ages 7–9)

1989. Farrar, Straus & Giroux, $11.95.

Babbitt, known for her popular fiction for older children, weaves a theme of self-reliance into this tale of a cat marionette. Nellie is owned by a clever old woman who can make her dance. But when her owner dies, Nellie thinks that she will never dance again. Big Tom, the old woman's real cat, brings her to the gathering where cats dance in the moonlight. She learns that not only can she dance on her own (with a little help from "moonshine"), but she likes it even better. Bold illustrations capture both the tranquil rural setting and the cats' cavorting.

Nettie Jo's Friends

by Patricia C. McKissack

(Ages 4–7)

Illustrated by Scott Cook.
1989. Knopf, $13.95.

Tomorrow is Cousin Willadeen and Charles Henry's wedding, and Nettie Jo has just one day to find a needle to sew a dress for Annie Mae, her favorite doll. She grabs her burlap sack and takes a walk through McKelvey Bottoms looking for her prize. Along the way she meets Miz Rabbit, Fox, and Panther, all of whom she helps despite the fact that they cannot help her. Depressed, Nettie Jo returns home for the evening. Then with a "Blat-a-tat-tum!" arrive her three friends bearing a needle and thank-yous. Cook uses shades of brown and yellow in his sunlit paintings that become more golden as the day ends. An imaginative and romantically wrought book.

A New Coat for Anna

by Harriet Ziefert

(Ages 5–8)

Illustrated by Anita Lobel.
1986. Knopf, $10.95.

Finding materials to make a coat in post–World War II Europe is no easy matter. But Anna's determined mother begins the long procedure of trading valuables for fabric and craftsmanship. She acquires some wool from a farmer, has it spun into yarn, dyes the yarn with berry juice, and takes it to a weaver. Family heirlooms are passed on for each of these tasks, and when the coat is completed at Christmas, a party is given to celebrate. Lobel's color illustrations give a real sense of the time, as if they were old photographs.

Nicholas Cricket

by Joyce Maxner

(Ages 5–8)

Illustrated by William Joyce.
1989. HarperCollins, $12.95.

Maxner's playful verse tells of the Bug-a-Wug Cricket Band that plays for the animals all night and into tomorrow.

If we're quiet and quick
we can find Cricket Nick
and the washboard strummers
and the slap-a-spoon drummers
and the crick-crick-crickety kazo hummers.

Joyce's moonlit paintings have a mysterious, seductive quality that entices children into his imaginative world. A delightful way to tuck children in on a warm summer's night.

Night on Neighborhood Street
by Eloise Greenfield
(Ages 5–8)
Illustrated by Jan Spivey Gilchrist.
1991. Dial, $13.95.

Leafing through Gilchrist's paintings to the rhythm of Greenfield's poetry feels like a stroll down an inner-city block. The people come to life. A church group is in midchorus. Kids play street games and walk away from a drug peddler hawking his wares on the corner. A reputedly haunted house lends mystery to the otherwise realistic territory.

Awards: Coretta Scott King Honor Book 1992; Notable Children's Book 1992

Oh, Brother!
by Arthur Yorinks
(Ages 6–8)
Illustrated by Richard Egielski.
1989. Farrar, Straus & Giroux, $15.95.

British twins are so wrapped up in their rivalry that they blow up a liner crossing the Atlantic and wind up in a U.S. orphanage. The boys escape from the foundling home to work in a circus, on street corners, and finally, in a tailor's shop, quarreling all the while. Egielski's large pictures, packed with period detail, mesh nicely with Yorinks's wry text,

guaranteeing appeal to both kids and adults. Look for other works by this team, including *It Happened in Pinsk* and *Hey, Al* (a Caldecott Medal winner).

On the Pampas
by María Cristina Brusca
(See Multicultural Fare, p. 37.)

The Patchwork Quilt
by Valerie Flournoy
(Ages 6–8)
Illustrated by Jerry Pinkney.
1985. Dial, $11.95.

A grandmother starts a quilt with the help of her granddaughter Tanya. A year's worth of memories go into the project, as remnants from some favorite jeans, a fancy dress, a Halloween costume, and other scraps are lovingly stitched in. No glamorous patterns can be found in this homespun quilt, as there are in *Sam Johnson and the Blue Ribbon Quilt* by Lisa Campbell Ernst. The simple square-patch pattern reflects the unassuming, homey character of the black family members who all pitch in to finish the project when Grandma falls ill. Pinkney's warm paintings have the depth of photographs, and the finished quilt is a masterpiece.

Awards: Coretta Scott King Award 1986

Paul Revere's Ride
by Henry Wadsworth Longfellow
(Ages 5–8)
Illustrated by Ted Rand.
1990. Dutton, $14.95.

Listen my children and you shall hear
Of the midnight ride of Paul Revere.

Rand's rich color paintings splendidly illustrate the words of Longfellow's classic poem about the Revolutionary War hero. Moonlit and lamplit scenes convey the drama of the verse. Endpaper maps help readers trace the route.

Pecos Bill
by Steven Kellogg
(Ages 5–8)
1986. Morrow, $14.95.

Separated from his parents' wagon train, Pecos Bill was raised by coyotes. This fiercely strong, fast, and clever fellow directed the first cattle roundups, invented the lariat, and tamed the wild horses of Texas. Kellogg improvises a bit on the legend and illustrates it in colorful, outrageous drawings so filled with action and particulars that they rekindle interest with every reading. Among the other folk heroes Kellogg has profiled in picture-book format are Paul Bunyan and Johnny Appleseed.

Peter and the Wolf
by Sergei Prokofiev
(Ages 4–8)
Illustrated by Barbara Cooney.
1985. Viking, $13.95.

Cooney's exquisitely designed version of the plot of the famous symphonic fairy tale is as close to a stage production as you can hold in your hands. After undoing the red ribbons that tie the cover closed and opening to the title page, one sees the first scene—the house of Peter's grandfather—spring into view. This three-dimensional tableau leads to four others, each more elaborate. Young readers can slide an arrow to animate the wolf's capture of the duck and Peter's capture of the wolf. The final scene at the zoo is a wonder,

complete with a caged wolf, balloon vendor in the midst of a sale, and a tall giraffe overlooking it all. An entrancing pop-up. (See also *Peter and the Wolf* in Audio.)

Pigs from A to Z
by Arthur Geisert
(See ABCs, p. 14.)

Poems of A. Nonny Mouse
by Jack Prelutsky
(Ages 6–12)
Illustrated by Henrik Drescher.
1989. Knopf, $12.95; paper, $4.99.

Prelutsky's cute introduction reveals that all these limericks, tongue twisters, and nonsense verses signed Anonymous should be attributed to Ms. A. Nonny Mouse, a rodent whose name keeps getting misspelled. What follows is a collection of such poems as:

> Algy met a bear,
> A bear met Algy.
> The bear was bulgy,
> The bulge was Algy.

Drescher's wild double-page spreads, done in bright colors and in the spirit of Edward Lear, add considerably to the kooky verses, four of which are original Prelutskys. Absurdity and irreverence will bring out the child in all readers. Look for Nonny in every picture. Just as much fun as Prelutsky's *For Laughing Out Loud*.

Awards: Notable Children's Book 1990

The Potato Man
by Megan McDonald
(Ages 5–8)
Illustrated by Ted Lewin.
1991. Orchard Books, $14.95.

A grandfather recalls the peddlers of his youth who sold their wares from horse-drawn carts along cobblestoned streets. The old man speaks to his grandchildren as the story opens, but soon all of the art is devoted to the old days. Full-color spreads show the knife sharpener and the potato man at work while the children watch in wonder.

Prehistoric Pinkerton
by Steven Kellogg
(Ages 4–8)
1987. Dial, $12.95.

Pinkerton, the irresistible, enormous Great Dane puppy, is teething. Look out. It's bad enough when he fells a tree holding a neighbor's hammock containing the sleeping neighbor. But when he heads to the museum with his owner, disaster occurs. All those tempting dinosaur bones are more than Pinkerton can resist. Kellogg's bright color drawings are filled with funny details that enhance the story line. The combination of dinosaurs and dogs make a book that kids will return to many times. Look for more of Kellogg's tall tales based on his own pup, such as *Pinkerton, Behave!*

Princess Furball
Retold by Charlotte Huck
(Ages 4–7)
(See Fractured Fairy Tales, p. 54.)

The Purple Coat
by Amy Hest
(Ages 5–7)
Illustrated by Amy Schwartz.
1986. Four Winds, $12.95.

Gabby decides that she wants a purple coat this fall instead of the standard navy blue one she has gotten every other year. Gabby and her mother ride into New York City to visit grandfather's tailor shop, where he manages to please both mother and daughter with a reversible coat—blue on one side, purple on the other. Schwartz's watercolors brightly depict city life and family relationships.

Awards: Notable Children's Book 1986; Reading Rainbow selection

Puss in Boots
by Charles Perrault
(Ages 5–9)
Illustrated by Fred Marcellino.
1990. Farrar, Straus & Giroux, $14.95.

In this magnificently crafted book, Marcellino's creamy illustrations lend a royal air to the famed cat—an ordinary tabby cat wearing nothing but an enormous pair of boots. The text is in large, gray type, befitting the soft pastoral setting of the story of the feline who rescued from penury a youngest son with no inheritance.

Awards: Caldecott Honor Book 1991; Notable Children's Book 1991

Ralph S. Mouse
by Beverly Cleary
(See Videos.)
1982. Morrow, $12.95; Dell, paper, $3.25.

Ramona Quimby, Age 8
by Beverly Cleary
(See *Ramona Stories* in Videos.)
1981. Morrow, $14.95; Dell, paper, $3.25.

Awards: Newbery Honor Book 1982

Ramona the Pest

by Beverly Cleary

(See *Ramona Stories* in Videos.)

1968. Morrow, $13.95; Dell, paper, $3.25.

The Relatives Came

by Cynthia Rylant

(Ages 5–7)

Illustrated by Stephen Gammell.
1985. Bradbury, $12.95.

Rylant captures perfectly the mayhem and glee produced by a visit from distant relatives. Even the smallest impact is noted, for example, at night, amid the murmurs and laughs there is "all that new breathing." Gammell's drawings fill this picture book with homey warmth.

Awards: Caldecott Honor Book 1986

Rumpelstiltskin

by the Brothers Grimm

(Ages 6–9)

Retold and illustrated by Paul Zelinsky.
1986. Dutton, $13.95.

Zelinsky's incredible paintings get better with each page in this familiar fairy tale about the impudent, cynical little man who makes a cheap deal with the miller's daughter to spin straw into gold in exchange for her first child. The pastoral detail is infused with gold—the rich colors of the illustrations pop from bright white paper. A truly special book.

Awards: Caldecott Honor Book 1987; Notable Children's Book 1986; Reading Rainbow selection

Runaway Ralph

by Beverly Cleary

(See *Ralph S. Mouse* in Videos.)

1970. Morrow, $14.95; Dell, paper, $3.25.

Scaly Babies: Reptiles Growing Up

by Ginny Johnston and Judy Cutchins

(Ages 6–8)

1988. Morrow, $12.95; paper, $4.95.

These striking closeups of charming baby boas, hatching gila monsters, and tiny turtles will diminish anyone's aversion toward reptilians. The text is packed with enough facts for a school report. General notes on the birth, life cycles, feeding, predators, and idiosyncracies of snakes, lizards, turtles, and crocodilians are followed by some specifics on particular species. The anecdotal writing and terrific illustrations make for fun science reading. The same approach is used in *Slippery Babies* by the same authors.

Shaka: King of the Zulus

by Diane Stanley and Peter Vennema

(Ages 7–10)

Illustrated by Diane Stanley.
1988. Morrow, $13.95.

Shaka was born in 1787 of the Zulu clan. Credited with being a military genius, he brought his clan power as a mighty nation. Stanley's pale yellow backgrounds are embellished with borders of beaded design. Detailed costumes portray the South African cultural style of another era. A pronunciation guide and sources are included for kids whose interest is piqued by this well-designed book.

Shari Lewis Presents 101 Things for Kids to Do

by Shari Lewis

(See Videos.)

Illustrated by Jon Buller.
1987. Random House, paper, $6.95.

FRACTURED FAIRY TALES

Here are some wacky or otherwise revisited versions of much-loved tales. Parodies can bring home the moral with humor and pizazz. Some of the darker tales, such as "Hansel and Gretel," do not translate well into spoofs for younger readers, the classic versions are the best bets, especially those retold and illustrated by Jan Brett, Paul Galdone, Trina Schart Hyman, and Paul Zelinsky.

A Frog Prince by Alix Berenzy   (Ages 6–9)   1989. Holt, $13.95.

"Once upon a time there lived a Frog who loved a Princess." Reworking the old Brothers Grimm tale about the frog who rescues the princess's gold ball and transforms into her prince, Berenzy rejects that premise altogether, giving the frog a shot at wish fulfillment. The King bestows ample means upon the frog to follow sun and moon to find another kingdom with "a *true* princess, of a different mind." Berenzy's spoof attacks the problem of this fairy tale—a spoiled brat of a girl abuses someone who is kind and gets rewarded in the end. The illustrations feature a human-sized frog with a heart and soul. A pleasure for all familiar with the original tale.

Goldilocks and the Three Bears by James Marshall   (Ages 4–7)   1988. Dial, $10.95.

Unlike other parodists who fracture fairy tales, Marshall stays close to the original story lines, but spices them up with sassy dialogue and madcap illustrations. His work is similar in tone to Steven Kellogg's *Chicken Little* (see p. 16), another not-to-miss picture book filled with modern wit and old-fashioned fun.
Awards: Caldecott Honor Book 1989

Jim and the Beanstalk by Raymond Briggs   (Ages 6–8)   1989. Putnam, paper, $5.95.

In Briggs's version of an old favorite the son of the giant from Jack and the Beanstalk appears. This second-generation giant has aged considerably and kindhearted Jim climbs the colossal plant to assist him. Jim locates a wig, spectacles, and false teeth for the balding, toothless gent. Turn to the 1992 ALA Notable *Jack and the Beanstalk* by Steven Kellogg for a conventional version of the popular tale.

Princess Furball Retold by Charlotte Huck   (Ages 4–7)   Illustrated by Anita Lobel.   1989. Greenwillow, $13.95.

Children's literature scholar Huck connects with the talented Lobel in a Cinderella variant set in medieval times. A clever, golden-haired princess is ignored, then promised in marriage to an ogre. Fleeing the castle with "one dress as golden as the sun, another as silvery as the moon, and a third as glittering as the stars," wearing a "coat made of a thousand different kinds of fur," and carrying treasure from her dead mother, Furball soon finds herself "servant to the servants" in another king's castle. There, with her goodly traits and magic gifts, she wins the king's love. This is a long but thoroughly entertaining tale. Lobel's frizzy-haired Princess Furball is a delight. *Sleeping Ugly* by Jane Yolen is another gem in this same vein.

Sidney Rella and the Glass Sneaker by Bernice Myers   (Ages 6–8)   1985. Macmillan, $13.95.

Sidney longs to be a football star, but he is forced to do all of the work around the house instead. The appearance of his fairy godfather changes all that in this wonderful "fracture" of a famous tale. (For more Cinderella versions, see Videos, p. 162.)

A Telling of Tales by William J. Brooke   (Ages 8–11)   1990. HarperCollins, $12.95.

Brooke adds unexpected twists that enliven five classic tales: "Sleeping Beauty," "Paul Bunyan," "Cinderella," "John Henry," and "Jack and the Beanstalk." Sleeping Beauty demands to see the prince's ID; Paul Bunyan learns to grow trees; Cinderella's foot doesn't fit the glass slipper, but the prince marries her anyway; a newspaper reporter invents the legend of John Henry to save face. Kids will enjoy dissecting the changes and creating their own.

The Waking of the Prince   The Working
Henry   The Fitting of the Slipper   The
Growin' of Paul Bunyan   The Telling of a T

Trail of Stones by Gwen Strauss   (Ages 12–17)   Illustrated by Anthony Browne.   1990. Knopf, $6.95.

In language both quaint and contemporary, Strauss reworks fairy-tale poems of childhood. Hansel and Gretel, Cinderella, Beauty and the Beast, and other familiar characters come alive, but without the softened edges of storybook memories. Instead, Strauss probes the heart of each character: the passionate Cinderella who loves the prince, the guilty father who's locked Hansel and Gretel out of his life. Black-and-white portraits by renowned picture-book illustrator Anthony Browne capture the intensity of the poems, which challenge readers to look for truth beneath the familiar, comfortable facades.

Awards: BBYA 1991

The True Story of the Three Little Pigs by Jon Scieszka   (Ages 5–8)   Illustrated by Lane Smith. 1989. Viking, $13.95.

The wolf plays on the reader's sympathy and gullibility as he narrates his version of what really happened concerning the Three Little Pigs. It seems he was making a birthday cake for his granny—whose portrait on the wall behind him reveals her to be the wolf of Little Red Riding Hood fame—when he ran out of sugar. So, it seems, his visits to the little pigs' homes were in search for the proverbial cup of sugar. In addition, the sneezing was just symptomatic of a terrible cold. And, of course, once the media got involved the whole thing was blown out of proportion. Smith's full-color illustrations are wacky and modern and funny.

Awards: Notable Children's Book 1990

Sidney Rella and the Glass Sneaker
by Bernice Meyers
(See Fractured Fairy Tales, p. 54.)

Sing a Song of Popcorn: Every Child's Book of Poems
Edited by Beatrice Schenk de Regniers and others
(Ages 4–12)
1988. Scholastic, $16.95.

Here's poetry that children can't put down. If the funny rhymes or thoughtful verses don't capture their fancy, the artistry of Maurice Sendak, Trina Schart Hyman, Arnold Lobel, and six other Caldecott-winning artists will. The topical arrangement allows readers to zero in on just the right verse for the right mood or school project. Also a must for family read-aloud sessions.

Awards: Notable Children's Book 1988

Song and Dance Man
by Karen Ackerman
(See Videos)
Illustrated by Stephen Gammell.
1988. Knopf, $11.95.

Awards: Caldecott Medal 1989; Notable Children's Book 1988

The Star Maiden: An Ojibway Tale
Retold by Barbara Juster Esbensen
(Ages 7–10)
1988. Little, Brown, $14.95.

Striking full-page watercolors are framed by Native American motifs in this beautiful retelling of an Ojibway legend. Members of the tribe spot a bright star almost reaching the earth. When the young braves are sent out to find it, one dreams of a silver maiden who longs to live among his people. The wise men of the council advise her to choose a peaceful resting place for her home. She at last settles on a quiet pond. Calling her sisters of the sky to join her, they become the stars of the water, the water lilies.

Storm in the Night
by Mary Stolz
(Ages 5–8)
Illustrated by Pat Cummings.
1988. HarperCollins, $12.95; paper, $4.95.

When the lights go out on a dark, stormy night, Thomas, a young black child, clutches his cat Ringo and tells his grandfather, unconvincingly, that he is not afraid. Grandfather, in turn, tells a story about the scariest moment in his own childhood. Cummings's artwork brings out the power of nature, while the story's ending shows Thomas bravely admitting his own fear. This book could open communication channels for kids reluctant to admit their worries.

The Story of Hanukkah
by Amy Ehrlich
(Ages 6–8)
Illustrated by Ori Sherman.
1989. Dial, $14.95.

The story of the Jewish Festival of Lights is conveyed in poetic prose and luminescent drawings. Sherman's gouache paintings impart the glory of the holiday and match perfectly Ehrlich's recounting of the successful fight for freedom underlying this annual Jewish observation.

Awards: Notable Children's Book 1990

Stringbean's Trip to the Shining Sea
by Vera B. Williams
(Ages 7–9)

Illustrated by Vera B. Williams and Jennifer Williams. 1988. Greenwillow, $11.95; Scholastic, paper, $3.95.

Stringbean Coe and his older brother, Fred, journey west from Kansas in a homemade camper, sending back postcards that tell of their adventures. The book consists of these postcards, fashioned in bright colors and filled with hand-lettered messages in various typefaces and styles. The Williamses' book, not unlike a photo album, reveals quite a bit about the cross-country road trip and the personalities of the two boys who accomplished it.

Awards: Notable Children's Book 1988

Susanna of the Alamo: A True Story
by John Jakes
(Ages 7–10)

Illustrated by Paul Bacon. 1986. HBJ, $13.95.

Davy Crockett is probably a more familiar defender of the famous old Spanish mission; but Susanna Dickinson's courage was equally tested. It was Susanna who carried a message directly from Santa Anna to General Sam Houston (who later defeated the Mexican dictator). The letter was "Full of false friendliness. [Susanna] was determined to deliver the message in a way that would make Santa Anna sorry he had ever sent it." She delivered an outraged narrative of the slaughter that raised the cry, "Remember the Alamo!" In this well-illustrated retelling Jakes has "Avoided legend, no matter how attractive," inventing only the dialogue. Bacon's maps, letters, historical

documents, and watercolor portraits enhance that sense of realism.

Swan Lake
by Margot Fonteyn
(Ages 6–9)

Illustrated by Trina Schart Hyman. 1989. HBJ, $14.95.

Esteemed ballerina Margot Fonteyn offers a captivating version of the beloved story of true love and the battle between good and evil. Hyman's paintings catch the feeling of the Rhineland. Her Odette is fragile and beautiful. On one side of each spread is a full-page painting, on the other is the text, accompanied by a small painting that reveals more about the particular scene. An added note about the history of the ballet brings even more meaning to the story.

The Tale of the Mandarin Ducks
by Katherine Paterson
(Ages 5–9)

Illustrated by Leo and Diane Dillon. 1990. Lodestar, $14.95.

Paterson's original tale about love and compassion, reward and principal, is enhanced by the Dillons' Asian-inspired artwork. When an evil lord assaults the natural world by stealing a mandarin drake for his personal viewing, Shozo, the emperor's steward, frees the duck, and is banished. But the drake, in turn, aids Shozo by helping his beloved, the kitchenmaid Yasuko, escape. The couple spend the rest of their days contentedly in a forest hut, living out the moral, "Trouble can always be borne when it is shared."

Awards: Notable Children's Book 1991

Talking Eggs

by Robert D. San Souci

(See Cinderella, p. 162.)

Illustrated by Jerry Pinkney.
1989. Dial, $12.95.

Awards: Caldecott Honor Book 1990; Notable Children's Book 1989

The Tenth Good Thing about Barney

by Judith Viorst

(See Videos.)

Illustrated by Eric Blegvad.
1971. Atheneum, $12.95; Aladdin, paper, $3.95.

That's Exactly the Way It Wasn't

by James Stevenson

(Ages 5–9)

1991. Greenwillow, $13.95.

Stevenson has written a whole series of wonderful picture books starring two tykes, Mary Ann and Louie, and their grandfather who tells them fantastic stories of, "When I was a boy . . . ." The balding, white-mustachioed gent is always clad in a suit—even in the scenes that portray his childhood recollections (then, his mustache is brown and his pants short). Grandpa's recollections are always an outrageous mix of fantasy and happenstance. Typically his brother Wainright figures prominently in the stories. In this tale, Mary Ann and Louie have been banished from home till they quit bickering, so they settle on Grandpa's porch to hear a twice-told tale—that is, versions from both Uncle Wainey and Grandpa about their own sibling rivalry. Stevenson's usual array of fantastic events and things—an exploding cherry pie and a giant armadillo—are in evidence. One of the best books in this series is *Worse Than Willy*—any family with a new baby will relish that tale.

The Three Little Pigs and the Fox

by William Hooks

(Ages 4–7)

Illustrated by S. D. Schindler.
1989. Macmillan, $13.95.

The Hooks/Schindler collaboration results in an entertaining rendition of a classic. Mama Pig and her three piglets—Rooter, Oinky, and Hamlet—lead a happy life in Appalachia's Black Mountains, eating their favorite foods. One by one, as they grow too big for the house, Mama sends them out to seek their fortune armed with motherly advice—"One: You got to watch out for that mean, tricky old droolymouth fox. Two: Build yourself a safe, strong house out of rocks. Three: Come home to see your mama every single Sunday." The first two piglets leave reluctantly and subsequently get into trouble. Only Hamlet, the littlest pig, learns Mama's lessons, and saves the day. Repetition of phrases helps move the story, and Schindler's watercolors render a fine family of pigs.

Awards: Notable Children's Book 1990

Tom Thumb

by Richard Jesse Watson

(Ages 5–8)

1989. HBJ, $12.95.

Weary from travel, Merlin approaches the cottage of a couple longing for a child ("even if the babe were no bigger than my husband's thumb," says the wife). In gratitude for their hospitality, Merlin grants them their wish. Tom Thumb, "the tiniest of tiny boys," loves adventure and because of his size is often found in the middle of it. In one of these adventures, Tom learns that Grumbong the giant is pacified only by a sea shell; this comes in handy when that same giant is waging war against King Arthur. Tom arrives on the scene riding a mouse and leading his own army of animals into battle. He thus becomes the smallest Knight of the Round Table. Watson's detailed, full-color illustrations depict a fairylike Tom amid the large world that surrounds him.

To Space and Back
by Sally Ride and Susan Okie
(Ages 8–12)
1986. Lothrop, $14.95.

In 1983, physicist Sally Ride became the first female American astronaut to travel in space. Her story of that space shuttle journey answers all the questions little ones are eager to ask. Amid the glorious color photographs of the earth ("a blue and white marble"), readers view the shuttle taking off and fellow astronauts working, playing, and sleeping. A picture of a fork in midair and tales of cookie fights explain the concept of weightlessness clearly and humorously. (See U.S. Space Camp in Travel, p. 334.)

Awards: Notable Children's Book 1986

The True Story of the Three Little Pigs
by Jon Scieszka
(See Fractured Fairy Tales, p. 55.)

Tuesday
by David Wiesner
(Ages 5–8)
1991. Clarion, $15.95.

Flocks of frogs leave their swamps aboard soaring lily pads and visit a sleepy town during the night, returning to their murky homes at dawn and leaving behind their no-longer-flightworthy lily pads all over the town. With only nine words, the story is told via Wiesner's stunning watercolors. A comical twist at the end implies an unending array of surprising Tuesdays. (See *Free Fall,* p. 117.)

Awards: Caldecott Medal 1992

Up Goes the Skyscraper
by Gail Gibbons
(Ages 5–8)
1986. Four Winds, $12.95; Aladdin, paper, $4.95.

Gibbons is a prolific author-illustrator of children's books on practical matters. This view of the design and construction of a large city building is true to her quality of work. Fine flat watercolors with bright yellows and blues demonstrate people hard at work. From earth samples and city inspections to the "evergreen salute" by the ironworkers and the final moving-in day, Gibbons covers the construction in every detail. Basic explanations of I-beams, screed, wind load, and more provide a new perspective for those who love to watch tall buildings rise.

The Very Best of Friends
by Margaret Wild
(Ages 5–8)
Illustrated by Julie Vivas.
1990. HBJ, $13.95.

James is William's cat; Jessie is William's wife. When William dies suddenly, Jessie and the cat grieve in their own ways, barely heeding one another. One day, Jessie realizes that the cat needs her care; soon James recognizes that Jessie can be his friend. This gentle study of grief is powerfully enhanced by Vivas's watercolors.

Awards: Notable Children's Book 1991

The Wall
by Eve Bunting
(Ages 5–8)
Illustrated by Ronald Himler.
1990. Clarion, $13.95.

The Vietnam Veterans Memorial, known as "The Wall," carries the names of 58,000 people who lost their lives in that war. Bunting's picture book sends a message about the purpose and solemnity of the memorial by describing the visit of one small boy and his dad. The father locates his father's name on the wall, commenting, "My dad. He was just my age when he was killed." Visits by other mourners and a class—"a bunch of big girls in school uniforms"—interrupt the pair's quiet for just a moment and demonstrate how personal yet universal The Wall is. Older children will appreciate Brent Ashabranner's *Always to Remember,* which has background on the memorial's creation.

Awards: Notable Children's Book 1991

Watch the Stars Come Out
by Riki Levinson
(Ages 6–8)
Illustrated by Diane Goode.
1985. Dutton, $13.95.

The story of a family's immigration to the United States opens with grandmother and granddaughter looking into a photo album. The bulk of the book then relates great-grandmother's departure from Europe as a young girl, the transatlantic boat trip, seasickness, the death of friends, sighting the Statue of Liberty, physicals on Ellis Island, and finally hugging mama, papa, and sister before getting ready for bed. With soft browns and pastel tones, Goode's color pencils evoke a turn-of-the-century atmosphere.

The Wednesday Surprise
by Eve Bunting
(Ages 8–10)
Illustrated by Donald Carrick.
1989. Clarion, $13.95; paper, $4.95.

A grandmother and granddaughter work together in secret every Wednesday night on Dad's birthday present—learning to read. Bunting's story offers the fun of birthday preparations and has a special surprise ending. Family cooperation and affection is conveyed throughout. An inspirational tale, graced by Carrick's subdued colors.

Awards: Notable Children's Book 1990

What's the Matter with Herbie Jones?
by Suzy Kline
(Ages 7–10)
Illustrated by Richard Williams.
1986. Putnam, $11.95; Penguin, paper, $3.95.

Herbie is lovestruck after he dances with classmate Annabelle for the first time. In other words, Herbie has the "G-disease" (*G* for girl). His best friend recognizes it right away and sets out to perform a cure. Kline captures the third-grade mentality, and the rescue efforts of Herbie's pal are hilarious. Graywash illustrations add to the fun of a delightful story for both sexes. Readers who are just moving into chapter books (with more text than pictures) will love this and Kline's other stories about Herbie Jones, including *Herbie Jones and the Monster Ball.*

When I Am Old with You
by Angela Johnson
(Ages 5–7)
Illustrated by David Soman.
1990. Orchard Books, $14.95.

A young black child envisions herself old like Granddaddy, doing the things they both do now: rocking on the porch, fishing, playing cards, sitting under a tree, rummaging through the attic, looking at old pictures, eating "bacon for breakfast and that's all," roasting corn on the fire, visiting the ocean, riding on a tractor, and walking through the woods. Respect and admiration for elders, loyalty, and love are transmitted through Soman's watercolors.

Awards: Coretta Scott King Honor Book 1991; Notable Children's Book 1991

Who Owns the Sun?
by Stacy Chbosky
(See Videos.)
1988. Landmark, $12.95.

The Wolf's Chicken Stew
by Keiko Kasza
(Ages 5–7)
1987. Putnam, $12.95; paper, $4.95.

An insatiably hungry Wolf hatches a plan to fatten up a chicken he'd like to eat. The first night he leaves 100 "scrumptious pancakes" on the chicken's porch. The second he leaves 100 scrumptious doughnuts. And the third

night, a 100-pound cake. Then he steals up to the door to grab his fat chicken and is surprised to find 100 chicks thanking "Uncle Wolf" and kissing him. The wolf, a lovable character with a heart of gold, walks home humbled.

Awards: Notable Children's Book 1987

The Year of the Perfect Christmas Tree
by Gloria Houston
(Ages 5–8)
Illustrated by Barbara Cooney.
1988. Dial, $12.95.

The Appalachian Mountains, from spring through winter, are beautifully evoked by Cooney's paintings. The folk-art style adds charm to Houston's family lore. In the small village of Pine Grove, a different family provides the church Christmas tree every year. In spring, Ruth and her Papa select the perfect tree, but this winter Papa has been called away to World War I. Ruth's mom is a determined woman who, with her daughter's help, delivers the tree late one night. Mom also stitches a wondrous dress for Ruth to wear as the angel in the town pageant and a doll to fill her daughter's Christmas wish.

Young Lions
by Toshi Yoshida
(Ages 7–10)
1989. Philomel, $14.95.

On the plains of Africa, three restless lion cubs go on their first hunt alone. The drawings give the crouching lions' view of rhinoceroses, water buffaloes, egrets, zebras, impalas, cheetahs, vultures, a lone hyena, and hunters' guns. Each of these animals has a defense

BEST OF THE BEST FOR CHILDREN

against predators, and they all get away. The three lion cubs return home from an unsuccessful hunt. Beautiful, accurate drawings are in warm earth colors, lit by an African sun. The author's comments on carnivores and population control in a concise note at the beginning of the book will invite readers to explore the subject further.

MIDDLE GRADERS

FICTION

Abel's Island
by William Steig
(See Videos.)
1976. Farrar, Straus & Giroux, paper, $3.50.

Awards: Newbery Honor Book 1977

The Accident
by Carol Carrick
(See Videos.)
1976. Clarion, $13.95; paper, $4.95.

Across Five Aprils
by Irene Hunt
(See Videos.)
1964. Berkeley, paper, $2.75.

Awards: Newbery Honor Book 1975

Afternoon of the Elves
by Jane Taylor Lisle
(Ages 9–11)
1989. Orchard Books, $12.95.

Buried within the unkempt lawn of scrawny, unfriendly Sara-Kate lies a perfectly formed elfin village complete with playground and Ferris wheel. Hillary, Sara-Kate's neighbor and only friend, is strongly attracted to the mysterious girl whose eyes shine in moonlight, whose house is shuttered and barren, and whose parents are never seen. Hillary wonders if they are all elves. When Sara-Kate is missing for several days, Hillary investigates and learns the truth. Sara-Kate is hiding and caring for her mentally ill mother. An eerie, contemporary tale forged with fantasy.

Awards: Newbery Honor Book 1990; Notable Children's Book 1990

Aldo Peanut Butter

by Johanna Hurwitz

(Ages 8–10)

1990. Morrow, $12.95.

Aldo has his hands full caring for and training his two new puppies, Peanut and Butter, gifts for his eleventh birthday. Then Aldo's grandfather suddenly becomes seriously ill, and Aldo and his two sisters have to make it on their own for a few days. Of course there are mishaps, but nothing capable kids can't (almost) handle. Another humorous hit from the author of *Aldo Applesauce* and *Much Ado about Aldo*.

Anne of Avonlea: The Continuing Story of Anne of Green Gables

by Lucy Maud Montgomery

(See Videos.)

1908. Bantam, paper, $2.95.

Anne of Green Gables

by Lucy Maud Montgomery

(See *Anne of Avonlea* in Videos.)

1908. Bantam, paper, $2.95.

Anne of the Island

by Lucy Maud Montgomery

(See *Anne of Avonlea* in Videos.)

1915. Bantam, paper, $2.95.

Babe: The Gallant Pig

by Dick King-Smith

(Ages 9–11)

Illustrated by Mary Rayner.

1985. Crown, $8.95.

When Farmer Hogget wins Babe the pig in a contest at the county fair, he quickly becomes fond of the small, cute animal. His wife is a practical woman, however, and she plans to have ham for Christmas dinner. Fly, a kindhearted sheepdog, takes pity on the homesick pig and raises him as one of her pups. Along with the others, Babe learns the commands and duties of a sheepdog. When Babe proves his courage and worth by saving the herd of sheep from rustlers, the Hoggets not only quit thinking of him as dinner, but start relying on him to be their number one sheeppig. The farmer's faith is justified when Babe wins the national sheepherding competition hooves down.

Bingo Brown, Gypsy Lover

by Betsy Byars

(Ages 10–13)

1990. Viking, $11.95.

Bingo Brown, of *Bingo Brown and the Language of Love* fame, is in a state of panic. It's almost Christmas, and his long-distance girlfriend, Melissa, has written to tell him that she's sending him a gift. Now Bingo is haunting the jewelry and perfume counters searching for a present worthy of a "gypsy lover." Life gets even more complicated when his mother goes into premature labor and has to be hospitalized. As usual, Bingo responds manfully to these and other crises. Byars's special blend of humor and warmth makes all of Bingo's adventures sure winners.

Awards: Notable Children's Book 1991

Blackberries in the Dark

by Mavis Jukes

(See Videos.)

1985. Knopf, $10.95; Dell, paper, $2.50.

A Blue-Eyed Daisy
by Cynthia Rylant
(Ages 10–12)
1985. Bradbury, $9.95.

Blue-eyed Ellie Farley's eleventh year unfolds in a series of vignettes. Ellie's family, living in the hills of West Virginia, is far from perfect. Her father is prone to drink; her four teenage sisters tend to keep their secret lives to themselves; her mother complains constantly. But it's a family that pulls together when times get tough. Getting her first kiss, learning to hunt with her father, watching her uncle go off to war, and sharing a very special Valentine's Day make this a year for Ellie to cherish.

Bobby Baseball
by Robert Kimmel Smith
(Ages 8–11)
1989. Delacorte, $13.95.

Ten-year-old Bobby "Baseball" Ellis has his career planned, from being the star pitcher on his dad's Little League team to achieving immortality in Cooperstown. But reality and fantasy seldom jibe, and having your father (a former minor league player) as coach is never easy. When tensions lead to an angry father-son confrontation on the mound, Bobby learns that it takes more than dreams to gain success. Loads of baseball trivia and realistic diamond action make this a hit for sports fans.

Borrowed Children
by George Ella Lyon
(Ages 11–14)
1988. Orchard Books, $12.95.

When her mother is bedridden after the birth of Willie, 12-year-old Amanda takes over. That means not only cooking meals, washing clothes, and caring for Willie and Mom; it also means leaving school. Life is hard in Kentucky during the Depression. Dad is away at the timber mill all week, and money is scarce. By the time her mother is back on her feet, Amanda has earned a vacation. She's thrilled when her grandparents in Memphis invite her to spend Christmas with them. Amanda loves the city and her Aunt Laura, who lives the childless life that Amanda envisions for herself. She soon finds, however, that she misses the warmth of her family and that other people's lives aren't always what they seem.

Bridge to Terabithia
by Katherine Paterson
(See Videos.)
1977. HarperCollins, $12.95; paper, $2.95.

Awards: Newbery Medal 1978

The Canada Geese Quilt
by Natalie Kinsey-Warnock
(Ages 9–11)
1989. Cobblehill, $12.95.

Ten-year-old Ariel, living on a Vermont farm in the 1940s, isn't sure she's happy when her mother tells her a baby is coming. But her grandmother's understanding and support help her adjust. Together they plan a special quilt for the baby, designed by Ariel and stitched by Grandma. Just before the quilt is finished and the baby is born, Grandma suffers a stroke. At first Ariel makes excuses to stay away from the gray, now-silent woman. But gradually, with gifts of apples, flowers, and slow walks outdoors, Ariel helps Grandma out of her depression. Together they finish the quilt and learn to cope with the changes that illness, birth, and the threat of death bring to a family.

Awards: Notable Children's Book 1990

A Child's Christmas in Wales
by Dylan Thomas
(See Videos.)
Illustrated by Trina Schart Hyman.
1985. Holiday House, $14.95.

Choosing Sides
by Ilene Cooper
(Ages 10–12)
1990. Morrow, $12.95.

Cooper has the attitudes, lingo, and worries of this age group down pat in her Kids from Kennedy Middle School series, which began with *The Winning of Miss Lynn Ryan.* The third in the series, *Choosing Sides,* focuses on the concerns of Jon Rossi, whose father is so thrilled his son is on the basketball team that the boy hesitates about following his own instincts to quit. Cooper's engaging stories for slightly younger readers (ages 8 to 10) include *Frances Takes a Chance.*

Chronicles of Narnia
by C. S. Lewis
(See Videos.)
7 Volumes.
1986. Macmillian, $79.95; paper, $39.95.

Dr. Dredd's Wagon of Wonders
by Bill Brittain
(Ages 9–11)
1987. HarperCollins, $11.50.

The peaceful town of Coven Tree—site of Brittain's other spooky tales, *The Wish Giver* and *The Devil's Donkey*—is in the midst of a drought when Dr. Dredd and his Wagon of Wonders arrive. In addition to the world's greatest wrestler, Dr. Dredd claims to have just what the town needs: a rainmaker. The mayor agrees to an unnamed fee if Dr. Dredd will make it rain. The evil Dr. Dredd plans to plant "seeds of greed" in every person's heart as his fee. When the rainmaker turns out to be a frightened captive boy, the town decides to rescue the boy. An action-packed tale from a master storyteller.

The Dragon's Boy
by Jane Yolen
(See *Merlin and the Dragons* in Videos.)
1990. HarperCollins, $13.95.

Dragonwings
by Lawrence Yep
(Ages 10–13)
1975. HarperCollins, $12.89; paper, $3.50; ABC-CLIO large-type, $15.95.

A Chinese youth who built and flew a biplane in 1909 is the inspiration for this story of Windrider, who dreams of flying. Told through the eyes of Moon Shadow, Windrider's eight-year-old son, the book depicts a child's love and respect for his idealistic father as well as a strong sense of the cultural adjustments made by Chinese immigrants in San Francisco.

Awards: Newbery Honor Book 1976

Encyclopedia Brown and the Case of the Disgusting Sneakers
by Donald J. Sobol
(Ages 9–11)
1990. Morrow, $12.95.

Ten-year-old Leroy Brown, better known in Idaville (and by his many fans) as "Encyclopedia Brown," solves ten new cases in this solve-it-yourself anthology. Kids get to match wits with the fifth-grade detective to whom coded clues and sinister slip-ups are elementary. (Look for *Encyclopedia Brown: The Boy Detective in the Case of the Missing Time Capsule* in Videos.)

Everywhere
by Bruce Brooks
(Ages 10–13)
1990. HarperCollins, $12.95.

When the grandfather of a 10-year-old white boy suffers a heart attack, a black nurse and her 11-year-old nephew, Dooley, arrive. Dooley claims that he and the boy can cure the grandfather (using an old Indian remedy) if they can find an animal that resembles the man and "switch souls." They settle on a turtle, and although the boy is reluctant to kill the animal, he agrees to let Dooley perform the rites. When the grandfather survives another attack and recovers, the boy believes in Dooley's magic—that is, until he finds the turtle alive.

The Facts and Fictions of Minna Pratt
by Patricia MacLachlan
(Ages 9–11)
1988. HarperCollins, $11.95.

Minna Pratt, already an accomplished cellist at 11, is searching for both her vibrato and answers about the facts and fictions of her life. When wealthy Lucas joins her chamber group and they become friends, Minna can't help but compare their lives. Lucas's world is so ordered his parents engage in conversations at the dinner table, not rowdy battles. The Pratt family, a colorful group of eccentrics, are more

disheveled and vital. As they prepare for a musical competition, Minna and Lucas learn to accept their families and themselves.

Awards: Notable Children's Book 1988

Free Fall
by David Wiesner
(See Picture Books for Older Readers, p. 117.)

The Friendship
by Mildred Taylor
(Ages 9–11)
1987. Dial, $12.95.

Mississippi in the 1930s was a time of racial boundaries and strict rules. Cassie Logan, the black heroine of Newbery Medal winner *Roll of Thunder, Hear My Cry* and *Let the Circle Be Unbroken,* knows enough of these rules to be shocked when Mr. Tom Bee not only calls a white shopkeeper by his first name but claims he saved the man's life. Readers won't easily forget the dramatic confrontation. This powerful slice of history will make an effective read-aloud by someone comfortable with dialect.

Awards: Notable Children's Book 1987; Coretta Scott King Award 1988

Fudge-a-Mania
by Judy Blume
(Ages 8–12)
1991. Dutton, $12.95.

Farley Drexel Hatcher, more commonly known as Fudge, is a definite source of amusement and annoyance to his older brother Peter. (He has been since his first appearance in *Tales of a Fourth Grade Nothing.*) In this novel, Fudge, 5, and Peter, 12—along with parents, baby sister, Grandma Muriel, Uncle Feather, the Myna Bird, and Turtle the dog— are off to Maine for a summer vacation. It turns out that Sheila Tubman (dubbed "The Queen of Cooties" by Peter) and her family are sharing the rental house. Sheila is familiar to Blume fans as the star of the book and movie *Otherwise Known as Sheila the Great*. Peter narrates the tale. Occasionally, sparks of enthusiasm interrupt his familiar, long-suffering, big-brother voice, telling of lost pets, new friends, marine disasters, a gymnast grandmother, and a surprising romance. Blume is a smooth storyteller whose characters ring so true that they stay around long after the novel is read.

A Girl of the Limberlost
by Gene Stratton Porter
(See Videos.)
1909. Dell, paper, $4.95.

The Great Dimpole Oak
by Janet Taylor Lisle
(Ages 10–12)
1987. Watts, $11.95.

Just outside the town of Dimpole stands an old oak tree. Its trunk is carved with initials, and everyone in town has memories of riding on its roots or sitting underneath its branches. To each person, the oak stands for something else. The old farmer who owns the land where the tree stands sees it as a storehouse of feelings. The town busybody plans to make it a shrine. Two 10-year-old boys dream of pirates' treasure under its roots. A schoolteacher and a postal clerk find it romantic. And a swami and his followers hail it as the source of mystical power. All are drawn to the tree for the Great Dimpole Day with surprising (and hilarious) results.

Henry
by Nina Bawden
(Ages 9–11)
1988. Lothrop, $13.

A young girl and her family are evacuated from London during the World War II bombings. They settle on a Welsh farm. In spite of missing their father (who is away in the navy), they try to make the best of it. When the youngest boy, Charlie, shoots a squirrel's nest out of a tree, a baby squirrel is rescued, and becomes a part of the family, who call him Henry. Lightened by the squirrel's antics, this is a careful portrait of a family trying to cope with change and loss.

Awards: Notable Children's Book 1988

Hiroshima No Pika
by Toshi Maruki
(See Picture Books for Older Readers, p. 117.)

Jellybean
by Tessa Duder
(Ages 9–11)
1986. Viking, $9.95.

Geraldine (nicknamed Jellybean) lives alone with her mother, an accomplished cellist. Their lives seem to revolve around Mom's busy schedule, and Jellybean sometimes resents being carted to concert halls or sitting through performances. But music is an important part of her life, too, and she dreams of someday being a conductor. She confides her ambition to her new friend, a shy man named Gerald (whom she suspects is her father), and then feels betrayed when he and her mother arrange to have Jellybean conduct the orchestra when it visits her school. Even though the New Zealand setting and slang may be unfamiliar, readers will recognize the ups and downs of the single-parent family.

Awards: Notable Children's Book 1986

Josie Gambit
by Mary Frances Shura
(Ages 10–13)
1986. Dodd, Mead, $10.95.

When Greg Farrell's mother leaves for a six-month business trip to Europe, he moves to a small Illinois town to stay with his grandmother. There Greg renews an easygoing friendship with Josie Nolan, a girl he's seen off and on since childhood and who shares his passion for chess. As an outsider, Greg is in prime position to observe Josie's beautiful but troubled friend, Tory Mitchell, play her own variation of the game—a real-life "gambit" (a chess move in which you sacrifice an important piece to better your position to win). Tory plans to destroy Josie's reputation and their friendship in a desperate attempt to force Tory's mother to turn over her custody to her father. Then Greg confronts Tory in a dramatic showdown.

Awards: Notable Children's Book 1986

Joyful Noise
by Paul Fleischman
(See Videos.)
Illustrated by Eric Beddows.
1988. HarperCollins, $11.95.

Awards: Newbery Medal 1989

The Kid in the Red Jacket
by Barbara Parks
(Ages 9–11)
1987. Knopf, $9.95.

Ten-year-old Howard Jeeter doesn't want to leave his friends in Arizona, even though his parents claim he'll "bounce back" after the move to Massachusetts. Being the new kid in school is as bad as he thought. Howard gets picked last for the playground soccer games, he eats lunch alone, and his only friend is a six-year-old neighbor, Molly, who follows him everywhere. Howard wants to be accepted so badly that he hurts Molly's feelings by siding against her. Eventually Howard's decency surfaces, but not before he learns some important lessons about friendship. The winning combination of laugh-out-loud dialogue and realistic situations gives this novel strong kid appeal.

King of the Cloud Forests
by Michael Morpurgo
(Ages 10–12)
1988. Viking, $12.95.

Fourteen-year-old Ashley Anderson is living with his missionary father in China when the Japanese invade. His father is determined to stay with the mission, but wants Ashley to escape to safety. So Ashley, disguised as a mute Tibetan boy, journeys with his Uncle Sung over the Himalayas to India. Hunger, illness, and wolves plague the trek. When Uncle Sung leaves Ashley in a deserted cabin to go for help, Ashley is rescued by Yetis. He soon realizes that they are confusing him with another traveler, one they treated like a god. Ashley stays with them for one year, before he escapes. He and Uncle Sung are finally reunited.

The Kitchen Knight: A Tale of King Arthur

by Margaret Hodges
(Ages 9–11)
1990. Holiday House, $14.95.

When a haughty lady arrives at King Arthur's court seeking a knight to free her captive sister, Gareth begs to be sent. Unknown to Arthur, Gareth is really his nephew. He's spent the past year working in the kitchen to gain humility. Now he's ready to earn knighthood by his own skill and courage. A rousing medieval adventure, based on Malory's tales and illustrated by lush, beautifully crafted drawings. Hodges's adaptation of *St. George and the Dragon* will thrill younger readers.

A Light in the Attic

by Shel Silverstein
(See Audio II: Stories,
Dramatizations and Folklore)
1981. HarperCollins, $14.95.

Like Jake and Me

by Mavis Jukes
(See Videos.)
Illustrated by Lloyd Bloom.
1984. Knopf, $12.95; paper, $4.95

Awards: Newbery Honor Book 1985

A Little Princess

by Frances Hodgson Burnett
(See Videos.)
Illustrated by Tasha Tudor.
1905. HarperCollins, $12.95; Dell, paper, $3.50.

Little Tricker the Squirrel Meets Big Double the Bear

by Ken Kesey
(Ages 9–11)
1990. Viking, $14.95.

Kesey, better known for his adult novels *One Flew over the Cuckoo's Nest* and *Sometimes a Great Notion,* creates a down-home fable (perfect for reading aloud) of a squirrel who outwits a grizzly bear. Little Tricker the Squirrel is snug in his bed when Big Double the Bear roars into the forest. The bear is hungry and able to outrun, outjump, and outclimb a woodchuck, a rabbit, and a marten (all of which he promptly eats). Now he challenges Little Tricker. But the wily squirrel claims he can outfly the bear and wins the contest when he "flies" to a tree at the edge of a cliff, and Big Double crashes to the ground. Bright, full-page watercolors add to the fun.

Awards: Notable Children's Book 1991

Maniac Magee

by Jerry Spinelli
(Ages 10–12)
1990. Little, Brown, $13.95.

"They say Maniac Magee was born in a dump. They say his stomach was a cereal box and his heart a sofa spring." Actually Jeffrey Lionel Magee was orphaned at age three and fled his uncaring relatives at age eight. On his own, he runs for his life. Spinelli imparts lessons about poverty, homelessness, and prejudice in a powerful contemporary novel that also shines with the qualities of old-fashioned tall tales.

Awards: Newbery Medal 1991

Me, Mop and the Moondance Kid
by Walter Dean Myers
(Ages 10–12)
1988. Delacorte, $13.95; Dell, paper, $3.25.

T. J., Mop (Miss Olivia Parrish), and the Moondance Kid have been friends for most of their lives at the Dominican Academy orphanage. Even after the two brothers are adopted, Mop still plays with them on the Elks Little League team. Mop is hoping that the Kennedys (their coaches) will want to adopt her, but with the orphanage closing, time is running out. While the Elks try to turn their season around, the members of this multiracial cast have their hands full with a missing pet llama, an accident-prone nun, and anxious new parents. Humor and plot lines mix comfortably to yield a sports book with wide appeal. Just as much fun is the sequel, *Mop, Moondance and the Nagasaki Knights.*

Awards: Notable Children's Book 1988

The Mermaid Summer
by Mollie Hunter
(Ages 10–13)
1988. HarperCollins, $12.95.

Eric Anderson scoffs at the legends of mermaids until a haunting song lures his crew and causes his fishing boat to crash. Eric survives, but, shunned by his fellow fishermen, leaves for foreign seas. His grandchildren, Anna and Jon, long for his return. He doesn't come back but sends, instead, wonderful gifts, including a magical conch shell and a jade comb. When Jon blows on the shell, he inadvertently summons a mermaid. She demands that Anna give her the comb or else she'll drown the town's entire fishing fleet. Anna stalls because she feels the comb is somehow linked to her grandfather's return. With the help of a wise old fisherman and the village witch, the children outwit the mermaid and bring their grandfather home. An enchanting folktale set in nineteenth-century Scotland.

Midnight Horse
by Sid Fleischman
(Ages 8–11)
1990. Greenwillow, $12.95.

An orphan boy called Touch arrives in the little town of Crinklewood to seek his only living relative, Judge Henry Wigglesforth. But there's a scheme afoot. It seems the judge has been spreading the rumor that a man was murdered in the local inn. Wigglesforth thus plans to buy the business for next to nothing. Touch, with a little help from a magician's ghost skilled at changing straw into horses, exposes the plot and saves the day. Good, old-fashioned storytelling from the author of the Newbery Medal–winning *The Whipping Boy.*

Millie Cooper, 3B
by Charlotte Herman
(Ages 8–10)
1985. Dutton, $9.95.

Millie Cooper, growing up in Chicago in the 1940s, dreams of owning a Reynolds Rocket ballpoint pen. She's sure it's just what she needs for that troubling composition, "Why Am I Special?" Millie doesn't feel special. She starts to cry when her teacher is too demanding, the class bully threatens to "beat her to a pulp," and she's never been good in art. But during the trials and tribulations of third grade, Millie finds her own special talents.

Period details give this pleasant story a strong sense of setting.

Molly's Pilgrim
by Barbara Cohen
(See Videos.)
Illustrated by Michael J. Deraney.
1983. Lothrop, $12.95.

Awards: Reading Rainbow selection

More Stories Julian Tells
by Ann Cameron
(Ages 8–10)
1986. Knopf, $10.95.

Julian, his younger brother Huey, and his best friend Gloria star in these vignettes depicting a close-knit African-American family. Sibling squabbles, pet rabbits, and bottles with messages sent out to sea keep Julian and company entertained through long summer days. As in the prequel, *Stories Julian Tells,* there is a strong sense of stability and warm, mutual affection.

Awards: Notable Children's Book 1986

Mrs. Frisby and the Rats of NIMH
by Robert C. O'Brien
(See *The Secret of NIMH* in Videos.)
1971. Atheneum, $14.95; Macmillan, paper, $3.95.

Awards: Newbery Medal 1972

My Book for Kids with Cansur
by Jason Gaes
(See *You Don't Have to Die* in Videos.)
1988. Melius and Peterson, $12.95.

Number the Stars
by Lois Lowry
(Ages 10–12)
1989. Houghton Mifflin, $12.95.

In World War II Denmark, friends Annemarie Johansen and Ellen Rosen fear the stern German soldiers that guard the street corners. But they fear the growing worry in their parents' eyes even more. When the Jews are threatened with relocation, Annemarie's family makes the dangerous decision to hide Ellen in their own home and to help the Rosen family escape. Based on real incidents, this powerful story evokes the strength of friendship and true meaning of courage.

Awards: Newbery Medal 1990; Notable Children's Book 1990

An Occasional Cow
by Polly Horvath
(Ages 9–11)
1989. Farrar, Straus & Giroux, $12.95.

Imogene, a native New Yorker, dreads the thought of spending all summer with relatives in Iowa surrounded by all those cornfields. But her cousins (who meet her airplane standing on their hands and waving their feet in the air) are a game bunch. Between midnight swims, blood oaths, secret societies, and training pigs to curtsy for the pig talent show, summer turns out to be fun. A fresh, hilarious story that will have kids laughing out loud.

On the Far Side of the Mountain
by Jean Craighead George
(Ages 9–12)
1990. Dutton, $13.95.

Since the last scene in 1959 Newbery Award winner *My Side of the Mountain,* two years have passed in the lives of Sam and his sister, Alice. Sam still lives in a tree trunk in the Catskill Mountains with his falcon, Frightful. Alice lives in a treehouse nearby. Sam is badly shaken when a conservation officer appears at his home and demands that he turn over Frightful. Even more disturbing, however, is Alice's sudden disappearance. Sam and his friend, Bando, track Alice and, along the way, uncover a ring of illegal falcon traffickers. In the end Frightful escapes, but Sam must weigh his love for the falcon against the bird's need for freedom.

Orp and the Chop Suey Burgers

by Suzy Kline
(Ages 9–11)
1990. Putnam, $13.95.

Orville Rudemeyer Pygenski, Jr., better known as Orp, enters a cooking contest sponsored by Fu Chow Soy Sauce. Using the sauce as his main ingredient, Orp creates the chop suey burger (a delicious blend of hamburger, Chinese vegetables, and soy sauce). Armed with his chef hat and accompanied by his favorite uncle, Orp takes on all challengers. Although he doesn't win the big prize—a trip to Disneyworld—readers entertained by Orp's high jinks in the original *Orp* will find a winner in this novel.

The Pigs Are Flying

by Emily Rodda
(Ages 9–11)
1988. Greenwillow, $12.95; Avon, paper, $2.75.

Sign painter Sandy claims, "Anything you can imagine is possible." But Rachel, stuck in bed on a rainy Saturday with a sore throat, isn't too sure. Her life seems dull, until Sandy leaves her a magical drawing that shows her riding a unicorn under a sky filled with flying pigs. Rachel is suddenly transported to the topsy-turvy world of "Inside." Whimsical drawings dot the pages as her frantic search for a way home builds to a suspenseful conclusion.

Quentin Corn

by Mary Stolz
(Ages 9–11)
1985. Godine, $11.95.

When a pig overhears the farmer planning to make him into prize-winning barbecue, he steals the farmer's clothes and runs away. With the clothes comes the ability to walk on two legs and talk like a human. Adopting the name Quentin Corn, the pig sets off to explore the world. He soon gets a job with a handyman and moves into a boardinghouse. The adults accept him as a strong young man with a healthy appetite, though three children see the pig beneath the clothing. A rousing tale (with some interesting insights on human behavior) that will make kids squeal with delight.

Racso and the Rats of NIMH

by Jane Leslie Conly
(Ages 10–12)
1986. HarperCollins, $12.50.

Conly, daughter of Robert C. O'Brien, has written a fast-paced sequel to her father's Newbery Medal winner, *Mrs. Frisby and the Rats of NIMH.* Descendants of both Mrs. Frisby and the original colony of superintelligent rats that escaped from the laboratory of the National Institute of Mental Health (NIMH) interact in this saga. On the road back to the Thorn Valley school, Timothy Frisby rescues a young rat called Racso from drowning. Racso, with his lies and bragging, gets off to a bad start at the school. But he proves his worth when the rats' home is threatened by the building of a dam, and he helps devise the plan that saves the valley.

Randall's Wall

by Carol Fenner
(Ages 10–12)
1991. McElderry, $11.95.

No one comes near fifth-grader Randall Lord. He's filthy. He smells. His home has no running water, and his mother has given up trying to keep either her children or their clothes clean. Randall hides his considerable artistic talent and his growing loneliness behind an invisible wall. He wants to be a part of his class, to be friends in particular with feisty Jean Worth Neary, but he doesn't know how. One day his wall of isolation begins to crack and crumble when he defends Jean from a bully, and she decides they should be friends. With humor and poignancy, this sensitively understated story reveals the plight of the poor.

The Remembering Box

by Eth Clifford
(Ages 9–11)
1985. Houghton Mifflin, $11.95.

Nine-year-old Joshua has spent every Sabbath since he was five with his Grandma Goldina. Together they light the candles and eat supper. Then Grandma, a "saving woman," goes to her "remembering box." Inside are mementos and photos that trigger stories of the old country and her childhood. These she shares lovingly with her grandson. The legacy of traditions and memories forms a special bond between the two that helps Joshua accept his grandmother's death in this tender, intergenerational story.

The Riddle of Penncroft Farm

by Dorothea Jensen
(Ages 10–12)
1989. HBJ, $14.95.

Lars is unhappy when his family abruptly leaves Minneapolis to live with his Great-Aunt Cass on her farm near Valley Forge, Pennsylvania. He's never been interested in history and starts out on the wrong foot with the kids in sixth grade, including his very likable cousin, Patience. But meeting Geordie, the ghost (or "shade" as he calls himself) of Lars's ancestor changes all that. Listening to Geordie's firsthand account of the Revolutionary War piques Lars's interest. When Aunt Cass dies, leaving only a vague clue to the whereabouts of her will, it's up to Lars and Geordie to solve the riddle and save the farm.

Risk n' Roses

by Jan Slepian
(Ages 11–14)
1990. Philomel, $14.95.

Eleven-year-old Skip and her older, mentally disabled sister, Angela, are newcomers to their Bronx neighborhood in August 1948. Skip is immediately drawn to charismatic Jean Persico, who challenges her followers with a series of destructive and sometimes dangerous dares. When Jean uses Angela in a cruel prank to get revenge on an elderly neighbor (a Holocaust survivor), Skip finds the strength to follow her own beliefs. Slepian portrays the conflict between peer pressure and family loyalty in this sensitive story.

Robin Hood
by Sarah Hayes
(Ages 7–12)
1989. Holt, $12.95.

Robin and company come alive in Hayes's spirited and accessible retelling of the tales. Beginning with Robin's rescue from Guy of Gisborne by Will Scarlet and his introduction to the outlaw band, the adventure is nonstop. As Little John, Maid Marian, and Friar Tuck join in Robin's escapades, life becomes delightfully miserable for the evil Sheriff of Nottingham. An inspired adaptation that showcases all the adventure, courage, loyalty, humor, and heartbreak of the original legends.

Rose Blanche
by Roberto Innocenti
(Ages 10–14)
1991. Stewart, Tabori & Chang, $15.95.

Rose Blanche is a young German girl who sees the escalation of World War II in terms of the changes it brings to her small town. She discovers a concentration camp nearby, and walks daily through the woods to bring food to the children she has met through the fence. Rose is killed in the closing days of the war. The Nazi insignias, concentration camp uniforms, and other visuals in this pictorial work assume a basic awareness of the events of World War II, and the horrifying scenes (of camp victims or the town mayor casually handing over a child who had fallen from a truck to a soldier) demand adult guidance.

Sadako & the Thousand Paper Cranes
by Eleanor Coerr
(See Videos.)
Illustrated by Ronald Himler.
1977. Putnam, $13.95; Dell, paper, $2.75.

Sarah, Plain and Tall
by Patricia MacLachlan
(Ages 8–10)
1985. HarperCollins, $10.95; paper, $2.50; ABC-CLIO, large-type, $15.95.

Anna can barely remember her mother, who died shortly after brother Caleb's birth. What she misses the most are her songs, which brightened their lonely lives on the prairie. When Papa advertises for a wife in an eastern newspaper, the children are delighted that Sarah (who describes herself as plain and tall) promises to come for a month's trial. They all love her immediately because she brings music and warmth back into their lives. But the children worry when Sarah speaks longingly of the sea. Will she stay? A poignant, unsentimental story of the struggles of pioneer life and the power of love.

Awards: Newbery Medal 1986

Saying Good-bye to Grandma
by Jane Resh Thomas
(Ages 8–10)
1988. Clarion, $13.95.

When seven-year-old Suzie's grandmother dies, she and her parents journey back to her grandparents' home to say good-bye. Suzie discovers that funerals are a curious mix of tears, laughter, and memories; of losing a loved one and finding family and friends. The kid's-eye view of the wake and funeral (complete with a game of "capture the flag" in the casket room) provides a gentle approach to the subject of death.

Awards: Notable Children's Book 1988

The Secret Life of Dilly McBean
by Dorothy Haas
(Ages 10–13)
1986. Macmillan, $12.95.

For years orphan Dilly McBean has been shuttled from boarding schools to summer camps. Now, to his delight, a new guardian places him in his own home surrounded by his family's belongings, hires watchful but unobtrusive caretakers, and enrolls him in public school. Even more important, his guardian arranges for Dilly to work with a scientist who can help him control his secret powers of magnetism. Throughout the story, shady figures plot to kidnap Dilly and hold him for ransom. But they aren't prepared for the strength of his powers or the combined forces of his new friends, faithful dog, and resourceful caretakers. A lively tale of high-tech high jinks.

The Secret of the Indian
by Lynne Reid Banks
(Ages 11–13)
1989. Doubleday, $13.95.

Omri has discovered that when he turns an old key (that his grandmother gave him) in the lock of a salvaged cupboard, he's not only able to turn plastic figures into tiny, real people, but he's able to send full-sized humans to other times and places. In part three of the saga, Omri's friend, Patrick, is transported to the Old West to search for "Boo-hoo" Boone. When he returns, he brings a tornado that causes havoc in England. Although there is

some backtracking to bring new readers up to date, kids should really begin with *The Indian in the Cupboard* and *The Return of the Indian* to fully enjoy this rousing sequel.

Shiloh
by Phyllis Reynolds Naylor
(Ages 9–13)
1991. Atheneum, $12.95.

Shiloh is a beagle puppy intended for hunting by owner Judd Travers—a nasty West Virginian who keeps his dogs chained up and kicks them about when they lose his favor. Shiloh captures the heart of Marty Preston, an 11-year-old neighbor whose honest parents insist that Marty return the pup to Judd even after it follows him home. Marty and Shiloh share anxious moments and real danger in this modern morality tale without easy resolutions.

Awards: Newbery Medal 1992

The Shimmershine Queens
by Camille Yarbrough
(Ages 11–13)
1989. Putnam, $13.95.

Life in the inner city is filled with violence. Ten-year-old Angie sees fear in everyone's eyes—in her father's as he walks out on the family, in her own as she faces taunts from classmates because of her dark skin and pronounced features. But Angie's 90-year-old cousin shares a gift with her: shimmershine. Shimmershine is the feeling you get when you're doing the best that you can do, when you're proud and respect yourself. Angie discovers it in herself when she begins to stand up to her classmates and later when she joins an African dance and theater group. Dialogue (some in black English), characters, and situations all ring true in this powerful novel.

Sign of the Beaver

by Elizabeth Speare
(Ages 10–13)
1983. Houghton Mifflin, $12.95; Dell, paper, $3.50.

From the author of the Newbery Medal winner *Witch of Blackbird Pond* comes another trip into America's past. This time, Speare conjures up eighteenth-century Maine and a remote cabin in the frigid wilderness. Young Matt is nervous as well as proud when he's entrusted to care for things while his father makes an arduous trip to Massachusetts to gather the rest of the family. When a disastrous attempt to rob a beehive leaves him desperately ill, Matt is nursed by the chief of the Beaver clan. Eventually, the chief's grandson becomes his teacher, his pupil, and his friend.

Awards: Newbery Honor Book 1984; BBYA 1983

Staying Nine

by Pam Conrad
(Ages 9–11)
1988. HarperCollins. $11.95.

Heather doesn't want to turn 10. Nine has been her best year so far, and she doesn't want anything to change. She wears the same clothes for her school picture as last year (even if they are a little tight), and she refuses to celebrate her birthday. She only agrees to a party when her mother promises no cake, no candles, and no presents. Only her Uncle Lou's girlfriend, kooky Rosa Rita, seems to understand. She makes Heather realize that

not all grownups are "grown up" and convinces her to give 10 a try.

Sticks and Stones and Skeleton Bones

by Jamie Gilson
(Ages 9–11)
1991. Lothrop, $12.95.

Hobie Hanson—star of five other hilarious novels beginning with *Thirteen Ways to Sink a Sub*—is back, and it's trouble as usual. Once again, Gilson is right-on-target with fifth-grade dialogue and humor. Hobie thinks his friend Nick will laugh at the old "snake in the can" trick. What he doesn't plan is the snake attaching itself to Nick's nose, and Nick being left with a "beet beak." Disasters snowball, rumors fly, and the friendship begins to crumble.

Strider

by Beverly Cleary
(Ages 9–14)
Illustrated by Paul O. Zelinsky.
1991. Morrow, $13.95.

In Cleary's Newbery Medal–winning *Dear Mr. Henshaw,* Leigh Botts worked through the trauma of his parents' divorce by writing long missives to his favorite author. What started as a dreaded school project ended in solace. Now Botts is back, four years older, an even better writer, and a runner as well. He also has a new dog, Strider, and a sense of resignation about his father's unreliability. Cleary's message is artfully understated.

The Trading Game

by Alfred Slote
(Ages 9–11)
1990. Lippincott, $12.95.

Ten-year-old Andy Harris comes from a family of baseball fans. His grandfather played in the major leagues for a short time, and his father was an avid baseball card collector. Andy's parents are divorced, but when his father dies, the boy inherits a valuable collection that includes a 1952 Mickey Mantle card worth $2,500. The only card that means anything to Andy, however, is Ace 459—his grandfather's card. His friend, Tubby, has it and will make a trade—but only for the Mantle. While negotiations continue, Andy's grandfather agrees to coach Andy's Little League team during one practice. Andy's baseball dreams and his relationship with his grandfather are almost shattered when the boy discovers that he doesn't have the killer instinct needed to play ball.

Up from Jericho Tell
by E. L. Konigsburg
(Ages 10–12)
1986. Atheneum, $13.95.

Eleven-year-old Jeanmarie Troxell and fellow latchkey kid Malcolm Soo (both destined to be famous) meet over the burial of a dead blue jay and become fast friends. While digging in their secret meeting place (dubbed Jericho Tel), they are suddenly summoned by the dead actress Tallulah. She sends them on a quest to find the three street performers who were with her when she died and to recover the fabulous, missing Regina Stone. The kids, armed with occasional invisibility and constant quick wits, track down the culprits.

Awards: Notable Children's Book 1986

Village by the Sea
by Paula Fox
(Ages 10–13)
1988. Orchard Books, $13.95.

Ten-year-old Emma dreads being sent to her aunt and uncle's home on Long Island while her father has bypass surgery. Uncle Crispin is a kind man whom Emma likes immediately; Aunt Bea is selfish and willful. Emma's only escape from her aunt's rampages comes when Emma befriends a girl named Bertie. Together they build a perfect miniature village by the sea. The night before Emma returns home, Aunt Bea viciously destroys their creation. Although heartbroken, Emma makes some great strides toward growing up when she understands and accepts her aunt's behavior.

Awards: Notable Children's Book 1988

Wayside School Is Falling Down
by Louis Sachar
(Ages 9–11)
1989. Lothrop, $12.95.

Welcome back to Wayside School, the wackiest elementary school in the world. Mrs. Jewls's class on the thirtieth floor is a "class where nobody was strange because nobody was normal." When Benjamin Nushmutt tells everyone his name is Mark Miller and Mrs. Jewls pushes a computer out of the window to teach the class about gravity, no one even thinks it's odd. As in Sachar's *Sideways Stories from Wayside School,* the schoolyard humor will have kids howling.

Westmark
by Lloyd Alexander
(Ages 10–13)
1981. Dutton, $15.95; Dell, paper, $3.25.

A young fugitive, a good-natured scoundrel who runs a traveling show, a street urchin who masquerades as an oracle priestess, an ineffectual king, and an evil prime minister are but a few of the unforgettable characters in this exciting picaresque tale. Combining political intrigue with high adventure and a dash of romance, this is the first book in a marvelous, award-winning trilogy that includes *The Kestrel* and *The Beggar Queen.*

Awards: American Book Award 1982

Where the Lilies Bloom
by Vera and Bill Cleaver
(Ages 11–14)
1969. HarperCollins, $12.95; paper, $2.95.

Afraid her family will be split up if authorities discover her father's death, Mary Call Luther decides to bury him herself. She then fights to put food on the table, cope with the whims of her feisty little brother, and misdirect unsuitable suitors who come to woo her serene, slow-witted elder sister. With its strong characters and vivid Appalachian setting, this is a wonderful portrait of a clever, resourceful girl who succeeds in preserving her family's dignity. Her story continues in *Trial Valley.*

NONFICTION

The American Family Farm
by Joan Anderson
(Ages 9–11)
Photos by George Ancona.
1989. HBJ, $18.95.

A photo essay tour of a dairy farm, chicken farm, and an organic hog and grain business. As the farming families are profiled, readers get a glimpse of the tremendous amount of work accomplished each day as well as the range of extended family, friends, and hired help needed to accomplish it. Even though family farming is, statistically, a dying enterprise, these families, through hard labor, care, and determination, are making it work.

Awards: Notable Children's Book 1990

Anno's Math Game III
by Mitsumasa Anno
(Ages 9–12)
1991. Philomel, $19.95.

Concepts as difficult and varied as topology, graphs, perspective, geometry, mazes, and left and right are depicted by Anno's droll, elfin figures, and transformed into challenging puzzles and clever games. Some kids may need a little help from parent or teacher, but even those who dislike math may be surprised to find themselves having fun.

Awards: Notable Children's Book 1992

The Big Beast Book: Dinosaurs and How They Got That Way
by Jerry Booth
(Ages 9–12)
1988. Little, Brown, $14.95; paper, $7.95.

Getting kids interested in dinosaurs isn't much of a challenge, but explaining a million years of fossil formation is something else. Booth shares a wealth of fresh ideas—including using city blocks to set up a time line, layering gelatin to show strata, and making carbon leaf prints—to simplify dinosaur lore. Part of the interactive Brown Paper School series, this is a storehouse of upbeat experiments and intriguing details.

Awards: Notable Children's Book 1988

Bill Peet: An Autobiography

by Bill Peet

(Ages 8–11)

1989. Houghton Mifflin, $16.95.

Through words and black-and-white pencil drawings, children's author Bill Peet recalls his childhood in Indiana during the Depression and his years as an artist at the Disney studios. Kids who know his picture books and those who love to draw will be enchanted with early sketches from such classic feature films as *Dumbo, Cinderella,* and *101 Dalmations* as well as other familiar Peet characters.

Awards: Caldecott Honor Book 1990; Notable Children's Book 1990

Bird Watch

by Jane Yolen

(Ages 8–11)

Illustrated by Ted Lewin.
1990. Philomel, $15.95.

Yolen's witty metaphors—for example, "over the mirror the noble swan slides, while under the surface she bicycle rides"—combine with Lewin's dramatic double-page watercolors to portray familiar birds in settings children will recognize. Brief notes on each featured bird help to make this beautifully crafted book appeal to both bird and poetry lovers.

Awards: Notable Children's Book 1990

The Book of Eagles

by Helen Roney Sattler

(Ages 9–12)

Illustrated by Jean Dray Zallinger.
1989. Lothrop, $14.95.

Full-page watercolors and sidebar art frame this comprehensive look at eagles. The readable text describes the bird's body structure, hunting abilities, rearing of young, and common habitats. Preservation programs are also discussed. A lengthy glossary lists various types of eagles by their common and scientific names; it also includes pictures of each bird and indications of its usual habitat.

Awards: Notable Children's Book 1990

Buffalo Hunt

by Russell Freedman

(Ages 9–11)

1988. Holiday House, $16.95.

Because the Plains Indians relied on the buffalo for food, clothing, utensils, and shelter, the buffalo hunt was an important ritual. Freedman details the roles played by the men, women, children, and shaman (spiritual guide) of the tribe in locating, hunting, butchering, and preserving the animal. Handsome reproductions of period paintings support this rich portrait of a people who treated the buffalo with respect and were almost destroyed when white settlers joined the hunt.

Awards: Notable Children's Book 1988

Cats Are Cats

Compiled by Nancy Larrick

(Ages 8–11)

Illustrated by Ed Young.
1988. Philomel, $17.95.

Alley cats, pampered cats, lost cats, and witches' cats purr, pounce, and scamper through this elegantly illustrated collection of poems. Authors such as Elizabeth Coatsworth, T. S. Eliot, and John Ciardi capture all the smug smirks, knowing nods, and mysterious movements in an appealing selection of verse. Any kid who has ever been "owned" by a cat will love it.

Awards: Notable Children's Book 1988

China Homecoming
by Jean Fritz
(Ages 10–13)
1985. Putnam, $11.95.

In *Homesick* Jean Fritz recalled her childhood in China and the upheaval that caused her missionary parents to return to the United States. Now, years later, Fritz returns to explore a China changed by Communism and revolution. Mixing travelogue with biography, she treats readers to a candid look at a country rich in tradition, yet striving frantically to be modern. In spite of China's drastic population controls and severely limited career choices for young people, Fritz finds the modern Chinese more content than the people of her past. Her keen observations and enlightening anecdotes make modern China fascinating and accessible to young readers.

Christopher Columbus: Voyager to the Unknown
by Nancy Smiler Levinson
(Ages 9–12)
1990. Lodestar, $15.95.

Excerpts from Columbus's letters and journals and facts culled from contemporary research document this chronological account of the explorer's childhood and his four historic voyages to the New World. Columbus, it seems, was a man so driven to finding a route to the Far East that he was willing to alter records and sway testimonies to prove that he had succeeded. Nevertheless, he was courageous and determined, facing hardships that included shipwrecks, threats of mutiny, and cannibals. Carefully selected photos of historic paintings add spice to this straightforward but intriguing biography.

Awards: Notable Children's Book 1991

Daniel Boone
by Laurie Lawlor
(Ages 10–14)
1988. Whitman, $11.50.

Lawlor sifts fact from legend in this carefully researched, lively biography of the famous frontiersman. Facts in this case are far from dull. Although his trapping and exploring treks were not always successful, Boone is remembered for his outright courage and love of adventure. Tales of his daring escapes, bold rescues, and frontier resourcefulness make for exciting reading.

Dawn to Dusk in the Galápagos: Flightless Birds, Swimming Lizards, and Other Fascinating Creatures
by Rita Golden Gelman
(Ages 10–12)
Photos by Tui De Roy.
1991. Little, Brown, $16.95.

Authenticity is the hallmark of this nature study. After providing background on the Galápagos's volcanic origins, Gelman depicts an ordinary day in the lives of the extraordinary creatures who inhabit these Pacific islands. The giant tortoises are probably the best-known residents, but there are also blue-footed boobies, sea lions, and giant iguanas, all featured in Tui De Roy's remarkable photographs.

Dinosaur Dig
by Kathryn Lasky
(Ages 9–12)
Illustrated by Christopher Knight.
1990. Morrow, $13.95.

Powerful text and photographs transport readers to the Montana Badlands to dig for dinosaur fossils. A history of the rugged terrain and its inhabitants precedes the sighting of what proves to be a triceratops vertebra and adjoining ribs. In the company of husband-and-wife team Kathryn Lasky and Christopher Knight (creators of the Newbery Honor Book *Sugaring Time*) and their two children, and guided by a paleontologist, readers share in discovering, extricating, fortifying, and transporting the delicate finds.

Exodus
Adapted from the Bible by Miriam Chaikin
(Ages 8–12)
1987. Holiday House, $14.95.

Bold illustrations accompany the tale of Moses leading the children of Israel out of Egypt. Unlike many Bible storybooks, this telling captures all the drama surrounding the great escape. Beginning with Moses' rescue from the bulrushes by the pharaoh's daughter, the book traces Moses' transformation from reluctant speaker to prophet of God. The familiar stories of the ten plagues, the parting of the Red Sea, and the deliverance of the ten commandments are included.

Fresh Brats
by X. J. Kennedy
(Ages 8–10)
1990. McElderry, $12.95.

Kennedy's brats freeze earthworms in ice cube trays, drizzle Vaseline on dance floors, weld school doors shut, and generally make life treacherous (yet entertaining) for unsuspecting adults. Kids will laugh out loud at the irreverent rhymes, caustic verse, and quirky illustrations in this wacky sequel to *Brats*.

Good Queen Bess: The Story of Elizabeth I of England
by Diane Stanley and Peter Vennema
(Ages 9–11)
1990. Four Winds, $14.95.

Elizabeth I of England, fondly known as Good Queen Bess by her people, ruled her country for 45 years (1558–1603). It was a time of religious and political strife in Europe, but Elizabeth I was both shrewd and just. Formal medieval paintings rich in the pageantry of the era embellish this readable account of Elizabeth's childhood and ascent to the throne. In an age when women were thought unfit to rule, Elizabeth proved her worth by sidestepping plots against her and commanding armies. A fascinating portrait of one of England's most influential rulers.

Awards: Notable Children's Book 1991

Growing Up Amish
by Richard Ammon
(Ages 10–12)
1989. Atheneum, $11.95.

A gently informative text follows Anna, a young Amish girl, through the activities of her day: from her early morning chores through classes in a one-room schoolhouse to an evening of reading and music, Ammon weaves in bits of history, tradition, and beliefs. Carefully separating myth from fact, he explains that the Amish accept only those modern things that will not interfere with their peaceful, structured lifestyle. Photographs by local Amish illustrate this enlightening study.

Indian Chiefs
by Russell Freedman
(Ages 11–15)
1987. Holiday House, $16.95.

Well known for histories and biographies for young people, Freedman supplies a thoughtful and thought-provoking look at six Indian chiefs who led their people during the latter half of the 1800s, when pioneering white settlers threatened Indian homelands and survival. Focusing on Red Cloud, Santanta, Quanah Parker, Washakie, Joseph, and Sitting Bull, he writes with compassion and power about how each dealt with the threat to their lands. A full-page portrait accompanies the profile of each chief, and numerous black-and-white photographs illustrate the text. The haunting pictures speak volumes about the tragedy and the heroism in this special chapter in America's history.

Awards: Notable Children's Book 1987; BBYA 1987

Inspirations: Stories about Women Artists
by Leslie Sills
(Ages 10–12)
1989. Whitman, $16.95.

Each of the four women profiled in this beautifully constructed book looked without and within for inspiration. Georgia O'Keeffe, child of Wisconsin farmers, found it in the outdoors, especially in the deserts of New Mexico. Mexican Frida Kahlo, crippled at 18, searched within herself and her heritage with often bizarre but moving results. Alice Neel set out to capture the poor, fearful, and vulnerable in her portraits. And Faith Ringgold used the images of Harlem in her fabrics, dolls, and quilts. An inspiring introduction to four talented and determined women.

Awards: Notable Children's Book 1990

In the Beginning: Creation Stories from around the World
by Virginia Hamilton
(See Multicultural Fare, p. 36.)

Joyful Noise: Poems for Two Voices
by Paul Fleischman
(See Videos.)
1988. HarperCollins, $11.95.

Awards: Newbery Medal 1989; Notable Children's Book 1988

The Last Princess: The Story of Princess Ka'iulani of Hawai'i
by Fay Stanley
(See Multicultural Fare, p. 36.)

Lincoln: A Photobiography
by Russell Freedman
(Ages 10–15)
1987. Clarion, $16.95.

Freedman searches beneath the myths to reveal Lincoln, a man of contrasts. Legendary anecdotes of his youthful wit, ambition, and thirst for knowledge are balanced by stories of personal and national tragedy that spawned depression, self-doubt, and fear of failure in the president's later years. What emerges is a very human hero, worthy of study and respect. Scrupulous research and carefully chosen photographs give readers a concise and readable account of both the origins and outcome of the Civil War and the contributions of our sixteenth president.

Awards: Newbery Medal 1988; Notable Children's Book 1987

Linnea's Windowsill Garden
by Christina Bjork
(Ages 8–11)
1988. Farrar, Straus & Giroux, $11.95.

Linnea calls herself an "asphalt flower" because she lives in the city. She has an indoor garden and is assisted by her friend, a retired gardener named Mr. Bloom (who also appeared in *Linnea in Monet's Garden*). The pair share a love of plants and a wealth of gardening knowledge. Whimsical drawings accompany concise directions on planting seeds and pits, pruning plants, watering, fertilizing, fighting bugs, and repotting. From starting plants with common household fruits and vegetables to organizing supplies, here is everything an aspiring young gardener needs.

Awards: Notable Children's Book 1988

Living with Dinosaurs
by Patricia Lauber
(Ages 8–12)
Illustrated by Douglas Henderson.
1991. Bradbury, $15.95.

Dinosaurs and the lands they roamed— swamps, forests, highlands—are seen through

Henderson's generous paintings and Lauber's descriptions of sights, sounds, and smells. Creatures from each habitat and how they lived are detailed. Lauber, an eminent science writer, is careful to distinguish between known facts and suppositions. She has written several previous books relating to this era, including *Dinosaurs Walked Here: And Other Stories Fossils Tell.* Notes on fossil searches today bring the reader back to the present and close this stunning journey.

Awards: Notable Children's Book 1992

Maggie by My Side
by Beverly Butler
(Ages 9–12)
1987. Dodd, Mead, $11.95.

Writer and teacher Butler, blind since age 14, is bereft when Una, her guide dog, dies suddenly of cancer. Not only did she love the dog, but she misses the mobility that the dog allowed. She decides to return to training school and several weeks later is training with a German shepherd named Maggie. Readers follow Butler and Maggie through the arduous course. When the two meld into a special team, Butler regains her fiercely sought independence. The author also provides background information on the history and training of Seeing Eye dogs.

Awards: Notable Children's Book 1987

Move Over, Wheelchairs Coming Through: Seven Young People in Wheelchairs Talk about Their Lives
by Ron Roy
(Ages 9–12)
1985. Clarion, $12.95.

Seven physically disabled children, ranging in age from 9 to 19, speak frankly about their daily lives. Each is remarkably resourceful, and readers will be amazed at how they've learned to adjust to school, exercise, eating, and communicating with friends and family. Candid information is given on the diseases at the root of their disabilities (including spina bifida, muscular dystrophy, and cerebral palsy), as well as the physical pain and emotional traumas they experience. Lively photos and the straightforward text reveal the determination and courage of these special kids. Another fine book is *How It Feels to Live with a Physical Disability* by Jill Krementz.

Neptune
by Seymour Simon
(Ages 8–11)
1991. Morrow, $13.95.

Little was known about Neptune, the eighth planet in the solar system, until *Voyager* sailed by it in August 1989. Simon, author of a string of award-winning science books for children (including *Galaxies, Earthquakes,* and *Icebergs and Glaciers*), matches the spacecraft's breathtaking photographs with a smooth, nontechnical text that shares these wonders with middle readers. An attractive photodocumentary that makes for a useful resource as well as a browser's delight.

Nightmare in History: The Holocaust 1931–1945
by Miriam Chaikin
(Ages 10–13)
1987. Clarion, $14.95.

A concise history of Judaism, the origins of anti-Semitism, and the rise of Adolf Hitler supply readers with vital background on the Holocaust. But it's the personal reminiscences and diary excerpts that give faces to the victims. Chaikin presents both the horrors and acts of courage forthrightly, without sensationalism. Twenty-five black-and-white photographs and prints visually document this account.

Awards: Notable Children's Book 1987

Painting Faces
by Suzanne Haldane
(Ages 8–10)
1988. Dutton, $13.95.

For thousands of years people all over the world have used face painting as part of religious rituals, as preludes to war, or as a means of celebration. Haldane gives a brief history of the art, mixing anthropology with theater. Full-page photos demonstrate designs that range from Native American, Kathakali (Indian dance dramas), Chinese opera, and Kabuki (Japanese theater) to African tribal masks and the more familiar animal and clown faces. In many cases step-by-step directions are given and needed materials detailed. A colorful, practical primer of an ancient art that continues to delight children everywhere.

Awards: Notable Children's Book 1988

Ramona: Behind the Scenes of a Television Show
by Elaine Scott
(Ages 9–11)
Photos by Margaret Miller.
1988. Morrow, $13.95.

Lively photos accompany this insider's view of the making of the television show *Ramona* from casting to postproduction. Details on the search (under the watchful eye of author

Beverly Cleary) for the perfect Ramona and the ideal Quimby house along with information on auditioning actors, building sets, and filming scenes will give kids some idea of all the backstage work needed to make a quality production. (See *Ramona Stories* in Videos.)

Awards: Notable Children's Book 1988; Reading Rainbow selection

Skeleton

by Steve Parker
(Ages 9–12)
1988. Knopf, $12.95.

Like *Arms & Armor* by Michele Byam and other entries in the Eyewitness series, Parker's book is packed with information. The evolution, structure, and function of both human and animal skeletons are described and amply illustrated. Pages are filled with drawings, photos, and X-rays of spines, teeth, skulls, and other assorted bones. From fossils to exoskeletons, from myths to medical facts, there's plenty to fascinate kids.

Awards: Notable Children's Book 1988

Something Big Has Been Here

by Jack Prelutsky
(Ages 9–11)
1990. Greenwillow, $14.95.

Poet Prelutsky's witty collection of verse, like his previous book, *The New Kid on the Block,* taps unerringly into kids' perspective and sense of humor. Mosquitoes and dinosaurs, brothers and sisters, and auks and paddlepusses romp through the pages. James Stevenson's black-and-white sketches washed in gray are the perfect complement for the wry humor

and spirited tone of the poems. Just right for reading aloud or chuckling alone.

Awards: Notable Children's Book 1991

The Story of Football

by Dave Anderson
(Ages 10–13)
1985. Morrow, $13.

Anderson traces the history of football from its origins in college rugby and soccer games to modern college and professional events. He highlights pioneering coaches and players. Each of the game's components—running, passing, receiving, kicking, blocking, tackling, and strategy—is explained in a clearly written text studded with anecdotes. Action photos add punch to the presentation.

Tales Mummies Tell

by Patricia Lauber
(Ages 10–13)
1985. HarperCollins, $11.95.

While the mention of mummies makes most people think of ancient Egypt, specimens have been uncovered in burial grounds in North America, peat bogs in Denmark, and tombs in Peru. Particularly fascinating are the stories mummies "tell" to the archaeologists who are investigating the bodies and trappings. Lauber offers details on everyday life of early civilizations as they are deduced by scientists using X-rays, autopsies, carbon dating, and plain old detective work. And kids will appreciate the gruesome aspects of embalming bodies and shrinking heads, complete with photos.

A Telling of Tales

by William J. Brooke
(See Fractured Fairy Tales, p. 54.)

TEENAGERS

A Special Note on Teen Reading

Books have loads of competition when it comes to today's young adults. MTV, the local mall, rock concerts, and sports demand the attention of even the most devoted readers. With the selections that follow, kids can also experience the marvelous, solitary pleasure of reading. We include the best of what's new in young adult publishing with selected award-winners and some old favorites. The range is broad, from tender romance and fantasy to modern advice. Indeed, many of the books deal forthrightly with important issues at the heart of adolescence—sexual development, family relationships, independence, and self-awareness. Because fewer young adult titles are published annually than other children's books, to assure a wide assortment, we've reached back a little further in time.

Often, parents who read some of the best "YA" books with their children find themselves delighted and intrigued by the writing and insights. It's one way to communicate with young teens. Although many books published for adult readers are great for teens, we have not listed any here—the better to focus on the exciting books written just for this audience.

FICTION

After the Dancing Days
by Margaret I. Rostkowski
(Ages 13–15)
1986. HarperCollins, $13.95; paper, $3.50.

This affecting novel set at the close of World War I combines a strong antiwar theme with the story of a young girl's coming of age. Undaunted by her mother's complaint that what she's doing is inappropriate for a young lady, 13-year-old Annie accompanies her physician father to work at the veterans' hospi-tal. While there, she reads to wounded soldiers who have returned from the front. She is particularly drawn to one terribly disfigured, solitary young man, who, it seems, has lost his will to live.

Awards: Notable Children's Book 1986; BBYA 1986

After the Rain
by Norma F. Mazer
(Ages 12–15)
1987. Morrow, $12.95; G.K. Hall, large-print, $14.95.

Rachel's grandfather, Izzy, has always been selfish, tyrannical, and rude. He's even worse now because he's ill. But when Rachel is forced to take over some of his care during the afternoons—"babysit" him, as it were—their relationship begins to change. He talks a bit about his life; she talks about hers. Izzy doesn't turn into the prototypical loving grandparent, but Rachel learns to love him anyway. When he finally goes into the hospital to die, she stands up to her parents so she can be with him at the end.

Awards: Newbery Honor Book 1988; Notable Children's Book 1987; BBYA 1987

Alan and Naomi

by Myron Levoy
(Ages 11–14)
1977. HarperCollins, $12.89; paper, $3.50.

A shading of humor helps temper this heart-wrenching novel set in the United States and dealing candidly with some of the consequences of World War II. Prompted by his parents, Alan reluctantly agrees to make friends with Naomi—"that crazy girl from upstairs." She is a war refugee whose awful memories of Nazi brutality have caused her to retreat from reality. A natural comic, Alan uses humor to break into her silent world, and he begins to truly like her—only to have her fragile sanity shattered forever when she sees him fighting with a Jew-baiting classmate.

The Alfred Summer

by Jan Slepian
(Ages 11–13)
1980. Macmillan, $11.95.

Lester is clever and funny, though cerebral palsy makes it difficult for him to talk. That doesn't seem to bother slow Alfred, or tough, boyish Claire, or Myron, who wants desperately to build a boat that will carry him away from the torments of his terrible family. Myron's boat becomes the group's special project, and their determined attempts to make it a reality present victories for them all—especially for Lester, who finds freedom in friendship.

All Together Now

by Sue Ellen Bridgers
(Ages 12–15)
1979. Knopf, $13.99; Bantam, paper, $2.75.

A humorous, heartfelt novel in which a 12-year-old learns about truth, acceptance, and herself. Casey is forced to spend the summer with her grandparents in a sleepy southern town. Her father is in Korea, and her mother works two jobs in the city. Casey feels lonely and lost when she meets gentle Dwayne Pickens, a 30-year-old man with the mind of a child. Their shared love of baseball draws them together, and by the end of the summer Casey has not only adopted Dwayne as her best friend, but has come to understand and treasure the other grownups she's met.

Awards: Christopher Award 1979; BBYA Nothin' But the Best 1966–1986

And One for All

by Theresa Nelson
(Ages 12–15)
1989. Orchard Books, $12.95.

The confusion and tragedy of the Vietnam war are captured in Nelson's poignant stateside story, told through the perspective of an apprehensive 12-year-old. It's 1967, the war is accelerating, and, like her father, a former marine, Geraldine's brother Wing is fiercely patriotic. Even Wing's best friend Sam, a devoted peace activist who lost his father in Korea, can't dissuade Wing from enlisting. Geraldine watches in anguish as the boys' differing political views tear them apart.

Awards: Notable Children's Book 1990; BBYA 1990

Badger on the Barge and Other Stories
by Janni Howker
(Ages 12–15)
1985. Greenwillow, $11.75; Puffin, paper, $4.95; ABC-CLIO, large-type, $14.95.

Each of the five stories Howker presents here has different characters and a distinctive plot, but all are set in the north of England and concern a pivotal encounter between a young person and an old, solitary stranger. In the title story, an independent old woman helps a grief-stricken girl deal with her brother's death; in another, when an old Nazi rescues a kidnapped child, a teenage boy regrets his past cruel taunting of the man. These complex stories are filled with images that express the fragility of love and the pain of loss in unforgettable terms.

Awards: Notable Children's Book 1985; BBYA 1985

Baseball in April and Other Stories
by Gary Soto
(Ages 10–14)
1990. HBJ, $14.95.

Written about Latino youth, the 11 short stories in this collection evoke a richness of a culture, language, and community. Like his characters, Soto grew up in Fresno, California, and he writes with warmth and candor about young people—Gilbert, the polite fifth-grader who dreams of being the Karate Kid; Veronica, who wants a blond, blue-eyed Barbie doll, not one that has her dark looks; and Manuel, who covers his confusion by spouting scientific jargon from magazines. Soto's stories blend a strong sense of what it's like to grow up Hispanic with a deep understanding of what it's like simply to be young.

Awards: BBYA 1991

Bearstone
by Will Hobbs
(Ages 12–15)
1989. Atheneum, $12.95.

Deserted by his parents and raised by his Ute grandmother, 14-year-old Cloyd Atcitty, filled with resentment and ready to run away, arrives at Walter Landis's farm. At school, the thought is that his stay with the lonely but kindhearted old miner will somehow make a difference. The visit begins encouragingly. Cloyd finds a turquoise bearstone, a symbol of luck to his people, and he seems to get along well with Walter. Their relationship is threatened when a hunter kills a bear and unleashes Cloyd's own round of destruction, which hurts Walter deeply. But when Walter is injured in a mining accident and Cloyd's frantic plan saves the old man's life, they admit their mutual love and respect. A heartwarming coming-of-age story with plenty of action.

Beyond the Divide
by Kathryn Lasky
(Ages 11–15)
1983. Macmillan, $13.95; Dell, paper, $3.25.

Knowing little of the world outside the shelter of her Amish community, Meribah Simon joins her father on a difficult wagon train trip west. The journey becomes a metaphor for her passage into adulthood: Meribah proves herself courageous in the face of loneliness and starvation, resourceful when she is deserted by the rest of the train, and loyal and understanding when her friend is raped and cruelly rejected. With Lasky's afterword to provide historical perspective, the book works both as a quintessential pioneer tale and a compelling story about growing up. Another unforgettable story of the west by Lasky is *The Bone Wars.*

Awards: BBYA 1983

The Blue Sword
by Robin McKinley
(See Fantasy Fiction, p. 90.)

Celine
by Brock Cole.
(Ages 12–15)
1989. Farrar, Straus & Giroux, $13.95.

Caught between innocence and maturity, Chicago high school senior Celine looks for truth in a phony conformist culture. She's drawn to Jake, her seven-year-old neighbor, with whom she shares a fascination for television. Cole finds poetry and laughter in the clichés of everyday life in this story of two lonely TV junkies who help each other overcome despair and make a home in the city.

The Changeover: A Supernatural Romance
by Margaret Mahy.
(Ages 13–15)
1984. McElderry, $12.95; Scholastic, paper, $2.50.

Love triumphs over evil in a tantalizing story mixing romance with supernatural goings on. Carmody Braque, a vampire of sorts, drains strength from his prey to prolong his life. When Laura Chant's little brother Jacko becomes his victim, she appeals to classmate Sorenson Carlisle, a white witch, for help. But Sorry can only do so much; it's Laura who must best the evil Braque. To do that, she must develop mystical powers of her own and "changeover" to the world one step beyond.

Awards: BBYA 1984

The Chocolate War
by Robert Cormier
(Ages 12–15)
1974. Pantheon, $18.95; Dell, paper, $3.50; G.K. Hall, large-type, $14.95.

Although selling chocolates for Trinity High School's fundraiser is supposed to be voluntary, Brother Leon, the teacher in charge, puts pressure on students who don't participate. When Jerry Renault refuses anyway, he become the school hero. When sales begin to drop because of his defiance, he becomes the target not only of the bullying cleric, but also of a brutal campus gang. A dramatic, controversial novel, now considered a classic of adolescent literature.

Awards: BBYA Nothin' But the Best 1966–1986

Come Sing, Jimmy Jo
by Katherine Paterson
(Ages 11–14)
1985. Lodestar, $12.95; Avon, paper, $2.95.

For more than 30 years, the Johnson family has performed its special brand of country music, and now it's 11-year-old James's turn

The Blue Sword by Robin McKinley   (Ages 12–15)   1982. Greenwillow, $13.95.

The mythical medieval kingdom of Damar is the setting for this fine sword-and-sorcery tale in which a young woman learns she possesses special powers. She is destined to become a warrior and help King Corlath's Riders defend their kingdom. Damar is also the backdrop for the Newbery Medal–winning novel *The Hero and the Crown,* which is actually a prequel to *The Blue Sword.* In that tale, the protagonist is the courageous daughter of the Damarain king, who bests a dragon and saves her people. Filled with romance, pagaentry and excitment, it was awarded the Newbery Medal in 1985. Don't miss McKinley's superb retelling of the "Beauty and the Beast" legend in *Beauty.*

Awards: Newbery Honor Book 1983; Notable
Children's Book 1983; BBYA 1982

Dealing with Dragons by Patricia Wrede   (Ages 11–15)   1990. HBJ, $15.95.

Princesses are supposed to behave; most of them do. Not Princess Cimorene, though. The youngest of seven daughters, she's a trial for her royal parents, preferring fencing to drawing, juggling to embroidery, and philosophy to etiquette. And she certainly wants nothing to do with dull-witted Prince Therandil. To escape them all, she volunteers to work for the powerful dragon Kazul and eventually finds herself battling some unscrupulous wizards who have invaded dragon territory. A spirited yarn that turns fairy tale convention on its head and is continued in a lively sequel, *Searching for Dragons* (a 1992 Notable selection).

Dragonsong by Anne McCaffrey   (Ages 11–14)   1976. Atheneum, $14.95.

Menolly wants desperately to be a Harper, but on the planet Pern women are not allowed to play and sing. Unwilling to abandon her gift for music, she runs away. Seeking refuge in a cave, she befriends nine Fire Lizards, small relatives of the huge dragons that protect Pern from the deadly, threadlike spores that threaten its survival. Menolly teaches them music, and they give her loyalty. This wonderfully intricate fantasy is but one in a series of titles about Pern and its imaginatively wrought creatures.
Awards: BBYA Nothin' But the Best 1966–1986

The Feast of the Trickster by Beth Hilgartner   (Ages 12–17)   1991. Houghton Mifflin, $14.95.

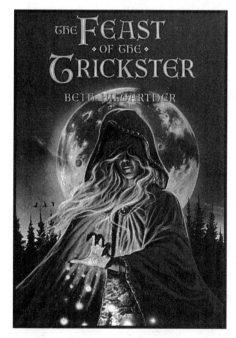

This novel is a rich sequel to *Colors in the Dreamweaver's Loom* (1989), in which sixteen-year-old Alexandra ("Zan") sought sanctuary in the woods to mourn the death of her father and was drawn into an alternate world. Zan, the champion of the Orathnis—gentle forest people—is now the victim of the Trickster and lost in a void. Her five quest companions—a Minstrel, a Swordswoman, a Shapeshifter, a Prophet, and a Heartmender—go in search of her. Highly comic moments occur when these transdimensional creatures arrive in New England and find escorts in three teenagers who offer their aid. Surprising twists, dramatic encounters, and a strong plot make this an especially worthwhile fantasy to explore.

Howl's Moving Castle by Diana Wynne Jones   (Ages 12–15)   1986. Greenwillow, $10.25.

Jones proves she's found the recipe for good comedy in this clever, lighthearted fantasy, filled with battling sorcerers, fire demons, sentient scarecrows, and doors that open into different dimensions. Turned into an ugly old crone by an unexpected witch's curse, Sophie Hatter wanders away from her boring existence, determined to make the most of her few remaining years. With newfound confidence, she bullies her way past the sentry at Wizard Howl's door, discovering, to her surprise, that he's not the evil sorcerer she expected. Instead, he's a handsome young wizard who needs a lesson or two in responsible behavior. The sequel, *Castle in the Air,* is an equally gripping saga that was selected as an ALA Notable in 1992.
Awards: Notable Children's Book 1986; BBYA 1986

Playing Beatie Bow by Ruth Park   (Ages 11–14)   1982. Atheneum, $13.95; Puffin, paper, $3.95.

While watching young Australian children play a game called "Beatie Bow," 14-year-old Abigail notices a strangely dressed child hovering on the fringes of the activity. As it turns out, the waif is the original Beatie Bow, for whom the game was named, but Abigail doesn't find out the girl's story until the the two travel back through time to Sydney, Australia, one hundred years in the past, where Abby discovers the intricate connections between herself and the Bow family, Beatie in particular.
Awards: Notable Children's Book 1982; BBYA 1982; Australian Children's Book of the Year 1981

Ratha's Creature by Clare Bell   (Ages 12–15)   1983. Dell, paper, $2.95.

An inventive fantasy set in a prehistory populated by intelligent cats. Cast out by her clan of herders for challenging its leader, precocious Ratha is taken in by an enemy tribe. Her curiosity and spirited nature cause her to be exiled by them as well, and she's scorned by both clans when a vicious war breaks out. It's her knowledge of fire that saves her and eventually brings her back into the fold of her original family—not as a novice herder this time, but as leader of the entire clan.
Awards: BBYA 1983

The Remarkable Journey of Prince Jen by Alexander Lloyd   (Ages 11–15)   1991. Dutton, $14.95.

When Prince Jen embarks on a journey to the legendary court of T'ien-kuo where he must learn how to rule, he carries six apparently ordinary gifts. The decisions the young prince must make about parting with these gifts, which save his own life and rescue others, effect a remarkable transformation during his coming-of-age quest through the Chinese countryside.
Awards: Booklist Top of the List 1992

to make a musical contribution. Wondering whether he'll actually be able to face an audience of strangers, he leaves behind the grandmother who raised him and joins his mother and his relatives as the youngest member of the group. As it turns out, stage fright is the least of his problems. The greater challenges include figuring out where he fits into the complicated dynamics of his family, and what to do about the stranger who claims to be his dad.

The Contender
by Robert Lipsyte
(Ages 12–15)
1967. HarperCollins, $12.89; paper, $2.50; ABC-CLIO, large-type, $14.95.

Life in Harlem has left 17-year-old Alfred and his buddy James angry and frustrated. But while James turns to crime and drugs, Alfred learns boxing, finding satisfaction and pride in his growing talent in the ring as well as the strength to help him cope with what he must face outside it. Filled with vivid fight scenes, this is a powerful novel. Look for its sequel, *The Brave.*

Cousins
by Virginia Hamilton
(Ages 10–13)
1990. Philomel, $14.95.

Cammy can't stand her cousin, Patty Ann, who patronizes her and is far too pretty, too smart, and too well behaved. Cammy manages to keep her feelings under control; but when Patty Ann makes some cracks about Cammy's beloved Gram Tut, a real feud breaks out between the girls. Cammy wishes her cousin dead, then despises herself for her angry words and thoughts when a freak accident

makes her wish come true. In exuberant language with cadences of certain African-American speech, Hamilton presents the contradictions that exist within each of us and explores the strange ways love and hate intertwine.

Awards: BBYA 1991

A Day No Pigs Would Die
by Robert Newton Peck
(Ages 11–14)
1972. Knopf, $16.95; Dell, paper, $3.50; ABC-CLIO, large-type, $14.95.

In an autobiographical novel set in Vermont during the 1920s, Peck evokes both the compassion and the harshness of the Shaker customs that shaped a young farm boy's life. Twelve-year-old Robert immediately loves the tiny newborn pig he is given by a grateful neighbor, but he helps his father slaughter Pinky when the time comes, a difficult task that gives him the strength he needs to assume grown-up responsibility when his father dies the following spring.

The Day That Elvis Came to Town
by Jan Marino
(Ages 12–15)
1990. Little, Brown, $14.95.

Filled with memorable characters, this rich story combines a sense of interracial understanding with the complicated dynamics of growing up and family relationships. Wanda hates her father's drinking problem and the strain it puts on her parents' marriage. She also hates the fact that her family must take in boarders to make ends meet. But her feelings change when she finds out that glamorous, generous Mercedes Washington, their newest lodger, went to school with her idol, Elvis Presley. Then Wanda's pathetic, mean-spirited aunt reveals that light-skinned Mercedes is black. In Wanda's 1963 Georgia, this still makes a difference. What Wanda must decide is whether the fact makes any difference to her.

The Day They Came to Arrest the Book
by Nat Hentoff
(See Videos.)
1982. Dell, paper, $3.25.

Dealing with Dragons
by Patricia Wrede
(See Fantasy Fiction, p. 90.)

Dixie Storms
by Barbara Hall.
(Ages 12–15)
1990. HBJ, $15.95.

A Virginia family suffering through hard times comes to life through the naive perspective of 14-year-old Dutch, who sees her parents' fortitude tested by a drought, her brother's marriage fall apart, and her own secret crush betrayed by her glamorous cousin. Told with vitality, the novel is a wryly affectionate, realistic portrait of a girl's coming to terms with her family and herself.

Awards: BBYA 1991

Dogsong
by Gary Paulsen
(Ages 12–15)
1985. Bradbury, $12.95; Puffin, paper, $3.95.

Eskimo youth Russell Susskit is reluctant to accept the modern world in which he lives. Mourning the loss of the old ways of his people, the songs they sang, and the stories that proclaimed their greatness, he embarks on a dog sled journey through the frigid north, a pilgrimage of learning, testing, and self-discovery, of tragedy and affirmation.

Awards: Newbery Honor Book 1985; Notable Children's Book 1985

Dragonsong
by Anne McCaffrey
(See Fantasy Fiction, p. 91.)

El Chino
by Allen Say
(Ages 12–15)
1990. Houghton Mifflin, $14.95.

Bong Way Wong, called Billy by his family, dreams of being a professional athlete. After all, his father always claimed, "In America, you can be anything you want to be." But in spite of his ability on the basketball court, Billy is just too short. He settles on a career as an engineer until a trip to Spain gives him a new ambition. Billy wants to be a matador. Being Chinese seems to be a drawback until Billy quits trying to be Spanish and becomes "El Chino," the first Chinese matador. Say's arresting watercolors add to the drama of this compelling biography that stresses not only following your dreams but knowing who you are.

The Empty Sleeve
by Leon Garfield
(Ages 11–14)
1988. Delacorte, $14.95.

Twins Peter and Paul Gannet were both born at a bad-luck hour, but according to superstitious Mr. Bagley, things will be far worse for

Peter. Fourteen years pass. Peter, now desperate to escape from his sickly brother, turns to petty crime to earn money for passage on a ship. What he doesn't realize is that each time he strays outside the law, he steps closer to fulfillment of old Bagley's prophecy. Garfield blends suspense with moral lessons in a crackerjack adventure set in eighteenth-century England and peopled with characters that Charles Dickens might have invented.

Eva
by Peter Dickinson
(Ages 12–16)
1989. Delacorte, $14.95.

A riveting, thought-provoking novel, set in an overpopulated future where human greed and indifference have taken a terrible toll. After an automobile accident, Eva wakes up in the hospital to discover that her mind, the only part of her body still whole, has been transferred into the agile body of Kelly the chimp, and that now she must integrate her human consciousness with her ape behavior patterns and instincts.

Awards: Notable Children's Book 1990; BBYA 1990

Fallen Angels
by Walter Dean Myers
(Ages 14–17)
1988. Scholastic, $12.95; paper, $3.50.

Less from patriotic impulse than from fear of a dead-end life in Harlem, Richie Perry, 17 and black, enlists in the army. What he finds in Vietnam is a war that breeds violence among comrades; a war in which parents betray their children and officers send men into combat only to reap honors for themselves; a war that

forces individuals to question their religion and their morality. But also in this harsh and terrifying foreign place, where tedium and terror are so closely entwined, Richie discovers himself and forges bonds of friendship and love unlike any he's ever known.

Awards: BBYA 1989; Coretta Scott King Award 1989

Father Figure
by Richard Peck
(See Fathers and Sons, p. 101.)

The Feast of the Trickster
by Beth Hilgartner
(See Fantasy Fiction, p. 91.)

Finding David Dolores
by Margaret Willey
(Ages 11–14)
1986. HarperCollins, $10.89.

Uncomfortable with her changing body and feelings, shy 13-year-old Arly struggles alone until she spots David Dolores, an older boy on whom she develops a crush. She tells no one. Instead, Arly happily watches David from afar, spying on him and on his artistic mother. But the situation changes dramatically after the lonely girl gets to know sophisticated Regina and shares her secret about David. Then fantasy smacks into reality, and Arly is forced to make herself known to the boy of her dreams.

Awards: BBYA 1986

A Fine White Dust
by Cynthia Rylant
(Ages 11–14)
1986. Bradbury, $11.95; Dell, paper, $2.95.

SEX EDUCATION

BOOKS

Asking about Sex and Growing Up: A Question-and-Answer Book for Boys and Girls by Joanna Cole   (Ages 9–12)   1988. Morrow, $12.95; paper, $4.95.

In an easy-to-read question-answer book illustrated with cartoon sketches and anatomical drawings, Cole considers fundamental concerns preteen boys and girls have about sex. A well-known author of children's nonfiction, she deals with the sensitive emotional and physiological material in an earnest, forthright fashion, speaking directly to kids in a tone that reassures them that it's okay to ask questions—whether they want to know about puberty, reproduction, wet dreams, birth control, or AIDS.

Being Born by Sheila Kitzinger   (Ages 7–Adult)   Photos by Lennart Nilsson. 1986. Grosset & Dunlap, $15.95.

Extraordinary full-color intrauterine photographs, taken by a renowned medical photographer, offer a glimpse of the miracle of developing human life. Kitzinger's almost lyrical text beautifully describes each stage in development, while the pictures dramatically explore what happens from the moment of conception right through to birth. A tender photograph of a newborn infant at its mother's breast concludes the book, which speaks to readers of many ages about an experience they all have in common.
Awards: Notable Children's Book 1986

Changing Bodies, Changing Lives by Ruth Bell   (Ages 13–17)   1988, rev. ed. Random House, $19.95; Vintage, paper, $12.95.

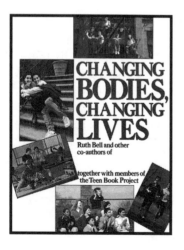

Colorful photographs on the cover will attract teenage readers to this comprehensive book, which supplies support and information about a host of growing-up issues. Answers to common questions about menstruation, intercourse, and homosexuality are combined with insights into such diverse subjects as depression, friendship, and getting along with parents. Frank comments from teenagers humanize the book, and black-and-white photographs scattered throughout capture real emotions on the faces of real kids.

Children and the AIDS Virus: A Book for Children, Parents, and Teachers by Rosemarie Hausherr   (Ages 6–9)   1992. Rev. ed. Clarion, $13.95.

Using the familiar cold virus as an example, Hausherr explains how microorganisms attack the body and how cells fight to defend against them. She then offers a concise description of AIDS, as a virus that renders the body powerless to protect itself. Reassuring yet precise, Hausherr explains that children are rarely stricken with AIDS, but she does introduce two who have contacted the virus, one through a blood transfusion and the other from a drug-addicted mother. A useful volume that brings the reality of the illness into focus for parents and children.
Awards: Notable Children's Books 1990

Safe, Strong, and Streetwise: The Teenager's Guide to Preventing Sexual Assault by Helen Benedict   (Ages 13–17)   1987. Little, Brown, $14.95; paper, $5.95.

Speaking directly to teenagers and including personal testimony from young adults who have survived attacks, Benedict discusses how to protect oneself from sexual assault. She emphasizes that "awareness and escape," rather than physical defense methods, are the most important factors in self-protection, and she provides sound guideposts for young people—young men as well as young women—confused by sexually exploitative situations on dates, on the job, or at school. Her book is explicit, as well as sensitive and practical.
Awards: BBYA 1987

The What's Happening to My Body? Book for Boys: A Growing Up Guide for Parents and Sons by Lynda Madaras and Dane Saavedra   (Ages 11–15)

The What's Happening to My Body? Book for Girls: A Growing Up Guide for Parents and Daughters by Lynda Madaras and Area Madaras   (Ages 11–15)   1988 Newmarket Press, $16.95 each; paper, $9.95 each.

Beginning with prefaces that urge parents to become involved in their children's sex education, these companion volumes contain a wealth of information related to the onset of puberty. Incorporating perspectives from her daughter, from Saavedra (the 15-year-old son of a friend), and from students she's taught in her California sex education classes, Madaras deals explicitly and authoritatively with a wide variety of sexual health and developmental issues. To encourage a better understanding of sexual development as a whole, she's included in each book a chapter that addresses young adults' curiosity about the opposite sex. Both books are illustrated with carefully executed drawings.

VIDEOS

See *Boy Stuff, Girl Stuff, Bodytalk, Double Dutch—Double Jeopardy,* and *It's Late* in Videos.

SOFTWARE

See *The Body Transparent* in Computer Software and *Dr. Know-It-All's Inner Body Works,* available in junior (Grades 4–6) and senior (Grades 7–12) versions from Tom Snyder Productions.

Though religion is not as important to his mother and father, it has long been a source of comfort and hope for 13-year-old Peter. His parents accept its importance in his life and do not hold him back, even when an itinerant revivalist preacher arrives in town, and Peter falls so completely under his sway that he's ready to leave home.

Awards: Newbery Honor Book 1987; Notable Children's Book 1986; BBYA 1986

The Friends
by Rosa Guy
(See Videos.)
1973. Holt, $10.95; Bantam, paper, $2.95.

The Ghost Belonged to Me
by Richard Peck
(Ages 11–14)
1975. Viking, $13.95; Dell, paper, $3.25; ABC-CLIO, large-type, $15.95.

Thirteen-year-old Alexander Armsworth is not exactly the kind of person anyone would consider a typical daredevil, even in his small turn-of-the-century Missouri town. Yet a hero he becomes, thanks to Inez, the rather watery ghost of a Creole Indian girl that appears in the barn to warn Alex of a calamity in the making. Discovering that poor Inez was once the victim of a similar misfortune, Alex enlists the aid of his 85-year-old great-uncle and an obstreperous girl named Blossom Culp to put Inez's uncomfortable spirit to rest. Equally clever and funny is *Ghosts I Have Been,* in which Blossom moves to center stage and discovers she has psychic powers.

Awards: BBYA Nothin' But the Best 1966–1986

The Goats
by Brock Cole
(Ages 12–15)
1987. Farrar, Straus & Giroux, paper, $3.50; ABC-CLIO, large-type, $14.95.

Two unpopular campers, Laura and Howie, are stripped of their clothing and marooned on an island in a cruel practical joke. Although frightened, they are determined not to return to camp. They escape under cover of darkness, and by rummaging through abandoned summer cottages are able to find both clothing and food. On the run, all the while trying to contact Laura's mother for help, they learn to depend on one another and use their own wits for survival. A powerful portrait of two outsiders, or "goats," learning their own worth.

Awards: Notable Children's Book 1987

Good-bye and Keep Cold
by Jenny Davis
(Ages 13–15)
1987. Orchard Books, $12.95; Dell, paper, $2.95.

Edda Combs, eight when her father dies in a mining accident, harks back to the years of her life after his death. Her unaffected narrative tells of their life in Cauley's Creek, Kentucky; Edda's lively little brother and the elderly eccentric relative who lives upstairs; unsettling discoveries about her father; and her mother's growing closeness to the man responsible for her father's fatal accident. The peculiarities of human nature shine clearly through her memories, which are ultimately more about her mother than they are about herself.

Awards: BBYA 1987

Good Night, Mr. Tom
by Michelle Magorian
(Ages 12–15)
1982. HarperCollins, $13.95; paper, $3.95.

Eight-year-old Willie, sickly and bearing the marks of child abuse, is terrified when he's evacuated from London at the outset of World War II. He is taken in by reclusive Tom Oakley, who has never recovered from the deaths of his wife and baby. As Willie gradually grows used to Tom and learns to trust him, Willie's emotional and physical wounds begin to heal. Country dialect and the atmosphere of wartime England enhance this compassionate story.

Awards: Notable Children's Book 1982; BBYA 1982

Half Nelson, Full Nelson
by Bruce Stone
(Ages 12–15)
1985. HarperCollins, $12.89; paper, $2.95.

Nelson Gato's 270-pound father dreams of big-time wrestling, while his mother wants a quiet life. When she leaves and takes seven-year-old Vanessa with her, Nelson vows to reunite his family. He fakes a kidnapping assisted by his friend Heidi. With Vanessa he begins a trek across Florida and Georgia to bring his beloved sister home.

Awards: BBYA 1985

A Hand Full of Stars
by Rafik Schami
(See Multicultural Fare, p. 36.)

Hatchet
by Gary Paulsen
(Ages 11–14)
1987. Puffin, paper, $3.95; ABC-CLIO, large-type, $15.95.

En route to visit his father in a remote part of Canada, Brian Robeson becomes so wrapped up in thoughts about his parents' divorce he's hardly aware of the parting gift his mother gave him—a hatchet, which he has strapped to his belt. When the small plane carrying him crashes and the pilot dies, Brian finds himself facing death in an unfriendly wilderness, equipped only with luck, brains, and his brand-new hatchet. A video made for the WonderWorks Family movie series, titled *A Cry in the Wild,* is based on this novel. Brian Robeson faces another test of his wilderness-survival skills in Paulsen's sequel, *The River.*

Awards: Newbery Honor Book 1987; Notable Children's Book 1987

Here at the Scenic-Vu Motel
by Thelma Hatch Wyss
(Ages 12–15)
1988. HarperCollins, $11.95; paper, $3.25.

When the board of education refuses to provide bus service to their remote homes in Bear Flats, Jacob Callahan and six other students are forced to take up residence in the distinctly unscenic Scenic-Vu Motel—boys and girls in separate rooms, of course—so they can attend school during the week. Responsibility for this displaced group falls to 17-year-old Jake, the oldest, who describes his stint as surrogate parent in warm, comic diary entries that capture his attempts to cope with everything from a stomach flu epidemic and parent-teacher

FATHERS AND SONS

These young adult novels about the father/son relationship are meant to be read by both; perhaps together. Hasn't it been too long since your boy and his dad shared a good book? "A father's involvement with books and reading can do much to elevate books to at least the same status as baseball gloves and hockey sticks in a boy's estimation," according to the Read-Aloud guru James Trelease.

Father Figure by Richard Peck (Ages 12–15)   1978. Dell, paper, $2.95.

When their mother dies, Jim Atwater expects to continue his role as substitute father for his eight-year-old brother, Byron, a job he's been doing since their father left the family years before. It comes as a nasty surprise when his grandmother decides to pack both boys off to Florida for a summer with Dad. An even greater shock for Jim is Byron's delight in their new surroundings and Byron's growing attachment to his real father.
Awards: BBYA 1978

Mariposa Blues by Ron Koertge   (Ages 11–15)   1991. Little, Brown, $15.95.

Things just weren't going well for 13-year-old Graham. His grades were slipping; he was constantly fighting with his parents, especially his father; and his body was changing in ways that surprised and embarrassed him. He fervently hoped spending the summer at Mariposa, where his dad trained thoroughbred race horses and where he could talk to his friend Lisa, would somehow enable him to figure out what was going on. Unfortunately, pretty Lisa is dreamy-eyed over a new boyfriend, and Graham finds himself battling jealousy at the same time that he's struggling to convince his father he's growing up.

On the Ropes by Otto Salassi   (Ages 11–14)   1981. Greenwillow, $11.25.

In order to save their farm from bank foreclosure, 11-year-old Squint Gains and his older sister, Julie, must find their long-lost father, Claudius. With more than a bit of luck, Squint succeeds, tracking Claudius down to a Dallas arena where the wrestlers he manages are entertaining cheering crowds. Then, wrestlers and father in tow, Squint returns home, where Claudius concocts a lively, thoroughly wacky series of wrestling matches to earn enough cash to keep the creditors at bay.

A Time of Troubles by Pieter Van Raven   (Ages 11–15)   1990. Scribners, $13.95.

With no home and no money coming in, 14-year-old Roy Purdy and his irresponsible father take their belongings and head west across the Dust Bowl. When their money runs out, they ride the rails and, later, join up with others, displaced by the Depression and lured to California by the tantalizing promise of work as fruit-pickers. What they discover when they arrive is not what they expect. A strike for higher wages promises bloodshed, and Roy and his father find themselves on opposite sides of the conflict.

conferences to discord in the ranks and his own case of first-romance jitters.

Awards: BBYA 1988

A Hero Ain't Nothin' but a Sandwich
by Alice Childress
(Ages 13–15)
1973. Avon, paper, $2.95; ABC-CLIO, large-type, $14.95.

Set in Harlem, this novel about 13-year-old Benjie Johnson, a heroin addict, offers a harsh but perceptive account of the complicated relationships that define his character and the agonizing struggle to beat his drug dependency. The distinctive voices of Benjie's mother, his stepfather, his friend Jimmy, and Benjie himself echo throughout the story, a compelling and timely commentary on society and personal values.

Awards: BBYA 1973; BBYA Nothin' But the Best 1966–1986

The Heroic Life of Al Capsella
by J. Clarke
(Ages 12–15)
1990. Holt, $14.95.

Fourteen-year-old Almeric Capsella wants desperately to fit in with his peers, but he's so embarrassed by his parents he doesn't think he has a chance. His touching, funny narrative articulates his woes and describes the wacky behavior of the unusual adults who cross his path—among them a mother who acts like "an alien from another planet" and a grandfather who stores garbage in the freezer so it won't smell. The sequel is *Al Capsella and the Watchdogs.*

Awards: BBYA 1991

The Honorable Prison
by Lyll Becerra de Jenkins
(Ages 13–17)
1988. Lodestar, $14.95; Puffin, paper, $3.95.

Marta loves her father and admires him for standing firm against the dictatorship that rules their Latin American country. However, when his critical editorials lead to the family's imprisonment in a remote village where they experience officially sanctioned torture, Marta begins to resent her father and his political ideals. Based on Jenkins's own experiences, this gritty, dramatic story makes clear the terror of daily life in a Latin American police state.

Howl's Moving Castle
by Diana Wynne Jones
(See Fantasy Fiction, p. 91.)

Incident at Hawks Hill
by Allan W. Eckert
(Ages 12–15)
1971. Little, Brown, $14.95.

An actual incident that took place in Canada around the turn of the century sparks this story of six-year-old Ben, small and shy, who communicates better with animals than with his own family. Lost on the prairie during a summer storm, Ben takes refuge in a tunnel. Here, he's accepted by its resident, a female badger, who nurtures Ben, allowing him to fill the place of the mate and the pups she's lost.

Awards: Newbery Honor Book 1971

In Lane Three, Alex Archer
by Tessa Duder
(Ages 12–15)
1989. Houghton Mifflin, $13.95.

A talented actress and an excellent swimmer, New Zealand teenager Alex Archer triumphs at everything she does. When a hit-and-run driver kills her boyfriend, her world falls apart. As she swims—thoughts whirling, heart pounding, muscles aching—toward a critical win that could send her to the Rome Olympics, she remembers the tragedy that shocked her from childhood into the adult world. An unforgettable book, as powerful for its depiction of the rigors of competitive sports as it is for its treatment of a familiar growing-up theme.

Awards: BBYA 1990

I Only Made Up the Roses
by Barbara Ann Porte
(Ages 13–15)
1987. Greenwillow, $10.25.

In a warm, wise, and funny book, Cydra James introduces her interracial family: seven-year-old Perley, black like Cydra's stepfather and clever beyond his years; her aunt Selina, who grew up in a segregated South; her loving stepfather; and, of course, herself, a keen observer of those around her. In a series of interconnected memories interlaced with myth and folklore, Cydra and her beloved family weave a strong patchwork of familial devotion that speaks straight to the heart.

I Will Call It Georgie's Blues
by Suzanne Newton
(Ages 13–15)
1983. Dell, paper, $2.75.

Fifteen-year-old Neal Sloan is the son of a Baptist minister who expects only perfection from his family and metes out harsh punishment when his expectations are not properly met. While Aileen, Neal's older sister, has chosen to rebel against her father's authoritarian rule, Neal finds a more private way to cope in his dysfunctional family. He's secretly learning to play jazz piano, and he's becoming a very good musician. Unfortunately, his seven-year-old brother Georgie isn't lucky enough to have an escape, and it's his tragedy that helps the family begin to heal.

Awards: Notable Children's Book 1983; BBYA 1983

Jacob Have I Loved
by Katherine Paterson
(See Videos.)
1980. HarperCollins, $12.95; paper, $2.95.

Awards: Newbery Medal 1981

The Keeper
by Phyllis Naylor
(Ages 11–15)
1986. Atheneum, $12.95; Bantam, paper, $2.95.

Nick's father, who is mentally ill, refuses to seek help even though his behavior is becoming increasingly bizarre. Powerless to defy him or interfere against his wishes, Nick and his mother must wait, watching in anguish as his illness worsens, until Nick finally takes it upon himself to secure the help his father needs. There's no sunny ending in this brutal portrait of a family in torment, but Naylor's portrayal of emotional strength in the face of tragedy speaks volumes about her faith in the human spirit.

Awards: Notable Children's 1986; BBYA 1986; BBYA Nothin' But the Best 1966–1986

Keeper of the Isis Light

by Monica Hughes

(Ages 12–15)

1981. Atheneum, $11.95.

Reared by a robot named Guardian, 16-year-old Olwen Pendennis has grown up without human contact, loving her life as Keeper of the Light for a galactic lighthouse built to guide space travelers. When a spaceship from Earth finally lands on her planet, Guardian insists Olwen wear a special coverall with an opaque face mask. Olwen doesn't understand why until Mark, a young settler whom she's grown to like, catches her unmasked, and she learns the truth about how she looks and who she is. A compelling, bittersweet story science fiction fans will love.

Awards: International Board on Books for Young People (IBBY) Honor List 1982

Language of Goldfish

by Zibby O'Neal

(Ages 12–14)

1979. Viking, $14.95; Puffin, paper, $3.95; ABC-CLIO, large-type, $14.95.

A middle child, 13-year-old Carrie Stokes is a talented artist and a gifted mathematician, but she lacks a sure sense of herself. She clings to the old days when she and her older sister, Moira, played by their backyard pond. With Moira now interested only in boys and her parents wrapped up in their own concerns, Carrie finds no one to cry to for help as she sinks deeper into an emotional abyss. It seems to her that death is the only way she can find peace. A gripping, affecting novel, this was one of the first children's books to deal openly with the sensitive subject of teenage suicide. That Carrie survives and gets well is a reminder to readers that there are always other choices.

Letters from Atlantis

by Robert Silverberg

(Ages 12–15)

1990. Atheneum, $14.95.

Told in the form of letters, Silverberg's inventive, witty mix of speculation and legend relates the experiences of a twenty-first-century time traveler, whose mission is to learn the secrets of the fabled Atlantis. While his body lies comatose in the Home Era, Roy's essence slips back centuries to merge with the mind of the Crown Prince of Atlantis, who, it turns out, knows full well that the kingdom is doomed but is not supposed to do anything about it.

Lyddie

by Katherine Paterson

(Ages 12–15)

1991. Lodestar, $14.95.

Thirteen-year-old Lyddie Worthen is tough. She has to be because she is alone. When poverty forces her family to separate, she's sent to work at a nearby tavern. Later she finds work in a Massachusetts mill, where illiteracy, industrial oppression, and sexual discrimination burden her hopes to earn enough money to buy back the family farm and gather her loved ones together again. Though the depiction of Lyddie's harsh mid-nineteenth-century life reads like melodrama, it is actually rooted in social history. Begun by Paterson as a part of the Women's History Project for the Vermont bicentennial, the novel is a vivid depiction of part of America's past as well as a moving portrait of an unusual individual who suffers great odds but still survives.

Awards: BBYA 1992

The Machine Gunners
by Robert Westall
(Ages 11–14)
1976. Greenwillow, $11.88; McKay, paper, $3.50.

A skillful, touching novel that captures a child's world changed by war. In a German plane that's crashed near his home in Garmouth, England, Chas McGill discovers not only the dead body of the pilot but also a Nazi machine gun still intact. Making off with the weapon, Chas and his friends build a sandbag fortress to contain it, then sit back awaiting the Nazi legions predicted by the newsreels.

The Man from the Other Side
by Uri Orlev
(Ages 11–15)
Translated from Hebrew by Hillel Halkin.
1991. Houghton Mifflin, $13.95.

Marek is a teenager who helps Antony, his Polish stepfather, to smuggle food and weapons in through the rank sewers below the Warsaw ghetto, and smuggle Jews out. Antony works for profit not altruism, and Marek is not fond of the man. When Marek discovers that his late father was Jewish, he focuses his paternal feelings on a refugee medical student named Jozek and smuggles him back into the ghetto to aid in the 1934 Passover uprising. Family conflict brings a personal level to this story of the Nazi bombardment of the ghetto and the deportation of the Jews. Orlev's earlier *Island on Bird Street* proved his skill with wartime adventure fiction. In this gripping new tale, the moral dilemmas are as labyrinthine as the sewers, both of which Marek must negotiate carefully to survive.

Awards: Mildred L. Batchelder Award 1992; BBYA 1992

Mariposa Blues
by Ron Koertge
(See Fathers and Sons, p. 101.)

The Moves Make the Man
by Bruce Brooks
(Ages 12–15)
1984. HarperCollins, $13.95; paper, $2.95; ABC-CLIO, large-type, $15.95.

Brooks makes basketball a metaphor for life's choices in a penetrating story about best friends. Jerome Foxworthy plays great basketball. He's also smart, savvy, and self-confident, with a loving family to help him cope with the racism he experiences as the first black student in his school. Bix Rivers, who is white, isn't as fortunate: his basketball is as bad as his life at home. Jerome tries to teach Bix what he knows about the sport. But Bix has trouble learning how to fake, and if he can't fool his opponents with the right moves on the court, he won't survive in any kind of game—certainly not real life.

Awards: Newbery Honor Book 1985; Notable Children's Book 1984; BBYA 1985

The Mozart Season
by Virginia Euwer Wolff
(Ages 12–15)
1991. Holt, $15.95.

Wolff makes the artistic experience special (as well as ordinary) in a story about a telling summer for 12-year-old baseball player and musical prodigy Allegra Leah Shapiro. As she practices diligently for an important youth music competition, Allegra begins to see how music relates to her life in Portland, Oregon, and to her family history, which stretches back to the Treblinka concentration camp. The passion Allegra feels for her music comes through in this novel. It will surely rouse teenagers who are themselves intense about something— whether it be collecting baseball cards, performing chemistry experiments, sewing, or, like Allegra, playing the violin.

Awards: BBYA 1992

My Brother Sam Is Dead
by James Lincoln Collier
(Ages 11–14)
1974. Macmillan, $13.95; Scholastic, paper, $2.50; ABC-CLIO, large-type, $15.95.

Told from the perspective of young Tim Meeker, this intelligent blending of fact and fiction reveals the effects of the Revolutionary War on one Connecticut family. What begins for Tim as a kind of strange adventure turns sharply disturbing. Tim witnesses his Tory father's imprisonment, the massacre of his neighbors by British troops, and finally the execution of his brother Sam, a soldier in the Continental Army, convicted of a crime he did not commit. It's the human cost of war, not the political issues involved, that Tim comes to understand.

Awards: Newbery Honor Book 1975

Nothing but the Truth:
A Documentary Novel
by Avi
(Ages 13–16)
1991. Orchard Books, $14.95.

In this deceptively simple story that evolves through a patchwork of memos, conversations, and diary entries, Avi cleverly challenges readers to explore the way emotions and preconceptions define and distort the truth. Phillip Malloy wants to run track, but his grade in Miss Narwin's English class isn't good

enough to allow him to try out for the team. When Narwin reprimands him for humming the national anthem in class instead of maintaining "respectful silent attention," he vents his anger by refusing to stop the disruption and is eventually expelled by the assistant principal. When the newspapers discover he's been kicked out for singing "The Star-Spangled Banner," Phil suddenly finds he's been declared a patriot. (What he really wants is a different English teacher.)

Awards: Newbery Honor Book 1992

One-Eyed Cat
by Paula Fox
(Ages 11–14)
1984. Bradbury, $11.95; Dell, paper, $3.50; ABC-CLIO, large-type, $15.95.

A Newbery Honor Book and recipient of a number of other awards, Fox's compelling novel revolves around a boy burdened by a guilty secret. From watching his mother struggle with crippling arthritis, Ned Wallis has learned about pain and tolerance; from watching his father, a country minister, he's learned about morality. From both he's learned about trust. But when he fires the Daisy air rifle his father has forbidden him to use, he betrays them, and when he thinks his single shot is responsible for the mutilated eye of a wild cat, his shame begins to corrupt his relationship with his loving family.

Awards: Newbery Honor Book 1985; BBYA 1984; BBYA Nothin' But the Best 1966–1986

On the Edge
by Gillian Cross
(Ages 11–14)
1985. Holiday House, $13.95; Dell, paper, $2.75.

Jinny is convinced that the new tenants at Mrs. Hollis's cottage have something to hide, and her suspicions are confirmed when the child who is with them tries to signal her secretly. Only then does she realize that the boy is Tug Shakespeare, son of a prominent British broadcaster, and that the strange people he's with are holding him hostage. Tug's struggle to maintain his sense of self while his kidnappers try to brainwash him makes for page-turning suspense.

Awards: BBYA 1985

The Pigman
by Paul Zindel
(Ages 12–15)
1968. HarperCollins, $13.95.

In alternating narratives, John and Lorraine, two clever high school sophomores who don't get along with their parents, describe their friendship with elderly Mr. Pignati, "the Pigman," and the bitter lesson they learn when they abuse his affection and betray him.

Awards: BBYA Nothin' But the Best 1966–1986

Playing Beatie Bow
by Ruth Park
(See Fantasy Fiction, p. 92.)

Prairie Songs
by Pam Conrad
(Ages 11–14)
1985. HarperCollins, $12.95; paper, $3.50.

With her loving family surrounding her, Louisa enjoys life on the Nebraska prairie despite the isolation and the hardships. Then the new doctor and his cultured wife, Emmeline, arrive from New York City. Louisa

adores Emmeline from the first, and the woman responds by sharing her books and her love of poetry and by helping Louisa's younger, less confident brother Lester learn to read. But as Louisa's love for poetry blossoms and Lester begins to thrive, Emmeline, unable to adjust to her new home, sinks deeper and deeper into despair.

Awards: BBYA 1985

Probably Still Nick Swansen
by Virginia Euwer Wolff
(Ages 12–15)
1988. Holt, $13.95; Scholastic, paper, $2.75.

Nick Swansen has minimal brain dysfunction. Although he isn't certain what that actually is, he knows he has difficulty spelling and writing. Also, he realizes his thoughts and actions are slow and that sometimes adults treat him differently from other 16-year-olds. But none of that stops him from wanting to take pretty classmate Shana to the prom. When she accepts, he is ecstatic; when she stands him up, he is devastated. In a halting, awkward, yet unforgettable narrative, Nick reveals the difficulties facing special kids who are caught between their limitations and their longing to be like everyone else.

Awards: BBYA 1989

The Rain Catchers
by Jean Thesman
(Ages 12–15)
1991. Houghton Mifflin, $13.95.

Grayling loves the old Seattle house where she has grown up. She loves her grandmother, too, as well as the circle of nurturing women who have raised her and shared with her their memories. But Grayling's fourteenth summer brings change: the mother who abandoned her wants her back; Gray watches her friend Colleen struggle in an abusive family; and sweet old "aunt" Olivia, who now suffers from cancer, decides it's time to die. Thesman deals perceptively with a variety of sensitive issues in this poignant, beautifully written story, rich in feeling and character.

Ratha's Creature
by Clare Bell
(See Fantasy Fiction, p. 92.)

The Remarkable Journey of Prince Jen
by Alexander Lloyd
(See Fantasy Fiction, p. 92.)

The Ruby in the Smoke
by Philip Pullman
(Ages 13–15)
1987. Knopf, $11.95; paper, $2.95.

The back streets of nineteenth-century London provide plenty of atmosphere for this crackerjack thriller filled with vivid characters. Still puzzled by the circumstances surrounding her father's shipboard death, orphaned Sally Lockhart arrives in London determined to investigate. With the help of a young photographer, his sister, and a lad who reads dime novels, she begins to unravel the eerie, convoluted truth, which involves a mysterious ruby connected to events that occurred during Sally's childhood. The first in a trilogy including *The Shadow in the North* and *The Tiger in the Well.*

Awards: BBYA 1978.

The Runner
by Cynthia Voigt
(Ages 12–17)
1985. Atheneum, $12.95; Fawcett, paper, $2.50.

Bullet Tillerman's father rules his family with an iron hand, but 17-year-old Bullet wants none of it. He hides his fear and anger in running, and he's the best cross-country athlete around. Then he's asked to coach Tamer, a black student on the school track team, and he learns through their relationship how to accept responsibility and overcome his prejudices as well as how to break away from his father's grip.

Awards: BBYA 1985

Running Loose
by Chris Crutcher
(Ages 13–17)
1983. Greenwillow, $13.95; Dell, paper, $2.95.

High school senior Louis Banks is thrilled to be a starter on his school's football team until the coach's racist pregame rhetoric results in the injuring of a black player on an opposing squad. With support from his girlfriend Becky, Louis takes an unpopular stand against the coach. Then Becky is killed in an accident, leaving Louis to wonder whether he's up to defending his principles alone. Crutcher evokes the rough-talking, macho ambience of high school sports in a keenly sensitive story about honor, fairness, and love.

Awards: BBYA 1983

Scorpions
by Walter Dean Myers
(See Videos.)
1988. HarperCollins, $12.95; paper, $2.95.

Awards: Newbery Honor Book 1989

Shabanu: Daughter of the Wind
by Suzanne Fisher Staples
(Ages 11–15)
(See Multicultural Fare, p. 37.)

The Shining Company
by Rosemary Sutcliff
(Ages 12–15)
1990. Farrar, Straus & Giroux, $13.95.

Sutcliff depicts a desolate seventh-century Britain at war, bringing it to life through the eyes of young Prosper, who leaves his home to become shield bearer to Prince Gorthyn, one of 300 Companions summoned by the king to fight. The story, based on an early British poem, is one of bravery and tragedy, with the Companion brotherhood riding courageously out to confront the enemy Saxons.

The Silver Kiss
by Annette Curtis Klause
(Ages 13–15)
1990. Delacorte, $14.95.

Shut out by her parents, who feel she won't be able to cope with her mother's dying, Zoë finds solace wandering through the park late at night. It's there she meets and falls in love with Simon, the strange silver-haired vampire—a compelling, sensuous creature who has pursued his vicious shape-changing brother through 300 years of history.

Awards: BBYA 1991

Sirens and Spies
by Janet Taylor Lisle
(Ages 12–15)
1985. Bradbury, $12.95; Macmillan, paper, $3.95.

Incorporating dramatic flashbacks to World War II France, Lisle fashions a riveting story that draws the fine line between loyalty and betrayal, between good and evil. American teenager Elise adores Miss Fitch, a talented French emigré who teaches violin and seems to embody the perfection that 13-year-old Elise hopes to attain for herself. One day, though, while looking through a book on the war, Elise comes across a photograph of Nazi collaborators and recognizes Miss Fitch as one of the traitors being jeered at by angry French villagers. This revelation of Miss Fitch's character drives Elise to watch her teacher to see what else there is to discover.

Awards: Notable Children's Book 1985

A Solitary Blue
by Cynthia Voigt
(Ages 12–14)
1983. Atheneum, $12.95; Fawcett, paper, $3.95.

Abandoned at the age of seven by his mother, a social activist, Jeff Greene tries very hard to please his father so he won't be rejected again. But he's never worked through his feelings for his mother, who he still hopes will accept and love him. When he receives an unexpected invitation to spend the summer with her in South Carolina, he's thrilled. Written by a prolific author who consistently writes with depth and feeling, this poignant novel explores the delicate ties among parents and children, especially between a boy and his caring but distant father.

Awards: Newbery Honor Book 1984; Notable Children's Book 1983; BBYA 1983; BBYA Nothin' But the Best 1966–1986

Strange Attractors
by William Sleator
(Ages 12–15)
1990. Dutton, $13.95.

A clever storyteller, Sleator knows how to take scientific fact and turn it into first-rate suspense. In this fast-paced story he plays with the complex theory of chaos. Science student Max finds a time-travel laser in his pocket and is suddenly the center of attention. It seems a top scientist and his daughter and their lookalikes from another time all want it. Max must determine to whom it belongs. First, though, he has to decide if he wants to give it up at all. *House of Stairs* is another popular, eerie tale from this author.

Awards: BBYA 1991

A String in the Harp
by Nancy Bond
(Ages 11–13)
1976. McElderry, $12.95; Puffin, paper, $5.95.

Unable to reconcile himself to his family's move from America to Wales, Peter Morgan becomes increasingly hostile and withdrawn. On the beach one day he discovers the magical tuning key of an old harp. The power of the key opens his way into the past, where the life of an old bard begins to unfold before his eyes, and he gradually finds himself involved in the man's history. Welsh legend and contemporary family drama come together in an evocative, award-winning fantasy.

Awards: Newbery Honor Book 1977

Summer of the Swans
by Betsy Byars
(Ages 10–13)
1971. Viking, $12.95; Puffin, paper, $3.95; ABC-CLIO, large-type, $15.95.

Fourteen-year-old Sara Godfrey is forced out of her self-absorption in this revealing story about family relationships and personal growth. Sara's developmentally handicapped brother, Charles, is lost while trying to find some swans that he had spotted on a nearby lake. Sara's frantic search for Charlie, which takes place over two agonizing summer days, helps her forget her own insecurities and gain new insight into herself. This is but one of Byars's many fine children's books.

Awards: Newbery Medal 1971

Sweetgrass
by Jan Hudson
(Ages 11–14)
1989. Philomel, $13.95.

Originally published in Canada in 1984, this powerful historical novel is a portrait of Dakota Indian life during the 1860s. It tells the story of 15-year-old Sweetgrass, who matures from a daydreaming child into a determined young woman on whose skills, intelligence, and sensitivity her entire family eventually come to depend.

Awards: Notable Children's Book 1990; BBYA 1990

Taking Sides
by Gary Soto
(Ages 11–14)
1991. HBJ, $14.95.

Lincoln Mendoza is a talented basketball player. He won't be stopped by minor injuries, nor by the difficulties of a move from his inner-city high school in San Francisco to a suburban one. Lincoln finds an ally in his mother's new boyfriend and an unexpected adversary in a best friend from his old school. The teen's comparison of the two communities and the thoughtful use of Spanish words throughout the text (a glossary is supplied) provide an added dimension to a universal story of growing up and adjusting to change.

Tex
by S. E. Hinton
(Ages 12–15)
1979. Delacorte, $13.95; Dell, paper, $3.25.

With his mother dead and his father out riding the rodeo circuit, often "forgetting" to send money home, 14-year-old Tex has only his older brother to depend on. Mason is serious and responsible; Tex is just the opposite— laid-back, funny, and a natural for attracting trouble. Tension between the two is an ongoing problem, aggravated by the possibility of Mason's leaving for college on a basketball scholarship. The prospect of life without Mason frightens and angers Tex more than he'll admit. He's angry, too, about his father's neglect, the reason for which becomes painfully clear when the old man finally comes home, a visit that brings the boys closer together than ever before.

Awards: BBYA 1979; BBYA Nothin' But the Best 1966–1986

Tiger Eyes
by Judy Blume
(Ages 12–15)
1981. Bradbury, $14.95; Dell, paper, $3.50.

Davey Wexler can't seem to accept her father's death. The well-meaning relatives with whom she and her family go to stay interfere too much, and her mother's problems coping with

grief complicate Davey's own healing. It's only after Davey gets to know Wolf, a young man whose father is dying, that she begins to understand and work through her sorrow. A sensitive, popular novel.

A Time of Troubles
by Pieter Van Raven
(See Fathers and Sons, p. 102.)

The True Confessions of Charlotte Doyle
by Avi
(Ages 11–15)
1990. Orchard Books, $14.95.

"Not every thirteen-year-old girl is accused of murder, brought to trial, and found guilty." So begins this spellbinding adventure that evokes the sights and sounds of the sea. Sailing from England to rejoin her family in America, prim schoolgirl Charlotte Doyle finds herself the sole female passenger on a rickety ship manned by a crew of vicious sailors and a captain who turns out to be a tyrannical madman.

Awards: Newbery Honor Book 1991; Children's Notable Book 1991; BBYA 1991

We Were Not Like Other People
by Ephraim Sevela
(Ages 13–17)
Translated by Antonina Bouis.
1989. HarperCollins, $13.95.

Translated from the Russian, these interconnected stories depict eight years of brutal struggle for an unnamed Jewish boy, separated from his parents during Stalin's great purge. In one riveting tale, the boy confronts

Stalinists who want him to betray his parents. In another, he and fellow factory workers huddle together in a cold dormitory dreaming aloud of food. Through it all the boy survives, often aided by a caring adult who helps him heal and also helps him discover moral values in his harsh, unstable world.

Wolf Rider: A Tale of Terror
by Avi
(Ages 12–15)
1986. Bradbury, $12.95; Macmillan, paper, $2.95.

Picking up the phone, 15-year-old Andy Zadinski hears a stranger, who calls himself Zeke, boast of a murder. After poking around a little, Andy discovers that Zeke's announcement was a little premature: Nina Klemmer, a student at the college where Andy's father teaches, is still very much alive. Is it all a joke? Neither Andy's father nor Nina believes that the heinous Zeke really exists. But Andy isn't crying wolf, and he sets out to prove it and protect the vulnerable girl. A suspense-filled mystery.

Awards: BBYA 1986

Words by Heart
by Ouida Sebestyen
(Ages 10–14)
1979. Little, Brown/Joy Street Books, $13.95; Bantam, paper, $2.95.

The only black family in a small western town feels the pressure of prejudice in the early twentieth century. When Lena bests another child by winning a scripture contest that demonstrates her intellectual abilities, the townsfolk grow angry. Her father's success on the farm angers them still more. But when they try to drive the family away, Lena's father refuses to give in to the hatred and pressure. His decision to stay becomes a source of tragedy as well as a source of hope for his daughter and the community.

Awards: American Book Award 1982

The Year without Michael
by Susan B. Pfeffer
(Ages 12–15)
1987. Bantam, $13.95; paper, $2.95.

Where is Michael? He promised he'd be home for dinner. He couldn't have simply disappeared without a trace. Yet that's exactly what happens to Jody's 13-year-old brother, who leaves one Sunday in September and never returns. Did he run away? Was he kidnapped? Can his family come to grips with the feelings his disappearance triggers? Will they pull closer together for comfort, or will they drift apart?

Awards: BBYA 1987

The Young Landlords
by Walter Dean Myers
(Ages 11–14)
1979. Puffin, paper, $3.95.

In their zeal to rehabilitate their neighborhood, five young friends suddenly find themselves the owners of a rundown apartment building populated by a slew of quirky tenants. The main responsibility for keeping the building operating falls to sensible Gloria and good-humored Paul, who narrates this funny, compassionate story of their day-today crises as landlords. Though wrapped in sharp comedy, the book's serious message still shines through: "The answers were a lot easier to come by when you stood across the street from the problem."

Awards: BBYA 1979; Coretta Scott King Award 1980

NONFICTION

Boy: Tales of Childhood
by Roald Dahl
(Ages 10–15)
1984. Farrar, Straus & Giroux, $12.95; Puffin, paper, $4.95; ABC-CLIO, large-type, $14.95.

Known for his ironic anecdotes, laugh-out-loud humor, and quixotic characters, as well as for occasional lapses into bad taste, the author of *The Enormous Crocodile, James and the Giant Peach*, and *The BFG* presents his most fascinating character—himself. Drawing on memories that have stayed with him for more than half a century, the controversial Dahl treats readers to a glimpse of a childhood every bit as bizarre as any of the make-believe he built for James or Willy Wonka. Dahl dwells more on the dismaying side of his childhood—beatings at British schools, a terrifying car accident, a frightful encounter with the witchlike Mrs. Prachett, who ran the local candy store—than on the laughter and love. But his candor is compelling and he mixes it with enough humor, irony, and horror to make readers laugh, wonder, and shudder at the same time.

Awards: BBYA 1985

Children of the Maya: A Guatemalan Indian Odyssey
by Brent Ashabranner
(Ages 10–14)
1986. Putnam, $14.95.

Ashabranner tells the compelling story of the Mayan Indian residents of Indiantown, Florida, who fled their strife-torn native country of Guatemala. Using a series of dramatic first-person narratives coupled with striking black-and-white photographs, he explores the trauma of a people caught between government forces and guerrillas who seek to overthrow their country's military dictatorship. Ashabranner makes it clear that while these Guatemalan Mayans live for now in safety, they are not free: many face the threat of deportation, which would mean certain death for all but a few.

Awards: Notable Children's Book 1986

Circus Dreams: The Making of a Circus Artist
by Kathleen Cushman and Montana Miller
(Ages 11–17)
Photos by Michael Carroll.
1990. Little, Brown/Joy Street Books, $15.95.

Eighteen-year-old Montana Miller put her college education on hold to fulfill a longtime dream. Traveling to France, she enrolled in the National Center for Circus Arts in Châlon-Sur Marne, where she learned not only how to fly through the air on a trapeze, but also how to juggle, clown, and walk a tightrope. Put together in collaboration with her mother, this combination of letters home, interviews with fellow circus students, and wonderful black-and-white photographs conveys the spirit of what Montana found at the Center: a taste of the circus magic that draws fans and performers to the Big Top season after season.

Awards: BBYA 1991

Columbus and the World around Him
by Milton Meltzer
(Ages 11–15)
1990. Watts, $13.95.

This polished biography sets the explorer squarely within the context of his times. Meltzer recognizes Columbus's navigational genius and his determination, but also his arrogance. Including primary source material from the Columbus Archives in Seville, Spain, Meltzer combines documentary information about the scientific, social, and intellectual climate of the Spain from which Columbus sailed with a colorful portrait of the man himself—from Columbus's humble origins to what has come to be regarded as his most famous discovery. He also looks critically at the cruelty with which New World peoples were treated by Columbus and the Spanish who followed him.

Awards: BBYA 1991

Flies in the Water, Fish in the Air: A Personal Introduction to Fly Fishing
by Jim Arnosky
(Ages 10–15)
1986. Lothrop, $12.95.

Arnosky celebrates his love for fly fishing through a collection of anecdotes that leaves no doubt about his respect for his finned adversaries. Incorporating information about the fish and the insects on which they feed as well as fishing how-to techniques, he quietly shares his knowledge and evokes his joy in the natural world. Beautiful, softly detailed pencil sketches surround the text, swirling down the margins and opening out on facing pages into delicate full-page drawings.

Awards: BBYA 1986

Franklin Delano Roosevelt
by Russell Freedman
(Ages 10–15)
1990. Clarion, $16.95.

The author of the Newbery Award–winning *Lincoln* (see p. 82) focuses here on an equally fascinating president. A marvelous assortment of photographs add visual appeal to the intriguing story, which follows Roosevelt from pampered, privileged child and handsome Harvard student through polio, paralysis, and the presidency. Concerned almost as much with the nation Roosevelt guided through depression and war as with Roosevelt's personal life, Freedman presents a record of the man's accomplishments during his three-plus terms as president and a candid assessment of the controversies that surrounded him throughout his administration.

Awards: BBYA 1991

From Hand to Mouth; or How We Invented Knives, Forks, Spoons, and Chopsticks & the Table Manners to Go with Them
by James Giblin
(Ages 10–14)
1987. HarperCollins, $12.95.

Giblin concerns himself with "that age-old problem: how to get food as swiftly, gracefully,

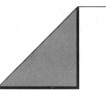

PICTURE BOOKS FOR OLDER READERS

Picture books aren't just for little kids. Middle graders and teenagers will relish the sly humor, serious topics, and splendid artwork in the following titles. Older readers should take another look at the work of illustrators such as Peter Spier, Ann Jonas, Chris Van Allsburg, Raymond Briggs, and those described here.

Black and White by David Macaulay   (Ages 8–15)   1990. Houghton Mifflin, $14.95.

Four stories in one, four separate stories, or one long story, or is it something else? Younger readers will enjoy the four humorous tales about a boy on a train, cows on the loose, commuters on the platform, and parents acting goofy. Older readers will pick up the subtle interactions and shared events among the stories, which feature an escaping convict who moves from the title page through each of the tales. Macaulay's book will leave readers happily puzzled and entertained as they pore over his distinctive artwork and wild plots. For readers who prefer facts to puzzles, Macaulay's books *Underground* and *Cathedrals* are heartily recommended.
Awards: Caldecott Medal 1991

Changes by Anthony Browne   (Ages 8–12)   1991. Knopf, $14.95.

A boy is told by his father that things are going to change. Do they ever! Even though Joseph's father merely means that their household is going to have a new member—a baby sister—Joseph takes his father literally. When he is left alone in the house, everyday items take on new and menacing images. Browne's art, likened to that of Salvador Dali, is surreal and unsettling. The drapes are transformed into green fingers with nails, the armchair turns into a huge gorilla; outside, on the clothesline, two socks become an animal skull. Intriguing in its spookiness, which is enhanced by the realism of the crystal-clear illustrations, Browne's book will also capture the interest of art students who recognize the takeoffs on Dali and other masters.
Awards: Notable Children's Book 1992

Free Fall by David Wiesner (Ages 8–12) 1988. Lothrop, $13.95.

Although there are no words in this fascinating picture book, it will take the mind of a sharp middle-grader to interpret the story. A young boy falls asleep clutching a book of maps. As pages fly from his book, the transformations begin. His quilt turns into a checkerboard, the site of a life-sized chess match. Castles with dragons to slay, pigs that carry riders, and swans that turn to drifting leaves follow. Images of *Alice in Wonderland* and *Gulliver's Travels* weave in and out of the pictures. This imaginative book could be used to spark creative writing projects, enliven group discussions, or provide solitary pleasure. Wiesner fans will also enjoy *Tuesday*. (See p. 59.)
Awards: Caldecott Honor Book 1989; Notable Children's Book 1988

Hiroshima No Pika by Toshi Maruki (Ages 8–14) 1982. Lothrop, $14.95.

"The Flash of Hiroshima" is the title's literal translation. It refers, of course, to the explosion of the atomic bomb in this Japanese city on August 6, 1945. Children who have seen war on television and hear annually of the anniversary of this World War II event will meet the grim reality in this blend of expressionistic and realistic art, tempered by few words. The impact of that bomb is told primarily through full-page paintings that follow a seven-year-old girl from her breakfast table across the racked city to a beach where she waits for days, with her mother and injured father, without help. This classic can overwhelm young readers and is best shared with an adult.

The Journey by Sheila Hanamaka (Ages 9–15) 1990. Orchard Books, $18.95.

This book combines brief, moving text and portions from a mural painted by Hanamaka to convey the injustices endured by Japanese-Americans during World War II. Quiet outrage and a sense of bitterness fuel the book, which draws on the experiences of the author's own family in its depiction of the blatant racism that became government policy during the war years. Hanamaka's text is passionate and personal; her paintings bring dignity to her people. These elements work beautifully together to expose a tragic episode in American history while delivering a message about bigotry that relates to us all.
Awards: BBYA 1991; Recommended Books for the Reluctant Young Adult Reader 1991

and as neatly as possible from hand to mouth." His illustrated text reveals our clever solutions to the dilemma, tracking our cutlery full circle across history and culture—from fingers and flint knives to modern utensils and back again to fingers, as fast-paced lifestyles prompt more and more people to eat on the run. Laced with lively wit and intriguing detail, Giblin turns the ordinary into the fascinating.

Awards: Notable Children's Book 1987

A Girl from Yamhill: A Memoir
by Beverly Cleary
(Ages 12–Adult)
1988. Morrow, $14.95; Dell, paper, $3.95.

Readers who have grown up reading stories about Ralph S. Mouse, Henry Huggins, Ribsy, and Ramona may love the funny childhood characters enough to be curious about their creator. Here, Cleary writes about her own growing-up in the 1920s and 1930s—her early years on a farm in Yamhill, Oregon, her difficult relationship with her mother, and, later, her life in Portland, where her family was to experience the Depression firsthand. It's a quiet, candid memoir that lends surprising insight into the woman behind the books while also capturing a time when automobiles and airplanes were not yet things people took for granted.

Awards: BBYA 1988

Going Over to Your Place: Poems for Each Other
(Ages 14–16)
Edited by Paul Janeczko.
1987. Bradbury, $12.95.

One of the best of Janeczko's anthologies, this collection is filled with poems that celebrate the excitement in ordinary things. Gathering work from small poetry magazines as well as from collected works of the famous, Janeczko presents a sampling of contemporary American poetry that reflects universal human experience in word pictures ranging from cozy and gently humorous to fierce and painful. The complex bonds between lovers, family, and friends are at the heart of the poems, which supply fresh perspectives on parts of life so familiar—a first kiss, a strong friendship.

The Journey
by Sheila Hanamaka
(See Picture Books for Older Readers, p. 117.)

Meeting the Winter Bike Rider and Other Prize Winning Plays
(Ages 10–17)
Edited by Wendy Lamb
1986. Dell, paper, $3.50.

One of the best collections in an ongoing series that showcases quality work from the Young Playwrights Festival Competition, a contest that culminates in an off-Broadway production of the winning play. Written by young people from 10 to 18, these eight winners of the 1983–1984 season all feature teenage or preteen characters. In *Tender Places,* one of the best inclusions, a troubled boy deals with divorced parents who vie for his love; two young men acknowledge affection for one another in *Liars,* a candid drama written by a 17-year-old student; and three old friends prepare to go in different directions after high school graduation in *Third Street.* Background on the festival is incorporated, as are remarks from each play's author.

Awards: BBYA 1986

Now Is Your Time! The African-American Struggle for Freedom
by Walter Dean Myers
(Ages 11–15)
1991. HarperCollins, $17.95.

Packed with political and personal stories, some from his own family, Myers's history of black Americans runs from the days of slavery through the civil rights movement of the 1960s. He tells of a Fula prince, Abd al-Rahman Ibrahima, brought to Mississippi in 1788 as a slave, of the brave 54th Massachusetts Volunteer Infantry during the Civil War, of artist/sculptor Meta Vaux Warrick, and many other well-known and less famous African-Americans. The narrative flow helps make history not only accessible but engaging. Myers's use of "we" and portraits from his own family tree inspire personal involvement.

Awards: Coretta Scott King Author Award 1992

Prairie Visions: The Life and Time of Solomon Butcher
by Pam Conrad
(Ages 10–17)
1991. HarperCollins, $16.95.

What was life like in nineteenth-century pioneer America? Solomon Butcher knew because he lived it. He also spent 15 years recording it on film. Conrad adds historical context and biographical detail to this photo-documentary of life in Nebraska. She incor-

porates some of the stories and anecdotes Butcher collected from the settlers he met over the years. The result is a connecting window to the past that exposes the harsh drama of daily life—the grim faces, the sod houses, the hard work—as it yields compelling vistas of unspoiled prairie and open sky.

Rescue: The Story of How Gentiles Saved Jews in the Holocaust
by Milton Meltzer
(Ages 12–16)
1988. HarperCollins, $12.95.

Meltzer records some of the finer instances that took place during the Holocaust by focusing on non-Jewish individuals who put themselves in jeopardy to save Jews. Organized roughly by country, the material he presents is a blend of historical background and exciting stories of personal courage, including eyewitness accounts contributed by persons who lived to tell the tale. Among the stories are those of Catholic priests, servants, and, as in the case of Denmark, the population of an entire nation, who came to the aid of friends but even more often helped total strangers. An inspiring history.

Awards: BBYA 1988

Seeing Earth from Space
by Patricia Lauber
(Ages 10–Adult)
1990. Orchard Books, $19.95.

A pioneer of the photo essay, Lauber uses that technique to present readers with a dramatic view of our planet. Full-color photographs, most supplied by the National Aeronautics and Space Administration, demonstrate with the verve of abstract paintings what technical advances such as radar and infrared sensing have enabled scientists to learn about the earth. Lauber's clear, expository text provides the background for the extraordinary graphics, explaining the mysteries the photos reveal and encouraging readers to protect our planet, "small and fragile, wondrous and lovely."

Awards: BBYA 1991

Smoke and Ashes: The Story of the Holocaust
by Barbara Rogasky
(Ages 12–17)
1988. Holiday House, $16.95.

Eyewitness accounts, statistics, narrative, and dozens of photographs, many taken by Nazis, blend together in a powerful lesson in history. Though Rogasky focuses mostly on Jews and what they suffered, she does not forget the millions of others the Nazis also persecuted. With the photos bearing witness to the terror, Rogasky quotes political doctrine on Hitler's "final solution" and explains how the nightmarish Nazi scheme was carried out against the Jews—from the enforcement of the Nuremberg laws and life for Jews in the ghettos to the concentration camps and the crematoria. A book written to inform as well as raise consciousness.

Awards: BBYA 1988

Somehow Tenderness Survives: Stories of Southern Africa
Selected by Hazel Rochman
(Ages 12–17)
1988. HarperCollins, $12.95; paper, $3.25.

Ten short stories and autobiographical accounts, written by southern Africans of various races, relate what it's like to grow up where racism is the law. Rochman has taken the book's title from a moving poem by Dennis Brutus. Her other selections include a piece by Nadine Gordimer, who dramatizes how prejudice infects the love between two teenagers, and an excerpt from Mark Mathabane's acclaimed *Kaffir Boy,* in which the author remembers a police raid when his father was arrested for not having his papers in order.

Awards: BBYA 1988

Sorrow's Kitchen: The Life and Folklore of Zora Neale Hurston
by Mary E. Lyons
(Ages 14–17)
1990. Scribners, $13.95.

Hurston, a folklorist, writer, and anthropologist who studied voodoo, celebrated black pride in her writing at a time when other intellectuals of the Harlem Renaissance focused on black suffering. Ostracized by them and accused of plagiarizing, she died poor and alone in 1960. In a fascinating biography that includes excerpts from Hurston's works, stirring quotes, and photographs, Lyons projects a broader image. She uncovers in Hurston's writings a richness and lyricism the folklorist's contemporaries missed and reveals Hurston's drive, her astonishing intellect, and her personal commitment.

Awards: Recommended Books for Reluctant Readers 1991

Starting from Home: A Writer's Beginnings
by Milton Meltzer
(Ages 12–17)
1988. Viking, $13.95.

Born in 1915, the son of Austrian parents, Meltzer was raised in an East Coast neighborhood where "almost everyone was an immigrant or the child of an immigrant." Set squarely within the social and political tumult of the early twentieth century, his charming, honest memoir captures his growing up in the midst of these multiethnic surroundings. With grace and humor, Meltzer recalls his family, his first love, his work, his school, and especially his love of books and reading, which helped shape his life and writing career. The gifted author of books for children and young adults weaves himself deftly into the fabric of history.

Trail of Stones
by Gwen Strauss
(See Fractured Fairy Tales, p. 55.)

Vietnam: Why We Fought
by Dorothy Hoobler and Thomas Hoobler
(Ages 11–17)
1990. Knopf, 17.95.

Beginning with an exploration of the political struggle that preceded the war, the Hooblers present a dynamic overview of the Vietnam conflict that carries its history through the postwar legacy. Dozens of candid, carefully captioned battlefield photographs capture the tragedy on the faces of soldiers—American and Vietnamese alike—while comments from politicians, soldiers, and individuals who observed, fought, and protested the war convey a clear sense of the complicated issues involved.

Why Am I Grown So Cold? Poems of the Unknowable
Edited by Myra Cohn Livingston
(Ages 10–14)
1982. McElderry, $14.95.

One hundred and fifty poems drawn from many cultures and centuries speak about the unexplained and unexplainable. Writers as diverse as Shakespeare, Shel Silverstein, Li Po, and Pablo Neruda explore the mystery of things that have intrigued us over time—spells and sorcerers, fairies and phantoms, enchantments and ghosts. A collection rich in language and imagery, with the special appeal of its eerie, supernatural theme.

Awards: Notable Children's Book 1986

Woodsong
by Gary Paulsen
1990. Bradbury, $13.95.

A popular author of young people's fiction turns to fact here. In language as stark as the environment he traveled, Paulsen records his experiences with sled dogs and sleds, first in his northern Minnesota home, then in frigid Alaska, where he and a team of 15 dogs participated in the grueling cross-country Iditarod race. Infused with a special reverence for the natural world and filled with descriptions of the harsh land Paulsen faced, his book is a compelling true-life account.

The Wright Brothers: How They Invented the Airplane
by Russell Freedman
(Ages 10–15)
1991. Holiday House, $16.95.

Biographer Freedman again demonstrates his soaring talent, so to speak, with this award-winning story of those two determined Americans who designed and tinkered in their cycling shop until they achieved the first powered, sustained, controlled airplane flight in 1903. The brothers also captured their trials on film, enabling Freedman to use many of their turn-of-the-century photographs, along with design drawings, to create a superb photo essay. For the enthused, lists of additional readings and of sites to visit are appended.

Awards: Newbery Honor Book 1992; *Booklist* Top of the List 1992

ENCYCLOPEDIAS AND DICTIONARIES

ENCYCLOPEDIAS

When choosing an encyclopedia for children, consider its suitability for the age of those who will use it. Often parents buy an adult encyclopedia, hoping their children will "grow into it" as they do a pair of shoes. However, by the time the children are able to benefit from the set, some of its contents will already be outdated. Meanwhile, the children may have become discouraged by trying to use an encyclopedia that is written at too high a level for them.

When buying an encyclopedia for elementary school children, it is best to select one written specifically for younger readers. They will be more likely to use the set and develop the habit of looking things up. Since young children are not able to get to the public library on their own, families with children of this age will especially appreciate having a set at home.

Among the factors to consider when purchasing an encyclopedia is the arrangement. In sets for children, it is best if the alphabet is divided so that all of one letter (or a combination of letters such as *W-X-Y-Z*) is in one volume. Only large letters like *C* and *S* should be divided between volumes. Decide whether the subject coverage is appropriate for children, who will be interested in pets, hobbies, sports, and how-to-do-it information as well as curriculum-related topics such as the states and U.S. presidents.

The timeliness of information is critical. There are many facts in encyclopedias that do not "date." Much of the information in the humanities—art, music, philosophy, for example—does not change dramatically over time. However, population statistics, election results, scientific breakthroughs, and sports records all need to be constantly updated. Most encyclopedias published in the United States are annually revised, but that doesn't mean that *all* facts are updated each year. Look up a topic about which you are knowledgeable to check for currency.

Encyclopedia articles should be written in a simple and direct style appropriate to the age of the audience, and new words should be defined when they are first introduced. Most encyclopedias include lists of further readings on many topics. The works listed should be current and appropriate for the age level of the readers. Bibliographies are most useful when they appear at the ends of articles rather than in a separate volume. Teachers sometimes discourage students from using encyclopedias when researching reports because they fear that they rely on them too much, but the bibliography at the end of an encyclopedia article can lead the child to further sources of information.

Illustrations are an important instructional component of encyclopedias. Since children are more dependent on pictures for meaning, parents selecting a set should pay special attention to them. They should be recent, large enough to be clear, and make good use of color.

The physical format of the set should also be attractive. Some sets are available in several bindings; the least expensive should be satisfactory for home use. Encyclopedias sometimes have extra features sold as part of a package—for example, yearbooks or dictionaries—and are meant to lure hesitant buyers. Do not let their presence distract you from assessing the encyclopedia's quality.

The following encyclopedias all meet the criteria just listed and are highly recommended. Visit a school or public library and examine them to see which set best meets your needs. When buying an encyclopedia from a salesperson in your home, remember that the Federal Trade Commission mandates a three-day "cooling off" period, during which you can cancel your order.

Compton's Encyclopedia
(Ages 10–18)
1992. Encyclopaedia Britannica, $599 (26 volumes).

Compton's emphasizes practical and curriculum-related information for students in the upper elementary grades through high school. The editors have chosen not to use a controlled vocabulary, but language is appropriate for young people. In addition to the sometimes lengthy text entries, there are Fact-Index capsule articles in the index. Illustrated, curiosity-raising "Exploring" questions are found at the beginning of each volume. Many articles end with lists of further readings appropriate for children.

The set is abundantly illustrated and two-thirds of the pictures are in color. Up-to-date and eye-catching, *Compton's* is sold in retail outlets, not in the home. Call 800-858-4895 for the name of the closest retailer. It is also available on a compact disc that is used in conjunction with a computer. This version, *Compton's Multimedia Encyclopedia,* also has sound and video. So, for example, Mozart's music can be played when that entry is summoned or a video of Martin Luther King may play when that entry is researched.

New Book of Knowledge
(Ages 7–14)
1992. Grolier, $995 (21 volumes).

This set is written specifically for elementary school children. Subject coverage is determined by both the school curriculum and the after-school interests of children. All articles are tested with the Dale-Chall readability formula to ensure that contents correspond to the interest and grade level at which the subject is generally taught. Most entries treat broad topics; a Dictionary Index at the end of each volume contains capsule entries on narrower topics. "Wonder" questions in some articles engage the child's interest; for example, in *elevator,* "How fast can the fastest elevator climb?"

New Book of Knowledge is heavily illustrated and almost all the pictures are in color. The set uses a larger typeface than other encyclopedias, one that is easier for beginning readers. There are no bibliographies in the main part of the set; they appear in a separate paperback volume, *Home and School Reading and Study Guides.* Parents can purchase this current and attractive encyclopedia from Discovery Toys salespeople (see p. 320) or by writing Lexicon Publications, 95 Madison Ave., Suite 603, New York, NY 10016 for the name of a local distributor.

World Book
(Ages 10–18)
1992. World Book, $599 (22 volumes).

The best-selling encyclopedia in America, *World Book* is useful for children in the upper elementary grades through high school. It is extensively revised every year, and coverage is very current. Articles are written at the appropriate level for the anticipated readership and thus vary in length and difficulty. The article *Dog,* for instance, is written on an easier level than *Computer.* There are bibliographies at the ends of many articles. It is heavily illustrated and almost all the pictures are attractive and in color. *World Book* is also available on a compact disc as *The Information Finder. Childcraft,* another multivolume set sold by World Book, is not really an encyclopedia but an anthology of readings for young children. *World Book* products are sold solely through home demonstrations. Look in the Yellow Pages under "Encyclopedia" for the name of a local *World Book* representative, or call the World Book toll-free customer service number, 800-621-8202.

DICTIONARIES

A dictionary is the reference work most commonly found in the home. Young children use dictionaries primarily to find correct spellings and definitions; older children use them for pronunciation, grammar, hyphenation, and word histories as well. Children's dictionaries are usually published in series and become more complex as children get older. Those for young children, for instance, have only a few thousand words defined in simple entries; dictionaries for older children have tens of thousands of words with more complicated entries. Four publishers do graded series of dictionaries for children: Houghton Mifflin, Macmillan, Merriam-Webster, and Scott, Foresman. They also publish school editions of their dictionaries under different titles. When choosing a dictionary, try to find out which series is used in your child's school.

All the dictionaries listed below are recommended. The differences among the dictionaries for an age group are usually minor—one may use photographs as illustrations rather than drawings. All these titles are published by firms with long-term commitments to dictionary publishing and are compiled by recognized specialists. Words are selected by researching the reading vocabulary of children and sometimes the spoken vocabulary as well. Attractiveness is an important consideration in engaging a child's interest in a dictionary. All the dictionaries here are well illustrated, and their clear typefaces and pleasing layouts make for readability.

Remember that the name *Webster* is in the public domain and can be used by anyone. While there are many excellent dictionaries with the name *Webster* in the title, the presence of that name is no guarantee of quality. Many inexpensive dictionaries for children are imports from Great Britain, and, though attractive, often are not appropriate for an American audience.

PRESCHOOLERS

Picture dictionaries help children learn to make associations between the printed word and objects, actions, and feelings. They are arranged by category rather than alphabetically and use pictures rather than words to give definitions. They each include fewer than 1,000 words.

The American Heritage Picture Dictionary
(Ages 4–6)

1986. Houghton Mifflin, $9.95.

This is a transitional dictionary; it depends on the illustrations to provide the definitions, but the four-color drawings are arranged in alphabetical order. Most entries also have a sample sentence.

Good Morning, Words!
(Ages 2–5)

1990. Scott, Foresman, $8.95.

This attractive book has words labeled on a series of four-color drawings and photographs. For example, in the category "Op-posites," a cityscape is shown with actions like *stop* and *go*. An index of all the words included follows the main text.

The Macmillan Picture Wordbook
(Ages 3–6)

1990. Macmillan, $8.95.

Words are labeled on drawings under 30 topics, such as homes, going places, and visiting the doctor. The same 12 characters are used in the drawings throughout the book to help direct the child's observation techniques. Words can be found quickly with the help of a word list. Color illustrations are in a consistent, attractive style.

EARLY GRADERS

These dictionaries are all in alphabetical order, but entries are simple, offering only a definition and a sample sentence using the word. The number of words defined ranges from about 1,000 to 4,000. Illustrations are used for one-quarter to one-third of all the words.

American Heritage First Dictionary

(Ages 6–8)

1986. Houghton Mifflin, $11.95.

This dictionary numbers additional meanings for a word. It gives the plural for each noun and the past tense of each verb. Attractive color drawings add to the book's appeal.

Macmillan First Dictionary

(Ages 6–9)

1990. Macmillan, $12.95.

Definitions are numbered, when necessary, and different forms of the word (plurals, other tenses) are found at the end of each entry. This book uses both photographs and drawings to highlight some of the definitions.

Words for New Readers

(Ages 5–7)

1990. Scott, Foresman, $10.95.

My First Dictionary

(Ages 6–8)

1990. Scott, Foresman, $12.95.

Words for New Readers is geared for the word-recognition of first-graders; *My First Dictionary* is designed for second- and third-graders.

MIDDLE GRADERS

Dictionaries for this age group have more complex entries. Syllabication is often indicated, and pronunciation and parts of speech are given. There may be occasional word histories and usage notes pointing out proper practice. These dictionaries often have elaborate appendixes: maps, tables of measure, historical facts, or other ready-reference information. The size of the vocabulary ranges from 28,000 to 35,000 words. The percentage of words illustrated is much smaller than in the reference books for younger users. These dictionaries have from 500 to 1,500 illustrations.

The American Heritage Children's Dictionary
(Ages 8–10)
1986. Houghton Mifflin, $12.95.

This dictionary makes word searches fun. Special features include homographs and homophones listed at the ends of entries; synonyms are boxed. Interesting facts about words are scattered throughout the dictionary in boxes labeled "Language Detective."

Macmillan Dictionary for Children
(Ages 8–10)
1989. Macmillan, $14.95.

Language notes and short essays about interesting facets of language appear in blue boxes throughout the text; word histories are also boxed.

Thorndike-Barnhart Children's Dictionary
(Ages 8–10)
1988. Scott, Foresman, $14.95.

In addition to definitions and word histories, this dictionary lists some word sources—that is, words in English that came from other languages.

Webster's Elementary Dictionary
(Ages 8–10)
1986. Merriam-Webster, $12.95.

In this dictionary, some entries offer usage notes, a history of the word, or synonyms along with the definitions.

Webster's New World Children's Dictionary
(Ages 8–10)
1991. Simon & Schuster, $15.95.

The newest dictionary in this group, this volume includes biographical and geographical entries as added features.

TEENAGERS

Entries in these dictionaries have the arrangement and most of the features of an adult dictionary, but the typeface is still larger and the number of words covered fewer, ranging from 35,000 to 100,000. Illustrations number from 1,000 to 2,000 and tend toward black and white. Sample sentences may not be given for all words. These dictionaries also usually have a reference section with metric equivalents, signs and symbols, or other facts. Biographical and geographical entries appear either in the main word list or in an appendix. For children of this age, it is advisable to purchase a recently updated dictionary that has clearly included new terms.

The American Heritage Student's Dictionary
(Ages 11–14)
1986. Houghton Mifflin, $12.95.

Macmillan Dictionary for Students
(Ages 11–14)
1984. Macmillan, $16.95.

A new edition was planned for 1992.

Thorndike-Barnhart Student Dictionary
(Ages 11–14)
1988. Scott, Foresman, $16.95.

Webster's Intermediate Dictionary
(Ages 11–14)
1986. Merriam-Webster, $11.95.

RESOURCES

American Library Association selected awards and notable lists. (See Key to ALA Awards, p. xvii)

The Best in Children's Books: The University of Chicago Guide to Children's Literature, 1985– *1990* by Zena Sutherland and others. 1991. University of Chicago, $37.50.

Book Links. Bimonthly (September–May). American Library Association, 50 East Huron Street, Chicago, IL 60611. $22/year.

BEST OF THE BEST FOR CHILDREN

Booklist. Biweekly, with single issues in July and August. American Library Association, 50 East Huron Street, Chicago, IL 60611. $56/year. (800) 545-2433.

Books Kids Will Sit Still For: The Complete Read-Aloud Guide by Judy Freeman. 1990. Bowker, $34.95.

Choosing Books for Children: A Commonsense Guide by Betsy Hearne. 1990, rev. ed. Delacorte/Delta, $16.95; paper, $9.95.

Choosing Books for Kids: Choosing the Right Book for the Right Child at the Right Time by Joanne Oppenheim et al. 1986. Ballantine, o.p.

Mother Goose Comes First: An Annotated Guide to the Best Books and Recordings for Your Preschool Child by Lois Winkel and Sue Kimmel. 1990. Holt, paper, $14.95.

The New Read-Aloud Handbook by James Trelease. 1989, rev. ed. Penguin, paper, $12.95.

The New York Times Parent's Guide to the Best Books for Children by Eden Ross Lipson. 1991, rev. ed. Times Books/Random House, paper, $15.

Parent's Choice. A quarterly journal of the Parent's Choice Foundation, P.O. Box 185, Newton, MA 02168, $15.

Purchasing an Encyclopedia: 12 Points to Consider. 1989, 3rd Ed. American Library Association, paper, $4.95.

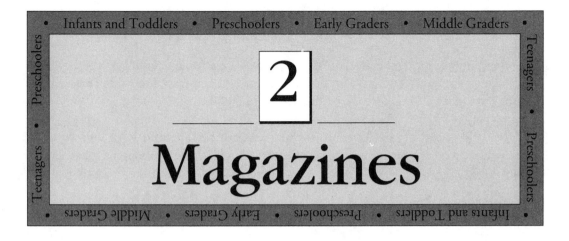

Infants and Toddlers • Preschoolers • Early Graders • Middle Graders •
Preschoolers
Teenagers
Teenagers
Preschoolers
Infants and Toddlers • Preschoolers • Early Graders • Middle Graders •

2

Magazines

INTRODUCTION

Magazines for children both stimulate and satisfy a youngster's curiosity. Up-to-date information and exuberant graphics offer an exciting complement to texts and other reading material. Moreover, youth with a creative bent can find outlets for their stories and illustrations in publications such as *Merlyn's Pen*. *The Market for Young Writers* by Kathy Henderson and *The Children's Writers and Illustrators Market* are guides that will direct youthful authors and artists to the periodicals that publish children's work (see Resources section at the end of this chapter).

Some magazines have the visual appeal of television with the added advantage of featuring fine writing. For children today there are specialized magazines on chess, sports, piano, ecology, space travel, wildlife, and more. A subscription is a way to spark an interest or ignite an ongoing passion. Many magazine articles list related books in each issue to encourage further reading.

Since there is an ever-growing number of consumer magazines for children, we decided to focus here on those most desirable for home use. Familiar classroom fare has, for the most part, not been included. Such titles are described in Selma K. Richardson's *Magazines for Children* (2nd ed., American Library Association, 1991) and *Magazines for Young Adults* (ALA, 1984).[1] We've also excluded magazines that are sheer imitations or spin-offs of popular TV shows or toys, though they can help motivate reluctant readers. Advertising is a controversial point in children's magazines, just as in children's television. Many quality periodicals eschew ads altogether. The type and content of ads are mentioned when considered important.

[1]The editors are grateful for the guidance provided by Selma K. Richardson in her two guides.

HOW TO USE THIS CHAPTER

Magazines can readily extend beyond the age groupings used throughout this guide; *Highlights,* for example, is suggested for children from 2 to 12. For ease of use, we first list the magazine at the youngest age level. Look throughout the chapter to find magazines that might interest your young reader.

Editorial addresses (edit:) are distinguished from subscription addresses (sub:) when they differ. This way children can write to the many magazines that call for kid participation, and subscriptions can be ordered easily.

Following this information is the rate for one year (as of late 1991) and the frequency of publication.

TODDLERS AND PRESCHOOLERS

Chickadee

The Magazine for Young Children from OWL

(Ages 3–8)

Edit: The Young Naturalist Foundation, 56 The Esplanade, Suite 306, Toronto, Ontario, Canada M5E1A7.

Sub: P.O. Box 11314, Des Moines, IA 50340.

$14.95; Monthly (except July and August).

Filled with animal and adventure stories, fiction, puzzles, craft ideas, and observation games, all illustrated with cartoons, drawings, and photographs. This nature magazine for preschoolers and children in the early grades is from Canada and has a French version called *Coulicou.*

Highlights for Children

(Ages 2–12)

Edit: 803 Church St., Honesdale, PA 18431.

Sub: Dept CA, P.O. Box 269, Columbus, OH 43216-0269.

$19.95; Monthly (one issue for July/August).

It's easy to see at a glance how *Highlights* can appeal to kids from ages 2 to 12. From the easy rebus stories to the "Headwork" that asks children to ponder interesting propositions— "If you could be invisible for just one day, what would you do?"—there is real diversity in the projects and the text. It may be difficult, however, to convince a child (of, say, 8 or 10) who has an eye for glitzier productions that there is still plenty of information and fun to be found in these familiar pages. Other features include recipes for cookery and crafts, puzzles, stories, and articles on science, sports, and various cultures.

Ladybug
The Magazine for Young Children
(Ages 2–7)
Edit: 315 Fifth St., Peru, IL 61354.
Sub: P.O. Box 58343, Boulder, CO 80321-8343.
$29.97; Monthly.

Despite its outdoorsy name, *Ladybug,* unlike *Chickadee* and *Your Big Backyard,* is not about nature. This preschool version of *Cricket* (see p. 134) is a fine literary magazine aimed directly at toddlers and preschoolers (not their parents). *Ladybug* does arrive with a separate parent's supplement, which includes an editorial on each month's theme, a list of extra reading (about a dozen titles), and the table of contents. *Ladybug* features colorful songs, rhymes, arts and crafts, read-aloud stories, fantasy, folk, and fairy tales. It's a delightful way for children to be introduced to terrific authors and illustrators, such as Helen Oxenbury and Tomie de Paola. The magazine is sturdily produced to survive sticky fingers and withstand frequent rereading.

Sesame Street Magazine
(Ages 2–6)
Edit: 1 Lincoln Plaza, New York, NY 10023.
Sub: P.O. Box 55518, Boulder, CO 80322-5518.
$14.97; 10 issues (monthly except February and August).

An exception to our exclusion of TV spin-offs, *Sesame Street Magazine* is based on the 20-year-old Children's Television Workshop production, which, after all, is no passing fad. The magazine draws easily upon the television show. For example, in one issue Big Bird announces, in a balloon caption, "This program is brought to you by the letters *O* and *P* and the number *8.*" Each issue, published on flimsy paper, is made to be used up; there are games to cut out and projects to complete while matching, sequencing, color recognition, and early reading and counting skills are playfully developed. A read-aloud photo essay about a serious issue, such as going to the hospital or starting school, is always included, as is a page full of letters and drawings from young readers. The accompanying parents' guide is as long, sometimes longer, than the regular issue. If this does not seem to be the most innovative of contemporary children's magazines, it is only because the sustained high quality of the program is now taken for granted.

Your Big Backyard
(Ages 3–5)
Edit and Sub: 8925 Leesburg Pike, Vienna, VA 22184-0001.
$12; Monthly (entire magazine is repeated every 3 years).

Truly in touch with its young audience, *Your Big Backyard* is packed with large color photographs and simple text in bold print. Throughout the 20-page magazine are pleasant learning games (circle the largest male mallard, then square the largest female mallard; count the raccoon babies; compare the lion to the lionfish; etc.). A little green furry creature acts as the host of this publication of the National Wildlife Federation. A white wraparound cover surrounds each issue with notes on the contents for parents and teachers, and advice on using the magazine for maximum fun and learning.

EARLY GRADERS

Boodle: By Kids for Kids
(See Write It Yourself, p. 135.)

Boomerang
(Ages 7–10)
Edit and Sub: Listen & Learn Home Education, 123 Townsend St., Suite 636, San Francisco, CA 94107. $39.95; Monthly.

Plug this magazine into your Walkman. That's right, it's an audio magazine. The voices on the tape are those of savvy kids asking tough questions about topical events, telling jokes, reviewing music, and enacting scenarios involving economics, science, and history. The flow of information on each 45-minute tape is phenomenal. The performances are polished and ingenuous. A print insert packaged with each cassette holds puzzles, games, answers to questions, and a summary of contents.

Cricket
(Ages 6–14)
Edit: 315 Fifth St., Peru, IL 61354.
Sub: P.O. Box 51144, Boulder, CO 80321-1144.
$29.97; Monthly.

"The very finest magazine for children," says Selma Richardson in her guide, *Magazines for Children* (see Resources section at the end of this chapter). Where else can young readers explore archaeology, fantasy, history, science, and much more through literature? Poetry, puzzles, and fiction also hook kids, bringing them to a world of excellent reading. The inviting, small magazine is without glossy photographs—the illustrations are more typically high-quality drawings, often by major illustrators. Some consider *Cricket* a bit intimidating, but in fact, the variety of fiction and nonfiction offers something for every interest, and the fine literary quality simply assures that reading it will be a pleasure.

Daybreak Star Indian Reader
(See Write It Yourself, p. 135.)

Games Junior
(Ages 6–12)
Edit: 810 Seventh Ave., New York, NY 10019.
Sub: P.O. Box 2082, Harlan, IA 51593.
$11.97; Bimonthly.

WRITE IT YOURSELF

Most magazines for kids feature a page or two of contributions from their readers. The magazines described below publish only the contributions of youthful authors, artists, critics, poets, and puzzlemakers.

Boodle: By Kids for Kids   (Ages 6–12)   Edit and Sub: P.O. Box 1049, Portland, IN 47371. $10; 4 issues/year.

Formerly called *Caboodle,* this quarterly magazine is nicely printed in a one-color, two-column format. Pensive, funny, imaginative stories, poetry, and drawings from children fill the pages. With more than 50 contributions per issue, there is room here for the work of many ambitious young writers and artists.

Creative Kids   (Ages 8–18)   Edit: 350 Weinacker Ave., Mobile, AL 36604.   Sub: P.O. Box 6448, Mobile, AL 36660. $24; 8 issues per year.

All kinds of contributions are printed in *Creative Kids,* including poetry, stories, reviews, limericks, puzzles, nonfiction, interviews, and artwork. Letter writing is also encouraged with a back page full of potential pen pals' names and addresses. The editors also challenge readers to invent games, "goofy gadgets," and other creative projects.

Daybreak Star Reader   (Ages 7–10)   Edit and Sub: United Indians of All Tribes Foundation, 1945 Yale Place E., Seattle, WA 98102. $20; Monthly (October through May).

Native American legends, history, and personal tales are reported by guest editors from different schools each month. The participants are chosen from fourth- through sixth-grade classes. They recount Indian lore they have learned from their families, travel experiences, and cultural history. Math puzzles, word games, letters, and crafts are also submitted. Reading and writing for this slim magazine would be a nice intercultural experience for children from any background.

Merlyn's Pen The National Magazine of Student Writing (Ages 12–15)   Edit and Sub: P.O. Box 1058, East Greenwich, RI 02818. $14.95; 4 issues (bimonthly from October through May).

A perfect market for junior high students not quite ready for the writing contests and literary publications aimed at older teens. Short stories, book and movie reviews, essays, parodies, travel pieces, poetry, drawings, cartoons, and other artwork created by students in grades 7–10 are considered. Notes by and about the author may be included, as well as readers' responses to pieces they have read. Cathartic writing often prevails; difficult issues such as teen suicide or child abuse may be covered. A good balance of humor, experience, and serious thinking is achieved.

Skipping Stones: A Multi-Ethnic Children's Forum   (Ages 7–13)   Edit and Sub: 80574 Hazelton Rd. Cottage Grove, OR 97424. $15; Quarterly.

Skipping Stones is a "playful forum for communication among children from different lands and backgrounds." The young readers are encouraged to correspond with pen pals (listed on the back page) and submit prose, poetry, drawings, and photographs about the traditions, holidays, and everyday life in their countries. The articles and stories are welcome in any language; English translations are set beside the originals. "Especially invited to submit their work," state the editors, "are children, youth, and adults from other cultural backgrounds, minorities, blacks, and under-privileged people from all parts of the world." One regular feature reports on the activities of associations and clubs for kids in the United States and other countries. There are also book reviews, games, songs, maps, crafts, and calendars that celebrate cultural diversity.

Stone Soup   The Magazine by Children   (Ages 6–13)   Edit: Children's Art Foundation, 915 Cedar St., Santa Cruz, CA 95060.   Sub: P.O. Box 83, Santa Cruz, CA 95063. $23; Bimonthly (September through May).

This small literary magazine publishes work by youthful writers based on personal experience, observations, and adventures. The art is set in small boxes amid clear typescript pages with large white margins. Stories and poems may contemplate grief, ambitions to travel the world and feed the hungry, or even sadness over losing a ball game. Brief profiles and small photographs of each contributor are included following their artwork, poems, or stories. International contributors add interest and distinction to this enterprise.

This junior version of *Games* for adults is a magazine of mental aerobics. It offers more complexity and variety than seen in *Hidden Pictures* (below). Five categories of games appear: Picture Puzzles, Word Play, Mystery, Logic & Numbers, and Games & Trivia. There are reviews of new commercial games and a comic strip that requires unscrambling. "The bountiful potpourri of any issue will amuse and fascinate the young while stimulating the thinking processes," says expert Selma Richardson.

Hidden Pictures Magazine

(Ages 6–10)
Edit: 2300 W. Fifth Ave., P.O. Box 269, Columbus, OH 43216.
Sub: P.O. Box 53781, Boulder, CO 80322.
$14.95; Bimonthly.

This spin-off from *Highlights for Children* (see p. 132) guarantees puzzle aficionados plenty of fun. It can be a blessing for travelers, keeping kids' minds and pencils active as they try to solve mazes, crossword puzzles, optical illusions, and hidden picture puzzles. The variety and challenge levels of the games are excellent, although there is not quite the diversity that appears in *Games Junior* (above).

Hopscotch

The Magazine for Girls
(Ages 6–12)
Edit and Sub: P.O. Box 1292, Saratoga Springs, NY 12866.
$13.50; Bimonthly.

Hopscotch's editors forthrightly state, "We believe that young girls deserve the right to enjoy a season of childhood before they become young adults; we are not interested in such topics as sex, romance, cosmetics, hairstyles, etc." They are interested, however, in recipes, games, crafts, pets, hobbies, and activities for girls. In each issue, appealing nonfiction articles (about collections, genealogy, girls in other countries, and so on) are accompanied by relevant, light fiction.

Kid City

For Graduates of Sesame Street
(Ages 6–10)
Edit: 1 Lincoln Plaza, New York, NY 10023.
Sub: P.O. Box 53349, Boulder, CO 80322-3349.
$13.97: 10 issues (monthly except February and August).

Formerly called *Electric Company,* after the public television show "for graduates of 'Sesame Street'," this magazine is full of items about popular culture balanced by pieces on such serious issues as racial inequity and handicaps and profiles of newsworthy kids. Created almost as filler between the preschooler periodical *Sesame Street* (see p. 133) and *3-2-1 Contact* (see p. 144), this magazine is rather superficial, but its range of topics and trendy look may capture and assist early readers.

Kids Discover

(Ages 5–12)
Edit: 170 Fifth Ave., New York, NY 10010.
Sub: P.O. Box 54206, Boulder, CO 80321-4206.
$14.95; 10 issues (monthly except June/July and August/September).

Each issue of this magazine (launched Summer 1991) covers one topic, such as trees, bubbles, pyramids, or airplanes. Great glossy photographs are accompanied by historical and scientific facts, "Discovery Zones" (single questions answered on the back cover), and "Think Pieces" (questions that require speculation and information assessment).

Relevant word searches, mazes, and craft projects conclude the magazine. Here is a good learning tool that is fun reading for both parents and children. As in *Zoobooks* (see p. 139), the glossy photos and short descriptive passages make it a good read-aloud for preschoolers as well.

P3
The Earth-Based Magazine for Kids
(Ages 7–10)
Edit and Sub: P.O. Box 52, Montgomery, VT 05470.
$18; 10 issues.

Called *P3* in reference to Earth as the third planet from the sun, this magazine (printed on recycled paper) helps clarify the threatening news about pollution, oil spills, and acid rain. It also offers down-to-earth suggestions for personal action, such as writing to authorities, conservation techniques, and bike riding (instead of asking for "limo service" from parents). Comics, rap songs, biographies, and news reports appear in this slick yet sincere publication. While coverage may gloss over some aspects of critical issues, the overall premise—to raise the environmental consciousness of kids—is a good one. Poetic kudos were sent in by one reader:

> Oil is bad
> Earth is rad
> P3 is no fool
> and it's so cool
> (Letter to the editor, May/June 1990)

Ranger Rick
(Ages 6–12)
Edit and Sub: 8925 Leesburg Pike, Vienna, VA 22184-0001.
$15; Monthly.

Membership in Ranger Rick's Nature Club includes this monthly from the National Wildlife Federation, featuring gloriously illustrated articles on animals and the environment. Exotic creatures, such as giant sea otters, are described by scientists in information-packed prose. The photography is excellent and the craft ideas, whether playful or aimed at backyard nature study, are always clever. A November issue displayed a rock collection in the design of a Thanksgiving feast. It looked good enough to eat. (Available on Talking Books.)

Seedling Series: Short Story International
(Ages 8–12)
Edit: 6 Sheffield Rd., Great Neck, NY 11021.
Sub: P.O. Box 405, Great Neck, NY 11022.
$14; Quarterly ($3.75 per copy).

Like *Student Series: Short Story International* (reviewed below) and the adult version *Short Story International,* this periodical arrives in paperback form and carries tales from modern authors throughout the world. Each edition features about ten (depending on length) short stories, often with a pointed moral or message, that are lively portraits of kids in various lands.

Skipping Stones
(See Write It Yourself, p. 136.)

Stone Soup
(See Write It Yourself, p. 136.)

U*S*Kids
(Ages 5–10)
Edit: 245 Long Hill Rd., Middletown, CT 06457.
Sub: P.O. Box 8957, Boulder, CO 80322.
$18.95; Monthly (except July and August).

Fitness tips, profiles of youthful achievers, general news, self-help suggestions, and light scientific articles fill this informal monthly. Crafts, easy recipes, memory tests, hidden puzzles, and match-ups carry on the seasonal or topical theme of each issue. The Pet Show—a poster on the back cover featuring pet of the month—is developed from pictures and messages sent in by readers, and an animal centerfold is carried in each issue. *U*S*Kids* is similar to *Kid City* (see p. 137) except for its self-help theme, which is most obvious in the "Kids Helping Kids" advice column, where questions and answers are supplied by the young readers.

Zoobooks

(Ages 6–10)

Edit and Sub: Wildlife Education, Ltd., 3590 Kettner Blvd., San Diego, CA 92101.
$15.95; 10 issues.

"Animal-of-the-Month" would be an appropriate subtitle for this magazine. Each issue is packed with dramatic color photographs and drawings that are clearly defined. The language is geared to school-age children, but the many stunning illustrations make it a good read-aloud for toddlers and preschoolers as well. The whole series, which consists of 58 titles that are updated regularly, is available in single issues or collected in hardcover versions.

MIDDLE GRADERS AND TEENAGERS

Boy's Life

(Ages 8–18)

Edit and Sub: 1325 W. Walnut Hill Lane, P.O. Box 152079, Irving, TX 75015-2079.
$15.60; Monthly.

Published since 1911, this official magazine of the Boy Scouts of America is no longer a members-only journal. It is aimed at kids ages 8–18; but with the birth of Tiger Cubs, first-graders may show an interest as well. The articles focus on sports players, distinguished scouts, popular hobbies, and heroic deeds. Exciting fiction comes in conventional short stories and in cartoons. Advertisements for scouting equipment, guns, and toys vie with the stories, craft projects, and features for kids' attention. The magazine still concludes with the long-standing "Think and Grin" pages, filled with riddles and wordplay sent in by readers.

Calliope
World History for Young People
(Ages 9–15)
Edit and Sub: 30 Grove St., Peterborough, NH 03458. $17.95; 5 issues.

Like *Cobblestone* and *Faces* (see pp. 140 and 141) from this publisher, each issue of *Calliope* has a single topic that is viewed from various angles by authoritative authors who speak clearly to young readers. Lost cities, great explorers, and famous battles are among the subjects covered in nonfiction, short stories (including fables and folklore), games, recipes, and crafts. Prior to September 1990, this magazine was called *Classical Calliope* and focused on the ancient world, especially Greek and Roman civilizations. Coverage is now international in scope, from ancient times through the Renaissance.

Clavier's Piano Explorer
(Ages 9–12)
Edit and Sub: 200 Northfield Rd., Northfield, IL 60093.
$6; Monthly (except July and August).

The piano is the star but not the whole show in this slim magazine. Pages are devoted to other instruments as well as composers, seasonal music, biographies, and clever quizzes and puzzles. Every issue carries two beginner pieces, submitted by young musicians (usually between the ages of 8 and 12). An attractive magazine that will surely entice eager young players to learn more about music theory and other musical subjects.

Cobblestone
The History Magazine for Young People
(Ages 9–15)
Edit and Sub: 30 Grove St., Peterborough, NH 03458. $22.95; Monthly.

The emphasis here is on American history. Engrossing articles and occasional fiction on such topics as the Alamo, television, suffrage, witchcraft, and the Pony Express are highlighted by period paintings, maps, photographs, watercolors, lithographs, and sketches. Readers need not be avid history buffs to find these pages absorbing. This acclaimed magazine is a pleasurable tool for broadening the whole family's sense of U.S. history.

Creative Kids
(See Write It Yourself, p. 135.)

Dolphin Log
(Ages 7–15)
Edit: 8440 Santa Monica Blvd., Los Angeles, CA 90069.
Sub: 930 W. 21st St., Norfolk, VA 23517.
$10; Bimonthly.

From the Cousteau Society comes this look into the world of underwater exploration and all types of water life. Gloriously illustrated articles on intriguing fish and other aquatic creatures, ecology, and marine biology are accompanied by clever quizzes and puzzles. The magazine keenly makes its point—to share the critical value, as well as the beauty, of our globe's water and its inhabitants.

Faces

The Magazine about People

(Ages 9–15)

Edit and Sub: 30 Grove St., Peterborough, NH 03458.
$21.95; Monthly (except June, July, and August).

A fine magazine on anthropology and natural history, from the publishers of *Calliope* and *Cobblestone,* created with the cooperation of New York's American Museum of Natural History. One entire issue covered chimps, apes, monkeys, and orangutans; another explored archaeology, courtship, and palaces. The articles, written by field scientists and acknowledged experts, maintain a scholarly but always youthful focus. A short story or folktale and recipes and crafts related to the issue's central theme are always included. A section called "Further Exploring" contains short reviews of relevant books and videos.

KidSports

(See Tune In and Tone Up: Sports Magazines, p. 142.)

Merlyn's Pen

(See Write It Yourself, p. 136.)

National Geographic World

(Ages 8–13)

Edit: National Geographic Society, 17th and M Sts., NW, Washington, DC 20036.
Sub: Dept. 00191, 17th and M Sts., NW, Washington, DC 20036.
$10.95; Monthly.

Not a scaled-down version of the Society's classic, *National Geographic,* this is, instead, a kid-oriented blend of popular science. An issue may feature incredible balloon art, a look at polar bears, or a visit to a famous dinosaur museum. The facts are reported in a journalistic rather than teaching style. Young readers' contributions enliven the art page.

Native Monthly Reader

A Scholastic Newspaper for Young Adults

(Ages 10–17)

Edit: RedSun Institute, P.O. Box 122, Crestone, CO 81131.
Sub: International Traditional Educational Systems, Inc., P.O. Box 217, Crestone, CO 81131.
$10 single subscriptions for museums and libraries only. (For schools: 20 copies/month, $98; 30 copies/month, $147.50); 8 times/year during the school year.

This slim (8–12-page) newspaper carries news and guidance for Native Americans from any background. Intended for use in "schools with significant Native American student populations," the paper projects to a broader audience, that is, readers of all backgrounds. Articles cover such topics as sports, geography, business, health, science, poetry, word puzzles, and contemporary news. A center insert featuring the work of a Native American artist often carries direct messages for kids. For example, from sculptor Roxanne Swentzell, "Don't be scared to express what you need to express. You have to dare to put your soul out for others to see or you'll never reach anybody."

Odyssey

(Ages 8–14)

Edit and Sub: Kalmbach Publishing Co., 21027 Crossroads Circle, P.O. Box 1612, Waukesha, WI 53187-1612.
$21; Monthly.

For kids intrigued by astronomy or space travel and technology, this is *the* resource.

TUNE IN AND TONE UP

SPORTS MAGAZINES

These three titles represent the quality sports magazines available for children, from the general to the specific—figure skating, hockey, cycling, canoeing, hiking, boating, soccer, you name it, there's a journal on it. Most of the specialized magazines are written for adults; but enthusiastic teens will enjoy them as well. Ask your librarian to help track them down.

KidSports   The Official Sports Magazine for Kids   (Ages 8–14)   Edit and Sub: 1101 Wilson Blvd., Arlington, VA 22209. $8.97; 6 issues.

Although the term "official" may be hype, this publication from ProServ, Inc. (a well-known sports marketing and management company) is an exciting one, filled with advice from professional athletes and admonitions to practice. Many articles feature the "When I Was Your Age" (an actual column title) approach, which differs from the kids-as-stars features in *Sports Illustrated for Kids*. There are plenty of ads, not all are directly related to sports. The supportive tone, advice from the stars, posters, and puzzles will draw and encourage readers.

Racing for Kids   (Ages 9–12)   Edit and Sub: Griggs Publishing Co., P.O. Box 500, Concord, NC 28026-0500. $25; Monthly.

From stock cars and funny cars to go-karts and modeling, all of the news about racing, cars, and drivers can be found here, plus feature stories, writing contests, kid profiles, quizzes, posters, puzzles, and model-building tips.

Sports Illustrated for Kids   (Ages 8–13)   Edit: Time & Life Building, Rockefeller Center, New York, NY 10020-1393.   Sub: P.O. Box 83069, Birmingham, AL 35283-0609. $17.95; Monthly.

One of the best scaledowns of a popular consumer magazine. The stories are about kids as well as the athletes they can admire. Comic strips supplement some of the stories to draw readers and focus interest (especially in the "I Learned My Lesson" tales from sports celebrities).

Odyssey carries informed, readable articles on up-to-the-minute space explorations, launch dates, and research, as well as NASA's plans for the future. Related experiments, puzzles, games, and projects are colorfully illustrated. The advertising is appropriate (related to space camps and sky-watching gear), and a section of classified ads gives readers a chance to exchange information on clubs, pen pals, equipment, and newsletters related to space exploration.

OWL
The Discovery Magazine for Children
(Ages 9–12)

Edit: The Young Naturalist Foundation, 56 The Esplanade, Suite 306, Toronto, Ontario, Canada M5E1A7.
Sub: P.O. Box 11314, Des Moines, IA 50340.
$14.95; Monthly (except July and August).

While the photographs are not quite as spectacular as those in *Ranger Rick,* they are charming. In addition, the many cartoon-style illustrations appeal even more to older readers. *OWL* covers areas of scientific and natural curiosity, including animals, space, biology, and ecology. The You Asked About . . . sections cover a variety of topics lightly, but with enough depth to answer basic questions and set seriously inquisitive minds in pursuit of more knowledge.

Piano Explorer
(See *Clavier's Piano Explorer* above.)

Plays
The Drama Magazine for Young People
(Ages 6–18)

Edit and Sub: 120 Boylston St., Boston, MA 02116.
$24.75; Monthly October–May (except January and February).

This magazine full of plays—one-acters, skits, and creative dramatic material suitable for productions by elementary, junior high, and high school students—is definitely school material. However, any family with kids serious about acting or playwriting would welcome this monthly arrival of comedies, dramas, satires, farces, melodramas, dramatized classics, folktales, fairy tales, and puppet plays. Subscribers may produce plays royalty-free; nonsubscribers must apply for performance permission and royalty quotations.

Racing for Kids
(See Tune In and Tone Up: Sports Magazines, p. 142.)

Sassy
(Ages 13–19)

Edit: 230 Park Ave., New York, NY 10169.
Sub: P.O. Box 57503, Boulder, CO 80322-7503.
$14.95; Monthly.

"Sassy" is a rather mild term for the brash tone of this magazine, where letters to the editor often open with, "You buttheads." It is the most contemporary of the teen magazines that flood the market. Advice on makeup and boys still abounds, but the approach is less silly and far more forthright than elsewhere. Quality short stories and reviews balance the glitz and beautification lessons. *Sassy* has inspired its own television show, and a print male counterpart, called *Dirt,* is in the works and is worth checking out.

School Mates
The U.S. Chess Magazine for Beginning Chessplayers
(Ages 8–18)

Edit and Sub: U.S. Chess Federation, 186 Route 9W, New Windsor, NY 12553.
$7.50; Bimonthly.

A celebration of tournament-level chess. A brief introduction to the magazine's methods for defining chess moves appears on the editorial page, but potential subscribers should have some experience with the game before taking on this journal's strategies and descriptions. Featured are reports on major competitions, profiles of champs, listings of upcoming junior tournaments, and tactical advice from other readers who send in their favorite chess problems and most successful maneuvers. Chess instructions are illustrated by black-and-white drawings against a lightly colored background. Ads are carefully limited by the U.S. Chess Federation. A crossword puzzle offers a change-of-pace challenge.

Sports Illustrated for Kids
(See Tune In and Tone Up: Sports Magazines, p. 142.)

Student Series: Short Story International
(Ages 12–18)

Edit: 6 Sheffield Rd., Great Neck, NY 11021.
Sub: P.O. Box 405, Great Neck, NY 11022.
$16; Quarterly ($4.25 per copy).

Each edition features about 10 (depending on length) contemporary short stories drawn from an international well of modern authors. "Multi-cultural to the Nth degree" according to the publisher Sam Tankel, "these unabridged stories from all over the world [are] written by living, indigenous authors who know their people and cultures well." He's absolutely right. The question remains: peri-odical or paperback? The tales arrive quarterly in a paperback format, so no ads, news, or fillers distract from the stories.

3-2-1 Contact
(Ages 8–14)

Edit: Children's Television Workshop, 1 Lincoln Plaza, New York, NY 10023.
Sub: P.O. Box 53051, Boulder, CO 80322.
$15.97; 10 issues (monthly except February and August).

Amusing and informative articles on science, computers, space, earth, animals, and the scientists and children who study such topics make up the bulk of this journal from the creators of *Sesame Street* (see p. 133) and *Kid City* (see p. 137). Fiction (usually just one story) and entertaining puzzles fill out this newsy, head-of-the-class magazine.

Zillions
Consumer Reports for Kids
(Ages 8–14)

Edit: 101 Truman Ave., Yonkers, NY 10703.
Sub: P.O. Box 54861, Boulder CO 80322-4861.
$13.95; Bimonthly (six issues).

Here are insights from kids on the meaning of the phrase "ripoff." Like its parent magazine, *Consumer Reports*, *Zillions* (formerly called *Penny Power*) relies on its audience for feedback. By asking young consumers what they think (about gimmicky clubs, peanut butter, dangerous toys, etc.), the magazine helps kids form sound opinions about the stuff they are endlessly exhorted to purchase (or ask their parents to purchase for them). *Zillions* gives kids credit for, and practice at, making practical consumer judgments.

RESOURCES

The Children's Writer's and Illustrator's Market. Annual. Writer's Digest, $14.95.

The Market for Young Writers by Kathy Henderson. 1990. Shoe Tree; dist. by Betterway Publications, $10.95.

Magazines for Children by Selma Richardson. 1991, rev. ed. ALA Publishing, paper, $12.50.

Magazines for Young Adults by Selma Richardson. 1984. ALA Publishing, paper, $22.50.

Magazines for Young People (formerly *Magazines for School Libraries*) by Bill Katz and Linda Sternberg Katz. 1991. Bowker, $34.95.

Of Cabbages and Kings by Kimberly Olson Fakih. 1991. Bowker, $29.95. (A topically arranged anthology of articles, short stories, and poems from children's magazines for ages 8 to 12).

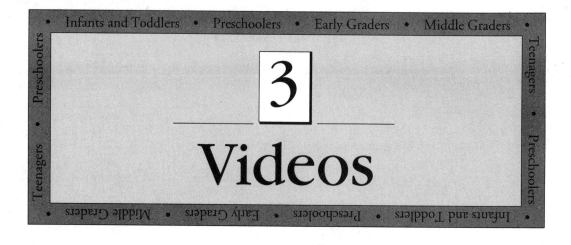

3

Videos

INTRODUCTION

Video and children's literature—how do they relate? Some of the best children's books have been transformed into videos, not always well. Some of the best videos are indeed based on children's literature; other videos are masterpieces on their own.

When it comes to adaptations, you simply can't judge a video by the book from which it is drawn. Often, there are several video versions of favorite children's stories. They can range in quality from wooden cartoons to productions filled with art and music worthy of the classic they portray. A quality video adaptation can surpass the print version or transform it into a new experience. Irene Wood, editor of the Audiovisual section of ALA's *Booklist* magazine, cites *The Snowman* as an example of a video that is even better than the wordless book on which it is based. And, in an interesting reversal, some book and audio products are now based on the art, narration, and music created for a video.

We present here more than a selective list of entertaining and educational videos. Here is the chance for children to gain "video literacy" by observing a range of production techniques, from live action to animation of all sorts. Through conversations about the videos, children can also learn how to watch, assess, and interpret—that is, how to think while viewing—and most of all, how to make connections with other experiences, including reading.

Few of the familiar feature films, such as *Peter Pan, E.T.,* and *Flight of the Navigator,* are listed here. Instead, we introduce children to some new faces, new stars, such as Ralph S. Mouse and the students of Degrassi High School. Videos of commercial films are easy to spot at your local library or video rental store and are mentioned in many other resources, such as *Parents' Choice Guide to Videocassettes for Children* (see Resources at the end of this chapter for more). They are also regularly listed in annual home video guides.

HOW TO USE THIS CHAPTER

Where can you find the videos recommended here? Most are at the library and many at the local video rental store. According to the American Library Association video *Choosing the Best in Children's Video,* "Some of the best children's video, especially book adaptations, are produced specifically for school and libraries and may be available to parents only through the library."

All, however, are available for purchase. Independent and specialty children's book and toy stores now offer videos. Many video rental companies will also handle purchases. The catalogs cited after our Toy and Audio chapters also list many of our video choices. We have identified the distributors (and listed their addresses and phone numbers) for all videos mentioned. For further information, consult *AV Market Place,* a reference book available in most public libraries, because distributors change, as do prices.

Do not be dismayed by the costs of some of these videos. The price discrepancy between the home video market and the educational market reflects the expenses faced by small independent artists and producers trying to create quality products. More and more school and library videos are being made available for home viewing, however, and the price gap is narrowing. Rabbit Ears and other producers are issuing quality videos at reasonable rates.

Just as you watch for favorite actors and directors in feature films, keep an eye out for directors and artists whose work stirs your children. By supporting quality video production (through library and rental requests as well as purchases) you'll help make more fine videos available.

Most home videos carry the label "For home viewing only." This label means that certain copyright restrictions exist regarding public showings of these tapes. The "public" is defined in copyright law as those "outside the normal circle of family and social acquaintances." Some home videos are available with public performance rights, and that fact is noted—only for home videos—by the designation "(pub. perf.)" following the price. If there is an additional cost for a video that carries the public performance rights, it is designated as "(pub. perf., $[*cost*])" when this information is known.

However, nonprofit educational institutions enjoy certain legal exceptions to the restriction. Librarians, teachers, and other educators using videos for group presentations may call the AIME Copyright Hotline (800-444-4203) to clarify issues concerning the right to show purchased, borrowed, or rented videotapes in classrooms and to the public.

SERIES

Some series have a boring sameness; others can be depended on to be consistently good. Exceptional series are those that offer consistently high production quality and fresh, varied approaches in visual style, mood, or story line, such as "Stories to Remember" and "We All Have Tales." Only a few productions from each series could be reviewed in this chapter; the rest will satisfy your passions for "more of the same." Here are a few series to note.

The American Storytelling Series (See Audio.)
Faerie Tale Theatre (CBS/Fox)
These live-action performances of classic fairy tales were created by Shelley Duvall, who stars in a few herself. Other sterling performers, such as Robin Williams, Jean Stapleton, and Billy Crystal, bring quirky humor to old favorites. Look for Duvall's new series called "Bedtime Stories."

Family Circle Storyland Theater (See Audio)
Reading Rainbow (GPN)
On every show LeVar Burton hosts a field trip that ties into the video adaptation of a great children's book. Reviews by kids of related titles follow. The range of topics and titles and the production quality are exceptional.

Stories to Remember (Lightyear Entertainment)
These book-based videos have elegant artwork and are narrated by such famous voices as those of Arlo Guthrie, Judy Collins, and Mia Farrow. The videos range from poetry for "babies" to Arthurian adventure for older viewers.

Storybook Classics (Rabbit Ears)
This series shines in its ability to match original artwork, narrative style, and music to the plot and period of the fairy tale. American folklore, fairy tales, and children's literary classics are part of the series.

Tell Me Why (Penguin Home Video; dist. by Prism)
Great for sparking interest in science, each of these nonfiction videos contains short features on topics such as Insects or Space.

We All Have Tales (Rabbit Ears)
International folklore with flair. Tales from Africa, Russia, Greece, Scandinavia, and elsewhere are narrated by well-chosen celebrities and produced with fitting artwork and music.

WonderWorks Family Movie (Home Vision)
The whole family can enjoy this mix of adaptations, such as "The Chronicles of Narnia," and original scripts. Fine acting and period detail highlight the productions.

INFANTS AND TODDLERS

Animal Alphabet

(Ages 2–5)

Producer and Director: Geoffrey Drummond.
Karl-Lorimar; dist. by Music for Little People, $19.95
(30 min.)

"This is an animal alphabet. How much more fun can an alphabet get?" asks composer/lyricist Elizabeth Swados. Each letter has its animal and each animal its tune. The variety of rap, pop, blues, and jingles tucks in a bit of music appreciation along with the news on animals and the way of the alphabet. The honored animals are seen in superb live-action shots drawn from *National Geographic* and *Encyclopaedia Britannica*'s film files. The music and chorus are fun, fresh, and memorable.

Baby's Bedtime

(Ages 1–4)

Stories to Remember series.
Producer: Joshua M. Greene.
Director: Daniel Ivanick.
Lightyear Entertainment, $14.95 each (pub. perf., $64.95)

In a sweet and supple singing style, Judy Collins vocalizes rhymes and poems from Kay Chorao's *The Baby's Bedtime Book*. Drawings glow with the moonlit blues and soft golds that radiate from the warmth of a cuddled infant or a toddler off to dreamland. Ernest Troost's musical score includes original, soothing lullabies and drowsy waltzes for the deepening night. A beguiling reflection of a small child's evening world. (Closed captioned)

CONNECTIONS

Books:
The Baby's Bedtime Book by Kay Chorao. 1989. Dutton, $13.95; book and cassette, $17.95.
The Baby's Good Morning Book by Kay Chorao. (See Books.)
Audio:
Baby's Bedtime and *Baby's Morningtime* sung by Judy Collins. Lightyear Records; dist. by BMG, $8.95.

Carnival of the Animals

(See Top Ten Music Videos, p. 223.)

Don't Wake Your Mom!

(Ages 2–5)

A & M Video, $14.98 (47 min.)

Ventriloquist Shari Lewis provides Mom with a naptime by encouraging youngsters to play along with Lewis and her puppets Lamb Chop, Charlie Horse, and Hush Puppy. Lewis regales her listeners with classics such as "Sleeping Beauty" and "Rip Van Winkle." Youngsters already thinking about time passing are then lured into a lesson on how to tell time. Magic acts, jokes, and more fun make the minutes pass all too swiftly.

Even More Baby Songs
(Ages 1–3)
Producer: Backyard Productions.
Video Treasures, $14.98 (30 min.)

Just one of a series of pleasing music videos for the youngest set, this title blends Hap Palmer's genial songs with appealing footage of cheerful toddlers and preschoolers happily engaged in the events of a day at home and around town. Upbeat or soothing melodies and lyrics treat themes of greeting a new morning, mastering finger foods, celebrating a beloved stuffed animal, or drifting off to sleep with favorite books. Forerunners to this title are *Baby Songs* and *More Baby Songs; Baby Rock* varies the format, with the tots cavorting to rock classics of decades past. Palmer's *Turn on the Music* (see Top Ten Music Videos, p. 223) is addressed to slightly older children. (Closed captioned)

Five Lionni Classics: The Animal Fables of Leo Lionni
(Ages 2–6)
Random House Home Video, $14.95 (30 min.)

Swimmy the brave fish, Frederick the poetic mouse, and Cornelius the upright crocodile appear in this collection that will lead children

straight back to Lionni's animal stories. Elegant cutouts and drawings by master animator Giulio Gianni vivify Lionni's original illustrations, which are rich with humor and meaning. Two more stories on this tape are "It's Mine" and "Fish Is Fish." (Closed captioned)

Awards: American Film and Video Festival Blue Ribbon

✐ CONNECTIONS

> Books:
> *Cornelius.* 1983. Pantheon, $13.99.
> *Fish Is Fish.* 1970. Pantheon, $12.99; Knopf, paper, $2.95.
> *Frederick.* 1967. Knopf, $14.95; paper, $2.95.
> *It's Mine.* 1986. Knopf, $14.95.
> *Swimmy.* 1963. Knopf, paper, $2.95.

Happy Birthday Moon and Other Stories
(Ages 2–6)
Children's Circle, $19.95 (30 min.)

When a little bear tries to give the moon a birthday present, his own wishes come true in a sweetly ironic fashion. The bear's echoing voice and determined pursuit of the moon's path is perfectly suited to video, creating a story easily followed by younger viewers. There is added humor and meaning for older children as well. Just as much fun is "The Napping House," which demonstrates the folly of too many heads in one little bed. The sensitive feelings of an only child about to become an oldest sibling are played out in "Peter's Chair." Two old favorites—"The Three Little Pigs" and "The Owl and the Pussycat"—finish out this balanced selection of short tales suited to young viewers.

Awards: Notable Children's Film 1987

⌒⌒CONNECTIONS

Books:

Happy Birthday Moon by Frank Asch. 1981. Simon & Schuster, $12.95; paper, $4.95.
The Napping House by Audrey Wood. Illustrated by Don Wood. 1984. HBJ, $14.95.
The Owl and the Pussycat by Edward Lear. Illustrated by Barbara Cooney. Little, Brown, o.p.
Peter's Chair by Ezra Jack Keats. 1967. HarperCollins, $13.95; paper, $4.95.
The Three Little Pigs retold and illustrated by Erik Blegvad. 1980, Atheneum, o.p.

Monster Hits
(Ages 2–5)
Sesame Songs Home Video.
Producer: Nina Elias.
Random House Home Video, $14.95 (30 min.)

Monster muppets Elmo and Herry Monster, familiar faces from "Sesame Street," host their own version of the Fuzzy Awards. This spoof on the Academy Awards is complete with "The envelope, please!" and selected performances of the prize-winning numbers from the long-running television series. Among the winners are "Comb Your Face" and Herry's own bluesy salute to Mommy Monster. More gems from Sesame Songs Home Video are *Sing Yourself Silly, Rock & Roll,* and *Dance Along.* (Closed captioned)

Musical Mother Goose
More Musical Mother Goose
(Ages 2–6)
Producer: David Yates and Joe Wolf for David Yates Productions.
Director: Alan Rogers.
Video Treasures, $9.95 each (55–60 min.)
Direct Cinema (pub. perf., $50 each) (5 min. each)

Whimsically rambunctious, these two videos present nursery rhymes and ditties in bright primary colors. An animated menagerie of fanciful creatures enacts the traditional nursery verses and jingles to captivating, rhythmic tunes. Short segments of the age-old favorites are imaginatively arranged around themes—for example, various songs about a boy named Jack—and are tied together by the memorable series refrain, "Rub a Dub Dub." A spirited British production. More Mother Goose in video is available in *Baby's Nursery Rhymes,* sassily narrated by Phylicia Rashad (see Audio).

Sharon, Lois & Bram: The Elephant Show
(Ages 2–8)
Producers: Arnie Zipursky and Bruce Glawson for Cambium Film and Video.
A & M Video, $14.95 each (30 min.)

The popular Canadian singing trio offers engaging entertainment in a series of programs from their television series. Whether visiting the zoo, preparing for a soap box derby, or tracking down missing cookies, Sharon, Lois, and Bram deliver appealing tunes from their enormous repertoire of classic folk songs, old popular standards, and other melodic delights. Along with the songs are playful interactions with young friends, silly puns and riddles, and guest appearances by other entertainers, such as singer Eric Nagler. The beat goes on with these polished, professional performers. (See also *Sleep Over* in Top Ten Music Videos, p. 225.)

The Teddy Bears' Picnic
(See Top Ten Music Videos, p. 225.)

Tin Toy
(Ages 2–Adult)
Direct Cinema, $19.95 (5 min.)

A drooling, diaper-clad infant pursues a mechanical toy—a one-man-band—around a spacious living room. Scooting beneath and behind the looming furniture, the mechanical figure evades the curious tyke, who takes a tumble into a howling cascade of tears. With sympathy for the bawling child replacing his fear, the tin toy attempts unsuccessfully to divert his former tormentor. Exquisite computer animation yields remarkably realistic characteristics in the baby and imbues the inanimate toy with lifelike emotions. A widely appealing technical tour de force.

Awards: Notable Children's Film 1990; YASD 1989; Academy Award Best Animated Film 1988

Turn On The Music
(See Top Ten Music Videos, p. 223.)

A Young Children's Concert
Raffi and the Rise and Shine Band
(Ages 2–Adult)
A & M Video, $19.95 (60 min.)

Raffi's originality is matched only by his flair for sing-along verses that bewitch young listeners and old. His use of an array of instruments introduces kids to great music, while his nonsensical, traditional, and enchanting tunes capture their musical imaginations. On this video: "Baby Beluga," "Down by the Bay," "He's Got the Whole World," and more, in a straightforward concert format.

PRESCHOOLERS

The Amazing Bone and Other Stories
(Ages 3–7)
Children's Circle, $19.95 (30 min.)

In "The Amazing Bone," a young pig named Pearl is strolling home from school when she meets a bone that once belonged to a witch.

After a cordial chat with this talkative skeletal fragment, Pearl pockets it. Later, the bone's verbosity protects her from harm when a menacing fox tries to turn Pearl into his evening meal. Among other stories on this imagination-stretching video is "A Picture for Harold's Room," in which a toddler draws a vivid scene on his wall and then enters it. In "The Trip," another journey is taken by a young boy who longs for friends from his old neighborhood. And "John Brown, Rose, and the Midnight Cat" will trigger thoughts of sibling rivalry as a new cat vies with the sheepdog John Brown for the attention of their owner, Rose.

Awards: Notable Children's Film 1987

CONNECTIONS

Books:
The Amazing Bone by William Steig. 1976. Farrar, Straus & Giroux, $14.95; paper, $3.95.
John Brown, Rose, and the Midnight Cat by Jenny Wagner. Illustrated by Ron Brooks. 1978. Puffin, paper, $3.95.
A Picture for Harold's Room by Crockett Johnson. 1960. HarperCollins, $10.89; paper, $3.50.
The Trip by Ezra Jack Keats. 1978. Greenwillow, $12.88; Mulberry, paper, $3.95.

Angus Lost
(Ages 3–8)
Producers: John Sturner and Gary Templeton for Evergreen.
Director: Gary Templeton.
Phoenix Films & Video, $150 (11 min.)

Against stirring background music, Angus, a black Scottish terrier, slips through a gate one day, has a few scares, meets some new friends, sleeps out in a forest, and hitches a ride all the way home on a dairy truck. Marjorie Flack's original story (from 1932) is appealingly embellished in this unnarrated dramatization.

CONNECTIONS

Books:
Angus Lost by Marjorie Flack. 1932. Doubleday, $12.95.

Colors and Shapes
(Ages 3–6)
Producer: Advanced American Communications. Coronet/MTI Film & Video, $250; rental, $75 (18 min.)

The live-action coverage of a day in the life of a five-year-old introduces concepts of shape and color. Sam helps carry in groceries and notes the shapes of common items. He points out to his mom the circles and triangles on his lunch plate and the rectangles on a neighborhood fence spotted as he walks to school. A similar video based on a book by Hoban is *Over, Under, and Through.*

CONNECTIONS

Books:
Circles, Triangles and Squares by Tana Hoban. 1974. Macmillan, $12.95.
Of Colors and Things by Tana Hoban. 1989. Greenwillow, $12.95.
Over, Under, and Through by Tana Hoban. 1973. Macmillan, $12.95; Aladdin, paper, $3.95.

Corduroy and Other Bear Stories

(Ages 3–7)

Children's Circle, $19.95 (35 min.)

The teddy bear Corduroy hops down from the toy department shelf in search of a new button for his green overalls. He is off on a series of wonderful adventures in the darkened department store—from a wild ride on a toy train, to a camping display, to the bedding department—with a suspicious security guard in pursuit. Eventually a young shopper provides the caring that Corduroy craves when she spots him and takes him home to lovingly sew on a new button. This beautifully realized dramatization warmly expands on Don Freeman's story. In *A Pocket for Corduroy* (Phoenix/BFA Films & Video), the little bear takes another journey, this time in search of a pocket.

Also on this tape is "Blueberries for Sal," the story of a little girl and a bear cub who lose their moms. Finally, in "Panama," a bear and a tiger pursue a quest for the perfect home. This tape is one of the many fine compilations of favorite picture book adaptations from Children's Circle.

∞ CONNECTIONS

Books:

Blueberries for Sal by Robert McCloskey. 1948. Viking, $13.95; Puffin, paper, $3.95.
Corduroy by Don Freeman. 1968. Viking, $13.95; Puffin, paper, $3.95.
The Trip to Panama by Janosch. 1978. Little, Brown, o.p.

Dr. DeSoto and Other Stories

(Ages 4–8)

Children's Circle, $19.95 (35 min.)

Whimsical animation and a wryly clipped narration, graced by delightful music, tell of the ingenious mouse dentist and his able wife assistant who successfully cure a wily fox's toothache. Although the carnivorous patient's thoughts begin to turn from dental distress to a tasty tidbit of mouse, the ingenious rodent manages to save both his practice and his own skin through an innovative treatment. This marvelous video, based on William Steig's book, heads a quartet of other adaptations of tales of fanciful derring-do. In "Curious George Rides a Bike," the impish monkey tries out a paper route and a circus act. "The Hat" brings fortune to an old soldier. "Patrick" is a wordless tale that demonstrates how all of nature is buoyed by beautiful music.

Awards: Academy Award

∞ CONNECTIONS

Books:

Doctor Desoto by William Steig. 1982. Farrar, Straus & Giroux, $13.95; paper, $4.95.
Curious George Rides a Bike by H. A. Rey. 1952. Houghton Mifflin, $12.95; paper, $3.95.
The Hat by Tomi Ungerer. 1970. Four Winds, o.p.
Patrick by Quentin Blake. 1969. Jonathan Cape, o.p.

The Dr. Seuss Video Festival
Horton Hears a Who and How the Grinch Stole Christmas

(Ages 3–8)

Producers: Chuck Jones and Theodor Geisel.
Director: Chuck Jones.
MGM/UA, $19.95 (60 min.)

Modern classics coproduced by the late Dr. Seuss himself (Theodor Geisel) and directed by renowned Hollywood animator Chuck Jones. When Horton the elephant spots a speck on a flower, he is addressed by the mayor of Whoville. All the Whos down in Whoville, no matter how small, have reason to be grateful to Horton and his belief that "a person's a person, no matter how small." Horton defends the Whos and himself against the taunts and threats of his neighbors, who deem him to be one crazy elephant. The opposite of the caring Horton is the Grinch, a creature whose heart is "two sizes too small." Narrated by Boris Karloff, this holiday classic beautifully celebrates the spirit of Christmas.

∞CONNECTIONS

Books:
Horton Hears a Who by Dr. Seuss. 1954. Random House, $9.95.
How the Grinch Stole Christmas by Dr. Seuss. 1957. Random House, $6.95.

The Emperor's New Clothes
(Ages 4–9)
Rabbit Ears Storybook Classics.
Director: Robert Van Nutt.
SVS/Triumph, $14.95 (30 min.)

Regal music and richly colored illustrations are used to depict the elegant formality of court life, setting the scene for the conceited ruler who falls under the sway of two dishonest weavers. They promise finery of such magnificence that it will remain unseen by the unworthy. John Gielgud's precise narration underscores the mounting trickery as the courtiers go along with the scheme to save their own positions. While the weavers run off with their booty, the emperor parades before

his subjects in naked pomposity. Sly wit and skillful animation convey the fable's timeless message of self-deception. (Closed captioned)

Fancy That
(See Top Ten Music Videos, p. 224.)

Frog and Toad Are Friends
Frog and Toad Together
(See Swamp Stars, p. 156.)

Frog Goes to Dinner
(See Swamp Stars, p. 157.)

Goggles
(Ages 4–8)
Coronet/MTI Film & Video, $250; rental, $75 (12 min.)

In this live-action dramatization, young actors relive the events of Ezra Jack Keats's Caldecott Honor Book starring Peter, his dog Willie, and his friend Archie. They outrun and outfox some bigger boys who try to claim a pair of goggles Peter has found. The chase scene, through a realistic inner-city setting, is accented by panpipe music. More stories by Keats and starring Peter are available in animated versions from Children's Circle.

∞CONNECTIONS

Books:
Goggles by Ezra Jack Keats. 1969. Aladdin, paper, $4.50.

The Happy Lion
(Ages 4–8)
Weston Woods, $100; rental, $20 (8 min.)

A genial lion residing in a French zoo is happy to greet the daily visitors who walk by the zoo

SWAMP STARS

Frog and Toad Are Friends / Frog and Toad Together   (Ages 3–8)   Director: John Matthews.
Producer: Churchill Media, $295 each; rental, $60 (18 min. each)

The everyday delights of friendship leap from the nine tales in these two videos. John Matthews's
incredible puppets are genuine re-creations of the characters from Arnold Lobel's popular books.
The simple dialogue comes straight from Lobel as well, while the setting is a perfectly constructed
realization of the illustrations. Kids will love visiting Toad's immaculate house, the river, and
woods.
Awards: Notable Children's Film 1987; Notable Children's Film 1989

∞CONNECTIONS

Books:
Frog and Toad Are Friends by Arnold Lobel. 1970. HarperCollins, $10.95; paper, $3.50.
Frog and Toad Together by Arnold Lobel. 1972. HarperCollins, $10.95; paper, $3.50.

Frog Goes to Dinner   (Ages 3–Adult)   Producers: Susan Osborn and Gary Templeton. Director: Gary Templeton.   Phoenix/BFA Films, $190 (12 min.)

A hilarious video about the mayhem that erupts when a pet bullfrog leaps out of his young owner's coat pocket at a fancy restaurant. Hopping from salad to soufflé to the chef's cutting board, the frog creates delightful havoc among the staff and customers. Viewers will savor the slapstick of the wonderfully improbable dining escapades. Two other froggy tales by Mercer Mayer, *A Boy, a Dog, and a Frog* and *Frog on His Own*—a Notable Children's Film for 1990—have also been made into live-action videos by Phoenix Films.

∞CONNECTIONS

Books:
Frog Goes to Dinner by Mercer Mayer. 1974. Dial, $8.95; paper, $2.95.
A Boy, a Dog, and a Frog by Mercer Mayer. 1967. Dial, $9.95; paper, $2.95.
Frog on His Own by Mercer Mayer. 1973. Dial, $9.95; paper, $2.95.

The Story of the Dancing Frog   (Ages 5–9)   Director: Michael Sporn. F.H.E.; dist. by Live Home Video, $14.95 (30 min.)   Lucerne Media, $295

The story of a frog who could outdance Gene Kelly (or at least keep up with him). The elegant, limber amphibian, named George, is found by a lovely lady who acts as his manager and brings his talents to the world in this charming animated film. (Closed captioned)

∞CONNECTIONS

Books:
The Story of the Dancing Frog by Quentin Blake. 1985. Knopf, $9.99; McKay, paper, $4.95.

and wish him "bonjour." However, when the lion takes a stroll through town after his cage door is left ajar, his friends become frightened. Panic ensues until a small boy fearlessly leads the lion back home. The cutout animation retains the charm and warm colors of the original story, now almost 40 years old.

CONNECTIONS

Books:
The Happy Lion by Louise Fatio.
Illustrated by Roger Duvoisin. 1954.
Scholastic, paper, $3.95.

Hey, What About Me?
(Ages 2–6)
KIDVIDZ, $14.95 (pub. perf., $34.90, including fifty activity guides and one leader's guide) (30 min.)

A baby brother or sister can be a real thrill or a genuine pain to an older sibling. The advice here on care and coping comes straight from the mouths of siblings three and up. They are seen in action and demonstrate how to feed a baby, hug one, and elicit smiles. They also share their anger and ways of releasing it. A nice film for parents and kids to share and a good one to have on hand when children are feeling left out.

In Search of the Wow Wow Wibble Woggle Wozzie Woodle Woo
(See Top Ten Music Videos, p. 224.)

Joe's First Video
(See Top Ten Music Videos, p. 225.)

King Bidgood's in the Bathtub
(Ages 3–7)
Director: Sara Kurtz.
Producer: Random House/Miller-Brody.
SRA Group, $37 (7 min.)

King Bidgood passes all his time in the tub. From there he wages war, dines, fishes, and even dances. He insists that his courtiers join him, until an exhausted page pulls the plug. This outstanding video features the lushly regal illustrations of Audrey and Don Wood's original picture book and carries off the whole narration in song. A delightful taste of operetta for a very young audience.

CONNECTIONS

Books:
King Bidgood's in the Bathtub by Audrey Wood. Illustrated by Don Wood. 1985. HBJ, $14.95.

Koko's Kitten
(Ages 4–10)
Producers: The Gorilla Foundation.
Churchill Media, $325; rental, $60 (17 min.)

After Koko the gorilla learned to communicate in sign language with her mentor, scientist Francine ("Penny") Patterson, the great ape indicated her desire for a pet. Wonderful sequences of Koko cuddling and playing with her new kitten are contrasted with the ape's distress when her pet was lost. This remarkable video documents a true and charming story of the rapport possible between animals of different species.

CONNECTIONS

Books:
Koko's Kitten by Francine Patterson.
1985. Scholastic, $9.95; paper, $3.95.

Let's Be Friends
(See Top Ten Music Videos, p. 224.)

Lyle, Lyle, Crocodile

(Ages 4–8)

Producer and Director: Michael Sporn.
Video Treasures, $9.99 (25 min.)
Ambrose Video Publishing (pub. perf., $69.95) (25 min.)

Although they hadn't expected to find a crocodile residing in their new apartment, the Primms happily come to appreciate genial Lyle's helpful and friendly participation in their household. When the former tenant, who was Lyle's original owner, comes to reclaim the reptile, the Primms discover just how much a part of the family the croc has become. This rousing animated musical production, adapted from Bernard Waber's book, overflows with energy and humor. The original musical score is by Charles Strouse, composer of *Annie* and other hit Broadway shows.

✑CONNECTIONS

Books:
House on East Eighty-eighth Street by Bernard Waber. 1973. Houghton Mifflin, $13.95; Sandpiper, paper, $4.95.

Madeline's Rescue

(Ages 4–8)

Children's Circle, $19.95 (23 min.)

Madeline is the impish red-haired girl created by Ludwig Bemelmans in his wonderful rhyming books. The three tales on this to-be-treasured tape will introduce younger children to Madeline, who is rarely found in her assigned "straight line" with the other young Parisian schoolgirls under the care of Miss Clavell. In the first, Madeline is rescued by Genevieve, a dog who is welcomed by Madeline's classmates but cannot stay. The next two tales depict the mischief Madeline contrives with help of the girls' bored neighbor, the son of the Spanish ambassador.

A video version of the original story, *Madeline* (Video Treasures), narrated by Christopher Plummer, is a perfect tape for a child facing minor hospitalization. Madeline fearlessly faces an appendectomy, and the questions posed by her peers (is it in her arm? her head?) speak directly to children's concerns.

✑CONNECTIONS

Books:
Madeline by Ludwig Bemelmans. 1958. Viking, $13.95; Puffin, paper, $3.95.
Madeline and the Bad Hat. 1957. Viking, $13.95; Puffin, paper, $3.95.
Madeline and the Gypsies. 1959. Viking, $13.95; Puffin, paper, $3.95.
Madeline's Rescue. 1953. Viking, $13.95; Puffin, paper, $3.95.
Toys:
(See the Madeline doll in Toys.)

Marc Brown Does Hand Rhymes

(Ages 3–5)

SRA Group, $62 (23 min.)

Marc Brown Does Play Rhymes

(Ages 3–5)

SRA Group, $51 (14 min.)
(Both videos, $97)

Author Marc Brown teaches timeless, humorous rhymes to an appreciative audience. His books, on which these videos are based, feature a boxed hand symbol for every gesture that accompanies a word or phrase. The Hand Rhymes video uses the charming illustrations from the book, then steps beyond that one-dimensional technique into scenes of Brown working and playing with a classroom full of children. Chipper music enlivens these lessons in rhythm, reading, and phonics. *Play Rhymes* is an equally enjoyable interactive video. Both videos can be purchased as a set. An unforgettable journey to the author's home and studio is found in *Meet Marc Brown* (SRA Group).

CONNECTIONS

Books:
Hand Rhymes. 1985. Dutton, $12.95.
Play Rhymes. 1985. Dutton, $10.95.
(See also *Party Rhymes* in Books.)

The Maurice Sendak Library
(Ages 3–Adult)
Children's Circle, $19.95 (35 min.)

This treasury contains wonderful adaptations of Sendak classics (some of which are Caldecott winners), sure to beguile parents and children. They include "Where the Wild Things Are," "In the Night Kitchen," and four stories from the Nutshell Library (see Connections below). Carole King, who composed the music for the tapes of the Nutshell Library, dynamically narrates and sings these stories, which also appeared on the video *Really Rosie*. She tells the plight of the exasperating Pierre who would only say, "I don't care," until a lion states, "I'll eat you if I may." Pierre learns his lesson well. Kids will learn to count forward and backward, recite the alphabet, and chant the months of the year with the other three Sendak/King collaborations.

Here too are the rambunctious wild things and the diaperless baby in the night kitchen,

sent on a mission to secure baking ingredients. A fine interview with Sendak caps the offerings. Besides telling of his own childhood (and the gargoylelike relations that inspired his wild things), Sendak talks about writing and choosing good books for kids. "A child isn't polite. . . . They don't care if a book's won 18 Caldecott awards. If they hate the first two pages . . . Zwammo—they throw it against the wall. You have to catch them." He does, on video as well as in print.

CONNECTIONS

Books:
Alligators All Around.
Chicken Soup with Rice: A Book of Months.
One Was Johnny: A Counting Book.
Pierre: A Cautionary Tale.
Above titles are available as a set in *The Nutshell Library.* 1962. HarperCollins, $11.89.
In the Night Kitchen. 1970. HarperCollins, $14.95; paper, $4.95.
Where the Wild Things Are. 1962. HarperCollins, $12.95; paper, $4.95.

Morris Goes to School
(Ages 4–8)
Director: John Matthews.
Churchill Media, $305; all rental, $60 (15 min.)

Morris the Moose wants to learn how to read and count, so he goes to school, much to the delight of his young classmates. Clever puppet figures and show-stopping songs follow the antlered student through his first scholastic experiences. Amid all the fun of slapstick comedy and a pun-filled script, this amusing musical acquaints young viewers with the routines and procedures of the elementary classroom and instills a vital message about the value of learning.

CONNECTIONS

Books:
Morris Goes to School by Bernard Wiseman. 1970. HarperCollins, $10.89; paper, $3.50.

The Mysterious Tadpole and Other Stories
(Ages 4–7)
Children's Circle, $19.95 (34 min.)

Every year Louis receives an unusual birthday present from his Uncle McAllister, who loves to explore the dales and lochs of Scotland. The tadpole that arrives this year seems to be just perfect for the small apartment Louis shares with his parents, but the gift soon outgrows the bathtub and shows no sign of stopping. Louis and his friend the librarian dream up an ingenious, daring plan to create the perfect home for the beloved, mysterious creature. Accompanying the title story are three more favorites. Drawn from the Bible, "Jonah and the Great Fish" is full of drama and suspense. Equally exciting is the fable "The Five Chinese Brothers," which shows how these siblings use their remarkable gifts to save one another. A mouse who aspires to a more formidable appearance visits a disorganized sorcerer in "The Wizard," and both learn valuable lessons.

CONNECTIONS

Books:
The Mysterious Tadpole by Steven Kellogg. 1977. Dial, $13.95; paper, $3.95.

The Five Chinese Brothers by Claire Bishop. Illustrated by Kurt Weise. 1938. Coward-McCann, $7.95; paper, $5.95.
Jonah and the Great Fish retold and illustrated by Warwick Hutton. 1984. McElderry, $13.95.
The Wizard by Jack Kent. Four Winds, paper, $5.95.

Noah's Ark
(Ages 3–8)
Stories to Remember series.
Producer: Joshua M. Greene.
Lightyear Entertainment, $14.95 (pub. perf., $64.95) (30 min.)

Peter Spier's wordless picture book of the biblical story is narrated by James Earl Jones, whose voice adds resonance to this elegant adaptation. The story of God's message to Noah unfolds through the animation of Spier's intricate paintings, rich in humorous detail. Poignant asides underscore the enormous task facing Noah, who constructs the ark, gathers and tends the pairs of beasts, endures the tedium of the long journey, and rejoices upon the boat's abrupt arrival on land. Stewart Copeland lends an expressive musical score. (Closed captioned)

CONNECTIONS

Books:
Noah's Ark by Peter Spier. 1977. Doubleday, $12.95; paper, $5.95.
Audio:
Noah's Ark narrated by James Earl Jones. Lightyear Records; dist. by BMG, $8.95.

CINDERELLA

Familiar folk tales appear again and again in different versions. For example, the following five videos bear a resemblance to the Cinderella story, yet each reflects an era, culture, and style different from the slickly animated, romantic Disney version. Here's proof that fairy tales are not just for the very young, but for all ages. Look for other fairy tales in video and book form that have a range of interpretations, such as "Beauty and the Beast."

Ashpet: An American Cinderella   (Ages 12–Adult)   Producers: Tom and Mimi Davenport. Director: Tom Davenport.   Davenport Films, $110; rental, $25 (45 min.)

Ashpet lives on a farm in Virginia and longs to attend a farewell dance for the soldiers departing to fight in World War II. Her wish is thwarted by her vain stepsister Thelma. A housekeeper acts as Ashpet's fairy godmother by providing a lovely gown and a horse to carry her to the ball. When Ashpet loses a beaded slipper as she departs, the good-looking soldier who was her dance partner fulfills the role of the handsome prince. A charming, live-action fairy tale performed in period attire.

Cinderella   (Ages 4–Adult)   Faerie Tale Theatre series.   Producer: Platypus Productions.   Director: Mark Cullingham.   Playhouse Video, div. of CBS/Fox, $14.95.

Jennifer Beals and Matthew Broderick star as Cinderella and the handsome prince, but Jean Stapleton steals the show as the droll fairy godmother with a Southern accent. Just one of the delightful Faerie Tale Theatre presentations masterminded by executive producer Shelley Duvall, this video brings contemporary wit and dynamite acting to the old legend. A romantic comedy for family viewing.

Mufaro's Beautiful Daughters   (Ages 4–8)   Directed by David R. Paight.   Weston Woods, $120; rental, $25 (14 min.)

Mufaro's daughters, Manyara and Nyasha, are summoned before the king so that he may choose a wife. The scheming, selfish Manyara plots to appear first at the palace while her gentle, loving sister takes time on the journey to care for hungry and elderly passers-by. Manyara's haste is her undoing. With an original score by Ernest Troost, this animated film uses Steptoe's original lush color drawings to evoke the African setting and emotional mood.

⌾⊃ CONNECTIONS

<u>Books:</u>
Mufaro's Beautiful Daughters: An African Tale by John Steptoe. 1987.
Lothrop, $13.95.

The Talking Eggs   (Ages 8–Adult)   Director: Rosemary Killen. SRA Group, $37 (21 min.)

Cajun music by Arthur Custer frames the tale of sweet Blanche, sorely tried by her malicious sister and taskmaster mother. No prince awaits. Instead a friendly witch grants Blanche a journey to a remarkable land of talking eggs and other treasures.

⌾⊃ CONNECTIONS

<u>Books:</u>
The Talking Eggs retold by Robert D. San Souci. Illustrated by Jerry Pinkney. 1989. Dial,
$12.95.
<u>Audio:</u>
Cassette and book available from SRA Group, $25.

The Tender Tale of Cinderella Penguin and Other Stories   (Ages 5–Adult)   Producer: The
National Film Board of Canada.   Smarty Pants Video, $14.98 (30 min.)

Cinderella has lost her flipper-slipper. Will the Prince be able to fit the mysterious apparel to the webbed foot from which it was lost? This animated spoof will delight young viewers and set them up for more fun in the four short films that follow: *The Sky's Blue, Mr. Frog Went A Courting, Metamorphoses,* and *The Owl and the Raven.* Originally created by the renowned Film Board of Canada, these films have been adapted for the home video market by Smarty Pants Video. Similar high-quality collections are available from this team.

Owl Moon and Other Stories

(Ages 3–7)

Children's Circle, $19.95 (35 min.)

Jane Yolen narrates her own book, *Owl Moon*, which tells of a father and daughter who walk the woods at night in search of a great horned owl. Colors capture the moods of the chill darkness outdoors and the warmth of parent and child. Other tales of exploration and animal life on this tape are "Hot Hippo," which explores the animal's plight as he tries to live in and out of the water, and "The Caterpillar and the Polliwog" and "Time of Wonder."

CONNECTIONS

Books:
The Caterpillar and the Polliwog by Jack Kent. 1982. Simon & Schuster, $12.95; paper, $5.95.
Hot Hippo by Mwenyee Hadithi. Illustrated by Adrienne Kennaway. 1986. Little, Brown, $12.95.
Owl Moon by Jane Yolen. Illustrated by John Schoenherr. 1987. Philomel, $13.95.
Time of Wonder by Robert McCloskey. 1957. Viking, $15.95; Puffin, paper, $4.95.

Paul Bunyan

(Ages 4–9)

Rabbit Ears Storybook Classics.
Director: Tim Raglin.
SVS/Triumph, $14.95 (30 min.)

Behind robustly exaggerated illustrations, the twanging narration of comic Jonathan Winters relates the larger-than-life exploits of the mythical lumberjack, his gigantic blue ox, and his gang of loggers. Devising a jumbo pancake griddle, straightening a logging road, or clear-

ing (and later reseeding) the Dakotas in record time are some of the Bunyanesque feats related with wide-eyed, tongue-in-cheek enthusiasm. Meanwhile, the camera finds some funny detail in each deed, and guitar music drives the spirited first-person retelling. If you enjoy this one, keep an eye out for *Pecos Bill*, also from Rabbit Ears.

The Pigs' Wedding and Other Stories

(Ages 3–Adult)

Children's Circle, $19.95 (39 min.)

Those invited to the wedding of Porker and Curlytail smell like pigs, which is what they are. The bride and groom solve this crisis by hosing down all their porcine guests, then painting delightful outfits that literally suit the nature of each excited squealer. The video's charming musical score is augmented by animal sounds and fun lyrics. This collection of nature tales with a twist includes "The Selkie Girl," which tells of the marriage of a sea maiden to a land-bound man and "The Happy Owls," in which two contented birds share their secrets with barnyard friends. Also on this tape are "A Letter to Amy" and "The Owl and the Pussycat" (the latter is also on the *Happy Birthday Moon and Other Stories* video, see p. 150).

CONNECTIONS

Books:
The Happy Owls by Celestino Piatti. o.p.
A Letter to Amy by Ezra Jack Keats. 1968. HarperCollins, $13.95; paper, $4.95.
The Owl and the Pussycat by Edward Lear. Illustrated by Barbara Cooney. o.p. (Jan Brett's version is in Books.)

The Pigs' Wedding by Helme Heine.
1979. McElderry, $12.95; Aladdin,
paper, $4.95.
The Selkie Girl by Susan Cooper.
Illustrated by Warwick Hutton. 1986.
McElderry, $13.95; Aladdin, paper,
$4.95.

Preschool Power!
(Ages 2–6)
Producer: Jacket Flips and Other Tips.
Concept Associates, $19.95 (30 min.)

Young children learn to manage new tasks by
themselves in this motivational video. In playful vignettes, fresh-faced kids demonstrate
how to put on a jacket, button a sweater, care
for a pet, make a simple snack, clean up spills,
and do other tasks. Catchy lyrics and melodies
break down each job into manageable steps,
promote pride in new skills, and encourage
preschoolers to greater heights of self-reliance.
This is a boon to both children and their
parents. There's a terrific sequel, *More Preschool Power!* (Jacket Flips).

Red Riding Hood and Goldilocks
(Ages 4–8)
Rabbit Ears Storybook Classics.
Director: Tim Raglin.
SVS/Triumph, $14.95 (30 min.)

Tongue-in-cheek retellings update two classic
stories in this appealing video duo, illustrated
with softly colored, naturalistic drawings and
expressively related by Meg Ryan. The ever-
so-virtuous Red Riding Hood strays from the
proper path in the woods, only to discover the
silver-coated, French-accented wolf, who later
"lifted the latch, lapped her up, and licked his
lips." It is the comforts of the upper-crust
lifestyle that do in the unendurably spoiled

Goldilocks, who just can't manage the rustic
housekeeping of the three bears. These tales
are memorable for the sass of Ryan's narration
and snap of contemporary humor.

The Robert McCloskey Library
(Ages 3–8)
Children's Circle, $19.95 (60 min.)

This single video features five of Robert
McCloskey's great stories and an interview
with the award-winning author. The tale of the
harmonica-player "Lentil" is here, along with
the classic "Make Way for Ducklings," featuring mom and dad ducks and their ducklings
waddling through downtown Boston. In
"Blueberries for Sal," a mother bear and
human mother find their offspring mixed up
on a fruit-picking expedition. "Burt Dow:
Deep Water Man" features an old sailor in a
rainbow-colored boat tending to a whale with
a sore tail. These animated adaptations carry
the lure of the original yarns. Sources for these
stories are revealed by the author in the closing interview.

ᏭᎧCONNECTIONS

Books:
Blueberries for Sal by Robert
McCloskey. 1948. Viking, $13.95;
Puffin, paper, $3.95.
Burt Dow: Deep Water Man by Robert
McCloskey. 1963. Viking, $15.95.
Lentil by Robert McCloskey. 1940.
Viking, $14.95.
Make Way for Ducklings by Robert
McCloskey. 1941. Viking, $12.95;
Puffin, paper, $3.95.
Time of Wonder by Robert McCloskey.
1957. Viking, $15.95; Puffin, paper,
$4.95.

The Sand Castle and Other Stories
(Ages 4–Adult)

Producer: The National Film Board of Canada.
Director: Co Hoedman.
Smarty Pants, $14.98 (30 min.)

Shifting sands reveal a genuine sand man, one more interested in creation than slumber. The large-limbed creature works in the dunes to create other equally fanciful sand critters, then inspires all of them to work together on a large castle. Music and sound effects reveal playful, diverse personalities, while a threatening sandstorm brings a note of sadness to critters and viewers alike. This Academy Award winner is presented with three other videos: a colorful version of Aesop's fable "The North Wind and the Sun," an amusing puppet presentation of the Eskimo legend "The Owl and the Lemming," and a splendid tour of the alphabet using only letters, drawings, and music. The rapidly changing shapes drawn for each letter will challenge children to create their own narration.

Awards: Academy Award, Best Animated Short Film, 1977 (*The Sand Castle*)

Sesame Street Home Video Visits the Firehouse
Sesame Street Home Video Visits the Hospital
(Ages 3–6)

Producer: Children's Television Workshop.
Random House Home Video, $14.95 each (30–34 min.)

Youngsters can join the Sesame Street gang to learn what happens when the firebell rings or someone has to go to the hospital. Information about the jobs of firefighters, both in the firehouse and at the scene of a blaze, incorporate basic fire-safety principles. When a visit to the emergency room extends to a short stay in the hospital, Big Bird's concerns and questions help demystify various hospital procedures and personnel. Instructive and reassuring, these titles reinforce concepts with song and address children's mixed feelings about new experiences. (Closed captioned)

Sleep Over
(See Top Ten Music Videos, p. 225.)

The Snowman
(Ages 4–Adult)

Producer: John Coates.
Director: Dianne Jackson.
Children's Circle, $14.95 (30 min.)

When a snowman comes to life, he returns a young boy's hospitality by taking him flying. Over the wintry landscape and across icy continents and seas they travel to a festive party of snowmen at the North Pole. Here, the lad meets Santa Claus. This fanciful, almost wordless tale has achieved the status of a holiday classic for its dazzling animation of pastel drawings and lush musical score. An artful recounting of a never-to-be-forgotten adventure.

Awards: Notable Children's Film 1990

✐CONNECTIONS

Books:
The Snowman by Raymond Briggs. 1978. Random House, $12.95; paper, $4.95; miniature edition, $4.95.
Toys:
(See the Snowman doll in Toys.)

Stanley and the Dinosaurs

(Ages 4–8)

Director: John Matthews.
Churchill Media, $325; rental, $60 (15 min.)

Brainy rather than brawny, inventive Stanley is scorned by his prehistoric peers who pursue their own boorish activities while Stanley relies on creative thinking to improve his lot. When Stanley saves the day by building the world's first house to shelter his compatriots from a band of voracious dinosaurs, the others gain new respect for his outlook on life. The underlying message of "working smarter, not harder" is conveyed by whimsical puppet figures, contemporary rap narration, and a bright musical score delivered by harmonizing dinosaurs and a chorus line of cavemen.

Strega Nona and Other Stories

(Ages 3–8)

Children's Circle, $19.95 (30 min.)

Strega Nona is a witch getting on in years who hires some help. Much like Mickey Mouse in Disney's animated "Sorcerer's Apprentice," the assistant steps out of line. This time the result is a house and then a town overflowing with pasta. In the first of the companion stories, "Tikki Tikki Tembo" captures the panicky haste of the young brother seeking to rescue his sibling from a well. "A Story—A Story" tells of Anansi the spider man, who looks to the heavens for more stories to tell. In the midst of these animated adaptations is "The Foolish Frog," a funny moral fable sung by Pete Seeger.

∽ CONNECTIONS

Books:
Strega Nona by Tomie dePaola. 1975. Simon and Schuster, $13.95.

Tikki Tikki Tembo by Arlene Mosel. Illustrated by Blair Lent. 1968. Holt, $14.95; paper, $5.95.
A Story—A Story by Gail E. Haley. 1970. Atheneum, $14.95; Aladdin, paper, $4.95.
Audio:
Birds, Beasts & Bigger Fishes & Foolish Frog by Pete Seeger. 1988. Rounder Records, $12.95.

Uncle Elephant

(Ages 4–8)

Director: John Matthews.
Churchill Media, $365; rental, $60 (26 min.)

Arnie is a nine-year-old elephant whose parents disappear during a boating trip. He is bereft. Old Uncle Elephant arrives to take Arnie home and works hard to cheer up his heartsick nephew. He soon has other animals dancing in the aisles of a train and singing up a storm to bring a smile to the little elephant. Arnie helps out his aging uncle after their day's exertions, and they talk about growing old, feeling sad, and being funny. Lots of serious moments slip into this entertaining elephant musical, leavened with calisthenics, dances, elephant jokes, and a celebratory revue when the parents arrive home safe and sound. Imaginative song and setting frame Matthews's excellent puppetry (seen in *Stanley and the Dinosaurs* and *Ralph S. Mouse*).

∽ CONNECTIONS

Books:
Uncle Elephant by Arnold Lobel. 1981. HarperCollins, $10.95; paper, $3.50.

What's Under My Bed and Other *Creepy Stories*

(Ages 4–7)

Children's Circle, $19.95 (35 min.)

Two kids, Louie and Mary Ann, cannot sleep after a scary bedtime story. They run to their grandfather for solace. The mustachioed gent treats his grandchildren to a version of "when I was a boy" that takes away their fears. Each scary scene, spookily enhanced by Ernest Troot's eerie sounds and background music, turns out to be a shadow or common household noise—the usual sources of nighttime fears. For the audience that loves spooky stories, the rest of the tape presents a ghost in "Georgie" and a courageous small boy who saves his older siblings in "Teeny-Tiny and the Witch Woman." "The Three Robbers" is an old favorite about marauders transformed by a young girl's wishes.

CONNECTIONS

Books:

Georgie by Robert Bright. 1944. Doubleday, $7.95; Scholastic, paper, $1.50.

Teeny-Tiny and the Witch Woman by Barbara Walker. Illustrated by Michael Foreman. 1975. Pantheon, o.p.

The Three Robbers by Tomi Ungerer. 1962. Atheneum, $14.95; Aladdin, paper, $4.95.

What's Under My Bed by James Stevenson. 1983. Greenwillow, $13.95; paper, $3.95.

EARLY GRADERS

Abel's Island

(Ages 6–12)

Producer and Director: Michael Sporn for Italoons Corp.

Random House Home Video, $14.95 (30 min.)

Lucerne Media (pub. perf., $295; rental, $60)

Swept away by a fierce rainstorm is a mouse named Abelard Hassam di Chirico Flint. A high-society creature, he is unaccustomed to fending for himself. Now, stranded on an island, he must do just that while striving to rejoin his beloved wife, Amanda. More than survival skills are developed, as the mouse begins to sculpt life-sized statues of his dear friends. Superb animation brings out the mauves and grays of William Steig's original illustrations, opening up this story from Steig's chapter-by-chapter text to a younger audience. (Closed captioned)

Awards: Notable Children's Film 1989

∽CONNECTIONS

Books:
Abel's Island by William Steig. 1976. Farrar, Straus & Giroux, paper, $3.50.

Alexander, Who Used to Be Rich Last Sunday
(Ages 5–9)

Producer: Bernard Wilets Productions.
Director: Dianne Haak.
AIMS Media, $295; rental, $50 (14 min.)

Alexander has great plans for the five-dollar gift from his grandparents, but by week's end he doesn't have much to show for it. A fine paid to his parents for unacceptable language and the hourly rental fee for a friend's snake are among the expenditures Alexander painfully incurs. On the other side of the ledger, he tries to raise cash for coveted walkie-talkies with a series of unsuccessful schemes. Humorously and sympathetically conveying the perils of risky financial management, this is a wonderfully acted adaptation of Judith Viorst's sequel to *Alexander and the Terrible, Horrible, No Good, Very Bad Day* (also available in video from AIMS).

Awards: Notable Children's Film 1991

∽CONNECTIONS

Books:
Alexander and the Terrible, Horrible, No Good, Very Bad Day by Judith Viorst. Illustrated by Ray Cruz. 1972.

Atheneum, $12.95; Aladdin, paper, $3.95.
Alexander, Who Used to Be Rich Last Sunday by Judith Viorst. Illustrated by Ray Cruz. 1978. Macmillan, $13.95; paper, $3.95.

Anansi
(Ages 5–10)

We All Have Tales series.
Rabbit Ears; dist. by UNI, $9.95 (pub. perf.) (30 min.)

Anansi, the amusing, mischief-seeking spider from traditional African folklore, is transplanted into a dazzling tropical world via Steve Guarnaccia's visuals. In the sugarcane fields of Jamaica, this Brer Rabbit of the insect world, adorned with a beard, top hat, and shades, outwits a snake by playing on his vanity. This scenario and further adventures are narrated by Denzel Washington, whose accent suits the tempo of the background reggae music of UB40.

Bach and Broccoli
(Ages 7–10)

Directors: Mahee Paiement and Raymond Legault.
Producer: Rock Demers.
Live Home Video, $14.95 (96 min.)

A middle-aged bachelor with a passion for Bach takes a sabbatical, planning to compete for a place on an international musical tour. Suddenly his ailing mother shows up on his doorstep, asking that he care for his orphaned niece. His solitary life is transformed by the 11-year-old and her pet skunk, Broccoli. This artfully directed joint Canadian/Polish production is dubbed—a fact that parents may note more than kids, who get wrapped up in the antics of the animal-loving girl and her new friends.

Awards: Chicago Film Festival

Beauty and the Beast
(Ages 3–Adult)
Stories to Remember series.
Producer: Joshua M. Greene.
Director: Mordicai Gerstein.
Lightyear Entertainment, $14.95 (pub. perf., $64.95) (26 min.)

Delicate animation brings to life Mordicai Gerstein's picture-book illustrations in this magical interpretation of the beloved fairy tale. Actress Mia Farrow intones the power and caged violence of the beast and the gentle sincerity of the woman he holds captive. Elizabethan melodies play through this enchanting lesson on the recognition and appreciation of genuine beauty. For fairy tale lovers, two more dazzling videos are *The Velveteen Rabbit* and *Thumbelina* (Rabbit Ears Productions, $9.95).

⌘CONNECTIONS

Books:
Beauty and the Beast by Mordicai Gerstein. 1989. Dutton, $12.95.
Audio:
Beauty and the Beast. Lightyear Records; dist. by BMG, $8.95.

Bodytalk
(Ages 5–8)
Producer: Bodytalk Programmes and CTVC.
Encyclopaedia Britannica, $99 each (9 min. each)

How the heart and circulatory system work to keep us healthy; how we taste, smell, and use our other senses; how we grow older—these are among the topics in this series of informative programs. Scenes of families at home and children at school are the backdrop, as two pleasing narrators offer lucid explanations. More complex concepts are made understandable with the help of animation and upbeat music. With its warm and forthright approach, this appealing British series capitalizes on children's curiosity about their bodies.

Awards: Notable Children's Film 1991; American Film and Video Festival Blue Ribbon

Cranberry Bounce
(Ages 5–11)
DeBeck Educational Video, $35 (pub. perf.) (30 min.)

A tour of a family cranberry farm leads into an entire show on the raising, cultivating, and use of this traditional American holiday food. The kids' lively songs and humorous asides add bounce to the video, which is further enhanced by animation, commentary on traditions, scientific details, and recipes. No side dish in this portrayal, the cranberry comes into the spotlight for one upbeat half-hour. (Closed captioned)

Dinosaurs
(Ages 8–Adult)
Will Vinton/Pyramid Films.
Golden Book Video, $9.95 (14 min.)
Pyramid Films (pub. perf., $195; rental, $75)

Claymation artist Will Vinton displays his now-familiar craft in this live-action video about a boy and a science project. As the lad broods about his assignment, the camera takes us straight into the Jurassic period, replete with active clay dinosaurs. A *Tyrannosaurus rex* let loose in an unruly classroom proves to be the highlight of this production.

Divorce Can Happen to the Nicest People
(Ages 5–10)
Producer: Peter Mayle.
Baker and Taylor Video, $19.95 (30 min.)

Concerto Grosso Modo   (Ages 8–Adult)   Producer: Yves Leduc for The National Film Board of Canada.   Distributor: Pyramid Film and Video, $175; rental, $75 (7 min.)

Musical notes are given arms and legs to gad about in a score and help explain musical structure and terms. Their explanation takes the form of a lively, original song that will entice anyone eager to learn more about music.
Awards: Notable Children's Film 1989

Sole Mani   (Ages 6–Adult)   Produced by Roberta Grossman.   Directed by Kyung-Ja Lee. Direct Cinema, $75; rental, $25 (4 min.)

Only a hand performs in this remarkable video. Painted to look like a tuxedo, the hand of conceptual artist Mario Mariotti portrays a temperamental conductor and his orchestra. At times, the digits portray the face or limbs of a single performer or even an entire choir. An amazing short production. (Closed captioned)
Awards: American Film and Video Festival Red Ribbon 1990

One couple's breakup is the central story in this reassuring video that seeks to take away some of the stigma caused by divorce. This production also tackles such abstract concepts as love. Animation, humor, and thoughtful explanations distinguish this video.

An Evening with Rick Charette

(See Top Ten Music Videos, p. 223.)

Every Dog's Guide to Complete Home Safety

(Ages 7–Adult)

Producer: William Pettigrew.
Director: Les Drew.
The National Film Board of Canada, $200; rental, $40 (10 min.)

Boy Scouts and Girl Scouts earning their home-safety merit points will relish this animated feature narrated by Wally, the safety dog. The adults are busy fixing dinner for the boss, so Wally is left in charge. He must keep the baby from the hazards of electrical sockets, a hot iron, open windows, and power tools. Wally is a bit like Roger Rabbit as a babysitter, since all the disasters befall him. An amusing video that stresses the importance of home safety.

Awards: Notable Children's Film 1988

The Fir Tree

(Ages 6–12)

Producer: Kevin Sullivan for Huntingwood Films.
Director: Martin Hunter.
Centre Communications, $395; rental, $50 (28 min.)

In a majestic forest, a small fir tree muses that one day it, too, will reach the stars like the surrounding conifers. Instead this perfectly shaped fir is chosen as a Christmas tree. The period costumes and touching music embel-

lish a beautiful retelling of Hans Christian Andersen's tale. This version has an interesting twist—a young girl carefully plants a seedling from the tree after it is turned into kindling at the end of the holidays.

CONNECTIONS

Books:
The Fir Tree by Hans Christian Andersen. Illustrated by Nancy Eckholm Burkert. 1986. HarperCollins, $13.95; paper, $3.95.

Follow the Drinking Gourd

(Ages 5–9)

SRA Group, $35 (11 min.)

In this story about Peg Leg Joe and the Underground Railroad, artistic camera work animates the bold folk images of Jeanette Winter's original picture book. Arthur Custer's score blends a banjo, guitar, and ocarina, lending just the right notes of optimism, tension, and woe to this portrayal of the fugitive slave experience. (See also *Underground Railroad* in Travel.)

CONNECTIONS

Books:
Follow the Drinking Gourd by Jeanette Winter. 1988. Knopf, $14.95.

Fool and the Flying Ship

(Ages 7–Adult)

We All Have Tales series
Producers: Mark Sottnick and Mike Pogue.
Rabbit Ears; dist. by UNI, $9.95 (30 min.)

Robin Williams affects a wonderful Yiddish accent, rich with colloquial humor, as he relates this tall tale of the simpleton from the shtetl who wins the czar's daughter in marriage. The fool is aided by a band of strangely talented eccentrics gathered during his travels aboard a magical flying ship. This droll production combines the outlandish exploits of colorful characters with the vigorous rhythms of the Klezmer Conservatory Band. A broad comedy for young and old.

Fun in a Box #1: Ben's Dream and Other Stories & Fun

(Ages 6–12)

Producers: Dirk Wales and David Angsten.
Director: Diane Kenna.
Made to Order Productions, $14.95 (30 min.)

While studying geography, Ben dozes off and dreams that his house has set out to sea. He drifts past such international landmarks—Big Ben, The Great Wall of China—as he has been studying in his textbook. Finally, he is awakened by the words, "Ben, wake up," being uttered by Mount Rushmore (but really being called at the window by his friend). Added to the fun is a howlingly funny rendition of the Fats Waller song, "Your Feets Too Big," and a none-too-serious private detective tale, "Fish."

CONNECTIONS

Books:
Ben's Dream by Chris Van Allsburg. 1982. Houghton Mifflin, $14.95.

Fun in a Box #3: The Birthday Movie

(Ages 6–Adult)

Made to Order Productions, $14.95 (30 min.)

This sprightly celebration of birthday lore and festivities entertains and informs. With fun and games come engaging facts about birthday customs—gathering friends, getting spanked, baking cakes, breaking piñatas. These doings

and more are woven into a birthday contest that challenges viewers. Meanwhile magic tricks, sound puzzles, and optical illusions provide other ways of participating in the revelry.

Harry Comes Home

(Ages 4–Adult)

Producer: Pete Matuvalich.
Barr Films, $420; rental, $50 (25 min.)

Adopted from the dog pound by a family willing to overlook his delinquent background, Harry, an appealing black-and-white border collie, finds a loving home with the Dobsons. But Harry's untamed nature and the taunts of the spoiled cat next door lead Harry into trouble (at a boot-camp-like obedience school) and eventually into total disgrace. This marvelous dramatization features stellar performances by both animal and human actors and leads viewers along on a hilarious slapstick romp. Harry eventually saves the day, the bullying feline, and his reputation. This original video is a sequel to the equally funny videos *Harry, the Dirty Dog* and *Harry and the Lady Next Door.*

Awards: Andrew Carnegie Medal 1991; Notable Children's Film 1990

CONNECTIONS

Books:
Harry the Dirty Dog by Gene Zion. Illustrated by Margaret Bloy Graham. 1956. HarperCollins, $12.95; paper, $3.95.
Harry and the Lady Next Door by Gene Zion. Illustrated by Margaret Bloy Graham. 1960. HarperCollins, $11.95; paper, $3.50.

The Hoboken Chicken Emergency

(Ages 6–12)

WonderWorks series.
Producer: Martin Tahse.
Director: Peter Baldwin.
Public Media Video, $29.95 (55 min.)

Henrietta, a six-foot, 266-pound chicken, is the creation of a mad scientist. She sets off the Hoboken Chicken Emergency when she escapes from Arthur Bobwicz. Arthur had purchased the enormous fowl (in lieu of a turkey) for Thanksgiving dinner, then tried to keep her as a family pet. This King Kong of the hen house tickles young viewers. The great costuming and fine acting will keep parents entertained as well.

∽ CONNECTIONS

Books:
The Hoboken Chicken Emergency by Daniel Manus Pinkwater. 1977. Simon & Schuster, $10.95; paper, $4.95.

Kickapie Kids in "Jailbirds"

(Ages 7–11)

1991. Video Reader Productions. $24.95 (pub. perf.) (40 min.)

A video comic book—is this the best or worst of both worlds? It's great, really. Balloon-encased dialogue motivates reluctant readers who can't resist following this adventure story about kids who foil a jail escape in a small town. It's rather like the silent films of the old days with a modern twist and plenty of action.

Let's Get a Move On!

(Ages 5–10)

Directors: Karen Tucker and Jane Murphy.
KIDVIDZ, $14.95 (pub. perf., $34.90, includes fifty activity guides and leader's guide) (30 min.)

Offering practical guidelines for coping with a family move, this upbeat video follows the relocation experiences of four kids in various family situations (including military and single-parent households). Rock songs, realistic domestic scenes, and kids' descriptions of their fluctuating emotions address each stage of the move: getting the news, preparing for the big day, living through the event, making new friends, and getting adjusted in the new home. This supportive resource includes helpful tips and offers a lighthearted perspective on this transition.

The Orchestra

(Ages 5–Adult)

Mark Rubin Productions, dist. by Music for Little People, $19.95 (40 min.)

The 1989 ALA Notable recording has been translated into video with splendid results. Peter Ustinov introduces the composer, conductor, and instruments of the orchestra with more than words. His musically accompanied explanations define the nature of the sounds made by each instrument played by the Toronto Philharmonic. Excerpts from some 30 classical pieces are selected to captivate his audience. Look for the original audio version (Music for Little People, $9.98). Also, don't miss Leo McKern's *Bring On the Brass* (see Audio).

Ralph S. Mouse

(Ages 5–9)

Producers: John Matthews and George McQuilken.
Director: Thomas G. Smith.
Churchill Media, $225; all rental, $75 (40 min.)

When he has to leave his home at the Mountain View Lodge, Ralph, the diminutive rodent

WHAT'S COOKING?

Kids Get Cooking   (Ages 6–10)   KIDVIDZ, $14.95 (pub. perf., $34.90, includes 50 activity guides and one leader's guide) (25 min.)

Four kids host this energetic, egg-focused mix of cookery, art, and science information, while a pair of puppets adds animated fun. The audience is bombarded with clever egg lore, ethnic treats and customs, science news, cooking safety tips, and jokes, accompanied by catchy tunes and some serious cooking of an unusual egg dish.

Kids' Kitchen: Volume 1, Cookies   (Ages 6–9)   Producer and director: Auntie Lee's Kitchen. $17.95 (pub. perf., $50) (23 min.)

The basics of cookie baking are presented by gray-haired Auntie Lee. A bit of homey nostalgia precedes the lessons of measuring and stirring for treats such as chocolate brownies, icebox cookies, and drop cookies. The on-screen list of ingredients is duplicated on a printed recipe card available with the video. The video could be a hit at a cookie-baking party for a holiday or birthday.

hero of Beverly Cleary's popular novels, rides to school along with his young human pal Ryan. Peering out from Ryan's shirt during Show and Tell, evading the janitor's state-of-the-art mousetrap, or starring during a visit of a TV news team, Ralph romps through a series of hilarious adventures. Here is an extraordinary melding of puppet figures and live-action dramatization. Winner of the first Andrew Carnegie Medal for Excellence in Children's Video, this witty and accomplished production is a fitting sequel to *The Mouse and the Motorcycle* and *Runaway Ralph* (both available in home video from Strand).

Awards: Andrew Carnegie Medal 1991; Notable Children's Film 1991

∞CONNECTIONS

Books:
The Mouse and the Motorcycle by Beverly Cleary. 1965. Morrow, $12.95; Dell, paper, $3.25.
Ralph S. Mouse by Beverly Cleary. 1982. Morrow, $12.95; Dell, paper, $3.25.
Runaway Ralph by Beverly Cleary. 1970. Morrow, $14.95; Dell, paper, $3.25.

Ramona Stories
(Ages 5–10)
Producer: Atlantis Films with Lancit Media and Revcom Television.
Warner Home Video, $29.95 each (30 min.)
Churchill Media (pub. perf., $59 each)

The Ramona stories appear in a series of ten hilarious dramatizations, with titles such as *Squeakerfoot, The Great Hair Argument,* and *Good Day/Bad Day.* Whether she walks barefoot down the aisle in her aunt's wedding,

discovers she has worn her pajamas to school, or tries her hand at a newly created dinner entree, Ramona has unforgettable experiences that will strike familiar chords with kids. These adaptations bring the misadventures, doubts, and successes of the young heroine to the screen with a fine feeling for Beverly Cleary's popular books starring the irrepressible youngster, her older sister Beezus, and her loving but long-suffering parents. Well cast and directed, these episodes are graced by genuine touches of family misunderstanding, affection, and humor.

Awards: Notable Children's Film 1989

∞CONNECTIONS

Books:
Beezus and Ramona by Beverly Cleary. 1955. Morrow, $13.95; Avon, $3.50.
Ramona the Pest by Beverly Cleary. 1968. Morrow, $12.95; Dell, paper, $3.25.
Ramona Quimby, Age 8 by Beverly Cleary. 1981. Morrow, $13.95; Dell, $3.25.
Ramona: Behind the Scenes of a Television Show by Elaine Scott. (See Books.)

Red Riding Hood and the Well-Fed Wolf
(Ages 8–11)
Churchill Media, $295; rental, $60 (15 min.)

Here is a parody with a point. After Red Riding Hood arrives at Granny's, she directs a nutrition lecture at the disguised wolf, delivers healthy foods, and helps him overcome his craving for meat. This live-action performance is enhanced by food-shaped puppets.

Shari Lewis Presents 101 Things for Kids to Do
(Ages 6–9)
Random House Home Video, $14.95 (60 min.)

More motivating than its print version, this video features Shari Lewis and her puppets—Lamb Chop, Charley Horse, and Hush Puppy—acting out suggestions to ward off boredom. They include magic tricks, brain-teasers, physical challenges, silly scorekeeping methods, and, of course, quick and easy puppetmaking. (Closed captioned)

✐CONNECTIONS

Books:
Shari Lewis Presents 101 Things for Kids to Do by Shari Lewis. Illustrated by Jon Buller. 1987. Random House, paper, $6.95.

Sole Mani
(See Visual Music, p. 171.)

Song and Dance Man
(Ages 5–8)
SRA Group, $41 (9 min.)

Vaudeville comes alive in the attic of Grandpa's house when he finds a dusty bowler and a cane and puts on a dazzling performance for his grandchildren. Stephen Gammell's Caldecott-winning illustrations are beautifully manipulated and Karen Ackerman's story seems even more heartwarming on screen.

✐CONNECTIONS

Books:
Song and Dance Man by Karen Ackerman. Illustrated by Stephen Gammell. 1988. Knopf, $11.95.

Song City U.S.A.
(See Top Ten Music Videos, p. 224.)

Squiggles, Dots, & Lines
(Ages 5–10)
KIDVIDZ, $14.95 (pub. perf., $34.90, includes 50 activity guides and leader's guide) (30 min.)

Ed Emberley shares his artistic skills with an enthusiastic group of kids who advance from the "I can't draw anything" stage to creators of impressive greeting cards, book illustrations, costumes, and party decorations. Six basic squiggles, dots, and lines serve as the building blocks to more complex drawings. Clever ditties with catchy tunes offer background to scenes of inspiring creations. Kids will not be able to resist picking up pencils and paper. Parents can learn a lot, too.

The Story of the Dancing Frog
(See Swamp Stars, p. 157.)

Take Me Out of the Ball Game
(Ages 6–10)
McGee and Me series.
Tyndale House Publishers, $19.95 (30 min.)

The McGee and Me series, starring 11-year-old Nicholas and three-inch-tall McGee, firmly promotes Christian values. Nicholas is a regular kid, except for the red-headed, leprechaun-sized conscience he carries around with him. McGee never tells Nicholas what to do, but he does remind him to look at the Bible and reflect a bit before making any irrevocable decisions. In this story, Nicholas's dad is coaching the all-star Little League team and wants to triumph even more than the kids. He puts all his faith in one star player and loses the sensible father image he wore in previous videos, such as *Do the Bright Thing*. The Christian perspective here is nicely interlaced with a good deal more subtlety than in earlier productions in the series. Books have been written based on each of the nine videos.

CONNECTIONS

Books:
Take Me Out of the Ball Game by Dennis Fertig. Illustrated by William F. McMahon. 1987. Whitman, $10.95.

The Tale of the Wonderful Potato
(Ages 6–Adult)
Producer: Filmsforsyningen.
Director: Anders Sorensen.
Phoenix/PBA Films & Video, $300 (24 min.)

History is ever so engagingly related in this saga of the lowly spud. With clever animation and tongue-in-cheek script, the fortunes of the potato are followed from its origins in the mountains of South America, to the shores of Ireland, to its welcome reception throughout Europe as a nutritious, easily grown food staple . . . and then, to its low times during the devastating potato blight of the mid-1800s. With asides on the vagaries of tastes and customs, this tuberous tidbit blends political, social, and gastronomic history.

The Talking Eggs
(See Cinderella, p. 163.)

The Tenth Good Thing About Barney
(Ages 5–10)
Producer: Bernard Wilets Productions.
Director: Dianne Haak.
AIMS Media, $260; rental, $50 (13 min.)

A young boy is saddened by the death of his cat, Barney. The video perfectly shares his mood by moving from a winsome photograph of the cat to the boy's untouched food and plaintive face at the dinner table. His mother suggests that her son think of ten good things about Barney to recite at the funeral they have planned for the morning. In this way, the boy's grief is given voice, and Barney is given new life in his memory.

CONNECTIONS

Books:
The Tenth Good Thing About Barney by Judith Viorst. Illustrated by Eric Blegvad. 1971. Atheneum, $12.95; Aladdin, paper, $3.95.

Tommy Tricker and the Stamp Travelers
(Ages 7–Adult)
FHE; dist. by Live Home Video, $12.98 (101 min.)

Can a boy actually shrink to the size of a postage stamp and travel on envelopes around the world from Canada to China, Australia, and England? It happens in this exciting adventure film. Along the way he encounters some terrifying moments and wonderful new acquaintances. The mystery, adventure scenes, and introductions to kids in foreign countries will sustain kids' interest in this feature-length movie.

Where Do You Think You're Going, Christopher Columbus?
(Ages 8–12)
Director: Chris King.
Producers: Paul Gagne and Chris King.
Weston Woods, $60 (pub. perf.) (35 min.)

Jean Fritz reads her version of Columbus's journeys in this video. New artwork by Margo Tomes blends well with the russet-toned illustrations of the original book (Putnam, 1980). The action in this primarily iconographic production is cleverly achieved with camera pans, zooms, and cuts. Many maps of the Old World and the present one give a good perspective, while Fritz's commentary brings Columbus to life.

∞ CONNECTIONS

Books:
Where Do You Think You're Going, Christopher Columbus? 1980. Putnam, $13.95; paper, $7.95.

Where in the World: Kids Explore Mexico
(Ages 5–11)
Encounter Video, $19.95 (pub. perf., $69.95) (30 min.)

From their treetop clubhouse, five inquisitive children use the resources of their hometown communities to explore new places around the globe. This creative geography video introduces Mexico through maps and camera footage of the land and its people. Pertinent historical and cultural highlights are noted by the clubhouse kids, who visit the library, the zoo, natural history and art museums, restaurants, and ethnic festivals to learn more about Mexican wildlife, artifacts, customs, and food. Other videos in this series visit Kenya, Alaska, and the U.S. National Parks. These engaging videos are structured into longer versions for classroom use.

Who Owns the Sun?
(Ages 5–9)
Producer: Disney Educational Productions.
Director: Mark Jean.
Coronet/MTI Film & Video, $280; rental, $75 (18 min.)

A six-year-old's father is a black field hand on a plantation in the 1800s. The boy, who lovingly cares for a horse that belongs to the plantation owner's daughter, asks his father,

"What does it mean to *own* a horse?" The boy's questions about ownership multiply when he overhears another farmer offer to purchase his father. The father's gentle, assuring response instills pride in his son, as he explains that just as no one can own the moon or the stars in the sky, no one can own what is inside of us. (Closed captioned)

∞ CONNECTIONS

Books:
Who Owns the Sun? by Stacy Chbosky. 1988. Landmark, $12.95.

You Can Choose
(Ages 6–10)
Producers: Elkind & Sweet Communications.
Live Wire Video Publishers; four programs $59.95 each (pub. perf., $219.95 for four programs) (25 min. each)

Dealing with feelings, peer pressure, responsibility, and cooperation are discussed by Michael Pritchard, who combines his talents as youth counselor and stand-up comedian. Funny skits performed by an ensemble group before an audience of San Francisco schoolchildren are followed by sensible talks on the vital issues. A companion to this series is available for teens (see *Power of Choice* on p. 197).

You Don't Have to Die
(Ages 6–Adult)
Producers: William Guttentag and Malcolm Clarke for Home Box Office.
Director: Malcolm Clarke.
Ambrose Video Publishing, $69.95 (30 min.)

To offer encouragement and help to others, this heartfelt portrait re-creates the cancer ordeal of 10-year-old Jason Gaes, who miraculously recovered after intensive chemotherapy, radiation treatment, and surgery at Minnesota's Mayo Clinic. The video consists of animated scenes and dramatic reenactments drawn from the book Jason wrote about his experiences. These are coupled with interviews with Jason and his articulate family. A low-key, affecting program that fosters respect, sympathy, and admiration for the Gaes family and their remarkably forthright sharing of traumatic events.

Awards: Academy Award 1989; American Film and Video Festival Blue Ribbon 1989

CONNECTIONS

Books:
My Book for Kids with Cansur by Jason Gaes. 1988. Melius and Peterson, $12.95.

MIDDLE GRADERS

The Accident
(Ages 8–13)
Producer and Director: Mark Chodzko.
Barr Films, $365; rental, $50 (22 min.)

Chris and his beloved dog, Badger, share sunlit adventures at a lakeside cottage in the opening scenes of this video. When Badger is killed by a car, Chris's shock and lingering grief are clearly felt by the viewer. The boy's feelings of guilt and sadness are less clearly understood by his parents. Eventually, they come to recognize their son's emotions and help him mark Badger's grave with a granite stone. A story in the *Old Yeller* (Disney, 1957) vein that focuses on the need for parent-child communication.

CONNECTIONS

Books:
The Accident by Carol Carrick. 1976. Clarion, $13.95; paper, $4.95.

Across Five Aprils
(Ages 10–Adult)
Producer: Learning Corporation of America.
Director: Kevin Meyer.
Coronet/MTI Film & Video, two programs, $250 each (32–34 min.)

Drawn from family records, this two-part, live-action film about the Civil War has an immediacy that brings the conflict to life.

Nine-year-old Jethro Creighton's favorite brother has joined the Confederacy; his other two brothers are Union soldiers. The splendid acting reveals a family dealing with distress while pursuing their everyday lives in a southern Illinois town. Teens absorbed by this film may want to watch the outstanding PBS video series, *The Civil War* by Ken Burns.

CONNECTIONS

Books:
Across Five Aprils by Irene Hunt. 1964. Berkeley, paper, $2.75.

Adventures of a Two-Minute Werewolf
(Ages 10–14)
Producer: Howard Meltzer for Scholastic.
Director: Mark Cullingham.
Distributor: AIMS Media, $99.95; rental, $50 (45 min.)

When Walt Cribbens celebrates his thirteenth birthday by going to a horror movie with his best friend Cindy, he turns into something more than a teenager. He becomes a werewolf! With Cindy's help, Walt learns to cope with his recurring transformation: he even turns it to his advantage when he runs into a bully. A made-for-television production that is ideally suited to the preteen sense of humor and adventure.

CONNECTIONS

Books:
Adventures of a Two-Minute Werewolf by Gene DeWeese. 1983. Doubleday, o.p.

All Summer in a Day
(Ages 9–Adult)
Producer: Karl Epstein.
Director: Ed Kaplan.
Coronet/MTI Film & Video, $250; rental, $75 (25 min.)

On the dismal planet Venus, the sun shines for only one hour, every nine years. Margot, recently from Earth, is the sole child in school who remembers the warmth of the sun, the smell of flowers, and the joy of butterflies. When a bully locks her in a school closet, Margot is deprived of the moments of solar bliss that she longed for. Stunning performances by young actors highlight this Ray Bradbury story.

CONNECTIONS

Books:
"All Summer in a Day" in *The Stories of Ray Bradbury* by Ray Bradbury. 1980. Knopf, $29.95.

American Portraits: Theodore Roosevelt—The Cowboy President
(Ages 10–14)
Producer: American Heritage Productions.
Clearvue-EAV, $59 (60 min.)

Theodore Roosevelt's boisterous nature comes to life in this well-edited video. Rich visuals, including portraits by Frederic Remington and clever cartoons, add depth and variety. Character voices and catchy music further enhance the presidential portrait. Roosevelt's biography is one of a series. Among the other presidents highlighted in this series are George Washington, Thomas Jefferson, Andrew Jackson, and Abraham Lincoln.

BEST OF THE BEST FOR CHILDREN

Anne of Avonlea: The Continuing Story of Anne of Green Gables

(Ages 10–Adult)

Producer and Director: Kevin Sullivan.
Walt Disney Home Video, $29.95 (122 min.; two tapes)

In this stunning sequel to *Anne of Green Gables* (Home Vision, $29.95), red-haired Anne Shirley is now a schoolteacher whose impetuosity continues to land her in the midst of both absurdly funny predicaments and heart-wrenching situations. As a teacher and boarder's chaperon in an all-girls school, Anne gets into as much trouble as her students. Some of the students are scheming, with parental approval, to get rid of this new schoolteacher; they connive to generate even more catastrophes, such as goats set loose across the lawns and fireworks in the classroom stove. Based on three of Lucy Maud Montgomery's novels written in the early 1900s, this lengthy film has old-fashioned charm and ongoing adventure to keep viewers engrossed. More of the author's Green Gables stories have been made into the 26-part series, filled with the shenanigans of girls and boys, *Return to Avonlea* (Direct Cinema). (Part One is an American Film and Video Festival Red Ribbon 1992.) (Closed captioned)

⌘CONNECTIONS

Books:

Anne of Avonlea: The Continuing Story of Anne of Green Gables by Lucy Maud Montgomery. 1908. Bantam, paper, $2.95.
Anne of the Island by Lucy Maud Montgomery. 1915. Bantam, paper, $2.95.

Anne of Windy Poplars by Lucy Maud Montgomery. 1936. o.p.
Anne of Green Gables by Lucy Maud Montgomery. 1908. Bantam, paper, $2.95.

Blackberries in the Dark

(Ages 8–10)

Director: Don MacDonald.
Producer: Walt Disney Educational Productions.
Coronet/MTI, $375; rental, $75 (27 min.)

When nine-year-old Austin visits the farm for the first time since his grandfather's death, he feels the old man's absence tremendously. The loss felt by both Austin and his grandmother gradually draws them together and helps them build a warm new relationship based on their fond memories of Grandpa. This beautiful, pensive adaptation of Mavis Jukes's story conveys the feelings of both generations and the steps taken haltingly to recover from the death of a loved one.

⌘CONNECTIONS

Books:
Blackberries in the Dark by Mavis Jukes. 1985. Knopf, $10.95; Dell, paper, $2.50.

Boy Stuff
Girl Stuff

(Ages 10–14)

Producer: Bob Churchill.
Director: Mark Chodzko.
Churchill Media, $270–$330; rental, $60 each (21 min. each)

Here's straightforward talk about puberty. Mixed with the irreverent wisecracks and humorous animation are direct answers to preteens' and teens' questions about their changing bodies. The narrator has a pleasant style that plays nicely against the realistic kids on camera. Personal hygiene is given top billing and sensibly explained. These videos, soon to be updated, offer a great response to questions kids are too shy to ask.

Bridge to Terabithia
(Ages 10–13)
WonderWorks series.
Public Media Video, $29.95 (60 min.)

Sensitive, artistic 10-year-old Jess Aarons doesn't fit in well with other fifth-graders in his isolated rural community. Then Aaron discovers a new friend in Leslie, a girl who understands him and excites his imagination with wonderful stories. Using rough boards, the two build a secret kingdom in the woods near their homes. They call it Terabithia and invent marvelous games and clever rituals for their private world. (Closed captioned)

Awards: American Film and Video Festival Blue Ribbon 1992

⌘ CONNECTIONS

Books:
Bridge to Terabithia by Katherine Paterson. 1977. HarperCollins, $12.95; paper, $2.95.

Buy Me That!
(Ages 6–10)
Films Inc., $79 (30 min.)

A genial host takes viewers behind the scenes of commercials in-the-making to help young consumers spot the deceptions of TV advertising. Enticing commercials promoting toys, games, dolls, and so forth, are contrasted with demonstrations of what they are really like off camera. This savvy guide offers the comments of disillusioned young customers who reveal their actual experiences with the highly touted items and their resentment of the tricks seen on TV.

Awards: Notable Children's Film 1991

The Cap
(Ages 7–12)
Director: Robert Duncan.
Producers: Seaton McLean and others for Atlantis Films and The National Film Board of Canada.
Beacon Films, $149; rental, $35 (26 min.)

A baseball cap signed by then–Montreal Expos Star Andre Dawson is Steve's prized possession. Forlorn when it is missing, Steve soon finds it—worn by the son of a wealthy attorney. Steve and his unemployed father attempt to retrieve the cap, but the attorney offers $100 instead and Steve's dad takes the money immediately, severely disappointing his boy. The reconciliation of father and son is a bit shallow, but realistic enough. The major-league baseball scenes will draw plenty of viewers to this video based on a short story—"A Cap for Steve" by Morley Callaghan.

A Child's Christmas in Wales
(Ages 8–Adult)
Producers: Atlantis Films, Cypress Films, and WTTW.
Director: Don McBreaty.
Home Vision, $19.95 (pub. perf., $149; rental, $35) (55 min.)

This video features Denholm Elliot as a grandfather recounting to his eager young grandson what Christmas was like when he was a boy in the early 1900s. Dylan Thomas's poetic memoir provides the narrative for beautifully filmed sequences: young boys mischievously haunting the snowy streets of a seacoast village; a large family's jovial exchanges of gifts and festive meals; and peaceful interludes in candlelit parlors as a raft of aunts and uncles sing goodnight to a sleepy lad. This transfixing dramatization of bygone times has become a Christmas tradition in its own right.

Awards: Notable Children's Film 1989

∞ CONNECTIONS

Books:
A Child's Christmas in Wales by Dylan Thomas. Illustrated by Trina Schart Hyman. 1985. Holiday House, $14.95.

Chronicles of Narnia
(Ages 8–13)

WonderWorks series.
Public Media Video, $29.95 each tape; $79.95 series (174 min.)

The three videos in this terrific WonderWorks series are based on events from several of the seven novels comprising the C. S. Lewis classic *Chronicles* fantasy. In *The Lion, the Witch, and the Wardrobe,* four children evacuated from London during the blitz slip into a wardrobe cupboard. In this, and the other two videos— *Prince Caspian/Voyage of the "Dawn Treader"* and *The Silver Chair*—the kids wind up in a fantasy world populated by nymphs, dwarfs, witches, talking animals, centaurs, and various elegantly costumed creatures. The child actors are delightfully natural, especially considering the exotic adventures they enact. Truly a magical production.

∞ CONNECTIONS

Books:
Chronicles of Narnia by C. S. Lewis. 7 volumes. 1986. Macmillan, $79.95; paper, $39.95.

The Lion, the Witch, and the Wardrobe by C. S. Lewis. 1950. Macmillan, $12.95; paper, $5.95.
Prince Caspian by C. S. Lewis. Macmillan, $12.95; paper, $5.95.
Voyage of the "Dawn Treader" by C. S. Lewis. Macmillan, $12.95; paper, $5.95.
The Silver Chair by C. S. Lewis. Macmillan, $12.95; paper, $5.95.

C'mon Geese
(Ages 10–Adult)

Produced and Directed by William Lishman for Cooper-Lishman Productions.
Bullfrog Films, $285; rental, $45 (28 min.)

As a boy, William Lishman imagined flying with the birds. Here he recounts just how he realized this incredible dream using his talents in metal sculpture. While raising a flock of young geese from goslings through fledglings to strong young fliers, Lishman devised various models of hang gliders. Through scenes of bumpy takeoffs and landings—and of the growing birds flocking after Lishman and around his experimental flying machines—the saga unfolds until both mechanical and avian wings are perfected. Soon the dreamer and the birds soar aloft as airborne partners.

Awards: American Film and Video festival Blue Ribbon

Double Dutch—Double Jeopardy
(See How to Say No, p. 192.)

Encyclopedia Brown: The Boy Detective in the Case of the Missing Time Capsule
(Ages 9–11)

Producer: Peter Johnson for Howard David Deutsch Productions.
Director: Savage Steve Holland.
Video Treasures, $9.99 (55 min.)

Popular pint-size sleuth Encyclopedia Brown and his musclewoman Sally show up the Idaville police force and the bad guys in this slick dramatization. A time capsule crucial to the town's centennial celebration has been stolen. Brown must figure out who stole it and why. Exciting chases and battles with adult villains make Brown's investigation satisfying viewing for armchair detectives of all ages. (See also Donald Sobol's *Encyclopedia Brown and the Case of the Disgusting Sneakers* in Books.)

Get Ready, Get Set, Grow!
(Ages 7–12)

Producer: Brooklyn Botanic Gardens.
Sterling Publishing Co., $29.95 (pub. perf.) (15 min.)

Cheerfully narrated by a participant in the Brooklyn Botanic Gardens children's program, this video describes the planting season, from planning to harvest. Great closeups of plant and insect life are used along with animation and cutaway views to explain plant development. Encouraging, informative fare for budding horticulturalists—and your everyday, backyard gardeners too.

Awards: Notable Children's Film 1988

A Girl of the Limberlost
(Ages 10–Adult)

WonderWorks series.
Home Vision, $29.95 (pub. perf.) (60 min.)

In Indiana of 1908, 15-year-old Elnora Comstock is torn by her duty to her widowed mother, who needs help on the family farm, and her desire to attend high school. Mother and daughter both feel the pressures of a timber company that wants to purchase their land. On her own, Elnora also faces the taunting of the town students who belittle her. The Limberlost Swamp—the site of her father's untimely death—becomes a refuge for Elnora. The story takes a turn when an adult friend, a naturalist and writer, pays the girl for collecting insects and butterflies from the marsh and listens sympathetically to her woes.

∞ CONNECTIONS

Books:
A Girl of the Limberlost by Gene Stratton Porter. 1909. Dell, paper, $4.95.

He Makes Me Feel Like Dancin'
(Ages 9–Adult)

Producer: Judy Kinberg for Edgar J. Scherick Assoc.
Director: Emile Ardolino.
Direct Cinema, $250; rental, $50 (51 min.)

Jacques D'Amboise of the New York City Ballet created the National Dance Institute to nurture the talents of children. From a program involving 30 kids, the NDI has grown to one that features some 1,000 children, professional dancers, musicians, and actors in an extravagant show. This Academy Award–winning video features scenes of the show's development from casting to curtain calls as well as voice-over remarks from children who share the value of their year with the NDI. The sincere reflections of tutor D'Amboise add depth to this beautiful production.

Awards: Academy Award Winner, Best Documentary Feature, 1983; American Film Festival, Best of Festival, 1985

Herschel Walker's Fitness Challenge for Kids
(Ages 9–12)
HPG Home Video, $19.95 (pub. perf.) (40 min.)

On his own turf—a football field—Heisman Trophy winner and Minnesota Vikings running back Herschel Walker exercises with a group of kids. The youngsters receive his counseling against drugs and alcohol as seriously as they do his stretching tips and fitness advice. Rap music and football footage add further appeal to this straightforward talk from a "once-chubby 12-year-old" who started exercising and hasn't stopped moving since.

Jack of Hearts
(Ages 9–13)
Director: Cynthia Scott.
Producer: The National Film Board of Canada.
Beacon Films, $149; rental, $35 (26 min.)

Elizabeth is devastated when she is chosen to play a male lead—the jack of hearts—in a dance recital. She handles the role with aplomb until the final curtain call when, provoked by the teasing of her peers, she announces, "I'm not a boy." After the show, a flamboyant houseguest teaches Elizabeth poker and a few lessons on dealing with life's humiliations. This sensitive dramatization portrays the pain of emerging adolescence.

∞ CONNECTIONS

Books:
"Jack of Hearts," a short story in *The Elizabeth Stories* by Isabel Huggan. 1987. Viking, o.p.

Joyful Noise
(Ages 8–11)
SRA Group, $83 (18 min.)

Based on the 1989 Newbery Medal book written by Paul Fleischman, this live-action video features cicadas, honeybees, grasshoppers, and other insects making a "boisterous, joyful noise." The narration is drawn from Fleischman's clever poetry, designed to be read aloud in alternating voices. The poet's fresh imagery and brisk pacing capture the life cycles and habits of insects. Nature study is rarely viewed with such elegant caprice and harmony.

Awards: Notable Children's Film 1991

∞ CONNECTIONS

Books:
Joyful Noise: Poems for Two Voices by Paul Fleischman. Illustrated by Eric Beddows. 1988. HarperCollins, $11.95.

Juke-Bar
(Ages 10–Adult)
Producer: Yves Leduc.
Director: Martin Barry.
The National Film Board of Canada, $200; rental, $40 (10 min.)

A bright, neon-wreathed jukebox is rolled into a greasy diner swarming with cockroaches. When the diner closes at the end of the day, the roaches blithely stream through the empty establishment and into the garish amusement center to party all night to the jukebox's big band sounds. Wonderful animation features crazy cockroach figures—with outlandish shoes and hats, frizzy hair, and bobbing antennae—heedlessly cavorting until all but two are trapped inside the jukebox. The owner returns and gleefully hauls away the machine, thinking he has captured all of the critters. Good fun and toe-tapping energy pervade this unusual approach to pest control.

Awards: Notable Children's Film 1991; American Film and Video Festival Blue Ribbon

Like Jake and Me
(Ages 8–11)
SRA Group, $37 (16 min.)

With original illustrations by Lloyd Bloom and lively music by Arthur Custer, this adaptation spins a well-known tale about stepfamily life. Alex is six years old, taking ballet lessons, and looking for common ground to share with his new father, a former cowboy. A comical misunderstanding gives Alex a chance to play the hero and brings the two closer together. A live-action version of this Newbery Honor Book is available from Coronet/MTI.

☞ CONNECTIONS

> Books:
> *Like Jake and Me* by Mavis Jukes. Illustrated by Lloyd Bloom. 1984. Knopf, $12.95; paper, $4.95.

Little League's Official How To Play Baseball
(Ages 8–14)
Producers: John Gonvalez and David Stern.
MasterVision, $19.95; video with book, $29.95 (70 min.)

"Advice comes straight from the players in terms kids understand," says one young viewer of this video. As the members of a Little League team practice, they share skills, lessons learned from mistakes, and facts on equipment and rules. The emphasis on practice stated by the young players is one of the many fine features of this useful video.

☞ CONNECTIONS

> Books:
> *Little League's Official How to Play Baseball* by Peter Kreutzer and Ted Kerley. 1990. Doubleday, paper, $9.95.

A Little Princess
(Ages 9–Adult)
WonderWorks series.
Public Media Video, $79.95 for 3 videotapes (174 min.)

Sara Crew arrives at her English boarding school with a personal maid, elegant wardrobe, and splendid accoutrements that impress the headmistress. Sara, who is motherless, has spent her childhood in India with her father, a soldier. She is clever as well as rich. The plot turns when the father is killed and the family fortune lost. Now penniless, Sara is forced to become a scullery maid at the school, but her cleverness and sterling qualities bring her good fortune once again. Shirley Temple played this role long ago in a feature film. In this WonderWorks version, a spunky Amelia Shankley stirs today's viewers.

☞ CONNECTIONS

> Books:
> *A Little Princess* by Frances Hodgson Burnett. Illustrated by Tasha Tudor. 1905. HarperCollins, $12.95; Dell, paper, $3.50.

BEST OF THE BEST FOR CHILDREN

Merlin and the Dragons
(Ages 5–12)

Stories to Remember series.
Producer: Joshua M. Greene.
Directors: Dennis I. Woodward and Hu Yihong.
Lightyear Entertainment, $14.95 (pub. perf., $64.95)
(26 min.)

The old wizard Merlin tells the youthful, newly crowned King Arthur a diverting tale. It concerns a fatherless boy whose powers of prophecy foretell the destiny of his native land and the birthright of its legendary ruler. Mysterious magicians mutter incantations, fearsome dragons emerge from beneath stone battlements, and riveting dream sequences portend all that comes to pass in this beautifully animated legend. Dynamic narration and an atmospheric musical score add to the spellbinding production. (Closed captioned)

CONNECTIONS

Books:
The Dragon's Boy by Jane Yolen. 1990. HarperCollins, $13.95.
Audio:
Merlin and the Dragons narrated by Kevin Kline. Lightyear Records, dist. by BMG, $8.95.

The Miracle of Life
(Ages 8–Adult)

Producers: Bo G. Erikson and Carl O. Lofman.
Random House Home Video, $19.95 (60 min.)

Narrated in reverent tones by June Lockhart, these views of the earliest stages of human life are remarkable. To ethereal melodies, closeups magnified a half-million times depict the processes of fertilization and cell division in an amazing array of colors. The film concludes at the seventh week, when every organ is present in an embryo the size of an adult thumb. This glimpse at the origin of life is a classic for all ages.

Molly's Pilgrim
(Ages 8–11)

Producers: Jeff Brown and Chris Pelzer.
Phoenix/BFA Films & Video, $325 (24 min.)

Different in speech and dress from her American schoolmates, a young Russian immigrant struggles to overcome her feeling of alienation. When Molly fashions a uniquely personal pilgrim figure for a school project, she bridges the gap between two cultures and enlightens her classmates on religious freedom. This poignant, beautifully filmed work, updated from Barbara Cohen's story, is a holiday classic that renews the meaning of the traditional Thanksgiving story.

Awards: Academy Award Winner, Best Live Action Short 1985; Notable Children's Film 1987

CONNECTIONS

Books:
Molly's Pilgrim by Barbara Cohen. Illustrated by Michael J. Deraney. 1983. Lothrop, $12.95.

One's a Heifer
(Ages 7–12)

Director: Anne Wheeler.
Beacon Films, $149; rental, $35 (26 min.)

A farm boy on the windswept Canadian plains of 1934 makes a solitary search for two missing calves. Peter feels certain that his calves are in the rickety barn of a reclusive, grizzled old man. Despite the geezer's guns and snarling demeanor, Peter confronts him about the animals. Peter finally returns home empty-handed, only to discover his calves have wandered back. The historical wilderness setting is established perfectly in scenic footage and expressive music. Fine dramatic viewing with plenty of character development.

Put on Your Own Show
(Ages 8–13)
Producer: Peg Emerson.
WGTE Home Video, $22 (pub. perf.) (55 min.)

Former ballerina Susan Zaliouk, now a dance and fitness instructor, takes youngsters from basic choreography to all the essentials of a performance. The dance routines are followed by lessons on makeup, props, staging, and costume. A group of peppy kids bounces through jazz, rock-'n'-roll, country, and school-spirit versions of the dances. Zaliouk's charisma has moved kids before in *Sue Zaliouk and the FunDance Kids*.

Realm of the Alligator
(Ages 9–Adult)
National Geographic Society Educational Services, $32.20 (59 min.)

Alligators haunting the Okefenokee Swamp of Georgia are tailed by two personable biologists whose narrative is as spellbinding as the up-close footage. This is just one of the many fine National Geographic Society specials that have been packaged for home video. Equally exciting portrayals are to be found in *Polar Bear Alert, The Sharks, Gorilla, The Rhino War, Rain Forest,* and *Volcano!* Excellent color photography and enticing narration make these some of the finest nature videos available.

The Red Shoes
(Ages 8–12)
Producer and Director: Michael Sporn.
Lucerne Media, $295; rental, $60 (25 min.)

Not a strict retelling of the Hans Christian Andersen tale, this modernized version comes with reggae music and narration by Ossie Davis. Lisa and Jenny, two preteens drawn together by their love of dance, are separated when Lisa's family wins a lottery and moves away from their old flat and their old neighbors. Jenny is left behind and ignored by her now upscale friend, but a pair of red shoes makes a magical difference in their lives, and the girls are reunited.

Sadako & the Thousand Paper Cranes
(Ages 10–Adult)
Informed Democracy, $195; rental, $45 (30 min.)

The true story of Sadako—a young Japanese girl who developed radiation-induced leukemia years after she was exposed to the Hiroshima atomic bomb—is related by Liv Ullmann and illustrated in pastel drawings. In her brave quest to defeat her illness, Sadako began folding paper cranes to fulfill the Japanese legend that a wish would be granted to anyone who folded 1,000 of them. Sadako died at the age of 12 in 1954, unable to complete her task, but her friends and classmates completed her mission. This adaptation of Eleanor Coerr's book beautifully relates how Sadako's courageous saga has become a symbolic longing for peace. *Hiroshima Maiden* (Home Vision, $29.95) is another story about a Japanese girl affected by the bomb who comes to the United States for treatment and has a powerful impact upon her American hosts.

Awards: Notable Children's Film 1991

⌘CONNECTIONS

Books:

Sadako & the Thousand Paper Cranes by Eleanor Coerr. Illustrated by Ronald Himler. 1977. Putnam, $13.95; Dell, paper, $2.75.

The Secret of NIMH

(Ages 8–Adult)

Producer: Don Bluth Productions.
MGM/UA Home Video, $19.95 (83 min.)

High-quality animation, a pleasing soundtrack, and endearing characters make a winning video out of Robert C. O'Brien's Newbery Award novel, *Mrs. Frisby and the Rats of NIMH*. Mrs. Frisby, a fieldmouse raising her children alone after the death of her husband, is alarmed when she hears that the farmer is beginning to plow and they must evacuate their home. Her son Timothy is sick and cannot be moved. She must find some way to delay the inevitable. Summoning her courage, she seeks advice from the Great Owl, who sends her to a colony of superintelligent rats that have escaped from the laboratory of the National Institute of Mental Health (NIMH). In the end, Mrs. Frisby saves her family.

⌘CONNECTIONS

Books:

Mrs. Frisby and the Rats of NIMH by Robert C. O'Brien. 1971. Atheneum, $14.95; Macmillan, paper, $3.95.
Racso and the Rats of NIMH by Jane Leslie Conly. (See Books.)

Victor

(Ages 9–11)

Producer and Director: Dianne Haak Edson.
Barr Films, $420; rental, $50 (27 min.)

At school, classmates taunt Mexican immigrant Victor, who is attempting to improve his English-speaking skills. At home, Victor speaks Spanish with his mother, who shies away from learning English. The fifth-grader is pulled between these two situations until his teacher bridges the gap with understanding and encouragement. At parents' night, the teacher welcomes Victor's mom and dad in Spanish; in return, Victor's mother pleases her son when she begins to converse in English. This beautifully acted dramatization underscores the tensions in bilingual families and encourages acceptance of new classmates. Look also for *Sweet 15* (Home Vision), a home video in the WonderWorks series about a traditional Mexican birthday celebration.

⌘CONNECTIONS

Books:

Victor by Clare Galbraith. 1971. Little, Brown, o.p.

Yosemite: The Fate of Heaven

(Ages 10–Adult)

Producer and Director: Jon Else.
Direct Cinema, $150; rental, $75 (58 min.)

The wonders of Yosemite, from tiniest plants to giant sequoias and cascading waterfalls, unfold in remarkable footage narrated by a reverent Robert Redford. A thoughtful script conveys the awe of the Miwok Indians for their mountain valley home of hundreds of years ago. Interviews with tourists and park rangers emphasize the fragile environment and its vulnerability to sightseers.

TEENAGERS

Cameramen Who Dared
(Ages 12–Adult)

Producer: David Clark.
National Geographic Society Educational Services, $32.20 (pub. perf.) (60 min.)

For those who marvel at the footage in National Geographic films, videos, and TV shows, here is the inside story. This chronicle of cinematographic daring offers such thrills as a great white shark descending with open jaws upon a caged, underwater camera operator; another scene catches a cameraman swinging from a vine in a rain forest alongside his primate subject. This skillfully edited video reveals the courage of the men and women who shoot memorable adventure, wartime, and wildlife footage. (Closed captioned)

Condor
(Ages 12–Adult)

Producers: Wolfgang and Sharon Obst for WETA-TV. Vestron; dist. by Live Home Video, $34.50 (60 min.)

The California condor, a stunning bird with a wingspan of nearly 10 feet, upstages even Robert Redford, who narrates this National Audubon Society special. Glorious footage of the bird in the wild is counterpointed by scenes of biologists and researchers taking measures to preserve these almost extinct creatures. (Closed captioned)

Awards: American Film and Video Festival Blue Ribbon 1987

The Day They Came to Arrest the Book
(Ages 12–Adult)

Director: Gilbert Moses.
FilmFair Communications, $395; rental, $50 (47 min.)

Teens become embroiled in a censorship issue that eventually involves the entire community. As the video opens, the editor of the high school newspaper and a friend disagree vehemently about the use of Mark Twain's *Adventures of Huckleberry Finn* in a history class. A parent complains to the principal about the word *nigger* in the book. At a school board meeting, parents, teachers, teens, and a librarian argue emotionally over language, censorship, and moral and social viewpoints. A stimulating video for both parents and kids.

Don't Say Yes When You Really Mean No   (Ages 10–14)   Magic Music, dist. by Partners in Learning, $39.95 (pub. perf.) (58 min.)

How children make choices about using alcohol and drugs is dramatized in rousing musical numbers. A 12-year-old has to decide between attending a best friend's party and accepting a date with an attractive new guy. Music, song, and choreography lay out her conflicts, possible solutions, and consequences of her actions. This fresh approach helps teach kids how and why to say "no" and examines the positive and negative influences of friends.

Double Dutch—Double Jeopardy   (Ages 8–12)   Produced and Directed by Ginny Durrin. Durrin Productions, $295; rental, $50 (20 min.)

Double dutch jump-rope champions and grade-school rap singers enliven this AIDS-awareness video. The songs performed by Washington, D.C., schoolchildren surround a candid classroom talk by a 20-year-old with AIDS, who warns the kids against the hazards of drugs, alcohol, and unprotected sex. (A version of this production that avoids the word *condom* is also available.)

Fast Forward Future   (Ages 8–10)   Producers and Directors: Harvey K. Bellin and Tom Kiefer. Instructional Media Institute, $95 (62 min.)

Three middle-grade children are drawn into a dark arcadelike room with flashing lights. Summoned by the "Mentor" who appears on a large video screen, each kid must reenact a stage in life when he or she was tempted by drugs or alcohol. While the kids observe their own mistakes, problem-solving and refusal techniques are offered by the Mentor. The sci-fi setting will sustain interest in a video sure to help other young people facing these dilemmas.

It Won't Happen to Me   (Ages 12–17)   Producer: Jerry Haislmaier. Directors: Jerry Haislmaier and Lillian Spino.   Coronet/MTI Films & Video, $495; rental, $75 (32 min.)

Marty is sent to a support group for teen alcoholics rather than face criminal charges when the police stop him for driving under the influence. The young man denies having a problem and scorns the company of his recovering peers. However, the 17-year-old athlete cannot help but realize, as he listens to the others, how many similar situations he has found himself in. Awareness does not come easily to Marty in this well-acted film; but when it does, other troubled teens will certainly feel the poignance and reality of his struggle.

See also *Herschel Walker's Fitness Challenge for Kids* (p. 186) for a more positive, upbeat approach.

∞ CONNECTIONS

Books:

The Day They Came to Arrest the Book by Nat Hentoff. 1982. Dell, paper, $3.25.

Forever Baseball

(Ages 12–Adult)

The American Experience series.
Producer: Irv Drasnin.
PBS Video, $59.95 (59 min.)

The ageless allure of the "supreme American invention" is chronicled in this nostalgic celebration. Against a backdrop of historical posters and game footage, famous baseball lovers, Little Leaguers, and major-league hopefuls tell of the game's appeal. Cameos of baseball heroes and legendary games of decades past affectionately trace the sport's irreplaceable role in American culture. (Closed captioned)

The Friends

(Ages 12–Adult)

Producer: Thames Television.
Director: Adrian Brown.
The Media Guild, $245 (25 min.)

An interview with novelist Rosa Guy is strategically placed within this dramatization of a scene from her novel, *The Friends*. Edith, who lives in a tenement, is visited by a wealthy school friend, Phylicia, whose disdain is obvious. The unique blend of fiction scenes and author interview overrides any preachiness. Guy is asked about her childhood in the West Indies and her feelings about moving to Harlem in the 1950s. The author's responses help to make the settings and morals of her stories achieve new life.

∞ CONNECTIONS

Books:

The Friends by Rosa Guy. 1973. Holt, $10.95; Bantam, paper, $2.95.

The Great Dinosaur Hunt

(Ages 12–Adult)

Producer: WQED/Infinite Voyage series.
Vestron Video; dist. by Live Home Video, $29.98 (60 min.)

This video focuses on the search for dinosaur bones and fossils from the late 1700s to the present. The presentation moves smoothly from archival footage of the early searches to interviews with modern-day paleontologists. Demonstrating with mechanically animated models, the scientists speculate, "Were dinosaurs the ancestors of today's birds?" Another NOVA presentation that probes this question is the two-part series *Dinosaur!*— "Tale of a Bone" and "Tale of a Tooth"—narrated by Walter Cronkite. (Closed captioned)

Help Save Planet Earth

(Ages 10–Adult)

UNI Distribution, $14.95 (pub. perf.) (70 min.)

Whoopi Goldberg, Jamie Lee Curtis, and John Ritter are among the celebrities who make appearances in this slick production encouraging environmental awareness. Tips include devising environmentally safe products, shopping with limited packaging in mind, and contacting pertinent agencies. Viewers are encouraged to conserve energy and resources and to get politically involved. The significant message is delivered in an entertaining, often tongue-in-cheek, way that will have special appeal to teens.

It's Late

(Ages 13–18)

Degrassi Junior High series.
Producers: Linda Schuyler and Kit Hood.
Director: Kit Hood.
Direct Cinema, $250; rental, $25 (30 min.)

One episode in a lengthy series starring Canadian junior high students facing up to adolescence. This video focuses on 14-year-old Spike, who is worried that she's pregnant. Spike talks to her mother, peers, and boyfriend, while related events keep viewers focused on the unfolding drama. There is a gripping realism in these programs that is enhanced by the polished filming and excellent plot development. This consistently top-notch series features a multiethnic group of Toronto youths. The original set of productions revolved around grade schoolers, known as The Degrassi Kids. (See also *Nobody's Perfect,* p. 196, for a sampling of the high school series.)

It Won't Happen to Me

(See How to Say No, p. 192.)

Jacob Have I Loved

(Ages 11–Adult)

WonderWorks series.
Producer: Richard Heus for KCET.
Director: Victoria Hochberg.
Public Media Video, $29.95 (pub. perf.) (55 min.)

Walking the seashore catching crabs, and storing up resentment over her twin sister's musical talent, 16-year-old Louise, played by Bridget Fonda, searches for an identity of her own. Her friendship with a sea captain in their close Chesapeake Bay community helps Louise rein in her jealousy and discover her own skills. There is nothing pat here about the depiction of the emotional quandary. The act-

ing, scenic detail, and subplots combine to make this a believable story that hits home.

Awards: Notable Children's Film 1991

CONNECTIONS

Books:

Jacob Have I Loved by Katherine Paterson. 1980. HarperCollins, $12.95; paper, $2.95.

Just for the Summer

(Ages 13–Adult)

Producer: Alzheimer's Association.
Director: James Moll.
Churchill Films Media; rental, $60 (30 min.)

When Phillip's grandmother comes to stay with the high schooler's family, her forgetfulness, outbursts, and irrational behavior distress the whole household. Phillip is confused by and resentful of his elderly grandmother, whom he remembers as a loving, active companion. He is dismayed when, in the middle of a crucial track meet, she runs out and interrupts the race to greet him. Scenes with Phillip's parents and classmates sensitively attest to the tensions and despair families face in coping with Alzheimer's disease. This well-acted video will help young people toward a better understanding of a prevalent degenerative disease.

The Making of Liberty

(Ages 12–Adult)

Guggenheim Productions, $29.95 (pub. perf.) (57 min.)

French sculptor Frédéric-Auguste Bartholdi's 20 years of work on the Statue of Liberty is given recognition in this exquisitely filmed video. Highlights of the monument's refurbishing give viewers an opportunity to explore in depth the grand lady's design and construction.

The Man Who Planted Trees
(Ages 9–Adult)

Producers: Société-Radio-Canada and Canadian Broadcasting Co.
Director: Frédéric Back.
Direct Cinema, $200; rental, $50 (30 min.)

A hiker in a barren land comes across a lone shepherd whose simple existence is dedicated to planting acorns throughout the hills. Exquisite animation of pastel drawings, a lush musical background, and Christopher Plummer's narration combine to produce an inspirational parable of a determined and generous creator. This timeless tale has much relevance in today's climate of environmental concern.

Awards: Academy Award, Best Animated Film, 1987; American Film Festival, Best of Festival, 1989

∽CONNECTIONS

Books and Audio:
"The Man Who Planted Trees," a short story by Jean Giono, is available in print with a cassette containing narration and original music by the Paul Winter Consort. (Music For Little People, $21.95)

Monterey Bay Aquarium
(Ages 10–Adult)

Producer and Director: Larry Taymor for Video Tours.
SelectVideo, $24.95 (pub. perf.) (30 min.)

In this tour of a California aquarium, ten different marine settings are explored in vivid underwater scenes. Staff members explain the sights as well as the institution's research. With frisky otters, mysterious fish, and exotic plants, this video tour will please families without a nearby aquarium and inspire those who plan to visit one. Similar videos are available from SelectVideo on the San Diego Wild Animal Park, Busch Gardens, and the New Orleans Zoo.

The Morning After: A Story of Vandalism
(Ages 12–Adult)

Producer: Greatapes, Minnesota.
Distributor: Pyramid Film & Video, $325; rental, $75 (27 min.)

When four Minnesota teens broke into a local high school one night, their vandalism was not limited to graffiti on the restroom walls. They went on a rampage using a blowtorch, forklift, paint, and open water hydrants, causing a million dollars in damages. In this study, each of the convicted vandals nervously and apologetically tries to explain and justify the group's motivation for such senseless violence. Although the causes of these irrational acts can never be fully explained, their aftermath is nevertheless documented in this indelible portrait of middle-class youths who succumb to alcohol and peer pressure. (See also *Vandalism Is Not Funny* on p. 198.)

Mr. Sears' Catalog
(Ages 12–adults)

The American Experience series.
Producers: Edward Gray, Mark Obenhaus, and Elizabeth Kreutz.
Directors: Edward Gray and Ken Levis.
PBS Video, $59.95 (59 min.)

From hams to corsets and houses to screws, a vast range of consumer goods were made available to the far-flung reaches of the United States through the entrepreneurial genius and mail-order catalog of Richard William Sears. This engaging tribute traces Sears's business career and gauges the impact of his "wish book" on rural America through vintage photographs, original entries from the Sears catalog, and snippets of customer correspondence. Like *Forever Baseball,* this is but one of several titles in the American Experience Series that bring fascinating immediacy to U.S. history. (Closed captioned)

Nobody's Perfect

(Ages 12–16)

Degrassi High series, Term 4.
Producers: Linda Schuyler and Kit Hood.
Director: Eleanor Lindo.
Direct Cinema, $250; rental, $25 (30 min.)

The kids from Degrassi Junior High (see *It's Late,* p. 194) have grown up into high schoolers with new conflicts, friendships, and concerns. This video centers on Kathleen and her boyfriend, Scott. Scott resents Kathleen's dramatic talent and the time she spends rehearsing. When he becomes abusive, Kathleen's friends step in. The discussion of friendships and relationships is heartening, and the show contains enough soap opera drama to keep viewers intrigued. Each entry in the series is a well-produced and realistically acted film that comes to a sensible, sensitive resolution. The series reached its conclusion with Degrassi High: Term 5 (1991).

Old Sturbridge Village

(Ages 10–Adult)

Producer: Eric Jones for Video Tours.
SelectVideo, $24.95 (pub. perf.) (30 min.)

Costumed guides re-create "the everyday way of life of everyday people" in an 1830s farming community. As they raise barns, care for plants and animals authentic to the period, and tend the homes and shops of Massachusetts's Old Sturbridge Village, the guides describe the daily activities of the people whose lives they are reenacting. More than just a travel video, this production reveals a sense of time and place in American history. *Sturbridge Village: Growing Up in New England* (SelectVideo) portrays the angst of farm youths choosing between life on the family farm or a move into the newly industrialized workplace.

Travelers and students will relish the other entries in this fine series: *Plimouth Plantation* (a seventeenth-century living museum with a re-created Wampanoag Indian encampment and a replica of the *Mayflower II* nearby), *Mystic Seaport* (a maritime history museum in Connecticut), *Henry Ford Museum and Greenfield Village* (a turn-of-the-century restoration in Michigan), and *Old Salem* (a reconstructed Moravian community of the late 1700s in North Carolina).

One More Hurdle

(Ages 11–16)

Producers: Barbara Klein and Beverly Raymond for Brookfield Productions.
Director: Mary Neema Barnette.
FilmFair Communications, $395; rental, $50 (47 min.)

Donna Marie Cheek is an African-American teenager who dreams of success as an equestrian competitor. In flashbacks and in scenes of Donna competing in jumping and hunting events, this video portrays the young woman's determination in the face of negative comments and financial difficulties. Fortunately, she has the support of her family.

The emotional hurdles and the dramatic tension in Donna's quest for the Olympics come through in this inspiring profile.

Power of Choice
(Ages 12–14)

Live Wire Video Publishers, 12 programs, $79.95 (30 min. each)

Stand-up comedian and youth counselor Michael Pritchard knows the problems of today's teens. Unlike his program for younger children (see *You Can Choose*, p. 179), this video has no fables about feelings or sharing. Here, Pritchard's mimicry targets uptight parents and troubled teens. He helps his audience laugh at themselves and put life in perspective. Stage antics are balanced by candid discussions with teen listeners in a very effective production.

Scorpions
(Ages 11–15)

Director: Robin Bossert.
SRA Group, $104 (37 min.)

Set in Harlem, this story about gang life and family ties focuses on Jamal, a 12-year-old torn between his affection for his imprisoned brother and his desire to reject the mantle of gang leadership. The drug scene, the violence of the streets, and the pathetic school situation are visualized with accuracy. The focus, however, remains on the kids and their feelings.

∞CONNECTIONS

Books:

Scorpions by Walter Dean Myers. 1988. HarperCollins, $12.95; paper, $2.95.

The Screaming Woman
(Ages 12–Adult)

Ray Bradbury Theater series.
Producer: Seaton McLean for Atlantis.
Director: Bruse Pittman.
Beacon Films, $149; rental, $50 (26 min.)

Heather can convince no one that the voice she hears of a woman screaming for help is genuine. A devoted reader of *Tales from the Crypt*, she is dismissed as overly imaginative. Yet Heather persists, and she discovers that a neighbor's wife is missing. Eerie music and haunting voices add to the mounting terror as Heather attempts a rescue. A well-realized Ray Bradbury story for fantasy and horror fans.

Awards: American Film and Video Festival Blue Ribbon 1989

Skin
(Ages 12–14)

Producer: Intercom Films.
Director: Gilbert W. Taylor.
Landmark Films, $195; rental, $50 (29 min.)

Bigotry against minorities is starkly conveyed in this film. Teens from East Indian, Vietnamese, and African-American backgrounds act out realistic confrontations in schools, stores, offices, airports, and on buses. The scenes are based on actual experiences. Guaranteed to sharpen one's perceptions of prejudice and its effects.

Awards: American Film and Video Festival Blue Ribbon 1990

Teen Workout
(Ages 13–18)

Random House Home Video, $14.95 (60 min.)

Bouncy, well-timed music sets the pace for Tamilee Webb's exercise video directed at teenage girls. The basics are covered: warm-ups, low-impact aerobics, toning and strengthening with ankle and wrist weights, and more intense routines. Choreography is precise and engaging. Teens will appreciate the well-coordinated pastel leotards worn by the instructor and her eager followers. Another fine video for aerobically inclined teens is *The Complete Teen Workout with Susan Zaliouk.*

Vandalism Is Not Funny

(Ages 11–Adult)

Directors: Sandra and Joseph Cosentino.
Karol Video, $59.95 (45 min.)

A comedic clip of kids smashing country mail-boxes turns into a serious look at the effects of vandalism on the victims, the community, the vandals, and their parents. Filmed in a rustic area of Connecticut, this video does not use professional actors, yet it offers a polished production. Interviews with kids, teachers, psychologists, school administrators, and others give a broad perspective on the problem. (See also *The Morning After: A Story of Vandalism* on p. 195.)

We Shall Overcome

(Ages 13–Adult)

Producers: Jim Brown and others.
Director: Jim Brown.
California Newsreel, $250; rental to colleges and universities, $75; rental to public libraries and high schools, $89 (60 min.)

Both before and after the years of the civil rights movement, the song "We Shall Overcome" summoned listeners to the struggle for justice. Its meaning and power are recalled by Pete Seeger, Joan Baez, and other performers, activists, and everyday folk who have sung it through the decades. In addition, news footage traces the song's history from the days of slavery and early labor strikes through sit-ins and "freedom rides" to rallies in South Africa and the People's Republic of China. This is a fascinating and meaningful video that makes history come alive.

The Wilds of Madagascar

(Ages 12–Adult)

Producer: Philip Chapman.
National Geographic Society Educational Services, $32.20 (pub. perf.) (60 min.)

Crocodiles, towering limestone cliffs, and unique fauna are hallmarks of the Ankarana plateau on the island of Madagascar. A team of naturalists treads lightly through this wilderness off the coast of Africa, planning how to best study yet protect the sanctuary for geckos, lemurs, mongooses, and other exotic inhabitants. The glorious photography is balanced by the informative commentary. (Closed captioned)

Wildwood Nights

(Ages 13–17)

Producer and Director: Karin Kelly.
Barr Films, $395; rental, $50 (29 min.)

Fourteen-year-old Stephanie Miller lies about her age to impress a collegiate hunk named David. The beach chatter goes smoothly, but when David invites Stephanie to go "partying," and she accepts, she is appalled by his raucous and boorish behavior. After the couple is detained by the police, Stephanie learns a few lessons about trusting appearances and about peer pressure. A good dramatization about the perils of a summer romance.

Awards: American Film and Video Festival Blue Ribbon 1991; Selected Film for Young Adults 1992

VIDEOS ON SELECTING BOOKS AND VIDEOS

Choosing the Best in Children's Video   Producer: Joshua Greene for ALA Video.
Library Video Network, $24.95 (35 min.)

Christopher Reeve hosts this tour through some of the best animated and live-action videos available. His narration, which tells how to select and locate quality viewing for children, is artfully interspersed with scenes from dynamite shows for children from infancy through age 12.

Sharing Books with Young Children   ALA Video; distributed by Library Video Network, $75 (25 min.)

Betsy Hearne, storyteller, children's book author, and editor of the *Bulletin for Children's Books,* shows and tells how to involve children with books. Her demonstrations of read-aloud and storytelling techniques will acquaint viewers with some popular children's books. (See also her guide, *Choosing Books for Children,* in the Resources section of Books.)

Tales of Love and Terror: Booktalking the Classics, Old and New   ALA Video; distributed by Library Video Network, $105 (25 min.)

Hazel Rochman's love of literature comes through in this video on book-talking for older kids. Designed as a tool for teachers and librarians, parents can also benefit from the introductions to noted young adult authors and their books. Rochman, a librarian, book reviewer, and editor of *Somehow Tenderness Survives* (see p. 120), shows exactly how to blend adult classics into conversations about relevant teen issues—a technique certain to aid any parent or professional.

VIDEO PRODUCERS AND DISTRIBUTORS

A & M Video
1416 North LaBrea Avenue
Hollywood, CA 90028
(213) 469-2411

AIMS Media
6901 Woodley Avenue
Van Nuys, CA 91406-4878
(800) 367-2467

Ambrose Video Publishing
1290 Avenue of the Americas
New York, NY 10104
(800) 526-4663

Auntie Lee's Kitchen
P.O. Box 25503
Portland, OR 97225
(503) 292-0467

Baker & Taylor Video
501 South Gladiolus
Momence, IL 60954
(800) 435-5111 (outside Illinois)
(800) 892-1892 (in Illinois)

Barr Films
P.O. Box 7878
Irwindale, CA 91706
(818) 338-7878

Beacon Films
930 Pitner Avenue
Evanston, IL 60202
(800) 323-5448

Bullfrog Films
Oley, PA 19547
(800) 543-FROG

California Newsreel
149 Ninth Street
San Francisco, CA 94103
(415) 621-6196

CBS/Fox Faerie Tale Theatre programs
1211 Avenue of the Americas
New York, NY 10036
(212) 819-3200

Centre Communications
P.O. Box 7878
Irwindale, CA 91706
(800) 234-7878

Children's Circle
Div. of Weston Woods
C.C. Studios, Inc.
Weston, CT 06883
(800) 243-5020

Churchill Media
12210 Nebraska Avenue
Los Angeles, CA 90025
(800) 334-7830

Clearvue-EAV
6565 North Avondale Avenue
Chicago, IL 60631
(800) 253-2788

Concept Associates
7910 Woodmont Avenue
Bethesda, MD 20814
(800) 333-8252

Coronet/MTI Film & Video
108 Wilmot Road
Deerfield, IL 60015
(800) 621-2131

Davenport Films
Route 1
P.O. Box 527
Delaplane, VA 22025
(703) 592-3701

Debeck Educational Video
314 East Holly #106
Bellingham, WA 98225
(604) 261-4791

Direct Cinema
P.O. Box 100003
Santa Monica, CA 90410
(800) FILMS4U

Durrin Productions
1748 Kalorama Road, NW
Washington, DC 20009
(202) 387-6700

Encounter Video
2580 NW Upshur
Suite 202
Portland, OR 97210
(503) 274-9476

Encyclopaedia Britannica Educational Corp.
310 South Michigan Avenue
Chicago, IL 60604
(800) 554-9862

FilmFair Communications
10621 Magnolia Boulevard
North Hollywood, CA 91601
(818) 985-0244

Films Inc.
5547 North Ravenswood
Chicago, IL 60640
(312) 878-2600

Golden Book Video
1220 Mound Avenue
Racine, WI 53401
(414) 633-2431

GPN
P.O. Box 80669
Lincoln, NE 68501
(800) 228-4630

Guggenheim Productions
3121 South Street, NW
Washington, DC 20007
(202) 337-6900

Home Vision
P.O. Box 800
Concord, MA 007142
(800) 262-8600

HPG Home Video
400 South Houston
Suite 230
Dallas, TX 75202
(214) 741-5544

Informed Democracy
P.O. Box 67
Santa Cruz, CA 95063
(408) 426-3921

Instructional Media Institute
c/o Weston Woods Studios
Weston, CT 06883
(800) 243-5020

Karol Video
350 North Pennsylvania Avenue
Wilkes-Barre, PA 18733
(717) 822-8899

KIDVIDZ
618 Centre Street
Newton, MA 02158
(617) 965-3345

Landmark Films
3450 Slade Run Road
Falls Church, VA 22042
(800) 342-4336

Lightyear Entertainment
Suite 5101
350 Fifth Avenue
New York, NY 10118
(212) 563-4610

Live Home Video
15400 Sherman Way
P.O. Box 10124
Van Nuys, CA 91410
(800) 423-7455

Live Wire Video Publishers
3315 Sacramento Street
San Francisco, CA 94118
(415) 564-9500

Lucerne Media
37 Ground Pine Road
Morris Plains, NJ 07950
(800) 341-2293

Made to Order Productions
Suite 400
535 Cordova Road
Sante Fe, NM 87501
(800) 232-5252

MasterVision
969 Park Avenue
New York, NY 10028
(212) 879-0448

The Media Guild
1722 Sorrento Valley Road
San Diego, CA 92121
(619) 755-9191

MGM/UA Home Video
10000 West Washington Boulevard
Culver City, CA 90232
(213) 280-6000

Music for Little People
P.O. Box 1460
Redway, CA 95560
(800) 346-4445

National Film Board of Canada
16th Floor
1251 Avenue of the Americas
New York, NY 10020-1173
(514) 283-9000

National Geographic Society
Educational Services
Washington, DC 20036
(800) 368-2728

Partners in Learning Programs
344 Seventh Avenue
San Diego, CA 92101
(800) 544-0844

PBS Video
1320 Braddock
Alexandria, VA 22314-1698
(800) 424-7963

Penguin Home Video
Prism Entertainment
1888 Century Park East
Los Angeles, CA 90067
(213) 277-3270

Phoenix/BFA Films & Video
468 Park Avenue South
New York, NY 10016
(800) 221-1274

Public Media Video
5547 North Ravenswood
Chicago, IL 60640
(800) 826-3456

Pyramid Film & Video
Box 1040
Santa Monica, CA 90406
(800) 421-2304

Pyramid Films
dist. by Golden Book Video
1220 Mound Avenue
Racine, WI 53401
(414) 633-2431

Rabbit Ears
dist. by UNI
Five South Sylvan Road
Westport, CT 06880
(203) 857-3760

Random House Home Video
400 Hahn Road
Westminster, MD 21157
(212) 572-2683

Reading Rainbow (See GPN)

SelectVideo Publishing
3301 West Hampden
Suite N
Englewood, CO 80110
(800) 346-5652

Smarty Pants Video
15104 Detroit Avenue
Suite 2
Lakewood, OH 44107-3916
(216) 221-5300

SRA Group
P.O. Box 4520
Chicago, IL 60680
(800) 843-8855

Sterling Publishing Co.
387 Park Avenue South
New York, NY 10016
(800) 367-9692

SVS/Triumph
1700 Broadway
New York, NY 10019
(212) 698-4814

Tyndale House
351 Executive Drive
P.O. Box 80
Wheaton, IL 60189
(800) 323-9400

UNI Distribution
70 Universal City Plaza
Universal City, CA 91608
(818) 777-4506

Video Reader Productions
10703 Maze Road
Indianapolis, IN 46259
(317) 862-3349

Video Treasures
500 Kirts Boulevard
Troy, MI 48084
(313) 280-1010

Weston Woods
389 Newton Turnpike
Weston, CT 06883
(800) 243-5020

Westport Media
dist. by Clearvue-EAV
6565 North Avondale Avenue
Chicago, IL 60631
(800) 253-2788

WGTE Home Video
136 Huron
Toledo, OH 43692
(419) 243-3091

RESOURCES

Booklist. Twice monthly with single issues in July and August. American Library Association, 50 East Huron Street, Chicago, IL 60611 (800) 545-2433. $56/year.

Children's Video Report. P.O. Box 3228, Princeton, NJ 08543-3228 (609) 452-3228

KIDSNET: A Computerized Clearinghouse for Children's Television and Radio. Suite 208, 6856 Eastern Avenue, NW, Washington, DC 20012 (202) 291-1400

Parent's Choice. A quarterly journal of the Parent's Choice Foundation, P.O. Box 185, Newton, MA 02168 $15 (617) 965-5913.

Parents' Choice Guide to Videocassettes for Children. 1989. Consumers Union, paper, $13.95.

Reading Rainbow: A Guide For Teachers 1992. GPN, P.O. Box 80669, Lincoln, NE 68501, paper, $10.50.

Video Source Book. Annual. Gale, $220.

(See also Key to ALA Awards, p. xvii.)

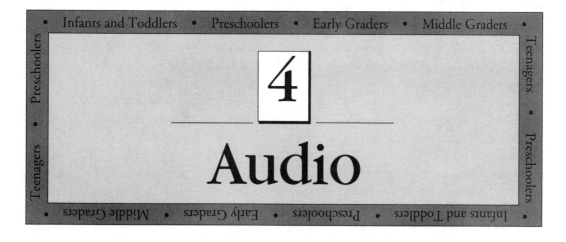

4

Audio

I. MUSIC MADE FOR CHILDREN

INTRODUCTION

"Where do my sneakers go at night, when I turn out the
    light?"[1]
"How did the turtle get his shell?"[2]
Who goes "In search of the Wow Wow Wibble Woggle Wozzie
    Woodle Woo!"?[3]

Answers to these questions plus a whole world more can be found in the new wave of musical recordings for children, represented in the choices below.

Children's music is undergoing a revolution, and the rebels are music masters whose work appeals to parents as well as kids. Some of the familiar names include Arlo Guthrie and Tom Chapin (brother of Harry Chapin and son of jazz pianist Jim Chapin), but many lesser knowns, who are talented singers, composers, and musicians, have devoted their talents to making great music with special kid appeal. Some of these artists work independently, and occasionally their treasures take a bit of mining.

Where do you find the recommended recordings? The library is the best place to start. If yours does not have a specific recording, the staff will be glad to track it down if possible or suggest

[1] Rick Charette, see p. 170
[2] Kathi Smith, see p. 235
[3] Tim Noah, see p. 224

similar works. When your child wants to hold on tight to a borrowed tape, record, or compact disc (CD), it may be time to buy a copy and add it to the home collection.

Locating quality children's music for purchase can be challenging at times. There are a few series, such as *Wee Sing,* that are widely marketed and show up in chain stores of all types. However, even in music stores children's fare is poorly represented; sometimes it must be sought under broad categories, such as folk music. Bookstores often carry book-tape combinations, but may be missing the excellent original story, comic, and dramatic recordings that are cited in the latter part of this section.

Children's bookstores, specialty toy shops, and catalogs are all good sources. Once you know the artists you like, you can check distributors' catalogs for new releases. Catalogs will not provide critical opinions, however. For reviews, look in parenting magazines and professional journals, such as ALA's *Booklist.* Along with the distributors for each of the titles reviewed (see pages 222, 226–227), we've listed a few catalogs. Ask your librarian about *AV Market Place* and other reference guides that provide the addresses of artists who distribute their own tapes.

HOW TO USE THIS CHAPTER

Because the cassette tape remains the most popular choice overall for cost, quality, portability, and children's handling, we have described recordings available in that format. Some items are available in records, and more and more children's audio is appearing in CD as well. The prices we've cited refer to the cassette tapes only.

Many of the tapes described in the following pages have won Notable Children's Recording awards from the American Library Association. Such awards represent the best opinions of outstanding librarians in children's services, basing their judgments on factors meaningful to children of all backgrounds and from all regions.

INFANTS AND TODDLERS

Babes, Beasts, and Birds
(Ages Infant–5)
Pat Carfra
Lullaby Lady Records; dist. by Alcazar, $9.98.

Carfra's lullabies and greet-the-day songs come from many lands and will lure responses from even the youngest listeners. Side 1 is full of wide-awake tunes about ducks, frogs, whales, bears, and babies; Side 2, "Dozing Off," weaves sweet music with evocative images.

Awards: Notable Children's Recording 1988

Earth Mother Lullabies: Volumes 1, 2, and 3
(Ages Infant–3)
Pamela and Tim Ballingham
Earth Mother Productions; dist. by Alcazar, $9.95 (per volume).

Soprano Ballingham sings an array of international lullabies, accompanied by soothing string and percussion instruments.

Awards: Notable Children's Recording 1988

Everything Grows
(Ages 2–6)
Raffi
A & M Records, $10.95.

Probably the best known of the many recordings by this popular singer for children, *Everything Grows* displays Raffi's typical magic and energy that invites—no, commands—children to sing along. His repeated verses, enjoyable nonsense, and unforgettable rhythms will stay with young listeners and encourage creativity. Raffi's terrific environmental recording *Evergreen, Everblue* (Silo) was selected as a Notable Children's Recording for 1991.

Awards: Notable Children's Recording 1988

Hello Everybody!
(Ages 1–4)
Rachel Buchman
A Gentle Wind, $8.95.

Rhymes, lullabies, and play-along songs for toddlers highlight this cheerful mix of original tunes and old favorites.

Awards: Notable Children's Recording 1987

I Wanna Tickle the Fish

(Ages 2–6)

Lisa Atkinson

A Gentle Wind, $8.95.

These bubbly bathtime, anytime songs will soothe the youngest listeners and tickle the imaginations of toddlers. Highlights are "Bathtub Queen" and "You Can be a Giant." Another fun record from this artist is *The One and Only Me*.

Lullabies Go Jazz: Sweet Sounds for Sweet Dreams

(Ages 1–Adult)

Jon Crosse

Jazz Cat Productions; dist. by Alcazar, $8.98.

Here's a great alternative to "Rock-a-Bye Baby." With sax, strings, and percussion, Crosse transforms the meaning of lullabies and leads tots (and parents) into sweet dreams with mellow jazz.

Awards: Notable Children's Recording 1987

Lullaby Berceuse

(Ages 3–5)

Connie Kaldor and Carmen Campagne

Music for Little People, $9.98.

Here are soothing lullabies in French and English—a charming combination. Kaldor's low, dreamy voice crooning in English is a pleasant counterpoint to the lilting French songs of Campagne. Light piano and guitar accompany the singers.

Marcia Berman Sings Lullabies and Songs You Never Dreamed Were Lullabies

(Ages 1–Adult)

Marcia Berman

B/B Records, $10.95.

Many of Berman's lullabies are Hit Parade songs from the 1950s, sung in a rich blues style. Also included are classic Russian songs that Berman recalls from her own childhood. A wake-up offering from this singer is *Marcia Berman Sings Malvina Reynolds' "Rabbits Dance" and Other Songs*.

Awards: Notable Children's Recording 1990

Peek-A-Boo

(Ages 2–5)

Hap Palmer

HAP-PAL Music; dist. by Alcazar, $9.95.

Palmer has spent more than two decades creating fine music for young children. These affectionate stylings of jazz, folk, and boogie-woogie tunes touch such basics as "Finger Foods" and "Gettin' Up Time." Palmer's *Zany Zoo* and *Homemade Band* recordings will delight older listeners as well.

The Rock-A-Bye Collection: Volume 1

(Ages Infant–Adult)

Tanya Goodman

J. Aaron Brown/Someday Baby; dist. by Alcazar, $9.95.

Backed by string orchestra, Goodman's vocals create an uplifting mood for parents and a nice listening experience for little ears. The flip side features instrumentals only. Also available from J. Aaron Brown is a Notable Children's Recording for 1989, *A Child's Gift of Lullabies*. (These nine contemporary lullabies are lovingly rendered and available in Spanish under the title *Un Regalo de Arrullos*.)

Sleepytime Serenade

(Ages 1–3)
Linda Schrade
A Gentle Wind, $8.95.

Accompanied by acoustic guitar and flute, Schrade encourages sing-along with her clear, spirited performance of traditional, classic, and modern songs. Just right for the youngest children.

Sleepy Train

(Ages 2–5)
Michael Mish
Mish Mash Music Records; dist. by Alcazar, $9.98.

A calming collection from Michael Mish, who combines bedtime stories with original lullabies. Side 1 has a variety of lullabies; Side 2 features "The Princess Story," a fine fairy tale enlivened by Mish's comical voices. The recording ends with "Sleepy Train"—a sure nap-inducer.

Songs and Games for Toddlers

(See Start Dancing, p. 210.)

Stardreamer, Nightsongs, and Lullabies

(Ages Infant–7)
Priscilla Herdman
Alacazam!; dist. by Alcazar, $9.98.

Fifteen lullabies, new and old, cast a magic spell via folksinger Herdman's acoustic guitar and mellifluous voice.

Awards: Notable Children's Recording 1989

PRESCHOOLERS

The Alphabet Operetta

(Ages 4–6)
Mindy Manley Little
MVO Records, $9.95.

Mindy Manley Little has composed an original tune for every letter of the alphabet, infusing each with a lively character of its own.

Beasties, Bumbershoots, and Lullabies

(Ages 4–8)
Mike and Carleen McCornack
Garden Variety, $9.98.

Sound effects (animal vocalizations, whizzes, clicks, and buzzes) punctuate the clear baritone and mezzo voices of the McCornacks,

START DANCING—
SONGS TO WIGGLE, WALK,
AND CLAP TO

Can a Cherry Pie Wave Goodbye? Songs for Learning through Music and Movement
(Ages 3–7) Hap Palmer   HAP-PAL Music; dist. by Alcazar, $9.95.

A gleeful children's chorus joins Hap Palmer in songs of early education—letters, numbers, phonics, days of the week, colors, animals, and more. Palmer is a singer and producer whose work belongs on everyone's shelves.

Songs and Games for Toddlers   (Ages 1–3) Bob McGrath and Katharine Smithrim   Western Publishing, $8.99.

Bob McGrath of "Sesame Street" is responsible for many lovely recordings for small children. The musical selections here incorporate instructions for play-along activities, familiar rhymes, and easily mastered sing-along tunes. McGrath's inviting voice and tone will have young listeners following his cue.

Steppin' to the Music   (Ages 2–5) Linda Saxton Brown   Linda Saxton Brown, $9.95.

Children will absorb musical principles as they sing, play, and dream along with Brown's action- and thought-provoking songs.

You'll Sing a Song and I'll Sing a Song   (Ages 5–8) Ella Jenkins   Smithsonian/Folkways; dist. by Rounder Records, $9.50.

An album full of songs meant to be imitated and improvised upon. Backed by the Urban Gateways Children's Chorus, Jenkins's rich, engaging voice moves from "Did You Feed My Cow?" to the "Maori Indian Battle Chant," bringing children to new musical and cultural experiences.

(See also *Marc Brown Does Hand Rhymes* and *Marc Brown Does Play Rhymes* in Videos.)

who present original and well-known songs that kids will savor.

Camels, Cats, and Rainbows
(Ages 2–8)
Paul Strausman
A Gentle Wind, $8.95.

Singer/songwriter Strausman is a former day-care teacher whose music sets little toes to tapping and imaginations to whirling with images of ants, peanut butter, drums, and more.

Awards: Notable Children's Recording 1982

Can a Cherry Pie Wave Goodbye? Songs for Learning through Music and Movement
(See Start Dancing, p. 210.)

Canciones para el Recreo/Children's Songs for the Playground
(Ages 4–8)
Suni Paz
Smithsonian/Folkways; dist. by Rounder Records, $9.98.

The Smithsonian has reissued some great classic children's music under its Folkways label. These 13 songs in Spanish by Suni Paz are a superb example. Five of the tunes have been translated into English on the tape (and print translations of all are provided). South American—particularly Chilean and Argentine—rhythms and instruments prevail.

Chanukah at Home: Holiday Songs for Children
(Ages 4–Adult)
Dan Crow, Marcia Berman, and others
Rounder, $9.50.

Six of the best children's recording artists join in offering both original and traditional Chanukah songs, sung in Yiddish, Hebrew, and English. Guitar, mandolin, banjo, and dobro accompany these joyous holiday tunes.

Family Concert
(Ages 4–9)
Barry Polisar
Rainbow Morning Music; dist. by Alcazar, $9.95.

This sampler from eight previous albums serves up some of the irreverent Polisar's best selections, including "My Brother Thinks He's a Banana" and "Underwear"—the latter, a surefire giggle-getter. Polisar's appeal stretches to older listeners, though he has been known to infuriate teachers, dubbed "boring" and "mean" in some of his outrageous songs.

Fran Avni Sings Artichokes and Brussels Sprouts
(Ages 3–8)
Fran Avni
Lemonstone; dist. by Alcazar, $9.95.

Accompanied by a chorus of children's voices, Avni moves from bluesy tunes to finger-snapping sing-alongs about vegetables, chicken pox, dancing, and other relevant aspects of childhood.

Happy Birthday!
(Ages 2–Adult)
Sharon, Lois, and Bram
Elephant Records; dist. by A & M Records, $8.98.

This well-known trio mixes calypso, country, waltz, and swing in their arrangements of birthday ditties. A family classic. Among the artists' many other popular collections are *Mainly Mother Goose* and *Sharon, Lois and Bram*

Sing A to Z, a Notable Children's Recording for 1991.

Awards: Notable Children's Recording 1989

Help Yourself!

(Ages 3–8)

Cathy Fink and Marcy Marxer

Rounder Records, $9.98.

Self-reliance and self-confidence are fostered through the charm and breezy rhythms of these original sing-along tunes. Lyrics address such childhood challenges as tying shoes, crossing streets, and learning to read. Fink is also responsible for putting together the wonderful recording *Grandma's Patchwork Quilt,* which features a range of talented performers and some very sensitive and delightful kids' songs.

Holidays and Special Times

(Ages 2–6)

Greg and Steve

Youngheart Records; dist. by Alcazar, $9.95.

More than Christmas and Chanukah are celebrated by Greg and Steve in this enticing medley of rock, pop, and rap. The songs encompass holidays all through the year, including Halloween and Martin Luther King's birthday.

Make Believe

(Ages 4–7)

Linda Arnold

Ariel Records; dist. by Alcazar, $10.

In original songs performed with her daughter, Arnold celebrates the child's everyday world as well as larger, general themes such as imagination and peace. Lovely

music enhances the upbeat ideas. Another fanciful collection by Arnold is *Peppermint Wings*. Arnold hosts "Pickleberry Pie," a weekly radio program for children. Look for it on local, college, and public radio stations.

Awards: Notable Children's Recording 1988

Rainy Day/Sunny Day

(Ages 4–7)

The Bumblebeez

The Bumblebeez, $7.99.

The trio of singers who call themselves the Bumblebeez (David Scheffler, Lianne Sterling, Laurie Hedlund) know how to keep kids happy, whatever the weather, through witty, bouncy songs that can be used for games, sing-along, or stormy-day listening.

Rhythm and Rhymes

(Ages 3–5)

Josh Greenberg and Bill Vitek

A Gentle Wind, $8.98.

Familiar tunes—for example, "Three Blind Mice" and "Simple Simon"—set to sophisticated jazz arrangements introduce children to new styles of music and a variety of instruments (and should dispel parental boredom).

Awards: Notable Children's Recording 1982

Shake It to the One That You Love the Best: Play Songs and Lullabies from Black Musical Traditions

(Ages 3–Adult)

Cheryl Warren Mattox (compiler)

Music for Little People, $9.

Caribbean, African, and African-American melodies are melded into this stirring, jazzy recording. Side 1 features playful tunes and Side 2, dramatic lullabies. The accompanying book is so beautifully illustrated that, on its own merits, it was named a Notable Children's Book of 1991.

SongPlay Hooray!

(Ages 3–5)
Dennis Hysom
Sleepwater Productions; dist. by Alcazar, $9.95.

Hysom's rock-'n'-roll and otherwise enhanced versions of traditional nursery rhymes tickle the funny bone in a musically imaginative fashion.

Steppin' to the Music

(See Start Dancing, p. 210.)

Uh-Oh!

(Ages 3–9)
Rosenshontz
Rosenshontz Records; dist. by Alcazar, $9.98.

Gary Rosen and Bill Shontz (Rosenshontz) are remarkable zanies whose rock-'n'-roll rhythms truly explore the concerns of children, from bugs to morning hugs, from sibling clashes to "Uh-Oh" crashes. The clarinet solos and full instrumental backgrounds appeal to adult listeners while training the ears of younger ones to more sophisticated music. The duo's lyrics are heartfelt. (See their video *The Teddy Bears' Picnic* in the Top Ten Music Videos list on p. 225.)

You'll Sing a Song and I'll Sing a Song

(See Start Dancing, p. 210.)

EARLY GRADERS

Animal Crackers and other Tasty Tunes

(Ages 5–8)
Kevin Roth
Sony Kids' Music, $8.98.

Roth's a favorite with children and adults because he can write and deliver a song with a new twist—even on familiar topics. Another favorite from Roth is *Dinosaurs, Dragons, and*

Other Children's Songs, which features a duet with Peter Yarrow of "Puff the Magic Dragon." *The Toymaker's Christmas* and *The Sandman: Lullabies and Night Time Songs* are two more award winners by Roth.

Awards: Notable Children's Recording 1990

Are We Almost There?
(Ages 6–12)
Troubadour
A Gentle Wind, $8.98.

Victor Cockburn and Judith Steinbergh (Troubadour) set comical, sensitive lyrics to rock music. Their songs give a kid's-eye view of common parental queries, such as "What did you do in school today?" The words as well as the feelings of kids are further represented with free-verse recitations by sixth-graders between the songs. Another Troubador recording, *On the Trail,* talks about chicken pox, loose teeth, and werewolves.

Chickens in the Garden
(Ages 5–10)
Phil Rosenthal and others
American Melody Records; dist. by Alcazar, $9.98.

Rosenthal, the bluegrass veteran known for *The Paw Paw Patch* (a Notable Children's Recording of 1988) offers country music for kids, with relevant lyrics on school days and swimming holes, all sung to the pulsating beat of mandolin, guitar, bass, and bongo drums.

Awards: Notable Children's Recording 1991

Diamonds and Dragons
(Ages 6–10)
Charlotte Diamond
Hug Bug Music; dist. by Alcazar, $9.

Here is fantasy on tape from a wizard with music and lyrics. Diamond's songs about imps, dragons, dinosaurs, and purple cats will enchant listeners, as does her Notable Children's Recording of 1987, *10 Carrot Diamond* (Hug Bug Music).

Diddy Bop Dinosaurs
(Ages 6–10)
Gary Lapow
Springboard Records, $10.

Peppy songs with a message—for example, "Look in a Book" and "Too Much Television"—are sung by Lapow to an appealing pop beat and electronic music. Parents may know Lapow from his folksinging days; kids may recognize him from his concerts on the Disney channel. Both will relish his inventive rock tunes.

Family Tree
(Ages 5–8)
Tom Chapin
Sony Kids' Music, $8.98.

Once they hear this verse from the title song, "We're a family and we're a tree/Our roots go deep down in history," kids won't be able to stop singing it. The dirgelike "Don't Make Me Go to School Today" is also intriguing. These are all terrific songs with music as catchy as the lyrics. Chapin's recording *Moonboat,* another original combination of the silly and solemn, is a Notable Children's Recording of 1990 and his *Mother Earth* is a 1991 Notable selection.

Awards: Notable Children's Recording 1989

TRAVEL TUNES

Any of the recordings in this chapter will brighten a trip for kids, but a few selections really nail the stresses and delights of a family vacation. The family sing-along is a time-honored way to pass the hours in a car. *KidsSongs* (see p. 217) is filled with repeatable verses and a lyric book large enough to share in the back seat; *KidsSongs Sleepyheads* will help out upon arrival.

A Car Full of Songs   (Ages 4–8) Tom Paxton   Sony Kids' Music, $8.98.

"Dad's Not Lost" and "I've Gotta Go" are two highlights of this recording, which also spins off into such keep-'em-busy activities as the license plate game. Paxton's bouncy music will ward off the driving doldrums.

Hopping Around From Place to Place   (Ages 4–7) Ella Jenkins   Educational Activities, Inc., $10.99.

Jenkins's work epitomizes children's music. This recording, featuring original tunes about international voyages, gives a good sense of varying cultures and geography. Instrumental flair comes from ukulele, guitar, accordion, bells, and percussion.

Imagination Cruise   (Ages 5–11) Chris Holder   A Gentle Wind, $7.95.

"Storysinger" Holder transports listeners with sparkling, funny tales. In "Wizard of the Highway," a twist on a Yiddish folktale, an already noisy car grows even worse until the normal din is downright peaceful in comparison. (Pack a print version of the tale, such as Margot Zemach's *It Could Always Be Worse,* for quieter times.)

Take Me with You!   (Ages 4–8) Peter Alsop   Yellow Moon Press, $9.95.

Alsop's folk tunes and lively rhythms will keep travelers amused. His "Irish Seatbelt Jig" is hilarious. And, in "It's No Fun When Ya Gotta Eat an Onion," he shows it's okay that not everyone likes the same things.

Traffic Jams   (Ages 3–6) Joe Scruggs   Shadow Play Records & Video, $9.

Silliness abounds in Scruggs's songs about traveling and encountering boredom, traffic, trolls, and  ogres. Scruggs is riotously funny and consistently original in his musical perceptions of childhood. His ability to see things from the child's point of view adds a lot to his verses.

The Farmer's Market

(Ages 4–10)
Timmy Abell
Upstream Records, $9.

The lyrics of Abell's upbeat country tunes are simple, direct, and often humorous, good for solo listening or family fun. Accompaniment features a flock of folk instruments, including the hammered dulcimer, banjo, fiddle, two-penny whistle, and mandolin.

Awards: Notable Children's Recording 1990

Friends of the Family

(Ages 5–Adult)
Jim Newton, Paul Stookey & Friends
Celebration Shop, $12.95.

Paul Stookey (of Peter, Paul and Mary), along with Newton and friends, developed this tape for seriously ill or handicapped children. Its message of hope and optimism can reach out to many others, of course. The recording is also available in Spanish, as *Amigos de la Familia.*

Growing Up Together!

(Ages 3–5)
Gemini
Gemini Records; dist. by Alcazar, $9.98.

Gemini are a set of twins—Sandor and Laszlo Slomovits—who celebrate families and growing up with a blend of folk, blues, and country music accompanied by the Ann Arbor Youth Choir. Their song "Hello" teaches salutations in several languages.

Awards: Notable Children's Recording 1990

I'm Gonna Reach!

(Ages 5–8)
Tom Pease
Tomorrow River Music; dist. by Alcazar, $9.95.

Pease sings both traditional and original songs, accompanied by a children's choir and fine backup musicians. Such numbers as "Bellybutton" and "Things Are Coming My Way" are sure to set young listeners in motion.

Awards: Notable Children's Recording 1990

I'm Just a Kid

(Ages 6–8)
Rory Zuckerman
Sony Kids' Music, $9.

Rory's first album introduced her own style of "kid-rock" with a great Motown beat and a sensitivity to children's concerns, such as shyness and self-esteem. Her newer recordings, especially *Little Broadway,* are just as zestful.

Improvise with Eric Nagler

(Ages 4–10)
Eric Nagler
Rounder Records, $9.98.

Folksinger Nagler performs an eclectic group of songs, joined by a children's and church chorus for some numbers. Throughout he addresses kids' emotions. The instruments are as varied as the titles, ranging from an electric guitar and psaltery to Nagler's own invention—a sewerphone.

Awards: Notable Children's Recording 1990

In the Hospital

(Ages 6–12)
Peter Alsop and Bill Harley
Moose School Records; dist. by Alcazar, $9.98.

Song and dialogue about illness and hospitalization are kept as lighthearted as possible. Children learn about sickness and hospital routines as well as find some morale boosters and humor amid the serious subject matter.

A Kid's Eye View of the Environment
(Ages 5–8)
Michael Mish
Mish Mash Music Records; dist. by Alcazar, $9.98.

Mish asks children questions about the earth and its future, and their concerns and responses inspire his music. The addition of practical suggestions and nature's sounds add further meaning to this quality production. Also recommended is *We Love the Animals*.

KidsSongs 1 and KidsSongs 2
(Ages 4–8)
Nancy and John Cassidy
Klutz Press, $10.95 (includes spiral-bound book).

Old favorites, many enlivened with funny lyrics, are sung by the Cassidys, who are sometimes joined by a chorus of children. "Holler-along Handbooks," full of colorfully silly illustrations on laminated pages, supply lyrics that encourage family singing and boost reading skills. *KidsSongs Jubilee* is another recording in this vein.

Mail Myself to You
(Ages 4–8)
John McCutcheon
Rounder Records, $9.50.

The sources of McCutcheon's lyrics stretch from Woody Guthrie to special-ed students, just as his musical treatments go from driving rock to folksy fiddling. He hits on all numbers in this appealing collection.

Monsters in the Bathroom
(Ages 4–8)
Bill Harley
Round River Records, $9.

From "Black Socks"—a dark comedy about laundry—to "That's What Friends Are For"—a rocking tune on sharing—Harley expresses a range of kids' feelings. The title song "Monsters in the Bathroom" confronts common childhood fears about darkness.

One World
(Ages 5–10)
Lois LaFond
Boulder Children's Productions; dist. by Alcazar, $9.98.

Beginning with the Latin-American beat of "Part of the Family," LaFond's music blends rhythms from around the globe to convey her title's harmonious premise. Reminiscent of Paul Simon's multicultural *Graceland, One World* integrates reggae, blues, and verses in various languages.

Oops!
(Ages 6–8)
Dan Crow
Sony Kids' Music, $9.50.

Crow's listeners have such a good time, they seem unaware that this entertainer is actually a teacher (specifically, a speech therapist) delivering covert lessons on the fun of language and correct usage within songs like "Kiss a Cow" and "Oops."

Piggyback Planet: Songs for a Whole Earth

(Ages 5–10)

Sally Rogers

Round River Records, $9.

An environmental serenade by a talented folksinger. Rogers draws from the rhythms of the earth and blends traditional Native American tunes with energetic, inspiring lyrics.

Shake Sugaree

(Ages 5–9)

Taj Mahal

Music for Little People, $9.98.

Taj Mahal delivers a "Funky Bluesy ABCs" and other terrific folk music with guitar and har-monica accompaniment. Here is an unforget-table musical tour through the South, the Caribbean, and West Africa. A children's chorus joins in the fun.

Awards: Notable Children's Recording 1989

Where Do My Sneakers Go at Night?

(Ages 5–9)

Rick Charette

Pine Point; dist. by Alcazar, $9.

Charette's witty, rhythmic reactions to lost socks and misplaced sneakers are irresistible, enhanced by great sound effects and original tunes. His songs are upbeat answers to everyday problems. (See Top Ten Music Videos, p. 223, for *An Evening with Rick Charette.*)

MIDDLE GRADERS AND TEENAGERS

[*Editor's Note:* Many of the songs for Early Graders are just as appropriate for 9- and 10-year-olds. Check the preceding section for choices. We have merged Middle Grader and teen titles here because music so readily transcends age categories. In fact, there are few "standard" titles for early teens, whose taste in music has reached what Jill Jarnow (author of *All Ears: How to Choose and Use Recorded Music for Children*) calls "The Age of Yuck"—anything *you* select for them is yucky.]

All for Freedom
(Ages 6–12)
Sweet Honey in the Rock
Music for Little People, $9.98.

Blues, gospel, jazz, and contemporary music are sublimely rendered by a quintet of women led by Bernice Johnson Reagon, a scholar, musician, and a curator at the Smithsonian. The collection is made up of traditional spirituals and folk songs rooted in the African-American experience.

Awards: Notable Children's Recording 1990

Christmas Day in the Morning
(Ages 10–Adult)
John Langstaff
Revels Records, $9.95.

Langstaff's music provides a classy alternative to conventional carols. Historical instruments, supplemented by a synthesizer, yield a joyous pageant of medieval song and dance rhythms.

Awards: Notable Children's Recording 1988

Daring Dewey
(Ages 8–12)
David Kinnoin
Song Wizard Records, $9.98.

Kinnoin's original tunes vary in rhythm from jazz to reggae, with stops at pop and rock-'n'-roll. Care for the earth and confidence in oneself are two of his more significant concerns, but he also sings blithely about veggies in "Eat Your Peas" and spiteful siblings in "A Thousand Stickers in His Underwear."

The Dinosaur and More
(Ages 9–12)
Karen & Tommy
Beanstalk; dist. by Alcazar, $8.

The song "R-E-A-D-I-N-G," based on Aretha Franklin's "R-E-S-P-E-C-T," is one of many high points in this grab bag for preteens. With rap, blues, and rock songs there's fun here, and relevant themes.

A Fish That's a Song
(Ages 8–14)
Smithsonian/Folkways; dist. by Rounder Records, $12.95.

American folk art and music are celebrated. The recordings were drawn from the Smithsonian archives, the artwork in an accompanying booklet culled from the Smithsonian's Hemphill Collection of American Folk Art. The music of Woody Guthrie, Pete Seeger, and Elizabeth Cotten are among these great selections.

Awards: Notable Children's Recording 1991

Hearts & Hands
(Ages 7–11)
Tickle Tune Typhoon
Tickle Tune Typhoon; dist. by Alcazar, $9.

With a mélange of musical styles, Tickle Tune Typhoon delves into matters of heart and mind. For example, "Brains" celebrates our thinking abilities, and "Grammar Rapper" talks about writing sentences. These are sensitive, uplifting songs from the creators of *All of Us Will Shine* and *Hug the Earth* (both Notable Children's Recordings). Look for *Let's Be Friends* in the Top Ten Music Videos, p. 224.

PETER AND THE WOLF

Peter and the Wolf (Ages 4–Adult) New York Philharmonic   Moss Music Group, $3.98.

Leonard Bernstein conducts the music of Sergei Prokofiev and narrates this tale of a disobedient little boy who snares a wolf by its tail.

Peter and the Wolf (Ages 3–8) Cincinnati Pops Orchestra   Caedmon/HarperCollins, $9.95.

Carol Channing's narration is beguiling and the musical sound effects from the Cincinnati Pops are terrific. "Tubby the Tuba" on the reverse side tells of a tuba who longs for a spot in the orchestra; meanwhile, the sounds of the orchestra are joyfully introduced to young listeners.

Peter and the Wolf (Ages 3–9) Dave Van Ronk
Alacazam!; dist. by Alcazar, $9.98.

Adapted for a jug band, Van Ronk's version remains faithful to characters and story but uses fiddle, clarinet, penny whistle, kazoo, mandolin, and guitar for instrumentation. A delightful folksy alternative by a blues artist.
Awards: Notable Children's Recording 1991

Peter and the Wolf (Ages 10–14) "Weird Al" Yankovich   Scotti Brothers; dist. by BMG Records, $9.99.

Yankovich keeps the music straight in his version, but adds rude sound effects and zany characterizations to his narration. A parody of Saint-Saëns's *Carnival of the Animals* is on Side 2.

Peter & the Wolf Play Jazz (Ages 4–Adult) Jon Crosse   Jazz Cat Productions; dist. by Alcazar, $9.

Crosse's excellent jazz rendition, narrated by LeVar Burton (host of the "Reading Rainbow" television series), will surely draw parents and children into a new appreciation of Prokofiev's story and Crosse's music. The reverse side carries Carmen McRae's jazzy rendition of nursery rhymes in "Cool Mother Goose Suite."
Awards: Notable Children's Recording 1990

Piqued an interest? Don't overlook *Peter and the Wolf,* illustrated by Barbara Cooney, in Books (on p. 50).

The Iron Man
(Ages 10–15)
Pete Townshend
Atlantic, $9.98.

Pete Townshend of The Who, creator of the rock opera *Tommy,* has produced another one based on a fable written by poet Ted Hughes. A 10-year-old (sung by Townshend) encounters the fearsome metal-consumer, Iron Man (played by blues legend John Lee Hooker), and a Space Dragon (sung by Nina Simone). The valorous child faces moral quandaries and experiences physical adversity before reaching his triumph. Grand rock music and poignant lyrics highlight this production.

Kaddywompas
(Ages 7–Adult)
Tim Noah
Noazart Records; dist. by Alcazar, $12.95.

The country-and-western beat of Noah's music, and the bucolic spirit of his songs, spin a mood of lazy summer days. Noah is a pro and this production shows it, from the original lyrics to the band's backup music. (See also Top Ten Music Videos, p. 224, for more of Noah's music.)

The Kids of Widney High
(Ages 9–11)
Special Music from Special Kids
Rounder Records, $9.98.

The kids of Widney High are a class of physically and developmentally disabled teens who have written lyrics that are fresh, earnest expressions of long-range hopes and everyday dreams. Excellent music supports the songs,

which are eloquently introduced by teacher Michael Monagan.

Awards: Notable Children's Recording 1990

Pete Seeger and Arlo Guthrie Together in Concert
(Ages 9–Adult)
Warner Bros. Records, $12.99.

This set of two recordings can introduce teens to classic folk and protest songs sung by two great artists. Among the tunes are "Yodeling," "Guantanamera," and "Declaration of Independence." The powerful, expressive singing of Seeger and Guthrie can also be found in a number of the releases from the Smithsonian/Folkways collection.

Somewhere in a Corner
(Ages 9–11)
Debbie Friedlander & Friends
Sound Creations; dist. by Alcazar, $10.

A pair of 12-year-olds are among the "Friends" responsible for the impressive lyrics in this collection of insightful, hopeful songs. The words call for an end to hunger, war, pollution, and racism. Rhythms of guitars and bongo drums echo these strong yearnings.

UHF
(Ages 12–18)
"Weird Al" Yankovich
Scotti Brothers; dist. by BMG Records, $9.99.

With his customary bravura, Yankovich parodies the serious-minded rock-'n'-roll performances of Dire Straits, R.E.M., and rapper Tune Loc. His send-ups feature comic references to popular American culture.

Yankovich's version of *Peter and the Wolf* is not to be believed (see p. 220).

Walk a Mile
(Ages 9–11)
Vitamin L
Lovable Creature Music; dist. by Alcazar, $9.95.

Sung by a multiethnic group of adults and teens, this mixture of pop, blues, and reggae emphasizes brother- and sisterhood and self-identity. "Think for Yourself," "Family," and "People Are a Rainbow" are some of the songs about peer pressure, human bonds, and valuing diversity.

Who Will Speak for the Children
(Ages 5–14)
Children of Selma and Rose Sanders
Rounder Records, $9.50.

Selma, Alabama, the historic site of the civil rights movement, is the home of the 24 children whose voices join Rose Sanders's in this stirring musical appeal for human rights.

MUSIC DISTRIBUTORS

A & M Records
1416 North La Brea Avenue
Hollywood, CA 90028
(213) 469-2411

Alcazar
P.O. Box 429
Waterbury, VT 05676
(800) 541-9904

Atlantic Recording Corp.
75 Rockefeller Plaza
New York, NY 10019
(212) 484-6000

B/B Records
570 North Arden Boulevard
Los Angeles, CA 90028
(213) 460-4387

BMG
One South 450 Summit
Oakbrook Terrace, IL 60181
(708) 268-6400

The Bumblebeez Records
859 North Hollywood
Suite 115
Burbank, CA 91505
(213) 654-9187

Caedmon/HarperCollins
1995 Broadway
New York, NY 10023
(212) 207-7000

Celebration Shop
P.O. Box 355
Bedford, TX 76095
(817) 268-0020

THE EDITOR'S TOP TEN
MUSIC VIDEOS

1. Turn on the Music   (Ages 2–7) Hap Palmer   Hi-Tops; dist. by Alcazar, $9.

Palmer reaches his young audience with a brilliant combination of animation, puppetry, and live performers (including little ones). His bright, funny tunes trigger hand clapping and singing along. A diner scene with exaggerated gum-chewing teaches manners. A journey to "Backwards Land" shows parents attending classes in mudpie creation conducted by small, serious teachers.

(See also *Baby Songs,* cited in the entry for Even More Baby Songs in our Videos chapter.)

2. Carnival of the Animals   (Ages 2–Adult) Camille Saint-Saëns   Gary Burghoff, narrator
TTE; dist. by Music for Little People, $16.98.

The whimsical poems of Ogden Nash are accompanied by the music of Camille Saint-Saëns performed by a youthful orchestra at the San Diego Zoo. Gary Burghoff (familiar to many from the television show "M*A*S*H") narrates, sharing the scene gracefully with the live animal stars.

3. An Evening with Rick Charette   (Ages 5–9) Rick Charette   Pine Point; dist. by Alcazar, $19.

Charette, accompanied by the Bubblegum Band, sings some of his favorite original numbers, such as "Where Do My Sneakers Go at Night?" and "I Love Mud." The bright images of Charette's most memorable tunes and lyrics are captured in several vignettes.
Awards: IRIS Award 1989

4. Fancy That   (Ages 4–8) Gemini   Gemini; dist. by Alcazar, $19.

A family concert featuring twin brothers Sandor and Laszlo Slomovits, who have adopted the fitting stage name of Gemini. Their virtuosity with instruments is as exciting to witness as their ability to pull their audience into action with effervescent songs about childhood. Music from around the world is another part of their repertoire.

5. In Search of the Wow Wow Wibble Woggle Wozzie Woodle Woo   (Ages 4–8) Tim Noah   A & M Video, $16.

Four Emmys were awarded to this production, which features special effects, amazing props and puppetry, and, most of all, Noah's energetic performance. Noah acts like a big kid in a child's room. The scene can be corny, but once he starts singing, wonderment soars and disbelief vanishes.

6. Let's Be Friends   (Ages 4–Adult) Tickle Tune Typhoon   Tickle Tune Typhoon; dist. by Alcazar, $19.98.

Do the "Vega-boogie" (and dance with a greater-than-life-sized ear of corn) and learn that "Everyone Is Differently Abled" with this joyous, interracial, multitalented group of exquisite song makers. This relatively long tape will have children returning to it again and again, drawing fresh fuel for the imagination and funny bone.

Awards: California Children's Video Award 1990

7. Song City U.S.A.   (Ages 5–10) Geoffrey Drummond, producer   IVE/FHE; dist. by Live Home Video, $14.95.

This outrageous rock-'n'-roll parody is hosted by Gus, whose silly antics in a 1950s diner gently spoof the songs performed by Rosenshontz and other stars of children's music. Original tunes such as "Peanut Butter Blues" and "Hippopotamus Rock," along with old favorites like "The Name Game," are all interpreted in rock video format, zany and appropriately juvenile. A sequel, *More Song City U.S.A.,* is also available.

8. The Teddy Bears' Picnic   (Ages 2–6) Rosenshontz   Rosenshontz; dist. by Alcazar, $24.

Gary Rosen and Bill Shontz ham it up for a delighted play-along audience of picnicking families as they sing the popular title tune and eight original creations. In with the fun are lyrics about divided families and kids with special needs. A bit of animation and a lot of horseplay between the singers liven up this video.

9. Joe's First Video   (Ages 3–7) Joe Scruggs   Shadow Play Records & Video, $19.

One mom on a skateboard and another scrounging for angel wings (for a costume) are typical of this off-the-wall video. Also featured is a reassuring music fable about where they put lost children. The mix of various animation styles (from Claymation to live-action) will distract some viewers, but entertain others.

Awards: U.S.A. Film Festival, 1st Place; California Children's Video Award

10. Sleep Over   (Ages 3–8) Sharon, Lois, and Bram   Elephant Records; dist. by A & M Video, $16.

Where can you find an elephant in a nightcap? At a sleepover held by the popular Canadian singing trio, who always have their elephant friend on stage. It's the night before a fishing trip and there's plenty of serious singing, silly jokes, and horse—er, elephant—play, for the multiethnic group of kids who sing and frolic in anticipation of the morning. Eric Nagler, a frequent guest on "Sharon, Lois, and Bram's Elephant Show," drops in for a rendition of "Does Your Chewing Gum Lose Its Flavor?" (See more about this group in Videos, on p. 151.)

Educational Activities, Inc.
P.O. Box 392
Freeport, NY
(800) 645-3739

Garden Variety Record Co.
1695 Holly Avenue
Eugene, OR 97401
(503) 485-0515

A Gentle Wind
P.O. Box 3103
Albany, NY 12203
(518) 436-0391

IVE/FHE
dist. by Live Home Video
15400 Sherman Way
P.O. Box 10124
Van Nuys, CA 91410
(800) 423-7455

Klutz Press
2121 Staunton Court
Palo Alto, CA 94306
(415) 857-0888

Linda Saxton Brown
P.O. Box 746
Carnelian Bay, CA 95711
(916) 583-6231

Moss Music Group
95 Commerce Road
Stamford, CT 06902
(203) 323-2999

Music for Little People
P.O. Box 1460
Redway, CA 95560
(800) 346-4445

MVO Records
Route 1
P.O. Box 274
Vashon, WA 98070
(206) 567-4831

Noazart Records
15920 177th Avenue
NE Woodinville, WA 98072
(206) 485-5357

Revels Records
Building 600
One Kendall Square
Cambridge, MA 02139
(617) 621-0505

Rounder Records
One Camp Street
Cambridge, MA 02140
(617) 354-0700

Round River Productions
301 Jacob Street
Seekonk, MA 02771
(508) 336-9703

Shadow Play Records & Video
P.O. Box 180476
Austin, TX 78718
(800) 274-8804

Song Wizard Records
P.O. Box 931029
Los Angeles, CA 90093
(213) 461-8848

Sony Kids' Music
P.O. Box 4450
New York, NY 10101

Springboard Records
2140 Shattuck Avenue
P.O. Box 2317
Berkeley, CA 94704
(510) 849-2400

Upstream Records
P.O. Box 8843
Asheville, NC 28814
(704) 258-9713

Warner Bros. Records
3300 Warner Boulevard

Burbank, CA 91505
(818) 954-6293

Western Publishing
1220 Mound Avenue
Racine, WI
(800) 558-5972

Yellow Moon Press
P.O. Box 1316
Cambridge, MA 02238
(617) 776-2230

II. STORIES, DRAMATIZATIONS, AND FOLKLORE

INTRODUCTION

In this section you will find select original tales, poetry, folklore, and dramatizations, performed by some of America's best readers and storytellers. There's a remarkable world of listening pleasure in audio, beyond the obvious benefits of the music and books available on tape. Storytelling and poetry performances are dramatic arts that weave their own kind of magic, accessible to all kids.

Joy Wilcox, a children's librarian and accomplished storyteller, reminds us that, "Storytelling perpetuates our English-language heritage" as well. "We don't practice the great forms of spoken English enough to maintain its richness and beauty. Our conversational speech is artless. Listening to and participating in good storytelling helps promote and sustain the oral heritage." Children develop an ear for expressive language.

Kids can curl up alone with a favorite story, or families can enjoy storytelling presentations together, listening at home, on the road, or in the library.

We've taken care to locate works that translate well to tape format. Listening to these spine-chilling, heartwarming, transporting tales will open new avenues for kids and adults. Perhaps these selections will prompt further explorations of storytelling, both live and recorded.

Videos of storytellers in action are also available; however, professional opinion is mixed on the use of this medium. Some hold that the storyteller should virtually disappear and let the story work its magic; others prefer a more flamboyant style that works well on the screen. Videos, at any rate, help spread the fame of storytellers and bring their work to a wider audience. Three special video series are cited below.

HOW TO USE THIS CHAPTER

The tapes listed can be tracked down in libraries, children's bookstores, and some music shops. The National Association for the Preservation and Perpetuation of Storytelling (NAPPS) publishes a national directory of storytellers, publications, festivals, and educational events. NAPPS also distributes many of the tapes cited in this section. Some of the tapes are privately distributed by the storytellers. Addresses are listed at the end of the section.

INFANTS AND TODDLERS

Baby's Nursery Rhymes
(Ages 1–6)
Stories to Remember
Lightyear Entertainment; dist. by BMG, $8.95.

Phylicia Rashad provides a sassy, sultry rendition of traditional Mother Goose rhymes. Set to Jason Miles's jazzy original musical score, this with-it treasury spins out 57 familiar nursery verses. (The video version is a terrific musical revue.) A refresher course in Mother Goose for parents.

Classic Children's Tales
(Ages 2–6)
Jackie Torrence
Rounder Records, $9.50.

With her impeccable timing and diction, Torrence tells six well-known stories, including "Little Red Riding Hood," "The Little Gingerbread Boy," and "Three Billy Goats Gruff." Torrence is a master of taletelling. Among her other outstanding recordings are *Country Characters, Legends from the Black*

STORYTELLERS PERFORM FOR THE CAMERA

The American Storytelling Series   (Ages 5–Adult)   Storytel Enterprises; dist. by H. W. Wilson Company. 8 videos, $99 each (Vols. 1–4 or 5–8 are $349).

Twenty-two American storytellers do their stuff in these video performances. Among them are Carol Birch, Brother Blue, Heather Forest, Jay O'Callahan, Michael Parent, Maggi Pierce, Laura Simms, Jon Spelman, and Elizabeth Ellis. Many American geographic regions and cultures are represented: Appalachia, New England, Native American, African-American, Caribbean, Irish, Far Eastern, and Eastern European.

Family Circle Storyland Theater   (Ages 5–Adult)   NAPPS, $14.95 each (4 vol.).

Each of the four volumes in this series of videos features a story apiece by Rafe Martin, Jay O'Callahan, and Laura Simms—three great storytellers.

The Storytellers Collection   (Ages 5–Adult)   Director: Tom Howard.   Producer: Peter Edwards. Atlas Video, $14.95 ($59 for series of 4 videos) (35 min. each).

Cultural diversity is a hallmark of this excellent four-video series, which features the Native American tales of Joe Bruchac, Olga Loya's Spanish-laced "Flying Skeleton," Alice McGill's African *pourquoi* stories, and the work of several other talents.

Tradition, and the ALA Notable, *Br'er Rabbit Stories.*

Good Morning, Good Night
(Ages 2–Adult)
Kathi, Milenko and Friends
Lightworks Productions, dist. by Music for Little People, $9.98.

Poems of William Wordsworth, Rudyard Kipling, Emily Brontë, Robert Louis Stevenson, and others gain dramatic force as accompanied here by woodwinds, guitars, saxophone, marimba, and percussion. Among the beguiling poems are Stevenson's "Block City" and "My Shadow." (See Books for picture book versions of these treasured poems.) *On the Way to Somewhere* is a sequel with more of the artists' original musical interpretations of famous verses.

Rockabye Bunny
(Ages Infant–2)
Linda Danly
Danly Productions, dist. by Alcazar, $9.

It is rare to find a story suited to the youngest listener, yet this tale of a baby bunny's day is truly that. The gentle, original music enhances the telling.

Awards: Notable Children's Recording 198

PRESCHOOLERS

Aesop's Fables
(Ages 3–Adult)
The Smothers Brothers
Music for Little People, $9.

Blending comic dialogue and music, Tommy and Dick Smothers wend their way through seven famous fables, among them "The Fox and the Grapes," "The Boy Who Cried Wolf," and "The Bird and the Jar." Silliness abounds, but the stories get across.

The Boy Who Loved Mammoths and Other Tales
(Ages 4–6)
Rafe Martin
NAPPS, $9.98.

Rafe Martin is an award-winning children's author and storyteller. This collection features his ALA Notable Book, *Will's Mammoth.* Martin's magic storytelling contains more words than the original picture book. Also in this collection are Native American stories and

Martin's special version of "The Three Little Pigs."

It's Thanksgiving
(Ages 4–7)
Jack Prelutsky
Scholastic, $5.95.

Prelutsky is a popular poet whose whimsy and sentiment are right on target. His delightful holiday presentations include Halloween, Christmas, and Valentine's Day collections. Also look for his other books, such as *The Poems of A. Nonny Mouse* and *Something Big Has Been Here* (see Books.).

Just So Stories
(Ages 4–8)
Graham Whitehead
Kids Records; dist. by Alcazar, $9.98.

Four of Kipling's short stories are performed by Whitehead—"The Elephant's Child," "The Sing-Song of Old Man Kangaroo," "The Cat That Walked by Himself," and "How the Camel Got His Hump." Film star Jack Nicholson has also narrated several Kipling tales for videos produced by Rabbit Ears. Cassette versions of Nicholson performing "How the Camel Got His Hump" and "How the Rhinoceros Got His Skin" are available from Windham Hill (dist. by Alcazar).

Awards: Notable Children's Recording 1988

Percival the Froggy
(Ages 3–5)
David Connolly
Music for Little People, $9.95.

Through narration, song, and vibrant sound effects, Connolly tells the tale of Percival, a young bullfrog who leaves his Louisiana

bayou for adventure and is caught by a little boy named Filbert. A joyful, down-home musical story about interacting with nature.

Prince Ivan and the Frog Princess
(Ages 3–6)
Natalia Makarova
Delos International, $7.98.

Prima ballerina Makarova narrates the romantic fairy tale in her richly accented English. The full score of the background music, Prokofiev's "Music for Children, Op. 65," is played following the tale. Another fine narration by Makarova is the Notable Children's Recording *The Snow Queen* (Delos), which features Tchaikovsky's "Album for the Young, Op. 39."

Awards: Notable Children's Recording 1991

Stories and Songs for Little Children
(Ages 2–10)
Pete Seeger
NAPPS, $9.98.

Seeger's trademark tale "Abiyoyo" (now a "Reading Rainbow" feature) is alone worth the price of admission. With it are more classics that kids will love to learn, including "Green Grass Grew All Around," "Raccoon's Got a Bushy Tale," and "Comin' Round the Mountain." (See also "The Foolish Frog" in Videos on p. 167.)

The Tailor of Gloucester
(Ages 3–6)
Meryl Streep and the Chieftains
Windham Hill, dist. by Alcazar, $9.50.

Streep's narration of the Beatrix Potter classic has something special. Is it her controlled voice that brings to mind Beatrix Potter spinning stories for her young friends? This Christmas tale about the mice who aid an elderly tailor gets a polished performance, one that will send story lovers back to Potter's adventures of Benjamin Bunny and Peter Rabbit. The Chieftains cloak Potter's words in the magic of their music. The fine video of this story, also narrated by Streep (produced by Rabbit Ears), prompted this tape.

Tales Around the Hearth
(Ages 3–8)
Heather Forest
A Gentle Wind, $8.95.

Forest's retelling of African, Swedish, and Russian folktales and fables retains their original flavor and highlights the positive messages. Includes pleasing vocal arrangements and sound effects.

EARLY GRADERS

Bring on the Brass
(Ages 6–9)
Mark Rubin Productions; dist. by Alcazar, $9.95.

Leo McKern introduces the brass sections of an orchestra in a splendid narrative. McKern, known to many as Rumpole of the Bailey from the PBS series, offers stately diction and a keen sense of humor. A similar recording, *The Orchestra,* featuring Peter Ustinov, is also available in video. (See Videos.)

Cabbage Soup
(Ages 5–12)
Children's Radio Theater
A Gentle Wind, $8.

Two fairy tales—"Beauty and the Beast" and "Cabbage Soup" (a zany, updated version of "Rapunzel")—are performed with zestful songs and dramatization. *Cabbage Soup* is one of many fine tapes from the Children's Radio Theater.

Awards: Notable Children's Recording 1984

Flying Africans
(Ages 6–Adult)
Alice McGill
Earwig Music; dist. by Flying Fish, $9.

Although she occasionally breaks into song, Alice McGill most often uses a straight narrative to relate these traditional and personal

CLASSICS COME TO LIFE

Mr. Bach Comes to Call   (Ages 5–10) Susan Hammond   Classical Kids, $9.98.

Johann Sebastian Bach pays a visit to a reluctant young pianist who becomes enthralled with the great composer's life story. Bach's tales about playing for royalty, his imprisonment, and composing are dramatically narrated to the child, while his stunning music is interspersed. See also *Bach and Broccoli* in Videos.
Awards: Notable Children's Recording 1989

Mozart's Magic Fantasy: A Child's Journey through *The Magic Flute*   (Ages 6–10) Susan Hammond   Classical Kids, $9.98.

A modern-day child, Sara, and a dragon are drawn into episodes within *The Magic Flute* in this audio adventure that playfully, sometimes poignantly, brings the world of opera and the music of Mozart to children.
Awards: Notable Children's Recording 1991

The Life and Music of Ludwig van Beethoven   (Ages 8–12)   North Star Records/The Classics 101, $9.95.

For good biographical detail look to the North Star series. On Side 1 of this tape, notes on Beethoven's early life, compositions, and hearing loss are interspersed with selections from his music. Side 2 is purely orchestral. Several other composers, such as Mozart and Bach, are featured in this series.

Vivaldi's Ring of Mystery: A Tale of Venice and Violins   (Ages 5–10) Susan Hammond Classical Kids, $9.98.

Katrina is left at the Pieta Orphanage as an infant, then grows to be an accomplished violinist determined to find her family. Aided only by a mysterious ring and a helpful gondolier, Katrina travels through eighteenth-century Venice, which inspired the music of Antonio Vivaldi. With this story base, Classical Kids producer Susan Hammond proceeds to acquaint young listeners with the fire and beauty of Vivaldi's creations.

African-American tales. The five stories with three songs feature guitar, banjo, and harmonica accompaniment.

Awards: Notable Children's Recording 1989

Granny Will Your Dog Bite and Other Mountain Rhymes

(Ages 6–10)
Gerald Milner
Knopf, $18.95 (cassette and hardcover book).

> Ducks on the millpond,
> Geese in the ocean:
> The devil's in the boys
> When they take a notion.

These Appalachian rhymes and songs will tickle listeners' funnybones while delivering a fine sampling of Americana. Banjo and fiddle music back the telling and singing. Homer Fleming and Sonja Bird talk deep "Southern" here, so much so that lines can be missed by young ears unaccustomed to the dialect. This makes the accompanying hardcover book, with its amusing, mood-setting illustrations, a valuable supplement.

Awards: Notable Children's Recording 1991

Joseph the Tailor

(Ages 7–12)
Syd Lieberman
NAPPS, $9.98.

Children will be spellbound by Lieberman's biblical tales and a voice that modulates perfectly as he moves from humor to serious themes. The title story demonstrates Lieberman's way of keeping his audience involved, and his version of "David and Goliath" thrusts listeners into a battlefield more dramatic than any Saturday-morning cartoon conflict.

Awards: Notable Children's Recording 1989

King Arthur and His Knights

(Ages 6–12)
Jim Weiss
Greathall Productions, $9.95.

Weiss is a gifted storyteller who speaks as if he were an Arthurian knight relating tales about others associated with the Round Table—King Arthur, Guinevere, Sir Kay, and Sir Percival. The crackling-fire sound effects in the background set the scene for these accounts of chivalry and the triumph of justice. Weiss's *Arabian Knights* and *Robin Hood/Three Musketeers* tapes (Greathall Productions) have similar appeal.

Awards: Notable Children's Recording 1991

Neighborhood Magic

(Ages 5–9)
Kendall Haven
Kendall Haven, $9.75.

Haven is adept at blending sound effects, background music, and unique vocal inflections. The two tales told here, "Bedtime Stories" and "Saturday," both show the calamitous effects an overactive imagination has on a young boy. The tales stir thoughts of building one's own stories and family legends.

Awards: Notable Children's Recording

Once Upon a Butterfly: A Narrated Musical Fantasy for Children

(Ages 5–10)
Carol Ann Eberle
Heart to Heart Music, $10.

NATIVE AMERICAN LEGENDS

The Boy Who Lived with the Bears and Other Iroquois Stories (Ages 6–10) Joe Bruchac
III Parabola; dist. by Bookpeople, $9.95.

Indian chants provide transitions between the moving and, sometimes, humorous traditional tales related here by a seasoned storyteller. In the title story, a boy who has been raised by bears is pursued in the forest by an ursine relative. Classic folklore rhythms and morals emerge, tantalizing astute young listeners. Another lively tape of classic legends is Bruchac's *Gluskabe Stories*.

Cherokee Legends I (Ages 4–10) Kathi Smith Cherokee Challenge, $10.

In a soft Southern accent, Smith tells folklore and animal stories learned from her ancestors. Native American chanting between each tale evokes a campfire or village setting. Listeners will be intrigued by the way the legends of Native Americans echo the themes of those from other nations. For example, the antics of the Cherokee Little People sound much like those of leprechauns, and Kipling's "Just So" stories are recalled by Smith's telling of "Why the Deer's Teeth Are Blunt."

Cherokee Legends I
by Kathi Smith

Eberle, a composer and singer, narrates a tale that was originally a ballet. Two dolls come to life in the toy room and dance through the night to elegant, original music.

Pegasus
(Ages 6–10)
Mia Farrow
Lightyear Entertainment; dist. by BMG, $9.50.

How Pegasus, once a winged colt, came to be a constellation of stars is related by Mia Farrow. When they hear this bewitching version of the Greek myth, kids may clamor for more. They might try Jim Weiss's tape, *Greek Myths* (Greathall Productions) and, for older listeners, *Greek or Whut?* (described below). *Pegasus* is also available as a video from Lightyear Entertainment.

Stories to Stir the Imagination, Number 1
(Ages 4–12)
Frances Kelley
Eye in the Ear Audio Publishers, $7.98.

"The Emperor's New Clothes," "Midas and the Golden Touch," "Toads and Diamonds," and "William Tell" are the four tales told by Kelley, a master at capturing each character. Music and sound effects liven the adventure. This is part of a four-part series, with such tales as "Pandora's Box," "A Mad Tea Party," and "The Dutch Boy and the Dike."

Sundays at Grandma's/Dimanches Chez Memére
(Ages 6–10)
Michael Parent
Michael Parent, $10.

Parent's stories from his childhood are mingled with traditional French songs. Both are gleaned from his French grandparents, who obviously imparted a love of his cultural heritage along with these fine anecdotes.

Three Hairs from the Devil's Beard and Other Tales
(Ages 7–Adult)
Rosalind Hinman
American Melody, $9.98.

Along with the title story (from the Grimm brothers), British storyteller Hinman dramatically narrates four other fables—English, Scandinavian, and Punjabi. Well-devised sound effects and connecting music by Phil Rosenthal enhance the tales.

Awards: Notable Children's Recording 1991

MIDDLE GRADERS AND TEENAGERS

The Adventures of Christina Valentine
(Ages 9–13)
Kendall Haven
Kendall Haven, $25 (3 tapes).

Christina Valentine suffers a "Twilight Zone" experience when she is sucked into her TV. Inside, Christina has disastrous run-ins with "laugh trackies" (hooded zombies), a chief executive pirate who wants to keep his profit-making secrets away from Christina's prying eyes, and others. This original tale raps commercial television along the way, deploring its role as little more than an advertising vehicle. Christina comes away from her encounters wiser about the realities of TV viewing. A bit heavy-handed in its message, it's still a great spoof and adventure tale. Haven's six-part series won the Corporation for Public Broadcasting's 1992 Silver Award for excellence in children's programming.

Cool in School: Tales from 6th Grade
(Grades 4–6)
Bill Harley
Round River Records, $9.98.

"Is it the way you tie your shoes . . . I got to know, what is cool in school?" After someone tells him to wear his shirt backwards and smear jelly on his hair, the singer decides, "From now on I'll do just what I want to do . . . I'll decide for myself." Highlighted by original songs, Harley's three stories about being cool, talking to girls, and surviving homework are excruciatingly true–funny.

Dreams and Illusions: Tales of the Pacific Rim
(Ages 10–Adult)
Brenda Wong Aoki
Rounder Records, $9.98.

Asian cultures of the world—China, Japan, Korea, Vietnam, Hawaii, and the Pacific coast of the United States—are represented in these six tales powerfully interpreted by actress Aoki. Traditional Asian wind and string instruments in Mark Izu's jazz scores lend atmosphere to these singular productions.

Ghostly Tales from Japan
(See Ghostly Tales, p. 239.)

Greek or Whut?
(Ages 12–Adult)
Barbara McBride-Smith
NAPPS, $9.98.

McBride-Smith is a riot as she parodies Greek mythology in contemporary vignettes. "Pandora," "Orpheus," and "Medea" will never be quite the same. Knowledge of the original tales makes these "fractured" versions work best.

Homespun Tales
(Ages 10–Adult)
NAPPS, $9.98 (Available as a hardcover book, $19.95).

If you don't know where to start your children listening, this is the place. Twenty-one stories from America's best taletellers are presented here. Donald Davis performs "Crack of Dawn." Jackie Torrence moodily renders her "Wily and the Hairy Man." Among the ghost stories, folklore, comedy, and nostalgic pieces are presentations by Elizabeth Ellis, Doc McConnell, and Kathryn Windham.

The Island
(Ages 10–Adult)
Jay O'Callahan
Artana Productions; dist by NAPPS, $10.

O'Callahan is simply one of the best storytellers around. This fantasy opens with a shipwreck that brings a character named Beals to an island inhabited by gruesome supernatural creatures. He lands in the midst of a confrontation between the evil Brineheart, master of the fog, and a fairy princess, Dardenelles, who is trying to save her mother, the queen. This primeval conflict of good and evil is given eerie voice by O'Callahan.

Jewish Tales from the Heart
(Ages 9–Adult)
Betty Lehrman
Tales for the Telling; dist. by NAPPS, $10.

Laughter and tears are induced by Lehrman's telling of Jewish folklore and family anecdotes. Europe and Israel are the settings for her stories, among them "Meshka the Kvetch," "Chicken Soup," and "Lena's Story."

Awards: Notable Children's Recording 1990

The Johnstown Flood of 1889
(Ages 9–Adult)
Syd Lieberman
The Telling Tale; dist. by NAPPS, $10.

Lieberman's account of the Johnstown Flood is remarkable. By introducing some of the people involved, especially one brave little girl, he personalizes the story of how heavy rains and a broken dam brought 40-foot waves that decimated the Pennsylvania city more than 100 years ago. The tape begins with a profile of an unsuspecting city and closes with the survivors returning to normal life, after the loss of some 2,000 lives and the entire city center.

Awards: Notable Children's Recording 1990

A Light in the Attic
(Ages 9–12)
Shel Silverstein
HarperCollins, $11.95.

Silverstein's whimsical verse is especially fun when read by the poet himself. Listening to these irreverent, comical, sometimes sad poems chosen from *A Light in the Attic* (the second children's book ever to appear on *The New York Times* Best Seller list, where it stayed for 186 weeks) is a pleasure.

Stories from the Other Side
(See Ghostly Tales, p. 239.)

GHOSTLY TALES

Ghostly Tales from Japan   (Ages 7–12) Rafe Martin   Yellow Moon Press, $8.98.

These four tales rooted in Japanese tradition are truly chilling. Martin tells how "late in the fall, the time we call Halloween, when the dead leaves rattled on the branches like bones," a young boy was sent by his parents to live in a temple so that he could survive a famine. But this "Boy Who Drew Cats" cannot stop drawing and is banished from the temple. Left on his own, the boy seeks sanctuary in a haunted temple and is attacked by a goblin. It is the cats he was forbidden to draw who rescue him. Another story, "Urashima Taro," will evoke shivers while it reminds listeners of "Rip Van Winkle." These eerie, sometimes gory tales are conveyed with disquieting laughter and moody narration.

Jump Tales   (Ages 6–Adult) Jackie Torrence   NAPPS, $9.98.

A jump tale has an ending so surprising and so skillfully delivered that listeners jump right out of their seats. Torrence ably carries out this old storytelling tradition in these humor-laced, spooky tales—"Blackbeard's Treasure," "Wiley and the Hairy Man," "Tailey-Po," and "The Yellow Ribbon," among others. Just as hair-raising are her *Tales for Scary Times* (Earwig).
Awards: Notable Children's Recording 1992

Stories from the Other Side   (Ages 10–Adult) Dan Keding   Turtle Creek; dist. by NAPPS, $9.

Chilling tales are rendered in measured tones by storyteller Keding. Visits from beyond the grave, ghostly apparitions, and dark shadows of folklore are summoned by the narrator's words. Two of these seven stories are sung in ballad fashion with spectacularly eerie results. Keding's *Dragons, Giants, and the Devil's Hide* is also worth a listen.

The Tell-Tale Heart and Other Terrifying Tales   (Ages 12–Adult) Syd Lieberman   Syd Lieberman Productions, $11.

Lieberman pulls from the classic works of Edgar Allan Poe, Ambrose Bierce, and even Chaucer for this well-conceived production. His tense narration of "The Pardoner's Tale," "An Occurrence at Owl Creek Bridge," a scene snatched from *Beowulf,* and three Poe stories will keep listeners on edge. *Awards:* Notable Children's Recording 1992

The Tricks of Life and Death
(Ages 11–Adult)
Olga Loya
Storyteller; dist. by NAPPS, $9.95.

Loya shares personal anecdotes and traditional Latin-American tales in this rich bilingual recording. She alternates her telling from Spanish to English, translating words, phrases, and sentences along the way in a clear and lyrical manner.

Awards: Notable Children's Recording 1990

Underground Railroad: Escape to Freedom
(Ages 9–Adult)
BackPax International, $9.95 (with paperback, $12.95).

Voices representing those of escaping slaves reveal terror, bravery, and yearning as they describe to an interviewer their means of flight through the Underground Railroad. Realistic sound effects and music add tension to these narratives, which are like a step back into American history. (See the Travel chapter for information on taking a real trip along such historic routes.)

Under the Greenwood Tree: Shakespeare for Young People
(Ages 12–Adult)
Claire Bloom and Derek Jacobi
Stemmer House, $8.95.

Renaissance music played on authentic period instruments provides the perfect mood for these excerpts from Shakespeare's poetry, drawn from both plays and sonnets. Claire Bloom and Derek Jacobi read like the superb actors they are.

Awards: Notable Children's Recording 1987

Weatherbeard and other Folk Stories
(Ages 8–12)
Tim Jennings
NAPPS, $10.

Jennings's tales range from the terror of the Norwegian folktale "Weatherbeard" to a comic view of geese and more sophisticated fare. The Sweet Corn Broadcasters add a musical finale.

DISTRIBUTORS

Alcazar
P.O. Box 429
South Main Street
Waterbury, VT 05676
(800) 541-9904

American Melody
P.O. Box 270
Guilford, CT 06437
(203) 457-0881

Atlas Video
4915 St. Elmo Avenue
Suite 305
Bethesda, MD 20814
(800) 999-0212

BackPax International
P.O. Box 603
Wilton, CT 06897
(203) 834-0669

Cherokee Challenge
P.O. Box 507
Cherokee, NC 28719
(704) 488-2988

Children's Radio Theater
1314 14th Street, NW
Washington, DC 20005
(202) 234-1436

Classical Kids
The Children's Book Store Distribution
67 Wall Street
Suite 2411
New York, NY 10006
(800) 668-0242

Delos International
1032 North Sycamore Avenue
Los Angeles, CA 9003
(213) 962-2626

Earwig Music Co., Inc.
1818 West Pratt Boulevard
Chicago, IL 60626
(312) 262-0278

Eye in the Ear Audio Publishers
P.O. Box 1005
Boston, MA 02103
(617) 267-1396

Flying Fish
1304 West Schubert
Chicago, IL 60614
(312) 528-5455

A Gentle Wind
P.O. Box 3103
Albany, NY 12203
(518) 436-0391

Greathall Productions
P.O. Box 813
Benicia, CA 94510
(800) 477-6234

Kendall Haven, Storyteller
5025 Occidental Road
Santa Rosa, CA 95401
(707) 577-0259

Knopf
400 Hahn Road
Westminster, MD 21157
(800) 733-3000

Lieberman Productions
Syd Lieberman
2522 Ashland Avenue
Evanston, IL 60201
(708) 328-6281

Lightyear Entertainment
350 Fifth Avenue
Suite 5101
New York, NY 10118
(212) 563-5135

Michael Parent
760 Lexington Avenue
Charlottesville, VA 22901
(804) 971-1829

Music for Little People
P.O. Box 1460
Redway, CA 995560
(800) 346-4445

NAPPS
P.O. Box 309
Jonesborough, TN 37659
(615) 753-2171

North Star Records
116 Chestnut Street
Providence, RI 12903
(401) 274-4119

Parabola
656 Broadway
New York, NY 10012
(212) 505-6200

Rounder Records
One Camp Street
Cambridge, MA 02140
(617) 354-0700

Round River Productions
301 Jacob Street
Seekonk, MA 02771
(508) 336-9703

Scholastic Productions, Inc.
730 Broadway
New York, NY 10003
(800) 325-6149

Stemmer House
2627 Caves Road
Owings Mills, MD 21117
(301) 363-3690

H. W. Wilson Company
950 University Avenue
Bronx, NY 10452
(800) 367-6770

Yellow Moon Press
P.O. Box 1316
Cambridge, MA 02238
(617) 776-2230

RESOURCES

All Ears: How to Choose and Use Recorded Music for Children by Jill Jarnow. 1991. Penguin, paper, $12.99.

Booklist. Twice monthly with single issues in July and August. American Library Association, 50 East Huron Street, Chicago, IL 60611. (800) 545-2433. $56/year. Reviews of recorded music, original stories, and books on tape appear regularly; Editors' Choice annually cites the best audio and video productions of the past year.

Mother Goose Comes First: An Annotated Guide to the Best Books and Recordings for Your Preschool Child by Lois Winkel and Sue Kimmel. 1990. Holt, paper, $14.95.

NAPPS Directory of Storytellers. National Association for the Preservation and Perpetuation of Storytelling, P.O. Box 309, Jonesborough, TN 37659 (615) 753-2171, $7.95.

(See also Key to ALA Awards, p. xvii.)

5
Computer Software

INTRODUCTION

Computers offer some of the most exciting ways for parents to play and otherwise interact with their children. The range of programs is enormous—from flight simulators and number crunchers to drawing, music, and writing programs. Many people have tuned into computers at work and readily accept the idea that a computer at home is a useful, even essential item. There are some nonbelievers, however, including those who feel there is no need for a computer in the home when popular arcade-game systems can be run on television equipment. But no such game system can stimulate intellectual activity and development the way good computer programs do.

These days, even in primary grades, major reports must be neatly presented. Children who start working on a keyboard at age four or even younger will have no trouble booting up the machine and sitting down to keystroke their own assignments in grade school. In many schools computer learning is part of the curriculum, and this way the basic skills are already in place.

Our focus is on computer software programs that offer positive reinforcement to kids. We've been somewhat wary of programs that jeer "boo, hiss, you lose" when a mistake is made. Kids get enough of that from their peers. A gentle reminder of the right answer is appropriate for youngsters, and an encouraging "try again" effective for older children.

Programs should develop thinking skills. Drills are okay and often more fun on the computer than anywhere else, but programs that continue to challenge and motivate a child to return and try again are the best investment.

Computer games can build skills in reading, math, geography, science, and foreign languages. We've gathered programs that provide some delight as they do so and that can be used at home, school, or the library.

As we've said earlier, please view our designated age levels as suggestions, not commandments. For example, the Middle Graders choices are strong on animal-oriented programs, and arithmetic is well represented under early grades, so feel free to drift accordingly. Many programs listed for the young are valuable even for adult use. The teen section is small because so many programs from the earlier grades serve older audiences as well. Most programs have levels of advancement that make the activities more challenging as the user's skill increases. Publishing or word-processing programs may be listed near programs for younger kids; many such programs are, in fact, suitable for all ages, depending on the user's skills.

The term *user* appears throughout this section as a good, bias-free word; sex or age should not restrict one's choices. Otherwise, we've kept computer jargon to a minimum.

HOW TO USE THIS CHAPTER

The software described below can be purchased, used at the library (or borrowed if copyright permits), and used at school. After each title, the software manufacturer and distributor are cited. Their addresses are provided at the end of this chapter, or they can be found in *The Software Encyclopedia*. Don't hesitate to write software providers for catalogs. Ask them about local outlets or order directly.

When you've identified a program you like, see if your local library has it, then give it a try before springing for the purchase. You might bring this book or a catalog along and suggest (to a librarian) that the library purchase or borrow an item. New software may not always be within the library's resources, but the librarians will be glad you asked; they want to know exactly what their patrons need.

All available formats, as of this writing, are cited before each annotation. The cost is listed only once if it is the same for IBM, Macintosh, Commodore, and Tandy as it is for Apple. If there are price variations, they are so noted. The notation *MS-DOS* means that a program will work with most IBM/Tandy systems. If a program is not available in a format compatible with your computer, it may be soon. Software manufacturers strive to match formats to demand. Ask at your local software store or check with the manufacturer or distributor. Ask what hardware is required before purchasing a program. Color monitors, joysticks, or other features may be necessary for its proper enjoyment. It is tempting, and often a fine idea, to seek out the most recent version of a program. Be sure, however, that it suits the hardware of your machine. Sometimes "newer" is not better. If your child has adjusted well to a program and not outgrown it, if it works fine, is the latest version necessary?

TRACKING BOOKS ON THE COMPUTER

BookBrain (Ages 6–14)   The Oryx Press.   Apple II, $195 (7 disks).

Available in three versions, for Grades 1 to 3, Grades 4 to 6, and Grades 7 to 9, *BookBrain* is a database of fiction and biographies. Catchy annotations for approximately 775 titles are on each program, but the *see* references can expand the book suggestions to more than 2,000. Comments by readers can be added to the database as well. The user simply looks for books by author, title, or subject, or plays with the "book detective" feature. In the latter, the computer poses a series of questions, then "detects" appropriate titles. Five books are suggested based on the user's responses.

BookWhiz Jr. (Ages 8–11)
BookWhiz (Ages 11–14)
BookWhiz for Teens (Ages 14–18)   Educational Testing Service.   Apple/Apple II, $199/each.
IBM (*BookWhiz for Teens* only).

Kids can use this customized book-selection software to look for certain types of books or define their own reading interests. In *BookWhiz Jr.,* there are 1,007 books in the database; *BookWhiz for Teens* has 755. Kids can look for a specific type of book or search according to reading level, main character, type of story, or length. A "choose-your-own-adventure" story game is available to help students pinpoint reading interests. The program will select 5 to 10 titles and offer intriguing annotations.

TODDLERS

Katie's Farm

(Ages 2–5)

Lawrence Productions.
Apple II, $39.95.
IBM/Tandy, Macintosh, Amiga.

McGee, an apple-cheeked toddler, tours his cousin Katie's farm, and the two kids hunt for eggs, visit animals, watch a scarecrow dance, and ride a horse. The extraordinary graphics and ease of use of this software allow a very young child to roam around a farm scene listening to realistic human speech and animal sounds while participating in the chores. The kids will think they are just playing while they are actually learning new words and concepts.

McGee

(Ages 2–5)

Lawrence Productions.
Apple IIGS, $39.95.
IBM/Tandy, Macintosh, Amiga.

McGee will be a familiar figure to parents of independent-minded toddlers. McGee has risen from bed before his family and travels throughout a six-room house and a backyard deciding whether to play with his toys, wake his mom, feed the dog, or engage in other toddler activities. This wordless, menuless software has pictures at the bottom of the screen that can be clicked into, so a young child can navigate the clever program solo. Talking with the child about places visited can help teach names for familiar places in a toddler's life—a significant learning experience. This software can acquaint youngest users with the computer (no drills, quizzes, right or wrong answers) and allows the more timid to explore imaginatively.

McGee at the Fun Fair

(Ages 2–5)

Lawrence Productions.
Apple IIGS, $39.95.
IBM/Tandy, Macintosh, Amiga.

McGee, accompanied by his mother, father, and an African-American friend, visits a carnival. There (via the joystick or cursor moves of the young computer user) the boys can pose for a street artist, gleefully polish off a Popsicle, play on a playground, and watch a clown blow up balloons and twist them into familiar shapes. Described as "wordless" because the instructions are all pictorial, this software is easy to master. Young children will relish the independence and decision-making allowed as much as they will enjoy the antics of McGee.

Muppetville

(Ages 3–5)

Sunburst.
Apple II, $65.
IBM/Tandy.

Kermit the Frog acts as host, bringing children along Main Street and into various interesting activities, including a shapes game with Miss Piggy, number recognition, and matching musical tunes.

Awards: Classroom Computer Learning Software Award 1988

Number Farm

(Ages 2–5)

DLM.
Apple II, $32.95.
IBM PC/Tandy, Commodore.

In this farmyard can be found a selection of counting and number-recognition games. Along with farm songs and barnyard noises, the six games feature clever lessons on the look of numbers both as words and in numeric form. Adult assistance is needed because titles must be read, since icons and picture screens are not exclusively used.

Ollie and Seymour

(Ages 2–4)

Hartley Courseware.
Apple, $49.95.

Ollie is a peddler of balloons whose pet monkey sends him on various expeditions. From these, small children learn direction, traffic safety, shapes and colors, number concepts, and caution with strangers. A colorful program just right for the youngest computer user.

PRESCHOOLERS

Bird's Eye View

(Ages 3–7)

Hartley Courseware.
Apple, $49.95.

Flying along with a bright-colored bird, children master abstract concepts about position and direction (over, beside, front, etc.). Users can rev up the game by introducing an airplane and trying to determine the bird's location in relation to the plane. Even though only two keys are used throughout—the space bar and return key—parental or teacher assistance is usually needed to guide youngsters at first.

Counting Critters

(Ages 3–6)
MECC.
Apple, $49.

Little ones enjoy painless learning as they work their way through five animated games that involve matching, number recognition, and counting from 1 to 20. In the sequel *Arithmetic Critters* (for ages 5–8), games teach addition, subtraction, counting by tens, and measurement with the same appealing critters.

Curious George in Outer Space

(Ages 4–8)
DLM.
Apple II, $24.95.

The familiar mischievous monkey is stranded on a planet inhabited by creatures of all sizes. Children can rescue him by correctly answering questions about shapes, sizes, and other comparison concepts. Younger players will require reading assistance; older ones will have fun following the story and playing space hero. Also available are *Curious George Goes Shopping* and *Curious George Visits the Library*.

Dr. Peet's Talk/Writer

(Ages 4–8)
Hartley Courseware.
Apple II, $69.95.

A program designed to help young children make the transition from letter recognition to writing. "The ABC Song" and "Big Letters" will help kids learn the alphabet, while the "Find Letters" game prompts them through the keyboard. With these skills mastered, children can write stories by inserting words into the sentences provided in 37 Talk/Writer activities. The sound, which requires an Echo or Cricket attachment, is more than a nice enhancement—it is particularly useful for visually impaired users. The program's author (Dr. Peet) offers special instructions for helping blind and visually impaired children learn the keyboard and use the program.

Awards: Classroom Computer Learning Software Award 1988

First Letter Fun

(Ages 3–6)
MECC.
Apple, $49.

After a scene is set, such as a circus, a new picture element is added, and the child must select the first letter of the name of that animal or thing from a choice of four possible letters. The name then runs under the picture to reward, or inform, the guesser. Another fine letter-recognition program is *Pictures, Letters, and Sounds* (Hartley).

Fisher-Price Firehouse Rescue

(Ages 3–8)
Gameteck.
Apple II, $14.95.
IBM.

The Fisher-Price "little people" can be rescued from a flaming building by a fire truck full of lookalikes. The young player must steer the truck through city streets to rescue a cat from a tree or a family from a house. No flames, sirens, or high-tension moments here, just good computer orientation. The street mazes (a variety of levels are available) are great for learning *left* and *right,* especially if played with a parental backseat driver. *Firehouse Rescue* is available in a Fisher-Price "Combo Pack" that includes two other good programs, *Little People Bowling Alley* and *My Grand Piano.*

Kidsmath

(Ages 3–8)

Great Wave Software.
Macintosh, $49.95.

Eight games, among them "Paddleball," "Frog Races," and "Tractors and Trucks," make this arithmetic and early math program an appealing one. Skills covered progress from counting through beginning fractions, and each game can be customized to suit the level of the player. For younger users, the difficult words can be translated into pictorial messages.

Awards: Technology & Learning Software Award 1990–1991

Letter Go Round

(Ages 3–6)

Hi-Tech Expressions.
Apple II, $9.95.
IBM/Tandy.

"Sesame Street" characters Big Bird, Bert, and Cookie Monster teach and tickle in this alphabet game played on a Ferris wheel. The easiest level involves matching a letter on the wheel with a letter carried by the Muppet. The program progresses through five more levels to a game involving scrambled word searches.

Mad Match

(Ages 4–Adult)

Baudville.
Apple IIGS, $39.95.

Players of this concentration game can range from preschoolers to adults. They must choose the matching pair from six images on the screen while super graphics, music, and stereo sound encourage them. The pictures increase in complexity, and a shorter time limit and the use of penalty points up the difficulty for older players.

Mask Parade

(Ages 4–12)

Springboard.
Apple, $39.95.
IBM PC.

Children can play creatively with dress-up clothes or fashion costumes to complement with glasses, badges, jewelry, ties, and hats. A picture menu, icons, and the use of a joystick make this an easy program for young users; the variety and novelty will sustain its appeal for older kids, too. A color printer is not necessary—children can complete their artistic lessons by cutting out and coloring the creations printed on a black-and-white model.

Math and Me

(Ages 3–6)

Davidson.
Apple, $29.95 (talking version for Apple IIGS, $49.95).
MS-DOS.

Youngsters will be up to plenty of "monkey business" while learning shapes, patterns, numbers, and simple addition problems using a mouse or keyboard. Animated monkeys glide across the screen to guide, reward, and entertain players/learners. Digitized speech enhances the version called *Talking Math and Me. Reading and Me* and *Talking Reading and Me* (both by Davidson) are two equally merry educational experiences for children aged 4 to 7.

Awards: Classroom Computer Learning Software Award 1989–1990

Mickey & Friends Fun Pack:
Donald Duck's Alphabet Chase
Mickey's Runaway Zoo
Goofy's Railway Express

(Ages 3–5)

Walt Disney Software.
IBM PC/Tandy, $39.95.
Programs also available individually.
Apple II, $14.95.
Commodore, MS-DOS.

A youngster can learn the alphabet and the keyboard while playing a game with Donald Duck, whose pets are hiding all over the rooms on the screen. In a similar game, *Mickey's Runaway Zoo*, Mickey and Goofy try to round up zoo escapees; the user must push the correct number keys to secure the animals. Lessons in letter and number recognition are smoothly delivered in these very basic programs. *Goofy's Railway Express* uses a circus setting to help users sort shapes.

Muppet Slate

(Ages 5–7)

Sunburst.
Apple II, $75.

Word processing for the youngest writers is available in this program, suitable for the regular keyboard or the Muppet Learning Keys—a colorful, alphabetically ordered keyboard for preschoolers. (An ongoing debate questions whether the Learning Keys, useful for teaching the alphabet, may inhibit computer users when a standard keyboard is introduced.) The program contains simple

words in large print and 126 rebus-style pictures of Muppets and other critters as well as houses and rainbows. Here's a great way to start story writing and word processing at the earliest level.

Awards: Classroom Computer Learning Software Award 1988–1989

The New Talking Stickybear Opposites
The New Talking Stickybear Shapes

(Ages 3–5)

Optimum Resource.
Apple IIGS, $49.95.

The Stickybear software will take children from recognizing shapes through multiplication. There is so much variety and consistent quality in this series that only a few sample programs are mentioned here. The digitized speech, sound, animation, and color graphics are consistently good, though nontalking formats are available for Apple II. The Stickybear host cajoles, congratulates, and rewards, with winning pictures demonstrating the right answers. In *Opposites*, 18 concepts (high/low, inside/outside, near/far, etc.) are presented in pictures, as words, and through sharp, digitized humanlike speech. The *Shapes* program has matching games and other challenges, with the same fine audiovisual reinforcement. Another good program for this age level is *The New Talking Stickybear Alphabet*. (See also *Stickybear Town Builder* on p. 258.)

Paint with Words

(Ages 3–8)

MECC.
Apple II, $49.

Select a word and the picture appears before your eyes—if that is not word recognition, what is? A choice of 12 backgrounds can be selected (school, lake, farmyard, etc.), and then eight words appear below the scene. Once a word is selected, it must be lifted to the picture (via joystick, mouse, or keyboard command), where it is transformed from print into a picture representing the word. Best of all, there is a voice option and a management system that allows the inclusion of synonyms as well as Spanish and other foreign languages.

Picture Chompers

(Ages 4–6)

MECC.

Apple II, $59.

A large set of chomping teeth appear on the screen and children are directed to "Chomp all the green things" or "Chomp all square things" in the 16-piece grid. There are more than 400 graphics and three levels of difficulty. The six levels of play (color, shape, size, design, class, and function) reinforce classification skills and provide a lot of fun in an arcade-style game. *Supermunchers* is another great game for early to middle grade computer users. (See also *Fraction Munchers* on p. 255.)

The Playroom

(Ages 3–7)

Broderbund.

Apple II, $49.95.

IBM/Tandy, $59.95.

Macintosh, $59.95.

Sound and color are phenomenal in this program, offering plenty of challenges and lots of rewards, even for the youngest user. The setting is a child's room (complete with toys on the floor and a small pile of laundry that contains a shirt that waves a sleeve). Activities involve clocks, a board game with three challenge levels, shape-matching, computer games, a radio that turns into a counting toy, and an ABC book that allows children to write a story by adding pictures to a castle scene or a neighborhood street scene. Arithmetic, reading, art, and silliness (popping balloons and waking a toy dinosaur that roars) can be practiced with ease. Once kids graduate from *The Playroom,* send them to *The Treehouse* (see p. 260).

Awards: ALSC Software of the Year 1989; *Technology & Learning* Software Award 1990–1991

Stars and Planets

(Ages 3–6)

Advanced Ideas.

Apple IIGS, $44.95.

Spaceships, stars, and planets serve as more than colorful backdrops in these six games. Moon rocks are collected by an on-screen astronaut, but only if the little one at the keyboard counts the number of rocks correctly. Early reading, arithmetic, and logic skills are equally tested in the other programs.

Talking First Reader

(Ages 4–8)

Orange Cherry Software/Talking Schoolhouse Series.

Apple IIGS, $49.

The inclusion of digitized speech has enhanced many juvenile software programs, and this is definitely one of them. New readers will appreciate the four relevant stories, large text, animation, and carefully articulated words that are augmented by extras, such as barking pups and bouncing balls. Children can learn directions from playing *Talking School Bus* in the same series.

PUZZLES

Jigsaw: The Ultimate Electronic Puzzle (Ages 5–Adult) Britannica Software. Apple IIGS (768K recommended), $39.95.

With four levels of difficulty (from 8 to 60 pieces) adaptable to 20 puzzle pictures, this program offers long-term challenge throughout the family. Experienced users can import new images from compatible software. The "puzzle maker" races a clock and can view the completed image (like checking the top of the puzzle box). Puzzles can be printed with the right hardware (ImageWriter I and II printers are recommended). Great sound and graphics add to the fun.

Mickey's Jigsaw Puzzles (Ages 4–10) Walt Disney Software, Inc. IBM/Tandy, $49.95.

Fifteen puzzles featuring Disney characters in space, in a haunted castle, on a beach, etc., can be selected and constructed on-screen. Players can request a puzzle with from 4 to 64 pieces. They can also choose whether the pieces will have square or traditional jigsaw shapes. Once built, a touch of a button will animate the characters briefly. Computer users with a sound device will hear lively voices and music upon completion.

The PuzzleMaker (Ages 5–9) Edmark. Apple II, $39.95.

The puzzles users make with the 50 pictures included here (or by accessing graphics programs to create original ones) remain on disk and are solved by shifting pieces from the puzzle page to the puzzle table. Each piece is rectangular in shape, so there are no corners or edges to give a head start as in conventional jigsaw puzzles. The level of difficulty can be changed from 12 to 24 pieces.

Tonk in the Land of the Buddy-Bots
(Ages 4–8)

Mindscape/SVE.
Apple II+/Apple IIGS, $19.95.
IBM/Tandy.

Developed by Mercer Mayer from his *Tink Tonk!* series of robot tales, this program sends kids on a search for missing robot parts. Tonk travels through Buddy-Bot Land via raft or cable car (as directed by the user). But beware of black holes that can swallow up Tonk and drop him into a maze in Gonk's castle. Before Tonk can even set out on his journey, the user must solve various recognition and memory challenges, such as matching the robot to its shadow or assembling a robot jigsaw puzzle. Robot music and bright color scenes highlight the play, which has four difficulty levels.

EARLY GRADERS

Easy Street
(Ages 5–8)
Mindplay.
Apple II, $49.99.

Better than a trip to the toy store, this program is a stroll down Easy Street with a shopping list in hand. Kids stop and purchase groceries, pets, toys, and other items (which can be designated by parent or teacher). A playful gorilla enhances the shopper's fun. This game has eight levels and is as educational as it is entertaining.

Awards: Computer Classroom Learning Software Award 1988–1989

Elastic Lines: The Electronic Geoboard
(Ages 7–12)
Sunburst.
Apple II, $65.
IBM/Tandy, $79.

The "geoboards" on the screen have pegs on which electronic rubber bands can be stretched to demonstrate geometric shapes, planes, and concepts such as area and perimeter. Shapes can be designed, then turned, flipped, or repeated to make patterns, all of which can be printed. The program offers an excellent visualization of mathematical concepts and a versatile creative outlet.

Awards: Classroom Computer Learning Software Award 1989–1990

ARTISTS ON-SCREEN

ColorMe: The Computer Coloring Kit   (Ages 3–10)   Mindscape/SVE.   Apple II, $44.95. IBM/Tandy.

The option of creating original pictures or altering those on the disk give this coloring program more depth than many others. Four types of crayons are available, and text can be added to a picture. Badges, cards, and coloring books as well as original art can be stored and printed by computer Rembrandts. This versatile program works easily with a mouse or joystick.

Color 'n' Canvas   (Ages 6–14)   Wings for Learning/Sunburst Communications.   Apple IIGS, $99.

An exemplary art program that provides an array of shapes and two palettes of colors (red, yellow, blue or red, green, blue) for creating original art. A template is available, to be filled in as a puzzle or a backdrop. Mirroring and zoom features expand the program's value and allow different challenge levels for young artists. A learning experience as well as an enjoyable venture into creative art.
Awards: Technology & Learning Software Award 1990–1991

Kid Pix   (Ages 3–Adult)   Broderbund.   IBM, $59.95.   Macintosh, Tandy.

One of the best features of this drawing program is the sound. The drawing tools and the colors, including a custom color feature, are super; but the sound effects really add to the fun of creating original pictures or working with ones imported from other graphics programs. Also available for labeling or enhancing drawings is the alphabet in English and Spanish. The drawing possibilities include a wacky brush, zigzags, bubbles, dot-to-dots, swirls, erasers, and "stamps." The menu offers easy access to all of the options.
Awards: Notable Children's Software 1992

Pow! Zap! Ker-Plunk! The Comic Book Maker   (Ages 7–Adult)   Queue.   Apple II, $49.95. IBM.

Once all the background, clip art, and additional features are loaded and accessible, amateur animators can call up sci-fi and other backdrops and establish villains and heroes in adversarial poses (or absurdly silly ones). Now the animators can fill balloon captions with original dialogue and, if they wish, print out a comic book. When an Echo speech synthesizer is attached, the characters actually talk.

Exploring Measurement, Time, and Money, Levels I–III

(Ages 5–11)

IBM PC Software Dept.
IBM, $202/each level.
Tandy.

Here is a classroom program with many levels that will instruct kids how to count money, tell time, and measure. To demonstrate these often difficult concepts, the software uses everyday situations, which helps show kids how vital the lessons are to their lives. Other helpful features in this easy-to-use program are encouraging pictorial instructions and a voice that informs players whether they are correct or not. Level I suits grades K–2; Level II, grades 3–4; and Level III, grades 5–6.

Awards: Technology & Learning Software Award 1990–1991; *Classroom Computer Learning* Software Award 1989–1990 (Level I)

Fraction Munchers

(Ages 7–10)

MECC.
Apple, $59.

A little green critter with safari hat and square eyes must elude the goofy but menacing Troggles while solving problems dealing with fractions, including equivalencies. Fractions can befuddle some, but concentration on rescue and escape missions can make the challenge a lot more fun. A more general program, but equally rewarding, is *Number Munchers* (also from MECC, but available in MS-DOS and Macintosh as well as Apple).

Hop to It!

(Ages 5–8)

Sunburst.
Apple II, $65.

Animation enlivens this addition and subtraction program that features ample skill challenges for early ages through third grade. For the latter group, there are multistep problems that restrict the numbers they can use to find the solution. A frog, spaceman, rabbit, or mouse character chosen by the child progresses along the line of numbers on the screen in response to the correct answers to the mathematical challenges. More fun than flashcards.

Awards: Technology & Learning Software Award 1990–1991

How the West Was Won + Three × Four

(Ages 8–Adult)

Sunburst.
Apple II, $65.
IBM/Tandy.

The player, driving either a stagecoach or a locomotive, pursues a number line to victory (at number 50). Addition, subtraction, multiplication, division, and order-of-operation skills are put to the test as players compete against one another or the computer. The Wild West theme is cleverly carried out.

Awards: Media & Methods Software of the Year 1988; *Classroom Computer Learning* Software Award 1988–1989

Jumping Math Flash

(Ages 6–10)

Mindscape/SVE.
Apple II, $39.95.

Kids will be so busy eluding the sea serpents by answering the arithmetic problems that they may not notice they are being drilled in the basics. A maze of numbers and threatening serpents cover the screen all through the 21 levels of this program, which also has three speeds to enhance the challenge.

Learn about: Animals

(Ages 5–8)

Wings for Learning/Sunburst.
Apple II, $75.

Kids can create imaginary animals and animal masks, but only after they have studied the real thing in this wonderfully animated program. Animal shelters, appearance, life span, food, and offspring make up the substance of some entertaining and unusually phrased questions. For example: "How many frogs long is this skunk?" There are also three animal masks that can be printed. Imagination and instruction fill the other programs in this series, too: *Learn about Plants* and *Learn about Insects.*

Awards: Classroom Computer Learning Software Award 1989–1990

The Little Shoppers Kit

(Ages 5–9)

Tom Snyder.
Apple II, $109.95.

Designed by teachers for group or classroom use, this program allows kids to create their own stores, handle sales, count change, even stock the shelves. Three store scenarios are already set up on the disk. This software comes complete with props, including toy groceries, play money, and a cash box.

LOGO PLUS

(Ages 6–17)

Terrapin Software.
Apple II, $119.95.
Macintosh (Terrapin LOGO), $99.95.

This powerful software can teach programming to first-graders through twelfth-graders. It has so many dimensions that it remains an important tool well after the basics are mastered. Students can use it to create their own challenges and continue to progress in computer logic. This version supplies new techniques for graphics, as well as additional text, music, and font capabilities. Lego Technic LOGO is a program especially designed to work with Lego models. It enables kids to visualize the effects of computer programming. See the Lego listing in Toys for more information.

The Manhole

(Ages 5–Adult)

Activision.
Apple, $49.95.
IBM PC.

Phenomenal adventures await the traveler through the manhole who journeys in a nonlinear fashion (forward, backward, sideways, up, and down) into more than 600 adventures, from a ship under the sea to a castle in the sky. Digitized voices and outstanding graphics highlight this entertaining program, which requires the use of a mouse. It can be enjoyed by the whole family.

Math Masters: Addition and Subtraction
Math Masters: Multiplication and Division

(Ages 6–9)

DLM.
Apple II, $46 each.

These two programs handle basics with pizzazz. Kids can pore over the electronic work sheets and move into arcade-style games featuring magic shows and robot/motorcycle Transformers. The menu bars, windows, and dialogue boxes allow easy access for individual players. If a parent or teacher reduces the number scale (of 0–25) to, say, 1–10, the games can be tackled by preschoolers.

Math Shop Jr
(Ages 6–9)
Scholastic.
Apple II, $69.95.
Macintosh, MS-DOS.

Here is math in a down-to-earth setting—shops and stores—rather than outer space or the Wild West. Students calculate costs and change, determine the area of a rug, estimate time, and convert measurements in this junior-scale version of the original *Math Shop* (for ages 10 and up). Another similar, quality program is *Algebra Shop* (see p. 270).

Awards: Classroom Computer Learning Software Award 1989–90

Microzine
(Ages 9–14)
Microzine Jr
(Ages 6–9)
Scholastic.
Apple II, $39.95/each issue.

Microzine is a software series that arrives quarterly to subscribers and contains four programs in each issue. Math, science, publishing, and social studies activities are found in each set. It's possible to select back issues if specific programs are desired.

Awards: Classroom Computer Learning Software Award 1986–1987

Nigel's World
(Ages 7–12)
Lawrence Productions, dist. by Broderbund.
IBM/Tandy (640K and hard disk required), $49.95.

It's easy to travel the world with Nigel—a red-headed Scotsman who produces spectacular photographs for Roxy, a magazine editor. Icons on the right of the program direct the user to Nigel's living room, where he receives his latest assignment from his fax machine. Then you must find his destination on the map. Novices, called *shutterbugs,* are given continent assignments, but the geography gets more specific with advancing levels. Fortunately, there are more than 40 maps and a variety of clues that can be easily called up using a mouse or keyboard. Social studies, geology, reading, and music recognition are some of the skills challenged by this remarkable program. Youngest users can simply travel around the world capturing animals, monuments, and people of various cultures in photographic images that appear on the screen with remarkable clarity.

NumberMaze
(Ages 5–11)
Great Wave Software.
IBM, $49.95.
Macintosh.

A castle awaits those who can wend their way through the arithmetic problems in the number maze. The graphics and sound effects extend the fun. Difficulty levels can be set by the player (or parent or teacher).

Awards: Classroom Computer Learning Software Award 1989–1990

PlayWrite

(Ages 7–11)

Sunburst.
Apple II, $75.

A dramatic production can be created by aspiring directors, playwrights, and stage managers, who create costumes, scenery, scripts, and sound effects with this easy-to-use point-and-click software. The play is acted out by puppets, including Bravo Dog and Encore Cat.

Poetry Palette

(Ages 7–Adult)

Mindplay.
Apple II, $59.99.

In the "palette," or database, there are more than 30 poetry forms that a user can call up, read about, then practice. While rhymes aren't mandatory, they are fun, and many will be found in the 12,000-word rhyming dictionary. The term *palette* has one more, deliberate use—there is also a graphics library, with which the accomplished poet can enhance the creation with a carefully selected picture.

Read 'n' Roll

(Ages 8–12)

Davidson.
Apple II, $49.95.
MS-DOS.

Bowling is the motivator here. Once the kids have worked their way through the skill exercises involving reading comprehension, inference deduction, sequencing, and recollection, they can bowl for vocabulary enhancement. (The game scores a strike in academic development, but don't let *that* distract the kids from all the fun.) In *Grammar Gremlins*

(Davidson), a haunted house is the setting for an arcade game that creates a lingering impression of language rules.

Stickybear Town Builder

(Ages 6–9)

Optimum Resource.
Apple, $39.95.
IBM/Tandy, Commodore 64.

Kids are given the keys to an on-screen car and instructed to cruise a brand-new town, with the aid of Stickybear. The goal is to follow the most effective route (a map appears at the top of the screen) to locate certain symbols. Among the other games that will hone map skills is the "Build a Town" option, in which roads appear to link the symbols chosen by the amateur civil engineer. The creative and timed challenges in this program lure kids back to play it over and over again. For graduates, try *Map Skills* (Optimum Resource), which has more than 100 trips and 10 levels of play.

Super Solvers: Treasure Mountain!

(Ages 5–9)

The Learning Company.
IBM PC, $49.95.

Players must call on science, math, reading, and thinking skills to resolve riddles and puzzles. In turn, they get to gather up treasure, fill the chest, and wrest the crown from evil hands. With sharp graphics and animation, this arcade-style game is fun and challenging on varied levels.

Trap-a-Zoid

(Ages 7–14)

Britannica Software.
Apple, $39.95.
IBM/Tandy, Commodore 64.

WORD PROCESSING AND MORE

The youngest computer users can try *Muppet Slate* and *Paint with Words* for story writing (see p. 251).

(see p. 251).

Appleworks 3.0   (Ages 8–Adult)   Claris Corporation.   Apple II, $169.

A classic word processor complete with a spell checker, flexible database, and a spreadsheet with more than 40 mathematical functions. The newest enhancements have made it more powerful and useful, not more complicated (as some say Appleworks GS is). The tutorial guides the novice smoothly, while the prompts keep the pro from getting stifled. The program still needs only 128K of memory and works well with 22 different printers.

Bank Street Writer III   (Ages 7–Adult)   Scholastic.   Apple, $29.95.   MS-DOS.

Motivation and much more can be found in this word-processing program, which includes a pull-down menu, a spell checker of 60,000 words, and a thesaurus with 50,000 synonyms. Frozen-text action allows teachers or parents to type in instructions that do not have to print out. Available only for the Apple computer is a 20-column format with large type. Among several excellent aids to this program are an organizational guide, *The Bank Street Prewriter,* and writing labs and activities.
Awards: Classroom Computer Learning Software Award 1988; *InCider Magazine* Incredibly Improved Product Award 1987

Magic Slate II   (Ages 7–Adult)   Sunburst.   Apple II, $129 for all 3 column formats; $65/each format.

This powerful, highly adaptable word-processing program is available in 20-column, 40-column, or 80-column formats. The smaller columns result in larger type, more suitable for the youngest users; the largest setting results in an acceptable program for adults. Depending on the age and reading level of the user, a family may purchase programs with one or all three of the formats along with spell checkers and lesson plans. Spanish type styles are available for all three column formats. *Magic Slate* is designed to interact exclusively with some of Sunburst's great creative writing programs, including *Write a Story!* (the science fiction story-writing guide) *Railroad Snoop,* and *Puppet Plays.*

When the zoids—creepy, polka-dotted creatures—are set loose, what can catch them? Only the correct geometric shape. Kids must draw the required triangle, square, parallelogram, or other shape to effect capture.

The Treehouse

(Ages 6–10)
Broderbund.
IBM/Tandy, $69.95.

An outstanding program developed along the lines of *The Playroom* (see p. 251). The setting is a treehouse filled with amazing activities. Among them are a road-rally "board game" of various levels that teaches counting, money estimation, and arithmetic skills; a silly sentence theater that coaches kids on parts of speech as they set up a funny play; a musical keyboard that allows song creation and instrument identification; and a musical maze that teaches notes, rhythms, and pitch. Other activities can be played along with the possums that hang out in this treehouse. Here is a well-designed and richly rewarding program.

Awards: Notable Children's Software 1992

Wood Car Rally

(Ages 8–13)
MECC.
Apple, $59.

The Pinewood Derby will never be the same once Cub Scouts start playing around with this program. The challenge lies in determining how certain variables (car weight, shape, friction/lubrication, and the ramp's angle and length) will affect a wooden car's performance. Three difficulty levels are available, including a challenge to create a variable to match a specific distance traveled.

Awards: Classroom Computer Learning Software Award 1989–1990

Writer Rabbit

(Ages 7–9)
The Learning Company.
Apple II, $69.95.
IBM PC/Tandy 1000.

Sheer fun, like The Learning Company's *Reader Rabbit,* this program has six games that teach parts of speech. Each of the games has varying levels of difficulty that can be adjusted to the skills of second-, third-, or fourth-grade students. The "silly stories" concocted by randomly selected phrases or words will demonstrate the functions of verbs, nouns, direct objects, etc., in a painless and amusing style.

Awards: Classroom Computer Learning Software Award 1988

MIDDLE GRADERS

Animal Trackers

(Ages 9–13)

Wings for Learning/Sunburst.
Apple II, $87.

A choice of three habitats—woodland, desert, or grassland—is offered to the "tracker," who must collect clues (such as footprints, food traces, burrows, and caves) and check them against a field guide in the database to discover what animal is lurking on the screen. Three levels of difficulty extend the usefulness of this nature program, which enhances deductive-reasoning skills.

Awards: Media and Methods Award 1991

Ant Farm

(Ages 8–12)

Sunburst.
Apple II, $65.

Kids study insect behavior but learn much more with this analytical software. Each ant must be paired with its particular work station, a task that involves problem-solving, memory, and creative strategies. Increasing levels of difficulty add to the interest of this program.

Audubon Wildlife Adventures: Grizzly Bears

(Ages 8–12)

Advanced Ideas.
Apple II, $49.95.
IBM.

Working as assistants to Dr. Potts, kids take on different roles—park ranger, oil company representative, biologist—in this environmentally educational program. The goal is to locate oil without disturbing the bears. Bear studies are extensive and include tracking, autopsies, and grizzly myth, mischief, and reality. The whales program in this series provides a similar educational challenge.

Backyard Birds

(Ages 8–14)

MECC.
Apple II, $59.

With a database of more than 120 North American birds, this challenging software transforms kids into scrupulous observers and detailed note-takers. The task is to carefully observe the looks and behavior of a bird before comparing it to the guide in the memory. This field-trip simulation sans raincoat or binoculars offers close-ups of more birds than a group of students will ever encounter.

Bank Street Writer III
(See Word Processing, p. 259.)

BannerMania
(Ages 7–Adult)
Broderbund.
Apple II, $44.95.
IBM/Tandy, $44.95.
Macintosh, $69.95.

While *The New Print Shop* (see Cards, Banners, and Books, p. 267) serves well for creating banners, this program offers more options in graphics, shapes, fonts, and colors. Best of all is the "transmogrify" option, which allows banner makers to see their messages on-screen in every one of the layout changes. "The banners made with this wonderful utility program are beautiful and easy to run," says one of our savvy school media specialists.

Awards: Technology & Learning Software Award 1990–1991

Call the Parrot
(Ages 8–10)
Hartley Courseware.
Apple, $39.95.

Buried treasure awaits on an island that also holds a truth-telling parrot and a mendacious pirate. The treasure hunter must dodge hazards, watch the lay of the land, and sort out clues (false and true) to find the booty. The island's layout and the hiding place change from game to game to keep clever players guessing and searching. With direction, children as young as four years old can enjoy this program.

Checkerboard Trails
(Ages 8–13)
Focus Media.
Apple II, $49.

A checkerboard filled with numbers and symbols for addition, subtraction, multiplication, and division gives players a chance to earn points as they practice their math skills. Using negative as well as positive numbers from −50 to 50, up to six players can choose their own level of difficulty as they chart a winning path across the checkerboard.

Crossword Magic
(Ages 7–Adult)
Mindscape/SVE.
Apple II, $59.
IBM/Tandy.
Macintosh, $49.95.

Creating crossword puzzles was too much like work before this truly magical program came along. Now one can simply type in a list of words and the structure forms itself to the size designations selected. Clues are added just as simply—the user is cued by the computer when to add each definition. Then the puzzle can be filled in, printed, copied, or edited. There is only one demo on this disk, so create you must if you want to play. (Ready-made crossword disks are available for classwork in math, science, social studies, reading, and language arts.) Crosswords are an inventive form of wordplay for all ages, and can be used for everything from study skills to greeting cards.

Design Your Own Home, Architecture
(Ages 10–Adult)
Abracadata.
Apple II, $89.95.
Apple IIGS, $89.95.
IBM, $99.95.
Macintosh, $99.95.

This outstanding program has a variety of uses, from instructing students in shapes, area, and basic architectural concepts to assisting adults who wish to lay out building and office designs. In the graphics toolbox is an array of essential shapes that are easily called up. The computer architect can draw and reorient walls and estimate the materials needed. Floor plans can be made using the dimension tool, which offers precise representations of furniture and fixtures. A color option allows for the use of patterns, shading, or blended colors. Two other versions of *Design Your Own Home,* which focus on interiors and landscaping, are available.

ESL Writer
(Ages 9–Adult)
Scholastic.
Apple II, $99.95.

Here is a spelling and grammar checker for those for whom English is a second language. Three dictionaries and grammar correction systems are installed: one for Spanish speakers, one for Asians, and a generic (adaptable) one. Almost any other word-processing document can be used with this program because it accepts material in ASCII format. Errors are highlighted, not corrected; the "help" screens and other hints suggest remedies.

Exploring Tidepools
(Ages 9–15)
Wings for Learning/Sunburst.
Apple II, $75.

Called an "electronic fieldtrip" by *Booklist* magazine, this program teaches about the formation of tidal pools and the life forms within them. The youthful scientist can choose to look through a microscope or underwater at different life forms, learning how and when they develop in the tidal cycles. The sample tidal pools are based on the California coast, but advanced users can compare East and West Coast pools and even develop their own on-screen.

The Factory
(Ages 9–16)
Wings for Learning/Sunburst.
Apple II, $65.
IBM/Tandy.

An on-screen assembly line allows kids to analyze and create multidimensional cubes while developing problem-solving skills. There are three progressive levels. First, the student learns how to move the cube and recognize its varying appearance; next, the student can create his or her own designs; the final challenge (with five levels of its own) requires that a cube already made be duplicated. Logic and spatial perceptions are put to work in this intriguing program, which is also available in Spanish as *La Fábrica.*

Awards: Classroom Computer Learning Software of the Decade 1990; *Classroom Computer Learning* Software Award 1987

Five-Star Forecast
(Ages 9–14)
MECC.
Apple II, $59.

By putting together variables such as wind direction and velocity, air pressure, temperature, and humidity, kids can become amateur weather forecasters. Once weather patterns are established and understood, predictions can be made. The technical terms can be replaced by everyday ones, if desired, and a choice between metric and standard measurements is possible. National Geographic's program *Weather Machine,* with its huge database, filmstrip, and other features, is another great program, but geared for older users and classroom settings.

Formula Vision

(Ages 9–17)

K-12 MicroMedia.

Apple II, $29.95.

A beginner's spreadsheet (with 15 cells) is one of the major assets of this program, which teaches the use of mathematical formulas. The spreadsheet allows the user to create tables and organize and manipulate values, units, labels, and formulas. Help screens and instructions are available throughout.

Fossil Hunter

(Ages 8–14)

MECC.

Apple II, $59.

Budding paleontologists can do their field work at home. The menu of icons readily offers the choices of digging, graphing, making lists and notes, and reviewing documents, while the screen shows layers of rock being studied by an on-site researcher. After a few finds, ranging from common fossils to extraordinary ones, kids are challenged to locate particular specimens and their geologic eras. One more program that will enthrall junior earth scientists is *Murphy's Minerals* (MECC).

Galactic Zoo

(Ages 10–15)

Focus Media.

Apple II, $85.

The characteristics of 60 endangered species fill the database and present a puzzle to kids, who must identify an animal on the basis of clues about habitat, diet, size, life cycle, predators, and so forth. Sharp graphics highlight this terrific instructional game.

Keep Your Balance

(Ages 9–14)

Sunburst.

Apple II, $65.

The pan of a balance fills the screen and on it may be apples, oranges, hammers, birds, or teacups. Once a particular goal is set, users must add, subtract, multiply, and divide their way to balancing equivalents. If necessary, the program will demonstrate the most efficient means to the solution, but it assesses no penalties for using additional steps.

The King's Rule

(Ages 9–Adult)

Wings for Learning/Sunburst.

Apple II, $65.

IBM/Tandy.

A math challenge without limitations. There are six levels, starting with knight's rule and rising to the king's. In each section three numbers appear at the top of the screen and the student must figure out their relationship (it may be as simple as adding 2 to each number, or far more complex). Division and multiplication are well tested in the higher levels, but most challenged is the user's sense of mathematical logic. Encouragement and plenty of practice space are offered, but no answers. There is a special guide, in code, to a teacher's answer book if the user really gets stuck. The flashing knights, magicians, and other guardians of the rules make for inspiring graphics.

Awards: Classroom Computer Learning Software Award Winner

Lunar Greenhouse
(Ages 8–11)
MECC.
Apple II, $59.95.

Botanical software with a lunar twist. Kids attempt to grow 15 vegetables on the moon and must keep their eyes on variable factors such as light, temperature, water, and growth cycles in order to gain the best crop in the shortest time.

Math Blaster Mystery
(Ages 10–17)
Davidson and Associates.
Apple II, $49.95.
MS-DOS.

Math is a mystery to many kids and adults, but this software program allows the user to play detective and absorb the lesson while working from Computation Cadet toward Arithmetic Agent status. Word problems, weight equivalencies, percents, and decimals all seem less sinister in the "whodunit" scenario.

Awards: ASLC Software of the Year 1989; *Technology & Learning* Software Award 1900– 1991

Mavis Beacon Teaches Typing
(Ages 9–Adult)
Software Toolworks.
Apple IIGS, $49.90.
IBM/Tandy, Macintosh, Commodore, Atari.

This is a must for kids and adults who still watch the keyboard more than the screen. Within this program, it's possible to work on typing skills in the classroom, the workshop, or the arcade. Outstanding graphics and sound are present in all four learning centers (lessons start at the chalkboard). The lessons become customized so the keyboarders can recognize their faults and strengths.

Midnight Rescue
(Ages 8–11)
The Learning Company.
IBM, $49.95.
Tandy.

Shady Glen School will turn invisible by midnight if the player cannot uncover the robot disguise of Morty Maxwell, master of mischief. Propelled by the user, a stylishly attired student moves through the halls of the school. He is on the lookout for robots, which he must photograph before they bop him, and for clues to uncover the robot that is Morty. Lots of reading, fact sifting, deductive reasoning, and high-tension fun are generated. Also from The Learning Company is *Outnumbered,* a similar program also set in Shady Glen, which calls on mathematical skills.

Miner's Cave
(Ages 9–15)
MECC.
Apple II, $59.

Caverns full of hidden gems entice users to extract them by employing four basic machines: a wheel and axle, pulley, lever, and ramp. It's essential to calculate the machine's purpose, force, and effectiveness as well as the work space available to successfully raise the jewels to the surface. A similar program, which focuses more on the minerals than the excavation process, is *Murphy's Minerals* (MECC). The novelty of the search, along with the straightforward instructions and colorful graphics, make these programs a hit with kids.

Mystery Matter

(Ages 8–12)

MECC.
Apple II, $59.
MS-DOS.

Aspiring chemists can play safely with mysterious substances in this program that challenges them to define a specific substance with given evidence.

National Inspirer

(Ages 10–13)

Tom Snyder Productions.
Apple II, $79.95.
MS-DOS.

This program is like a scavenger hunt through the United States. Players are challenged to locate two resources by traveling through 10 consecutive states and ending up in one that fulfills certain conditions (population, elevation, etc.). Maps are included for route planning. Another challenge awaits in *International Inspirer* (Tom Snyder).

Awards: Technology & Learning Software Award 1990–1991

Odell Lake

(Ages 9–12)

MECC.
Apple II, $55.

The adage "Eat or Be Eaten" was never truer. In this wonderful simulation, the user adopts the role of a fish and must seek out food and steer clear of predators. There are six kinds of fish present in the mountain stream, each offering a lot to learn about nature and survival.

Awards: Classroom Computer Learning Software Award 1988; Classroom Computer Learning Software of the Decade 1990

The Oregon Trail

(Ages 9–Adult)

MECC.
Apple II, $59.
MS-DOS.

The nitty-gritty of wagon-train life is reenacted in this simulation of a 2,000-mile westward trek. The player must outfit the covered wagon, cope with disasters, track the weather, and select efficient routes. An absorbing program that intimately reveals history while demanding astute planning skills. Similar software includes *Wagons West* (Focus Media) and *Sante Fe Trail* (Educational Activities).

Awards: Classroom Computer Learning Software of the Decade 1990

Rebus Writer

(Ages 8–Adult)

Mindscape/SVE.
Apple II, $49.95.

With a database called a "Pictionary" (a file of 300 pictures or icons), this program allows children to write their own mysterious messages in words and pictures. Kids must also strive to solve the messages created by the computer, which gives plenty of hints by accepting any correct letter and omitting the

CARDS, BANNERS, AND BOOKS

HOMESTYLE PUBLISHING

Children's Writing & Publishing Center   (Ages 7–Adult)   The Learning Company.
Apple II, $89.95 (family school edition).   IBM PC.

Crossing all age and interest levels, this well-established software is flexible, practical, and productive. Kids—parents, teachers, and librarians, too, for that matter—can create newsletters, reports, certificates, and other messages with flair. The variety of type styles and sizes, headings, and graphics take the drudgery out of learning word processing and teach page layout as well.

Awards: Classroom Computer Learning Software Award 1989–1990

The New Print Shop   (Ages 5–Adult)   Broderbund.   Apple II, $59.95.   IBM/Tandy, $69.95.
Macintosh, $69.95.   Commodore, $54.95.

This creative publishing program, considered one of the best around, offers enjoyable and practical activities. Greeting cards, invitations, certificates, and banners are easy to create in color (if a color printer is available) using different fonts, borders, and special graphics. New to a recent edition (1990) is the ability to stretch, reduce, copy, and flip pictures, placing them anywhere on a page. Daily, weekly, monthly, and yearly calendars can also be produced. Sizes for banners range from a nine-foot poster to a mouse-sized sign.

Awards: Technology & Learning Software of the Year 1990

Publish It! 4.0   (Ages 10–Adult)   Timeworks.   Apple II, $149.95.   IBM (*Publish It 2.0*).
Macintosh.

On-screen help, as well as the manual and reference card, make it fairly easy to operate this publishing program's graphics, word-processing, page-layout, and typesetting features. With 1,200 type combinations, established layouts, borders, and fonts available, the program has ample material in its own right. For the more adventurous, word-processing data from *Appleworks* or *Bank Street Writer* (see Word Processing, p. 259) is readily accepted, and additional clip-art sources, such as *The Print Shop,* are easy to assimilate. Suited to both practiced and beginning publisher, the program can serve older kids and their parents for elegant school and work reports as well as award certificates, newsletters, and other documents. (See also *Writer's Helper Stage II* on p. 275.)

inaccurate ones. With a mouse or a joystick, even freehand drawings are possible. Any child or adult who fancies this sort of wordplay will also enjoy *Riddle Magic* (Mindscape).

Scoop Mahoney: Investigative Reader
(Ages 9–14)
DLM.
Apple II, $46.

Playing investigative reporter, kids locate information via interviews, phone calls, etc., which are accessible through icons. After gathering the facts, the user must put the story together. Concrete answers are required at first; but the user soon learns to take careful notes, sift data, and make deductions. With five stories available at each of the four levels, there are many challenges and much fun for readers of varying skills.

Space Station Freedom
(Ages 10–12)
MECC.
Apple, $59.

No flying asteroids or meteor belts in this thought-provoking program. The players must match astronauts to missions by drawing biographical information, letters of recommendation, and other details from the database. One interesting facet is the mix of fact and opinion that must be carefully measured. Repeated play is possible because of the depth and mix of the data. Results are scored with an eye toward arcade appeal.

Spell-It Plus!
(Ages 10–Adult)
Davidson and Associates.
Apple II, $49.95.
MS-DOS.

This program is great for an early speller, but it is equally terrific for grownups. There are more than 1,000 commonly misspelled words plus spelling rules in the database. The program also supports five activities that involve decoding, unscrambling, and correcting, and an involving arcade-style game. French, Spanish, German, or additional English words may be added to all of the activities from the foreign language fonts included.

Awards: Technology & Learning Software Award 1990–1991

Super Solvers: Challenge of the Ancient Empires
(Ages 10–14)
The Learning Company.
IBM PC, $49.95.

An Indiana Jones–style adventure is possible here, as kids journey to ancient China, Rome, Egypt, India, and the Near East searching for buried cultural artifacts. Vivid sound effects, graphics, and animation highlight the searches through 20 underground caverns, which must be carefully navigated to avoid falling rocks, scary creatures, and other obstacles. Challenging on several levels, this is a game kids will return to.

The Voyage of the Mimi and The Second Voyage of the Mimi
(Ages 9–Adult)
Wings for Learning.
Apple II, $1,399 for Voyage 1; $1,050 for Voyage 2 (includes videos, books, and software materials).

The Voyage of the Mimi and *The Second Voyage* are an integration of video, print, software, audio, and hype (that is, posters and T-shirts). As complete units they are quite expensive, but they also offer an incomparable learning experience. The first voyage is a scientific exploration of humpback whales off the coast of New England. The related software includes *Maps and Navigation, Whales and Their Environment, Whale Databases, Ecosystems,* and *Island Survivors.* On the second voyage, students travel to Mexico, where they study Mayan civilization. The related software includes *Maya Math* and *Sun Lab.* All of these software items are available individually. These ventures offer a real feeling for environmental issues, history, and archaeology, along with some entertaining software challenges, such as *Island Survivors.* (See also *Children of the Maya: A Guatemalan Indian Odyssey* by Brent Ashabranner in Books.)

Awards: Classroom Computer Learning Software Award

What Do You Do with a Broken Calculator?

(Ages 8–Adult)

Sunburst.
Apple II, $65.
IBM/Tandy, Macintosh, $69.

If some of the keys on a calculator are broken, then one must devise alternative problem-solving methods. That is exactly what this software program demands—imaginative use of numbers and operations. The user can establish which keys are "broken" or nonfunctional and how to compensate. (For example, if the addition key is out, the users subtract or multiply to arrive at an answer.) Here are good problems that will challenge a child well beyond story problems and drills.

Winker's World of Numbers

(Ages 9–13)

Wings for Learning/Sunburst.
Apple II, $65.

A grid of numbers appears on the screen, and then Winker the Worm slithers into view and covers some of the entries. The pattern to the hidden numbers must be deduced by the user via addition, counting, or multiplication. There are three levels of difficulty in this unusual program. *Winker's World of Patterns* (Wings for Learning/Sunburst) is another puzzle program that involves colors, numbers, and word patterns.

TEENAGERS

Alge-Blaster Plus!
(Ages 12–18)
Davidson and Associates.
Apple II, $49.95.
MS-DOS, Macintosh, $59.95.

The challenges of first- and second-semester algebra can be met and conquered through five learning activities. Extensive practice is given in graphing and translating story problems into algebraic expressions. More than 500 equations and different levels of difficulty will suit a range of learners. Once mastered, the graphing skills can be used to ward off asteroids threatening a space station in the Alge-Blaster game.

Algebra Shop
(Ages 12–15)
Scholastic.
Apple II, $69.95.
Macintosh, MS-DOS.

For kids addicted to the mall, here's a relevant program to help them work on their fractions, square roots, factoring, equation reduction, and function-solving. Each of the ten shops in the computer-screen mall calls for a different mathematical skill. Varying games test how many customers users can serve in a given time, or how many shops can be managed at once.

Blue Powder, Grey Smoke
(Ages 12–Adult)
Core Group.
Apple II, $49.95.
Macintosh, IBM PC, Commodore 64/128.

This simulation of three Civil War battles will challenge historical knowledge and planning ability. Players must consider weaponry type and use, field supplies, even battle fatigue and morale, along with military tactics in following an actual battle or creating one of their own. An excellent tutorial leads the novice through the steps, and minute-by-minute reporting keeps the user on target. One can play against the computer or with two or more players. Four levels of difficulty are available. Superior visuals and sound effects.

The Body Transparent
The Grammar Examiner
States & Traits
(Ages 12–17)
Compton's NewMedia.
Apple II, $29.95 (for 3 programs).
IBM PC/Tandy, Commodore.

HYPERSOFTWARE FOR MULTIMEDIA PRODUCTIONS

School reports may never be the same once creative students are introduced to "hyper" software, which can readily incorporate graphics, text, and sound. Below are two popular programs. Some electronic encyclopedias can also interact with this software, including *Compton's Multimedia Encyclopedia* and *The Information Finder*. They are available in compact disc (CD-ROM) format, which, with the necessary equipment, can be read and listened to on home computers. (See Books.)

Hyperstudio: (Version 2.1)   (Ages 10–Adult)   Roger Wagner Publishing.
Apple IIGS with 1MB (4 disks, sound digitizing hardware card, microphone) $149.95.

Art, sound, text, and graphics can be blended into "cards" that are stacked in sequence to result in a vivid multimedia production. The sound card with this program allows for ready use of music, recorded speech, and other customized sound effects. More than 250 art clips are available along with the paint tools to create original artwork. Use of a scanner enables the incorporation of photographic images, and a video overlay card will allow video- and laser-disc images to be pulled in. It's easy to see how these programs could enhance a term paper, but the whole family can use the system for fun or credit.

Scholastic Hyperscreen   (Ages 12–Adult)   Scholastic.   Apple II, $99.95.   MS-DOS.

Speech, music, narration, visuals, and headings can be added together to form a presentation that is built screen by screen. The user can draw from various fonts, backgrounds, and clip art within the program, or use drawing tools and "hotspots" that allow integration of speech or frames from a videodisc. Once created, the disks can be used without the program disk (so a project made at school can be worked on at home or worked on by several people at once). Handicapped students are aided by a special scanner feature that allows participation in interactive stories.

Take a tour of the digestive or skeletal system with flashy graphics and irresistible computer challenges. Players can learn both the function and placement of body parts within the major systems by pitting their skills against one another or the computer. In *The Grammar Examiner,* newspaper articles must be written to please a strict editor. History and geography are tested in an entertaining fashion in *States & Traits.* Another excellent anatomical program is *Dr. Know-It-All's Inner Body Works,* available in "junior" (Grades 4–6) and "senior" (Grades 7–12) versions from Tom Snyder Productions.

Colonial Merchant

(Ages 12–18)
Educational Activities.
Apple II, $69.

The dangers faced by sea captains transporting goods in the eighteenth century are brought to life in this arcade-style history lesson. The user begins as a Boston merchant who, with a ship and 500 pounds sterling, must buy, sell, and transport merchandise. Historical trading measurements, methods, and hazards are vividly presented on-screen.

The Fidelity Chessmaster 2100

(Ages 10–Adult)
Software Toolworks.
Apple II and Apple IIGS, $49.95.
IBM, IBM Windows, $59.95.
Macintosh, Commodore, Amiga.

With seven levels for beginners and an equally outstanding range for intermediate and advanced players, this program will challenge a wide range of participants. Participants can play against the machine or other players. The computer can be adjusted to "Best Play," so that it always makes a winning move, or to the "Coffeehouse Style," which offers a variety of interesting, but not necessarily best, moves.

Music Studio

(Ages 9–Adult)
Activision.
Apple IIGS, $89.95.

Music and lyrics can be created and printed out by a novice or an experienced musician with this program. A music paint box allows the computer musician to apply notes of varying colors and sizes using a keyboard, mouse, or joystick. The compositions can be readily played back, allowing the effect of single note alterations to be easily recognized. A serious composer can interface the program with a MIDI and a synthesizer.

Awards: Classroom Computer Learning Software Award 1988

Revolution '76

(Ages 11–Adult)
Britannica Software.
Apple IIGS, $49.95.
IBM PC.

Kids become personally involved in the Revolutionary War by severing ties with Great Britain, building the army and calculating its movements, handling financial questions such as taxes and inflation, negotiating with allies, and even considering what form of government to institute. By playing out scenarios that differ from real events, students can rewrite history—and certainly learn from it.

Awards: Technology & Learning Software Award 1990–1991

The Ripple that Changed American History

(Ages 12–Adult)

Tom Snyder Productions.
Apple II, $79.95 (includes *Encyclopedic Dictionary of American History,* teacher guides, and worksheets).
IBM.

The "Ripple" is a disturbance in time that must be located as quickly as possible. It should be a cinch with only 200 years of American history (1775–1975) to search through. It's not—but it *is* plenty of fun. Players sharpen their geography and sense of period events. With more than 20 levels of difficulty, this program suits youth and adults on a level with the *Carmen Sandiego* series (see p. 274).

Sim City

(Ages 12–18)

Broderbund.
IBM/Tandy, $59.95.
Macintosh, Commodore, $39.95.
Amiga, $59.95.

Create your own city—or use one of the cities in the program—and participate in its growth. Among the tough issues to contend with are pollution, power supplies, crime, taxes, traffic congestion, and housing costs. The Sims are simulated residents whose needs must be met and complaints answered. A Sim City Terrain Editor (sold separately) enables the user to create the landform or terrain to exact specifications in order to re-create a genuine city. Rich in imagination, this program will capture a variety of interests, whether played as a game or a civics lesson. For another challenge, try *Sim Earth* (Broderbund).

Awards: Technology & Learning Software Award 1990–1991

Super Story Tree

(Ages 9–13)

Scholastic.
Apple II, $79.95.
MS-DOS.

Young authors can feel like film directors with this program that allows them to enhance a story with music, speech, and sound effects as well as through visuals (with original drawings and backgrounds). The readers move the plot along its electronic pages and decide the outcome.

Awards: Classroom Computer Learning Software Award 1989–1990

Time Navigator Leaps Back

(Ages 12–Adult)

MECC.
Apple II, $59.

Driving an on-screen "chronomobile," users travel throughout American history from 1790 to 1900. After being thrown back in time, the student must navigate forward by selecting the correct clues, which could be artifacts, headlines, works of literature, or even bits of dialogue. The program can be played competitively, for points, or not. While it doesn't have quite the flair of *Where in Time Is Carmen Sandiego?* (see p. 274), it does have more history and specific facts. A great sequel to the exciting program *Time Navigator* (MECC).

Who'll Save Abacaxi?

(Ages 12–18)

Focus Media.
Apple II, $89.

Political science in action. Acting as a leader of a Third World country, the user must secure

WHERE OH WHERE IS CARMEN SANDIEGO?

This excellent series of programs challenges people age 8 and over to capture an international spy ring and its leader, whose name is Carmen Sandiego. The program is so popular it has even spawned its own TV quiz show for kids on public television.

Where in the U.S.A. Is Carmen Sandiego?　(Ages 10–Adult)　Broderbund.　Apple II, $54.95. Macintosh, $59.95.　IBM/Tandy, $59.95.　Commodore, $49.95.　Amiga, $59.95.

The wily villain Carmen Sandiego, who first appeared in the global *Where in the World Is Carmen Sandiego?* (now available in French, too), can also be pursued through the United States. Carmen is aided by gang members who must first be tracked down before the player achieves the status of master detective and is allowed to pursue the leader. Clues are followed along a cross-country trail. *Fodor's USA Travel Guide* comes with the software to help out. An animated chase sequence complete with a paddy wagon provides a smashing finale—but only for the most dogged sleuths and geography buffs. *Where in America's Past Is Carmen Sandiego?* is another gem in this series. The archcriminal has also been tracked through time in *Where in Time Is Carmen Sandiego?* and through 35 European nations in *Where in Europe Is Carmen Sandiego?*. Consistent fun and learning for the whole family.

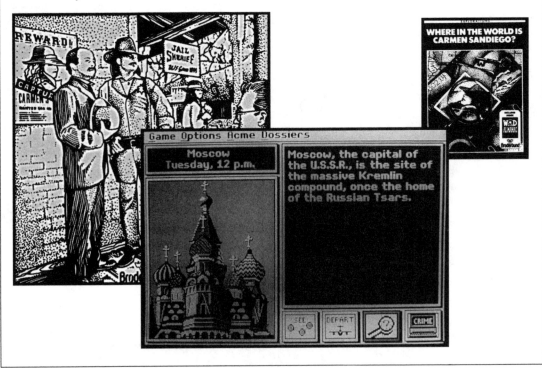

internal harmony, balance the economy, ensure a growth of services and reduction of population, and attain reelection. Definitely a challenging program, but a helpful database is available. A similar program, *Hidden Agenda* (Springboard Software), is available for IBM PC and Macintosh computers.

World GeoGraph
(Ages 11–Adult)
MECC.
Apple IIGS, $89.

Around the world on a computer! This software makes it possible, allowing the user to graphically visit 177 countries. With more than 50 categories of information (cultural, socioeconomic, climatic, geologic, etc.) in the database, the program will do a lot more than satisfy simple curiosity. It's also a treasure trove for creating reports, graphs, and tables. A unique way to study the world's peoples and places. Equally valuable is *USA GeoGraph* (MECC), a *Technology & Learning* Award winner for 1990–1991.

Awards: Classroom Computer Learning Software Award 1989–1990

Writer's Helper Stage II
(Ages 12–18)
CONDUIT.
Apple II, $35.
IBM, Macintosh.

Defined as a "prewriting and revising" program, *Writer's Helper* contains various routines for overcoming writer's block and honing organizational skills. There's a slot machine for ideas (just push an "alt" key and a number and see what turns up) as well as other devices designed to spark ideas. Few of the ideas seem geared for fiction writers; most of the suggestions are oriented toward nonfiction, making this useful for school assignments. Organizational and developmental plans are just as creative and practical. A "Notepad" segment can serve as the word processor, or the user can create a file and move to a more sophisticated word-processing system.

Awards: Technology & Learning Software Award 1990–1991

Zoyon Patrol
(Ages 12–18)
MECC.
Apple, $59.

Armed with maps, reports, and a database, the user must capture the dangerous Zoyons and restore them to their natural habitat. The intelligent creatures are more than a match for the director of the search, who must also stay within a budget and sustain a good public image. This clever, multifaceted program demands sharp analytical, planning, and research abilities.

MANUFACTURERS AND DISTRIBUTORS

Abracadata, Inc.
P.O. Box 2440
Eugene, OR 97402
(800) 451-4871

Activision, Inc.
11440 San Vicente Boulevard
Suite 300
Los Angles, CA 90049
(310) 207-4500

Advanced Ideas, Inc.
591 Redwood Highway
Suite 2325
Mill Valley, CA 94941
(510) 526-9100

Baudville Software & Accessories, Inc.
5380 52nd Street
Grand Rapids, MI 49512-9765
(800) 728-0888

Britannica Software (see Compton's New-Media)

Broderbund Software, Inc.
P.O. Box 6125
Novato, CA 94948-6125
(800) 521-6263

Claris Corporation
5201 Patrick Henry Drive
Santa Clara, CA 95052
(408) 987-7000

Compton's NewMedia
722 Genevieve Street
Suite M
Solana Beach, CA 92075
(619) 259-0444

CONDUIT
University of Iowa
Oakdale Campus
Iowa City, IA 52242
(800) 365-9774

Core Group
P.O. Box 1265
Madison, CT 06443
(203) 458-9363

Davidson and Associates, Inc.
P.O. Box 2961
Torrance, CA 90509
(800) 545-7677

DLM, Inc.
P.O. Box 4000
One DLM Park
Allen, TX 75002
(800) 527-4747

Edmark Corporation
P.O. Box 3218
Redmond, WA 98073-3218
(800) 426-0856

Educational Activities, Inc.
1937 Grand Avenue
Baldwin, NY 11510
(800) 645-3739

Educational Testing Service
School Services, 88-D
Rosedale Road
Princeton, NJ 08541
(800) 545-2302

Focus Media, Inc.
485 South Broadway
Suite 12
Hicksville, NY 11801
(800) 645-8989

Great Wave Software
5353 Scotts Valley Drive
Scotts Valley, CA 95066
(408) 438-1990

Hartley Courseware, Inc.
133 Bridge Street
Dimondale, MI 48821
(800) 247-1380

Hi-Tech Expressions
584 Broadway
Suite 509
New York, NY 10012
(212) 941-1224

IBM PC Software Department (see Lexmark
International, Inc.)

K-12 MicroMedia Publishing, Inc.
6 Arrow Road
Ramsey, NJ 07446
(800) 292-1997

Lawrence Productions, Inc.
1800 South 35th Street
Galesburg, MI 49053-9687
(616) 665-7075

The Learning Company
6493 Kaiser Drive
Fremont, CA 94555
(800) 852-2255

Lexmark International, Inc.
1221 Alverser Drive
Midlothian, VA 23113
(800) IBM-2468

MECC
6160 Summit Drive North
Minneapolis, MN 55430-4003
(800) 685-MECC

Mindplay
Department D5
Unit 350
P.O. Box 36491
Tucson, AZ 85740
(800) 221-7911

Mindscape/SVE Corp., Inc.
Department E
1345 Diversey Parkway
Chicago, IL 60614-1299
(800) 829-1900

Optimum Resource, Inc. (see Weekly Reader
Software)

Orange Cherry Software, Inc.
P.O. Box 390
Pound Ridge, NY 10576
(800) 672-6002

Oryx Press
4041 North Central Avenue at Indian School
Road
Suite 700
Phoenix, AZ 85012-3397
(800) 279-6799

Queue, Inc.
338 Commerce Drive
Fairfield, CT 06430
(203) 333-7268

Roger Wagner Publishing, Inc.
1050 Pioneer Way
Suite P
El Cajon, CA 92020
(619) 442-0522

Scholastic
2931 East McCarty Street
P.O. Box 7502
Jefferson City, MO 65102
(800) 541-5513

Software Toolworks
60 Leveroni Court
Novato, CA 94949
(800) 231-3088

Spinnaker Software Corp.
201 Broadway, 6th Floor
Cambridge, MA 02139
(800) 826-0706

Springboard (see Spinnaker Software Corp.)

Sunburst Communications (see Wings for
Learning)

SVE (see Mindscape/SVE Corp., Inc.)

Terrapin Software, Inc.
400 Riverside Street
Portland, ME 04103
(207) 878-8200

Timeworks, Inc.
625 Academy Drive
Northbrook, IL 60062
(800) 535-9497

Tom Snyder Productions, Inc.
90 Sherman Street
Cambridge, MA 02140
(800) 342-0236

Toucan (see Queue, Inc.)

Walt Disney Software Co.
P.O. Box 290
Buffalo, NY 14207
(800) 688-1520

Weekly Reader Software/Optimum Resource,
Inc.
10 Station Place
Norfolk, CT 06058
(800) 327-1473

Wings for Learning/Sunburst Communications
P.O. Box 660002
Scotts Valley, CA 95067-0002
(800) 628-8897

RESOURCES

Booklist. Twice monthly with single issues in July and August. American Library Association, 50 East Huron Street, Chicago, IL 60611 (800) 545-2433. $56/year. Reviews of new software appear regularly; an annual list of the past year's best software appears in "Software's Greatest Hits" each January.

High/Scope Buyer's Guide to Children's Software 1992. High/Scope Educational Research Foundation. 600 North River Street, Ypsilanti, MI 48198-2898. $19.95. A good preschool resource for software selection.

Only the Best: Preschool-Grade 12: The Annual Guide to Highest Rated Software by Shirley Boes Neill and George W. Neill. Annual. Bowker, paper, $29.95.

Science Fare: An Illustrated Guide & Catalog of Toys, Books, and Activities for Kids by Wendy Saul and Alan Newman. 1986. Harper-Collins, paper, $14.95.

Software Encyclopedia. Annual. Bowker.

Technology & Learning (formerly *Classroom Computer Learning*). Peter Li, Inc., 2451 East River Road, Dayton, OH 45439. September–May. Software is regularly reviewed, and "Only the Best" list appears annually.

(See also Key to ALA Awards, p. xvii.)

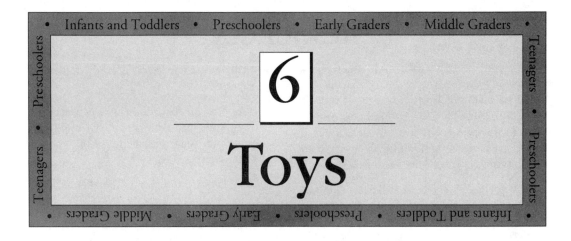

6

Toys

INTRODUCTION

Every other cartoon character on television, it seems, has its face replicated in an action figure. The value of such spin-offs is, to be generous, mixed. Here we look at high-quality playthings that echo the rich experiences found in good books, videos, software, music, and storytelling. The toys described below will enhance the playing, learning, and caring experiences of the material already presented.

Only toys that inspire imaginative play are recommended here.* While we recognize fully the value of musical instruments, bikes and trikes, physical equipment, and other kinds of playthings, only so much space is available in this volume. Books offering broad coverage of suitable toys for all age groups are cited at the end of this chapter.

Toys whirl in and out of the marketplace according to trends and fashions; we have tried to gather well-established items as well as brand-new creations. Also suggested are ways to create your own family favorites, such as bubble wands and a year-round costume box.

Mary Sinker of the USA Toy Library Association, and author of *Toys to Grow On*, explains that there are two categories of toys: mass-market toys, like Fisher-Price, and toys for the specialty market, such as Brio and educational toys. Sinker states that the two rarely meet on the shelves. Because the chain stores don't often carry the specialty items, many of the toys described here must be sought in catalogs, independent toy shops, museum stores, and children's bookstores. They can also be found in your local Toy Library, if you have one. If you don't, write: USA Toy

---

*Our recommendations follow principles embraced by the American Library Association for selecting quality children's media. ALA does not itself evaluate toys, however, and the appearance of a toy in this selection does not constitute endorsement by ALA. Our research incorporates experience from some of the many libraries that buy and circulate toys, as well as advice of parents, educators, children's booksellers, toy shop proprietors, and independent authorities. —*Ed.*

Library Association, 2719 Broadway Ave., Evanston, IL 60201, for more information on creating a community resource for borrowing toys and developing playgroups. Another excellent resource is Lekotek—a toy-lending and information center geared to the needs of children with disabilities (see Resources at the end of this chapter).

When you buy, evaluate toys for long-term stimulation and diversity of play. Joanne Oppenheim's *Buy Me! Buy Me!* gives excellent selection advice for each age level. Look past the bright packaging whenever possible and read the contents thoroughly. The video *Buy Me That!* (see Videos) offers families a lesson on toy advertising. Toy selection is a perfect way to introduce one's child to consumer awareness.

HOW TO USE THIS CHAPTER

Described below are specific toys, their manufacturers and/or distributors, and prices, current as of this writing. If the toy is widely distributed by department stores and toy store chains, the label "mass market" is appended. If the toy is a catalog-only item, a catalog is listed. Popular toys will certainly appear in more than one catalog, so watch for price differences. If the toy is widely available in the specialty market—children's toy and bookshops, museum stores, hobby shops, and catalogs—the manufacturer and distributor are cited.

You can write or call toy suppliers (see addresses and phone numbers at the end of this chapter). If they cannot sell directly, they will suggest a local source. Most toy companies are pleased to hear from consumers; your feedback can help them make better products.

Because toy availability is subject to vagaries of demand and distribution, some items cited may simply be unavailable; however, the information we've provided may lead you to similar toys. Sometimes the desired product has been repackaged or updated.

To help extend the learning experiences that come from play, we've connected many of our selected toys to related media: books, magazines, videos, music, stories on tape, and software. Some of these items are mentioned in the earlier chapters, and we've provided a *see* reference to the descriptions; but we have also used this toy section to extend the number of media titles we could recommend to you for purchase or to find in your library. In "Connections," the abbreviation (o.p.) means that a book is out of print and is more likely to be in your library than in your bookstore.

Good toys don't have to be loaded down with "learning assignments" to make them worthwhile, but when a child's interest in a subject, character, or style is stimulated, that interest seeks further expansion. Our "Connections" can help provide it—and plenty of fun besides.

INFANTS

Boomerings

(Ages 6 months–3)
Discovery Toys, $6.98.

These 24 plastic links hold toys to cribs, playpens, strollers, and car seats, and they can be strung to make a colorful chain for baby to observe. Their bright hues and connections will also intrigue toddlers and help them distinguish colors and develop small motor skills. Similar links are widely available in catalogs and toystores.

The Bubble Whale

(Ages 6 months–3)
Hearth Song catalog, $12.95.

Set in the water, this small yet magnificent wooden blue whale emits bubbles as it submerges. When captured by a tiny hand and turned over, the whale is a water scoop as well. The small painted eyes look mischievous on the sleek surface, which is covered with a nontoxic and water-resistant finish. The Hearth Song catalog is a treasure trove of finely crafted wooden toys, art supplies, and fanciful, inspiring playthings.

CONNECTIONS

Books:
Bunny Bath by Lena Anderson. 1990. R&S Books, $3.95.
Spot Goes Splash by Eric Hill. 1990. Putnam, $3.95. A submersible plastic book.
Wally Whale. 1990. Child's Play, $4.99. Another fun-to-dunk book.
Audio:
Bathtime Magic by Joanie Bartels. Discovery Music, $9.95.
I Wanna Tickle the Fish by Lisa Atkinson. (See Audio.)
[*Reminder*: Never place a tape player or any electrical device where it may fall in the water.]

Double Feature

(Ages Infants–18 months)
Wimmer-Fergusen, $24.95.

Double Feature is a reversible toy with an unbreakable mirror and the stark black-and-white images that many say best stimulate a baby's visual perception. On one side is a series of sharp line pictures (a sailboat, circle, etc.) and on the other is a 12-by-16-inch acrylic mirror. Corner ties allow this toy to be attached to crib or playpen so a newborn can stare for hours at a wondrous face.

Musical Mobile
(Ages Infant–18 months)
The Right Start catalog, $29.95.

Five clowns upside down. This mobile has the right idea, since the clowns are facing the baby, not the ceiling or the adult standing next to the crib. The clowns dance to a gentle tune when the mobile is wound up. They are available dressed in primary colors, pastel shades, or black and white. For newborns *The Right Start* catalog has plenty of other stimulating mobiles featuring mirrors, fish, animals, and more.

(Whether you buy a mobile or make one, be sure it provides something for a baby's-eye view. One child recently received a beautiful Peter Rabbit scene, but all he could see from his crib were the bunnies' white plastic bottoms.)

∞CONNECTIONS

Books:
Baby's World: A First Catalog by
Stephen Shott. (See Books.)

Red Rings, Blue Ball
(Ages 3–18 months)
Gruner & Jahr; dist. by International Playthings, $5.

One of a series of excellent *Parents Magazine* Child Development Toys, this teether contains a smaller ring within a larger one and a bright blue ball in the middle that holds a bell. The teether can be chewed, swung, tugged, or (using the Boomerings cited above) hung up for batting practice.

The other Child Development Toys are just as irresistible. The Stand-up Man falls to pieces in a second, but has a suction cup to keep him in place while a sturdy cord is pulled by a yellow teething ring to restore him. Basic fluid dynamics can be observed by infants as they watch a red bead slide top to bottom in the Tracking Tube, which at one end has a squeaker and at the other bells encased in soft yellow plastic. All of these toys come with Play and Learning Guides for parents. To babies, of course, play and learning come naturally.

Skwish
(Ages Infant–24 months)
Pappa Geppetto's Toys, $18.

A ball made entirely of heavy-duty elastic, bright colored dowels, and bells. Also available in black and white, it will lay flat to be stuffed in a bag and easily regain its shape. Light enough for an infant, the toy is perfect for games of "Mommy/Daddy-fetch" that babies like so well.

TODDLERS

Blocks

(Ages 18 months–6)

Childcraft catalog, $36.95 (32-piece beginner set).

These plain wooden blocks made of hard maple can be transformed into almost anything the child imagines, and they can be used for years. For the youngest child, blocks are nice for exploring shapes, balance, and structures. Fine motor skills and patience are well tested. In Childcraft's classic set, the basic unit block is 1⅜ by 2¾ by 5½ inches. Small hands can make some impressive projects even with the beginner set, which has 32 pieces in 8 shapes. The largest set (the Olympic Set) has 161 pieces in 19 shapes. All of these shapes—pillars, arches, ramps, curves, squares, triangles, and so forth—can be purchased individually. This unique feature (most companies sell the various shapes only in sets) allows you to collect blocks geared to your child's building inclinations. Wooden people, signs, and rolling vehicles are also available.

∞CONNECTIONS

Books:
Block City by Robert Louis Stevenson. (See Books.)

Bumblebee

(Ages 2–4)

National Wildlife Federation catalog, $9.95.

When a child unzips a yellow fabric beehive, a striped bee appears, complete with yellow wings formed from the walls of the hive. The zipper clasp needs a larger ring for little hands, but children will love the texture and versatility of this fuzzy pet.

∞CONNECTIONS

Books:
A Colorful Adventure of the Bee Who Left Home One Monday Morning and What He Found Along the Way by Lisa Campbell Ernst. Illustrated by Lee Ernst. 1986. Lothrop, $11.75.
Magazines:
Your Big Backyard. (See Magazines.)
Videos:
Insects from the "Tell Me Why" series. Penguin Home Video; dist. by Prism, $19.95.
Software:
Learn about Insects. Wings for Learning/Sunburst, $65.

Circus Caravan

(Ages 2–5)

Lego/Duplo, $35.25, mass market.

A ringmaster in black top hat leads a short parade of three cars carrying a black dog, a horseback rider, a clown sitting atop an elephant, and another clown who is actually shot out of a cannon. A little imagination and, perhaps, some items from the Lego/Duplo zoo, firetruck, and regular block sets can add to the fun.

⌒ CONNECTIONS

Books:

The Clown's Smile by Mike Thaler. Illustrated by Tracey Cameron. 1986. HarperCollins, $10.89.
Harriet Goes to the Circus by Betsy and Giulio Maestro. 1977. Crown, paper, $2.50.
Software:
First Letter Fun. (See Computer Software.)
Goofy's Railway Express. (See Computer Software.)
Videos:
"Curious George Rides a Bike." (See *Dr. Desoto and Other Stories* in Videos.)
Circus 1,2,3. F.H.E., a div. of Live Home video, $14.95.

Crayola Sidewalk Chalk

(Ages 2–8)

Binney & Smith, $ .89, mass market.

Oversized chalk in pastel colors—blue, yellow, and pink—can entertain kids for hours. Uses include creating outlines essential for sidewalk games and drawing imaginative scenes.

⌒ CONNECTIONS

Books:

Blackboard Bear by Martha Alexander. 1969. Reprinted in a miniature edition with three related titles as *4 Bears in a Box.* 1991. Dial, $8.95.
Hopscotch Around the World by Mary D. Lankford. 1992. Morrow, $15.
Hopscotch, Hangman, Hot Potato, & Ha Ha Ha: A Rulebook of Children's Games by Jack Maguire (Introduction by Captain Kangaroo). 1990. Prentice Hall, $13.95.
Videos:
Mary Poppins. Disney, $19.95. (In one memorable scene, Dick Van Dyke is a street artist who transports the children and their governess into a magical world via his sidewalk sketches.)
Software:
ColorMe: The Computer Coloring Kit. (See Computer Software.)

Mr. Potato Head

(Ages 2–6)

Playskool, $5.99, mass market.

With flexible arms, and with storage inside the plastic potato for all the changeable features, this old favorite still delights children who like to put the face together just right or in silly disorder. An entire bucket of 38 silly pieces is available for $19.99.

⌒ CONNECTIONS

Books:

Tail Toes Eyes Ears Nose by Marilee Robin Burton. (See Books.)

BEST OF THE BEST FOR CHILDREN

Software:
The Playroom. (See Computer Software.)
Facemaker Golden Edition. Queue, $39.95.

Sand and Water Activity Table
(Ages 2–6)
Playskool, $99.95, mass market.

A standout favorite among preschoolers who love to dabble in water, sand, clay, bubbles, and anything squishy. This table can seat from 4 to 6 little ones. The moist material can be kept in one sink and dry material in the other (but with the littlest users, everything gets mixed up, so plan accordingly or count on seeing mud). Drain holes make this portable, heavy-duty plastic table easy to clean. The benches fold up to create a flat surface for an art table or a little desk. Use some of the creations suggested in *Mudworks* (see Resources)

A smaller sand/water toy is the Sand-Water Wheel (available, although not exclusively, from Discovery Toys, $11.98).

∞CONNECTIONS

Books:
I'm King of the Castle by Shigeo Watanabe. Illustrated by Yasuo Ohtomo. 1982. Putnam, paper, $3.95.
Videos:
The Sand Castle. (See Videos.)

PRESCHOOLERS

Alphabet Letters and Numbers
(Ages 3–5)
Playskool, $4.99 to $6.99 (magnetic sets).

Alphabets come in all styles, shapes, textures, and toy concepts. There are vinyl puff letters that stick to any shiny surface, felt letters, puzzle pieces, cards, and an old favorite, magnetic letters. Playskool's magnetic ones can be used in the carrier board, on a refrigerator, or on any other magnetic surface. A single set is great for learning the basics (though it doesn't have enough duplicates to spell much of anything). Jars of letters that help the new speller are available from Childcraft and other companies.

One inexpensive way to create a lasting alphabet board is to attach a large square of heavy felt to a kitchen or playroom wall, and then cut out felt letters. Other shapes created

BEYOND BEARS

There are plenty of cuddly bears out there—Paddington, Corduroy, Winnie-the-Pooh, to name just a few. For a change, here are some other lovable critters spun off from literary creations that will appeal to children of many ages. Although many of these creatures have appeared in a series of books, usually only a single title is mentioned in our Connections. A special Connection also appears in this section: posters that endorse reading and libraries.

Unless otherwise noted, all prices are taken from Listening Library's BookMates catalog. (Weston Woods offers all but Clifford and Spot, priced individually or as sets that include video, book, and stuffed toy.) If a single size designation appears beside the price (e.g., 12″), it refers to the height of the toy.

Clifford $17.95 (12″ long, 6″ tall) ($399 for the 4′ version).

Even the huge (four-foot) version is scaled down considerably from the Big Red Dog in Norman Bridwell's many stories. Why, Clifford is larger than owner Emily Elizabeth's house! Bridwell's picture books entertain kids and teach manners, reading, numbers, and more.

∞CONNECTIONS

Books:
Clifford: The Big Red Dog by Norman Bridwell. 1963. Scholastic, paper, $1.95.
Videos:
A music video, *Clifford's Sing-a-Long Adventure,* is available, as is a series of learning videos, such as *Clifford's Fun with Letters.*

Curious George   Gund, $14.95 (11″) ($299 for 4½′ version), mass market.

H. A. and Margaret Rey's books about this mischievous monkey and the man in the yellow hat have delighted generations of kids. The monkey's high jinks have been spun off into new books, videos, and even software programs.

✐ CONNECTIONS

<u>Books:</u>
Curious George written and illustrated by H. A. Rey. 1941. Houghton Mifflin, paper, $3.95.

<u>Videos:</u>
"Curious George Rides a Bike." (See *Dr. Desoto and Other Stories* in Videos.)

<u>Audio:</u>
Curious George Learns the Alphabet: Three Stories read by Julia Harris. Caedmon, $9.95.

<u>Software:</u>
Curious George in Outer Space. (See Computer Software.)

<u>Poster:</u>
Curious George sits munching donuts and poring over a book with the caption, "Curious? Read." ALA Graphics, $5 (17″ by 22″ poster).

Max   Weston Woods, $8.95 (9″).

The white rabbit who hops through Rosemary Wells's popular board books comes complete with the familiar red vest. Clad in a candy-cane decorated nightshirt and nightcap trimmed in white fake fur—as he appeared in *Max's Christmas*—he looks full of mischief.

✐ CONNECTIONS

<u>Books:</u>
Max's Christmas by Rosemary Wells. (See Books.)

<u>Videos:</u>
Max's Chocolate Chicken. 1991. Weston Woods, $100; rental, $15.

Max and the Wild Things $15.95 each (12″) ($135 for 3′ version).

This Max is a mischievous little boy in a white wolf suit. Also available as toys are three of the Wild Things who first appeared with Max in Maurice Sendak's Caldecott-winning *Where the Wild Things Are.* The author has based an opera on this story. Some kids find it sleep-inducing, others find it scary, still others are intrigued.

✐ CONNECTIONS

<u>Books:</u>
Where the Wild Things Are by Maurice Sendak. 1962, HarperCollins, $12.95; paper, $4.95.

Maurice Sendak Library. (See Videos.)

Where the Wild Things Are—Opera. Home Vision, $29.95.

Poster:

The Wild Things march with Max surrounded by the caption, "Your Library. Where The Wild Things Are." ALA Graphics, $6 (22″ by 34″ poster). Wild Things bookmarks are also available, $7 (200 bookmarks).

Audio:

Where the Wild Things Are read by Maurice Sendak. Children's Book & Music Center, $8.95.

Snowman $19.95 (11″).

The snowman in a green felt hat and scarf is based on Raymond Briggs's magical, wordless book about a young boy and his snowy creation that comes to life. There is a Snowman Game for young players available from the Museum of Fine Arts of Boston, $19.95.

∞ CONNECTIONS

Books:

The Snowman by Raymond Briggs. 1978. Random House, $12.95; paper, $4.95.

Videos:

The Snowman. (See Videos.)

Spot $8.95 (7″).

With this golden, spotted puppy, little ones will have fun reenacting all the hide-and-seek games suggested in Eric Hill's lift-the-flap and board books. The popular Spot books have been translated into Spanish, French, and German and are useful for foreign language lessons for the young.

∞ CONNECTIONS

Books:

Where's Spot? by Eric Hill. 1980. Putnam, $10.95.

Videos:

Spot's First Video and *The Adventures of Spot* (in French, German, and Spanish—not in English). Gessler catalog, $29.95 each.

by parents, relatives, and kids can be added to this homemade toy. (Also, it's a good gift-by-mail idea for grandparents.)

CONNECTIONS

Books:
A is For Animals by David Pelham. 1991. Simon & Schuster, $14.95.
Build Your Own Alphabet by Joy Nagy. 1990. Abrams; paper, $17.95.
I Can Be the Alphabet by Marinella Bonini. (See also ABCs, p. 13.)
Magazines:
Sesame Street Magazine. (See Magazines.)
Videos:
Animal Alphabet. (See Videos.)
"Alphabet" on *The Sand Castle* video. (See Videos.)
Dr. Seuss's ABC. Random House Home Video, $9.95.
"Alligators All Around" on *The Maurice Sendak Library.* (See Videos.)
Audio:
The Alphabet Operetta. (See Audio.)
Software:
Donald Duck's Alphabet Chase. (See Computer Software.)
Dr. Peet's Talk/Writer. (See Computer Software.)
Letter Go Round. (See Computer Software.)

Animal Soundtracks
(Ages 3–8)
Living and Learning; dist., although not exclusively, by Childcraft, $10.95.

Songs like "Old MacDonald" are fun, but "with an oink oink here . . ." does not give the real sense of how a pig, or cow, or turkey sounds.

This lotto game does. Each player must listen carefully to the voices of 30 animals played in random order on an accompanying cassette. When the players recognize who (or what) is talking (or mooing or rat-a-tat-tatting), they put a bingo chip over that face on the card. The cards contain nine lifelike color photos of animals; no cards are exactly the same. A crib sheet is available that lists the order of the sounds on the tape. Also in the instructions are brief introductions to the domestic and wild creatures.

CONNECTIONS

Books:
Gobble Growl Grunt by Peter Spier. 1988. Doubleday, $5.95.
Magazines:
Your Big Backyard. (See Magazines.)
Zoobooks. (See Magazines.)
Videos:
Animal Babies in the Wild. Scholastic, $16.95.
Audio:
We Love the Animals by Michael Mish. Silo/Alcazar, $9.

Bubble Kit
(Ages 5–Adult)
Nature Company, $29.95.

Bubbles are a surefire favorite for toddlers and older kids. There are also adults who can't resist taking a turn. Nature Company has the Ultimate Bubble Kit, containing a video with "Bubble-ologist" Louis Pearl, a 32-page book on the physics and how-to's of bubblemaking, two bubble trumpets, and a secret solution. Kids can make bubbles as large as themselves, or form intricate shapes.

For a simpler approach, large bubble

wands are available from toystores, catalogs, and craft fairs. Or the same fancy wands can be made at home with a few feet of vinyl-coated wire, a pair of wire cutters, and some artful twists. The secret recipe for a gallon of bubbles: Mix, then chill, 6 cups water, 2 cups Joy dishwashing liquid, ¾ cup Karo syrup; use at room temperature.

⌒CONNECTIONS

Books:
Soap Bubble Magic by Seymour Simon. Illustrated by Stella Ormai. 1985. Lothrop, $11.95.
The Unbelievable Bubble Book by John Cassidy in collaboration with David Stein; comes with a fabric loop/wand (David Stein's Bubble Thing) that makes body-size bubbles. Klutz, $9.95.
Videos:
Our Unbelievable Bubble. A Cannes Film Festival award-winning video, available from Klutz, $15.95.

Cassette Player
(Ages 3–8)
Fisher-Price, $49.99.

A sturdy cassette player designed for children, such as this one by Fisher-Price, will allow rough-and-ready access to the exciting music and original stories described in the Audio chapter as well as books on tape. A personal cassette player gives a child a level of independence in selecting what to listen to; it also spares parents who are less thrilled by endless repetition of favorite tunes or tales. The accompanying microphone lets kids make their own recordings. Besides encouraging young recording stars, the taping feature can be used

for such purposes as special messages to distant grandparents.

⌒CONNECTIONS

Books:
The books-on-tape selections are almost endless. Many of the titles in this guide are available in recorded versions.
Magazines:
Boomerang. (See Magazines.)
Audio:
(See selections throughout Audio.)

Clay and Play Doughs
(Ages 3–10)
Playskool, $2 to $20, mass market.

The traditional Play-Doh is now accompanied by a wide variety of gadgets and toys, not all of which stimulate the imagination. There are many other offerings in clay and modeling dough, but which are best depends on the age and intent of the youngster.

One sure way to provide variety is to use the recipes in *Mudworks: Creative Clay, Dough, and Modeling Experiences* by MaryAnn F. Kohl (see Resources). With 125 types of edible and incredible dough, these fairly easy recipes will keep any budding artist busy.

Costumes/Dress-up Clothing
(Ages 3–10)
Kid-Size Career Hats from Educational Insights, $12.95.
Uniforms and costumes from Childcraft, $14.95–$32.95.

The career hats from Educational Insights are for a race-car driver, police officer, construction worker, and firefighter. The four plastic hats make a nice start toward a dress-up box. Childcraft offers an array of uniforms—nurse, doctor, firefighter, mail carrier, and police officer—as well as a trunk of accessories, such as capes, moustaches, clown tie, witch's hat, and an ostrich plume.

The do-it-yourself approach to filling a dress-up box actually yields more variety and greater durability. For girls, prefab items are often limited to wedding dresses, fairy garb, or princess (never queen) attire. For boys, the prefab dress-up items available as toys are too often battle gear from one era or another. Inspired by some of the Connections below, haunt a few garage sales, poke through the attic, ask around, and you'll turn up a fine collection of graduation gowns, ties, vests, dresses, slips, shirts, hats, etc., which will serve children's imaginations. Dressing up gives kids a chance for self-expression and an opportunity to try on "what I'm going to be when I grow up." And when the inevitable plays, skits, and school programs come around, parents are prepared.

CONNECTIONS

Books:
Easy Costumes You Don't Have to Sew by Goldie Taub Chernoff. 1975. Four Winds, $11.95.
Martin's Hats by Joan Blos. Illustrated by Marc Simont. 1984. Morrow, $11.95.
Whose Hat? by Margaret Miller. 1988. Greenwillow, $12.95.
Videos:
Caps for Sale. Children's Circle, $19.95.
"Oh, By the Way" in *Joe's First Video.* (See Top Ten Music Videos in Audio.)

Maurice Sendak's Really Rosie. Children's Circle, $19.95.
Audio:
"Really Rosie" sung by Carole King is available on cassette.
Software:
Mask Parade. (See Computer Software.)

Count and See
(Ages 3–6)
Troll Learn and Play catalog, $24.95.

The traditional abacus is expanded upon with 17 math tiles. Alongside the three sliding rows of colored disks are cork-lined rows waiting for placement of corresponding number and symbol tiles. The relationship of a numeral to an amount can be easily introduced, along with the concepts of addition and subtraction. The colorful beads are irresistible (and safely anchored), and the blocks provide a smooth introduction to arithmetic.

CONNECTIONS

Books:
Anno's Counting Book by Mitsumasa Anno. 1977. HarperCollins, $15.95; paper, $5.95.
How Much Is a Million? by David M. Schwartz. 1985. Lothrop, $15; paper, Scholastic, $2.95.
26 Letters and 99 Cents by Tana Hoban. 1987. Greenwillow, $14.95.
Magazines:
Sesame Street Magazine. (See Magazines.)
Videos:
"One Was Johnny" in *The Maurice Sendak Library.* (See Videos.)

Audio:
Counting Games and Rhythms for the Little Ones by Ella Jenkins. Smithsonian/Folkways; dist. by Rounder, $9.95.
Software:
Counting Critters. (See Computer Software.)
Number Farm. (See Computer Software.)
Ollie and Seymour. (See Computer Software.)

Dress-Me-Up

(Ages 2–5)
Battat Games, $10.88.

This new twist on paper dolls will suit boys as well as girls. The substantial cardboard figures are anatomically correct and ready to don winter and summer clothes, including shoes, boots, and play gear. Fitting the laces through the holes prepares a preschooler for shoe-tying and challenges fine motor skills.

Four First Games

(Ages 3–5)
Ravensburger; dist. by International Playthings, $16.

Simply and aptly called Bird Game, Castle Game, Flower Game, and Sausage Game, these are fine introductory games that will not bore parents. There are two reversible game boards, a die with colors rather than numbers, cards, and wooden play markers. The colors and drawings on the boards are bright and interesting. In the Bird Game the players (up to six) must travel seven spaces to the nest in the center. The Castle Game is reminiscent of Candy Land. The German Ravensburger company—a name to look for in good children's games—shows its ethnicity in the Sausage Game, which has a border filled with snapping dachshunds.

Harvest Time

(Ages 4–7)
Family Pastimes; dist. by Animal Town catalog, $17.

A simple board game whose object is to bring in the carrots, peas, corn, and tomatoes on time. Picture cards and a die with colors make this game easy for the youngest user. Best of all, the real winner is the one who learns to help out his or her neighbor.

Once the gardening bug has bit, kids will enjoy gardening tools scaled to their size. Constructive Playthings and True Value hardware carry sets that include a rake, shovel, and hoe. A hand-tool set is available from the Animal Town catalog. A kit for an Atlantic Giant Pumpkin can be ordered from the Insect Lore Products catalog.

☙CONNECTIONS

Books:
Growing Vegetable Soup by Lois Ehlert. 1987. HBJ, $10.95.
Linnea's Windowsill Garden by Christina Bjork. (See Books.)
Miss Penny and Mr. Grubbs by Lisa Campbell Ernst. 1991. Bradbury, $13.95.
More Than Just a Flower Garden by Dwight Kuhn. 1990. Simon & Schuster, $12.95.
The Victory Garden Kids Book: A Beginner's Guide to Growing Vegetables, Fruits, and Flowers by Marjorie Waters. 1988. Houghton Mifflin, paper, $12.95.
Videos:
Get Ready, Get Set, Grow! (See Videos.)

Audio:
"Vega-boogie" from *Let's Be Friends* by Tickle Tune Typhoon. (See Top Ten Music Videos in Audio.)
Software:
Lunar Greenhouse. (See Computer Software.)

Let's Pretend . . .

(Ages 3–6)
Creativity for Kids, $9.90.

Let's Pretend . . . Travel Agency and Let's Pretend . . . Restaurant are two of the sets in this series of career toys. Each box holds simple props, such as notepads, badges, or tickets.

Parents and teachers can add to these sets with items from a local office-supply store. Play money, cardboard signs, travel posters, fancy pencils, and safe occupational gadgets or tools would make Let's Pretend even more fun, as would a few costumes from our dress-up suggestions, given earlier. Add a scarf, tie, or garage-sale jacket for an office look.

∞ CONNECTIONS

Books:
When We Grow Up by Anne Rockwell. 1981. Dutton, $10.95.
Videos:
Kidsongs: What I Want to Be. Viewmaster Video/Warner, $14.95.
Software:
The Little Shopper's Kit. (See Computer Software.)

Music Maestro II

(Ages 4–Adult)
Aristoplay, $25.

Players of all ages can learn about the look, sounds, and functions of 48 instruments. Jazz, bluegrass, folk, rock, and classical instruments appear on the game board; the two tapes were created by musicians at the Oberlin College Conservatory of Music. With five different games to play at various levels, this toy will not go "out of tune." Older players may want to move on to The Game of Great Composers. (See p. 312.)

∞ CONNECTIONS

Books:
I Like the Music by Leah Komaiko. 1987. HarperCollins, $12.95.
The Philharmonic Gets Dressed by Karla Kuskin. 1982. HarperCollins, paper, $3.95.
Magazines:
Clavier's Piano Explorer. (See Magazines.)
Videos:
Bach and Broccoli. (See Videos.)
Audio:
(See Classics Come to Life in Audio.)
Software:
(See *The Treehouse* in Computer Software.)

Noah's Ark

(Ages 3–5)
Discovery Toys, $34.98.

The wooden ark is accompanied by nine pairs of brightly colored animals and Noah and his wife. It has a loading ramp that slips into place and closes up the side of the ark. For children ages 7 and up, there's a board game called Noah's Ark (International Games, Inc.) with question-and-answer cards to acquaint kids with the biblical tale.

CONNECTIONS

Books:
Aardvarks, Disembark by Ann Jonas. 1990. Greenwillow, $14.95. (See ABCs, p. 12.)
Inside Noah's Ark by Laura Fischetto. Illustrated by Letizia Galli. 1989. Viking, $13.95.
Noah's Ark by Peter Spier. 1977. Doubleday, $12.99; paper, $5.99.
Videos:
Noah's Ark. (See Videos.)
Audio:
Noah's Ark. Lightyear Records, dist. by BMG, $8.98.

Post Office
(Ages 3–6)
Fisher-Price, $28.99.

A blue plastic mailbox, which looks like a miniature of the one on the corner, opens up to reveal a carrier basket, stamps, clock, and calendar—all the necessities for a home-based, portable postal station. An old book bag or purse can readily serve as the young letter carrier's bag. There's enough junk mail in any household to fill it up and keep a child busy. Small U.S. Postal Service jeeps and vans (Siku; dist. by Playspaces), though on a different scale, could add to the fun.

CONNECTIONS

Books:
The Jolly Postman and *The Jolly Christmas Postman* by Janet and Allan Ahlberg have special delivery envelopes on every other page addressed to nursery rhyme characters. 1986. Little, Brown, $15.95.
Post Office Book by Gail Gibbons. 1982. Crowell, $12.95.
What the Mailman Brought by Carolyn Craven. Illustrated by Tomie dePaola. 1987. Putnam, $12.95.
Videos:
The Post Office. National Geographic "Our Town" series, $68.
Audio:
Mail Myself to You by John McCutcheon. (See Audio.)

Puppets
(Ages 3–10)
Listening Library's BookMates catalog, $11.95–$29.95.

Mice, spider, raccoon, turtle, and pig puppets from this catalog can be used with an endless number of treasured children's stories, such as *The Very Busy Spider* or *Pig Pig and the Magic Photo Album*. Also available from Listening Library are a reversible polliwog/frog puppet and a caterpillar that turns inside out to become a butterfly. Children can dramatize some terrific tales with these hand puppets. A puppet theater can be made by draping a curtain across a doorway. A more elaborate model is offered in the Childcraft catalog.

20 Puppets for Kids (from Creativity for Kids, $15) is a kit for making finger puppets. There are 20 small tubes and disks along with plenty of sequins, feathers, pipe cleaners, lace,

fake fur, plastic eyes, ribbons, and felt. Also supplied are tickets, scripts, construction suggestions, and two backdrops.

CONNECTIONS

Books:
The Very Busy Spider by Eric Carle. 1985. Putnam, paper, $4.95.
Pig Pig and the Magic Photo Album by David McPhail. 1986. Dutton, $10.95; paper, $3.95.
Magazines:
Plays. (See Magazines.)
Videos:
"The Caterpillar and the Polliwog" in *Owl Moon and Other Stories.* (See Videos.)
Shari Lewis Presents 101 Things for Kids to Do. (See Videos.)
Software:
McGee. (See Computer Software.)
PlayWrite. (See Computer Software.)
Puppet Maker. Wings for Learning/ Sunburst, $75.

Puzzles

(Ages 3–6)
JTG, $12.95.

There are plenty of puzzles with scenes from nursery rhymes and fairy tales to connect kids to books, but JTG has an especially nice series called the "Award Puzzles" that are based on scenes from Caldecott Medal and Honor books. These framed jigsaw puzzles range in difficulty from the 14-piece Color Zoo to the 40-piece St. George and the Dragon.

CONNECTIONS

Books:
Color Zoo by Lois Ehlert. (See *Color Farm* in Books.)
St. George and the Dragon retold by Margaret Hodges. Illustrated by Trina S. Hyman. 1984. Little, Brown, $14.95; paper, $5.95.

Robin Hood Game

(Ages 3–8)
Ravensburger; dist. by International Playthings, $25.

Players must count the arrows on the cards they draw to determine their move; drawing a Sheriff of Nottingham card may bring on a chase or a duel. Adventure, danger, and gold await the merry children who play this board game. Inevitably, they will be caught up in the Robin Hood legend as well.

CONNECTIONS

Books:
Robin Hood by Sarah Hayes. (See Books.)
Videos:
Robin Hood. Disney, $19.99.
Magazines:
Calliope. (See Magazines.)
Audio:
The Adventures of Robin Hood. Listen for Pleasure, $14.95.
Robin Hood/Three Musketeers by Jim Weiss. Greathall Productions, $9.95.

Solar Cash Register

(Ages 3–8)
Childcraft, $19.95.

The eight-digit calculator operates on solar power or the bright lights of an ordinary classroom. The young cashier can add, subtract, divide, multiply, and compute percentages. Paper money is included in the cash drawer, and a paper receipt is issued. This is a perfect prop for *Let's Pretend . . .* (see p. 294).

CONNECTIONS

Books:
Dollars and Cents for Harriet by Betsy Maestro. Illustrated by Giulio Maestro. (See Books.)
If You Made a Million by David M. Schwartz. Illustrated by Steven Kellogg. (See Books.)
Software:
Exploring Measurement, Time, and Money. (See Computer Software.)
The Little Shoppers Kit. (See Computer Software.)
Money Works. MECC, $59.

Space Shuttle
(Ages 3–8)
L'il Playmates, $24.98, mass market.

L'il Playmates offers more than a space shuttle in this brightly colored, multifaceted toy. There is a launching platform with a mission control base, radar unit, flatbed truck, rescue trucks, five astronauts, the shuttle, and booster rockets. The plastic unit may lose appeal for kids past preschool ages, however.

Tonka has a comparable toy called the "Space Shuttle Gift Set" ($19.99). What it lacks in detail (astronauts, radar unit, etc.) it makes up for in realism, although the scale of shuttle to trucks is still not even close. These are fine toys to tie to a trip to the Kennedy Space Center or, even, Space Camp. (See Travel.)

CONNECTIONS

Books:
I Want to Be An Astronaut by Byron Barton. (See Books.)
Monster Trucks and Other Giant Machines on Wheels by Jerry Bushey. 1985. Carolrhoda Books, paper, $4.95.
Software:
Stars and Planets. (See Computer Software.)
Curious George in Outer Space. (See Computer Software.)

Tangram
(Ages 3–Adult)
Quercetti; dist. by International Playthings, $10.

The tangram is an ancient Chinese puzzle made up of a square cut into a rhomboid, five triangles, and a square. These seven pieces can be formed into limitless combinations. Twenty-four basic shapes are demonstrated on the cue cards that come with this magnetic set, which is well suited to young children. They can make a camel, rabbit, person doing a headstand, evergreen, and more. Older kids and adults can tackle more complicated challenges with this endlessly fascinating puzzle.

CONNECTIONS

Books:
A Children's Zoo. by Tana Hoban. 1985. Greenwillow, $13.95.
Grandfather Tang's Story by Ann Tompert. 1990. Crown, $12.95.

The Tangram Magician by Lisa Campbell Ernst and Lee Ernst. 1990. Abrams, $16.95 (includes three small stick-on tangram sets).

Magazines:

Games Junior. (See Magazines.)

Videos:

Colors and Shapes. (See Videos.)

Software:

Stickers. Queue, $34.95.

Toy School Bus

(Ages 2–5)

Playmobil, $29.99.

The Playmobil school bus contains four children with backpacks, a crossing guard/bus driver, street signs, and a stop light. It will merge nicely with the Playmobil school set, playground, and other realistic settings that are widely available. In fact, it's getting hard to imagine a scenario that is not available in Playmobil toys. There are schools, pirate caves, Victorian homes, farms, hospitals, western forts, teepees, construction sites, and medieval castles. All the little plastic figures wear appropriate costumes and carry authentic props. Preschoolers, just beginning to sort the real from the make-believe, revel in these toys.

CONNECTIONS

Books:

The *Magic School Bus* series by Joanna Cole. (See Books.)

School Days by B.G. Hennessy. Illustrated by Tracey Campbell Pearson. 1990. Viking, $13.95.

Wheels on the Bus by Paul Zelinsky. 1990. Dutton, $14.95.

Software:

Talking School Bus. Orange-Cherry, $59.

School Bus Driver. Fisher-Price, dist. by Gametek/IJE, $9.95.

EARLY GRADERS

Capsela

(Ages 6–12)

Sanyei American Corporation, $15.99–$84.99.

Plastic bubbles are transformed into robots, trucks, and all sorts of land and water vehicles or machines when kids add the gears, wheels, propellers, axles, hoists, lights, and pumps included in these remarkable sets. These bubble-shaped vehicles and other creations encourage the testing of scientific concepts—electricity, force, energy, buoyancy, propulsion, and traction. There is a wide range of building kits, from the introductory one that makes five projects ($15.99) to the expert set ($84.99), which can be used to build more than 100 models. More sophisticated systems ($119) allow the builder to create vehicles that move by voice-activated or remote-control commands.

CONNECTIONS

Books:
Einstein Anderson, Science Sleuth by Seymour Simon. Illustrated by Fred Winkowski. 1986. Puffin, paper, $3.95.

Cards
(Ages 7–12)
Aristoplay, $6–$7.

A simple game of 21 (blackjack) can improve arithmetic and analytical skills. Other games—war, rummy, poker, fish—are equally beneficial. "Authors" and "Children's Authors" are two old favorites that painlessly acquaint kids with the classics. Created by Whitehall Games, both are widely available in mass-market and specialty stores. Aristoplay has sets of playing cards featuring inventors, explorers, and scientists and some with famous figures in black history. The Animal Town catalog includes three sets of playing cards featuring famous women: "Foremothers," "Poets and Writers," and "Founders & Firsts" ($6.50 each). (While a player is awaiting his or her turn, there's a lot to be learned.)

The Smithsonian has created three card games (available from Education Insights), each with 400 questions and answers— "Presidential Quiz," "American History Quiz," and "U.S. Space Exploration Quiz"—that will challenge parents at least as much as their kids.

CONNECTIONS

Books:
Cards for Kids by Elin McKoy. 1991. Macmillan, $13.95.
The Klutz Book of Card Games: For Sharks and Others by the editors of Klutz Press. Klutz, $9.95.
Software:
Ted Bear Games. Baudville, $29.95.

Crayola Designer Kits
(Ages 7–10)
Binney & Smith, $20, mass market.

Plastic sketch boards, templates, paper, pencils, and design manuals fill both the Crayola Designer Kit for Vehicles and Crayola Fashion Designer Kit. Kids without artistic talent can produce polished sketches of clothing, cars, and spaceships. These valuable sets offer just enough help and plenty of possibilities. Another option is the Create a Critter set for younger kids, with its 30 rubbing plates. Kids can make tops, middles, and bottoms that match or don't, like the creations possible in *The Playroom* software.

CONNECTIONS

Books:
Draw 50 Beasties and Yugglies and Turnover Uglies That Go Bump in the Night by Lee J. Ames. 1989. Doubleday, $12.95.

The Drawing Book by Leon Baxter.
1990. Ideals, $13.95.
Magazines:
See Write It Yourself in Magazines.
Videos:
Squiggles, Dots, & Lines. (See Videos.)
Software:
The Playroom. (See Computer
Software.)

DetectoLab
(Ages 7–12)
Educational Design, $30.

This home crime lab contains suggestions for
80 crime-detection experiments. Kids can
work with invisible ink, coded messages,
fingerprint collection and analysis, a code
wheel, and a 30-power minimicroscope to
devise and resolve mysteries on their own.
Creating and solving codes offers an instructive way to play with language. This company
also makes smaller, less expensive minilabs,
such as a Fingerprint Kit and an Electro-Mag-
netix Kit.

⌒CONNECTIONS

Books:
*The Cat's Elbow and Other Secret
Languages* by Alvin Schwartz. 1982.
Farrar, Straus & Giroux, $12.95.
The Kids' Code & Cipher Book by
Nancy Garden. 1992. Linnet Books,
$17.50.
Videos:
*Encyclopedia Brown: The Boy Detective
in the Case of the Missing Time Capsule.*
(See Videos.)
Software:
Midnight Rescue. (See Computer
Software.)

Scoop Mahoney: Investigative Reader.
(See Computer Software.)

Electronic Sketch Pad
(Ages 5–Adult)
Sony, $114.95, mass market.

The television monitor becomes an artist's
sketchpad (and the VCR tape a sketchbook)
when this toy is hooked up. Drawing is done
on a gridded mat using a special pen, but the
work appears on the TV screen in color or
black and white. Sound effects can be added
to enhance the fun and eye/hand coordination.
The toy's potential is vast. Older kids can use
a camcorder to create animation.

⌒CONNECTIONS

Books:
The Big Red Drawing Book by Ed
Emberley. 1987. Little, Brown, $12.95.
*Make Your Own Animated Movies and
Videotapes* by Yvonne Anderson. 1991.
Little, Brown, $19.95.
Near the Sea: A Portfolio of Paintings by
Jim Arnosky. 1990. Lothrop, $13.95.
Videos:
Be a Cartoonist. Family Express Video,
$19.95.
Squiggles, Dots, & Lines. (See Videos.)
Software:
ColorMe: The Computer Coloring Kit.
(See Computer Software.)
Color 'n' Canvas. (See Computer
Software.)
Kid Pix. (See Computer Software.)
(See also the cartooning and home
publishing programs in Computer
Software.)

Erector Set

(Ages 7–Adult)

Meccano/Erector, $15.95 (103-piece set), mass market.

Erector sets are back, complete with Allen key wrenches and 100–600 metal parts, including a variety of bolts, metal rectangles, squares, and uniquely shaped pieces. Kits for older builders come with essential gears and transmissions necessary to make an electric motor powered by batteries. The "Ultimate Erector Set" is a truly deluxe version containing over 3,100 parts in an impressive five-drawer wood cabinet.

CONNECTIONS

Books:
Up Goes the Skyscraper by Gail Gibbons. (See Books.)
Unbuilding by David Macauley. 1987. Houghton Mifflin, $15.95; paper, $6.95.

Face Painting

(Ages 6–10)

Klutz, $14.95.

A paint box comes attached to a spiral-bound, laminated book that reveals the secrets of successful face painting. This is a Halloween necessity, but it's also fun all year long. Using the enclosed brush and sponge, kids can decorate feet, arms, torsos, and faces with pirate's patch, puppy spots, ballet toe slippers, fire-breathing dragon, and lots more. True to the manufacturer's name, even a klutz can become an artist with this equipment.

CONNECTIONS

Books:
Painting Faces by Suzanne Haldane. (See Books.)
Be A Clown! The Complete Guide to Instant Clowning by Turk Pipkin. (o.p.)

Grow a Frog

(Ages 6–10)

Three Rivers Amphibian; dist., although not exclusively, by Insect Lore, $12.95.

A small square plastic aquarium comes with a bit of frog food, instruction booklet, decorative rocks, and a coupon for one tadpole. Receiving the tadpole by mail is almost as exciting as witnessing its transformation. (A closeup view of the transition from tadpole to frog is not to be missed.) This is an easy pet for children to care for as long as they refrain from overfeeding. Three Rivers (P.O. Box 406, Massapequa, NY 11758) is ready to supply extra food and housing, or the supplies can be obtained at a local pet shop.

CONNECTIONS

Books:
Amazing Frogs and Toads by Barry Clarke. 1990. Knopf Eyewitness Junior Series, paper, $6.95.
Frogs, Toads, Lizards, and Salamanders by Nancy Winslow Parker and Joan Richards Wright. 1990. Greenwillow, $13.95.
Magazines:
OWL. (See Magazines.)
Videos:
The Mysterious Tadpole and Other Stories. (See Videos.)
(See also Swamp Stars in Videos.)

Tadpoles and Frogs. National Geographic, $56.

Audio:
"Frogs" and "Dodge City" on *Earth Songs* by Jay O'Callahan. Artana Productions; dist. by Silo, $9.95.

Software:
Odell Lake. (See Computer Software.)

Knights and Dragons

(Ages 6–10)

Britain's Petite Limited; dist. by Reeves, $1.99–$3.99.

Here's an alternative to the battling action figures so popular from TV cartoons. Around a castle, children can encamp these plastic armored knights on foot, a fire-breathing dragon, and moving jousting knights on horseback. For the full effect, Britain's sells a plastic Lion Castle with a movable drawbridge, scaling ladders, moat, and courtyard interior. The Hearth Song catalog carries a beautiful wooden castle that these toy warriors can defend. Older children will enjoy constructing and reconstructing the Lego castle systems.

∞CONNECTIONS

Books:
The Kitchen Knight: A Tale of King Arthur by Margaret Hodges. (See Books.)
St. George and the Dragon by Margaret Hodges. Illustrated by Tina Schart Hyman. 1984. Little, Brown, $14.95; paper, $5.95.
Tom Thumb by Richard Jesse Watson. (See Books.)
Tournament of Knights by Joe Lasker. 1986. HarperCollins, $12.95; paper, $4.95.

Young Merlin by Robert D. San Souci. 1990. Doubleday, $13.95.

Magazines:
Calliope. (See Magazines.)

Videos:
Castle (based on the book by David Macauley). PBS Video, $19.95.
Merlin and the Dragons. (See Videos.)

Audio:
King Arthur and His Knights read by Jim Weiss. (See Audio.)

Software:
NumberMaze. (See Computer Software.)
The King's Rule. (See Computer Software.)

Land Ho! Tierra Tierra!

(Ages 8–Adult)

Aristoplay, $22.

Sail the oceans of the fifteenth century aboard the *Niña, Pinta,* or *Santa Maria* by playing this game of discovery modeled on the journey of Christopher Columbus. All of the cards, instructions, and playing aids are in English and Spanish. Play the game in either language or in both for a greater challenge. If history games are a hit, try Made for Trade (also by Aristoplay, $22), about colonial America.

∞CONNECTIONS

Books:
Christopher Columbus: Voyager to the Unknown by Nancy Smiler Levinson. (See Books.)
Columbus and the World Around Him by Milton Meltzer. (See Books.)
I Sailed with Columbus by Miriam Schlein. 1991. HarperCollins, $13.95.

Pedro's Journal: A Voyage with Christopher Columbus by Pam Conrad. 1991. Caroline House, $13.95.
Videos:
The Discovery of the Americas. Spoken Arts, $44.95.
Where Do You Think You're Going, Christopher Columbus? (See Videos.)

Leaf and Flower Press
(Ages 6–10)
Woodcrafter Kits; dist. by Nature Company, $9.95.

This leaf and flower press is constructed of 7-inch-square birch plywood end-pieces. Screws tightened with wing nuts flatten the collector's treasures. Blotting papers and cardboard compressing sheets are also supplied. This set includes the "Backyard Explorer Kit," which contains *The Leaf and Tree Guide* and *The Leaf and Tree Album*, both by Rona Beame (Workman Publishing).

✑CONNECTIONS

Books:
Discovering Trees by Douglas Florian. 1990. Macmillan, $10.95; paper, $3.95.
The Giving Tree by Shel Silverstein. 1964. Harper & Row. (o.p.)
Videos:
The Man Who Planted Trees. (See Videos.)
Audio:
The Man Who Planted Trees. Earth Music Productions, $9.95; with book, $21.95.

Make-A-Mask Kit
(Ages 6–Adult)
Educational Insights, $9.95.

Be a clown, duck, monster, pharaoh, or whatever—just make the mask. The kit includes one basic face form, one roll of pretreated sculpting gauze, paints, and a paintbrush—enough craft materials to make one mask. Gauze refills are available at $6.95 per roll. More creative types may find a substitute for the pretreated gauze in *Mudworks* (see Resources). Masks are often taboo at Halloween because they restrict the vision of trick-or-treaters; but masks are great for cultural studies and supervised imaginative play.

✑CONNECTIONS

Books:
Animal Faces, Fun Faces, and *Dinosaur Faces* by Pierre-Marie Valat. 1988. Dutton, $14.95 each. (Each volume contains between 5 and 15 punch-out masks.)
Software:
Mask Parade. (See Computer Software.)
Learn about: Animals. (See Computer Software.)

Mousetrap
(Ages 6–10)
Milton-Bradley, $12.99.

Players move small plastic mice around the board in pursuit of cardboard cheese wedges, while building a complicated trap piece by piece, according to the instructions. The player who snares the cheese without getting caught in the trap wins. Younger players (ages 4 to 6) often prefer to skip instructions and simply hook up the configuration of staircases, falling marbles, and seesaw, and then send the whole thing whirring into action.

✑CONNECTIONS

Books:
Anatole and the Thirty Thieves by Eve Titus. Illustrated by Paul Galdone. 1969. Bantam, paper, $4.95.
The Mouse and the Motorcycle by Beverly Cleary. 1980. Morrow, $12.95; Dell, paper, $3.25.
Videos:
Abel's Island. (See Videos.)
Ralph S. Mouse. (See Videos.)
Software:
The Playroom. (Hosted by a mouse, this program also has a mouse vs. monster "board" game). (See Computer Software.)

Mysteries of Magnetism
(Ages 8–12)
Educational Insights, $14.95.

Magnets fascinate, yet few people stop to consider the pull they exert on everyday life, from electric motors to the tug of the poles. With advances in the study of superconductivity, magnetism will become an even more pervasive aspect of our daily lives. Playing with magnets, especially in well-designed kits such as this one, can build an appreciation of magnetic facts and mysteries. The principles of magnetism are covered at various levels in these games and experiments. Compass techniques are also demonstrated in this set, which includes a 32-page booklet and essential test equipment. (See also the Edmund Scientific catalog, which has magnets galore.)
[*Reminder:* Never bring magnets near a computer or software.]

✑CONNECTIONS

Books:
Forces in the Earth: A Book About Gravity and Magnetism by R. J. Lefkowitz. (o.p.)
Magnets to Generators: Projects with Magnetism by Peter Lafferty. 1989. Watts, $11.95.
The Secret Life of Dilly McBean by Dorothy Haas. (See Books.)
Magazines:
Boy's Life. (See Magazines.)

Pallino: The Mosaic Machine
(Ages 5–12)
Quercetti; dist. by International Playthings, $29.99.

This looks and even plays like a pinball game, but there is more to it than scoring points or vanquishing foes. The object is to make colorful mosaics with marbles, and the challenge is more a matter of skill than luck. A button has to be pressed to release a single marble and another button (out of 12) has to be pushed to draw it into the right slot. Six cards, filled with bright random patterns, are used to match the marbles to the colors on the board. Kids can also design their own patterns on a blank card.

Presto-Change-O
(Ages 8–Adult)
Educational Insights, $19.95.

Unlike Monopoly (which is still a lot of fun), this is a more realistic board game that teaches players how to earn, save, and spend money. As the players move around the board, chores help them earn a dollar or two, while arcades and other items tempt them to spend it. The goal is to reach $10, and each player must keep change and bills in the highest denominations (five $1 bills must be changed into a $5 bill, just as four quarters must be turned into the bank for a dollar).

∞**CONNECTIONS**

Books:
Making Cents: Every Kid's Guide to Making Money by Elizabeth Wilkinson. Illustrated by Martha Weston. 1989. Little, Brown, paper, $8.95.
Magazines:
Zillions. (See Magazines.)
Software:
Exploring Measurement, Time, and Money. (See Computer Software.)
Money Works. MECC, $59.
The Treehouse. (See Computer Software.)

Time Capsule
(Ages 6–10)
Workman, $15.95.

A silver-colored plastic tube unscrews to hold selected treasures. Inside are two small envelopes labeled "Historic Object Containment Envelopes." The accompanying guide has plenty of ideas for filling the capsule and for occasions to use it. Bury it at a birthday party or on the first day of school. There are also basic instructions on mapmaking to help the seeker relocate the capsule once it's buried in the backyard or hidden in the attic or a closet.

∞**CONNECTIONS**

Books:
Steven Caney's Kids' America by Steven Caney. Workman, paper, $11.95.

Videos:
Encyclopedia Brown: The Boy Detective in the Case of the Missing Time Capsule. (See Videos.)
Software:
Math Blaster Mystery. (See Computer Software.)
Scoop Mahoney: Investigative Reader. (See Computer Software.)

Young Storytellers
(Ages 5–9)
Patail Enterprises, $19.95.

This spiral-bound book with blank vinyl pages is waiting for children to fill it with their own stories by using 256 vinyl stick-on words and phrases. Composition is easy, even for non-readers, who can simply match the color of the word or phrase with the colored rectangles at the bottom of the page. While children have fun making silly or sensible stories, they are learning, through the color-coding, parts of speech and correct word order. Original artwork is encouraged in the space above the sentences; four wipe-off markers are supplied. The envelope-style carrying case keeps the pieces together. A good traveling toy.

∞**CONNECTIONS**

Books:
A Bundle of Beasts by Patricia Hooper. Illustrated by Mark Steele. 1987. Houghton Mifflin, $12.95.
A Cache of Jewels and Other Collective Nouns by Ruth Heller. 1987. Putnam, $10.95; paper, $5.95.
Herds of Words by Patricia McCarthy. 1991. Dial, $11.95.

Kites Sail High: A Book about Verbs by Ruth Heller. 1988. Putnam, $10.95; paper, $5.95.

Magazines:

See Write It Yourself in Magazines.

Videos:

The Maurice Sendak Library—especially the interview with the author at the end of the tape. (See Videos.)

Audio:

"Grammar Rapper" on *Hearts & Hands* by Tickle Tune Typhoon. (See Audio.)

Software:

Grammar Toy Shop. MECC, $59.

Poetry Palette. (See Computer Software.)

Read 'n' Roll. (See Computer Software.)

Writer Rabbit. (See Computer Software.)

Yo-Yo

(Ages 5–Adult)

Duncan Toys, $3.49, mass market.

Yo-yos are an eternal toy. Although frustrating at times, they are fun and enhance manual dexterity. Yo-yos come in silly designs or shapes, but it's best to start with a conventional one. Duncan, the best-known yo-yo company, provides instructions for three yo-yo games on the package and supplies a coupon to purchase a 48-page how-to book. Yo-yoing is a serious skill to many adults, including Tommy Smothers (of the Smothers Brothers), who has performed—with his yo-yo—with the Boston Pops orchestra.

∞ CONNECTIONS

Books:

The Klutz Yo-Yo Book by John Cassidy. Klutz, $9.95, including a maple yo-yo.

Videos:

Yo-Yo Man by The Smothers Brothers. Music for Little People, $14.98, including a yo-yo.

DOLLS WITH A STORY

All of these dolls are stars in popular children's stories. They will appeal to children of many ages. Usually only one title in a series is mentioned in our Connections. A special Connection also appears in this section: posters that endorse reading and libraries.

Prices are drawn from the Listening Library BookMates catalog, except where another catalog is cited. Most of the dolls are available in specialty shops and other catalogs as well. The size designation beside the price (e.g., 18″) refers to the height of the doll.

Angelina Ballerina $15.95 (11″).

This determined little mouse faces troubles that will ring true to many little ones. Both her worries and her triumphs can be relived with this posable doll in a pink tutu.

✐CONNECTIONS

Books:
Angelina Ballerina by Katherine Holabird. Illustrated by Helen Craig. 1983. Crown, paper, $8.95.
Audio:
Angelina Ballerina and Other Stories read by Sally Struthers. Caedmon, $9.98.

Felicity Merriman   Pleasant Company, $88 (one doll plus hardcover book) (18″).

Felicity joins Kristen, Samantha, and Molly in the American Girls Collection. Each doll represents a specific era in American history. Period clothing, accessories, and toys have been created to suit each doll and the books that feature them. The books in themselves are delightful—the dolls and their accoutrements are splendid, but pricey. Felicity, the redhead from 1774, currently has six stories and a video filmed at Williamsburg in her collection.

CONNECTIONS

Books:

Meet Felicity by Valeria Tripp. 1991. Pleasant Company, $12.95 each; paper, $5.95 each.

Videos:

Felicity's Elegant Tea Party. Pleasant Company, $22.

Linnea $12.95 (11").

Linnea in Monet's Garden by Christina Bjork features a small girl wandering through the famous impressionist's grounds at Giverny. Accompanied by this dark-haired doll in an apron smock and straw hat, children can explore many gardens and works of art.

CONNECTIONS

Books:

Linnea in Monet's Garden by Christina Bjork. Illustrated by Lena Anderson. 1987. R & S Books; dist. by Farrar, Straus & Giroux, $10.95.

Linnea's Windowsill Garden by Christina Bjork. (See Books.)

Madeline $15.99 (14″) ($29.95 for 18″ version).

Madeline, the book, tells about the high jinks of a Parisian schoolgirl who falls ill and needs an emergency appendix operation. The impish Madeline as a cloth doll has bright red rag hair, a blue coat, and even the famous appendectomy scar. Here's a perfect toy and tale to minimize the worries of a sick child. The 18″ doll even has a proper schoolgirl hat.

✑ CONNECTIONS

Books:
Madeline by Ludwig Bemelmans. 1939. Viking, $13.95; Puffin, paper, $3.95.
Videos:
Madeline's Rescue. (See Videos.)
Audio:
Madeline and the Gypsies & Other Stories and *Madeline & Other Bemelmans* read by Carol Channing. Caedmon, $9.95 each.

Ramona $17.95 (16″).

Ramona, with her tomboy attire and tousled brown hair, suits the image portrayed in Beverly Cleary's beloved novels about this younger sibling who has her own way of doing everything.

✑ CONNECTIONS

Books:
Ramona the Pest by Beverly Cleary. 1968. Morrow, $12.95; Dell, paper, $3.25.
Videos:
Ten videos starring Ramona are available, including *Siblingitis* and *The Great Hair Argument.* (See *Ramona Stories* in Videos.)
Audio:
Beezus and Ramona, Ramona, the Brave, and *Ramona Quimby, Age 8* are just a few of the many cassettes available. Random House, $9.90 each.
Poster:
Ramona with her arms loaded with books stands under the proclamation "Libraries are Forever." ALA Graphics, $6 (22″ by 34″ poster); Ramona bookmarks are also available, $7 (200 bookmarks).

MIDDLE GRADERS AND TEENAGERS

Ant Farm
(See Critter Condo.)

BanKit
(Ages 8–12)
Kidscorp, available from Discovery Toys, $19.98.

BanKit, billed as "The Home Checking Account and Money Management System for Kids" can clarify the basics of banking, checks, and other money matters. The set comes with two checkbooks, deposit slips, registers, and a manual for parent and child. This is a great way to work on basic arithmetic skills or save for a rainy day (or a skateboard).

✏CONNECTIONS

Books:
Making Cents: Every Kid's Guide to Making Money by Elizabeth Wilkinson. Illustrated by Martha Weston. 1989. Little, Brown, paper, $8.95.
Smart Spending: A Young Consumer's Guide by Lois Schmitt. 1989. Scribners, $11.95.

Magazines:
Zillions. (See Magazines.)
Boomerang. (See Magazines.)
Videos:
Alexander, Who Used to Be Rich Last Sunday. (See Videos.)
Audio:
Boomerang. (See Magazines.)
Software:
Exploring Measurement, Time, and Money. (See Computer Software.)
Money Works. MECC, $59.

Chess Set
(Ages 9–Adult)
Workman, $14.95.

A basic chess set for beginners with plastic pieces and a large board. The instruction book enclosed, *The Kids' Book of Chess,* offers a little history of the game as well as the basics for new players. The book's full-color drawings of knights, kings, queens, and bishops lend fun and authority to the well-orchestrated lessons. Available in the U.S. Chess Federation catalog (cited at the end of this section) are portable, magnetic, leather, talking, correspondence, and computer chess games.

CONNECTIONS

Books:

Bobby Baseball by Robert Kimmel Smith. (See Books.)

Chess for Juniors by Robert M. Snyder. 1991. Random House, paper, $13.

Magazines:

School Mates. (See Magazines.)

Videos:

Masters of Disaster. Indiana University, $150.

The Mighty Pawns. WonderWorks series; Home Vision, $29.95.

Software:

The Fidelity Chessmaster 2100. (See Computer Software.)

Critter Condo

(Ages 8–12)

Educational Insights, $14.95.

For long-term insect observation, the condo can serve as an ant farm, butterfly nursery, frog hatchery, hermit-crab shelter, or even a terrarium or cactus garden. A booklet on insect observation and care is supplied along with coupons and alternate sources for ants and other critters. Frog eggs, silkworm eggs, and live lady bugs can be ordered from Insect Lore (the address is at the end of this section). Hermit crabs are available at most pet stores.

You can also pick up a *Critter Carnival* (Educational Insights, $12.95), which is actually a "bug playground." Using the supplied tweezers, you carefully place the insects amidst the swings, tracks, slides, and other playground equipment. Youngsters with a fascination for insects will enjoy this opportunity to see them in such an environment.

Don't overlook the traditional ant farm, which is available from Running Press for

$12.95 along with *The Ant Rancher's Handbook.* The book offers descriptions of ant types and behavior, then leads into explanations on how to create a colony and perform experiments (e.g., "pass the chow" and "ant racing"). A coupon for ordering ants is found at the end of the book.

CONNECTIONS

Books:

Ant Cities by Arthur Dorros. 1987. HarperCollins, $13.95; paper, $4.50.

The Ant Rancher's Handbook by George S. Glenn. 1990. Running Press, paper, $7.95.

A House for Hermit Crab by Eric Carle. 1987. Picture Book Studio, $15.95.

Insect Metamorphosis: From Egg to Adult by Ron and Nancy Goor. (See Books.)

Two Bad Ants by Chris Van Allsburg. 1988. Houghton Mifflin, $16.95.

Magazines:

National Geographic World. (See Magazines.)

Ranger Rick. (See Magazines.)

Videos:

Backyard Bugs. National Geographic Society, $59.99.

Honey, I Shrunk the Kids. Disney; dist. by International Video Entertainment, $22.99.

Insects from the "Tell Me Why" series. Penguin Home Video; dist. by Prism, $19.95.

Joyful Noise. (See Videos.)

Family Album

(Ages 8–Adult)

Childswork/Childsplay; dist. by Animal Town catalog, $16.

This game calls for players to portray people and situations from their own families using charades or drawings. Some sample challenges are "the whole family involved in painting a room," or "the funniest friend you ever had," or "the TV parent that you'd like to be." There are stacks of cards for parents and children as well as a general category. Special blank cards can be used as wild cards to write in personal scenarios about family memories, members, and situations. A twist of the spinner determines whether the player must draw or "act." Among other values, Family Album serves as a perfect icebreaker for a family reunion. (See Travel.)

CONNECTIONS

Books:
Do People Grow on Family Trees? Genealogy for Kids and Other Beginners by Ira Wolfman. 1991. Workman, paper, $9.95.
Videos:
Make a Family Video Album. Produced by Christopher Stanton for Edgewater Productions, $19.95.
Audio:
Family Tree by Tom Chapin. (See Audio.)

Fun with Hieroglyphs
(Ages 8–Adult)
Metropolitan Museum of Art, $19.95.

Hieroglyphs can suit almost any occasion. (One child used this set to make Valentine's Day cards for school.) This hands-on introduction to the Egyptian alphabet is a great lesson in phonics, because each image must be translated by sound. Creator Catherine Roehrig keeps her explanations simple in the trans-

lation chart and accompanying booklet. Twenty-four stamps and an ink pad are the essence of this toy.

CONNECTIONS

Books:
Ancient Egypt (Exploring the Past series) by George Hart. Illustrated by Stephen Biesty. 1990. HBJ, $13.95.
Mummies Made in Egypt by Aliki. 1979. Crowell, $12.95; paper, HarperCollins, $4.95.
Magazines:
Calliope. (See Magazines.)
Kids Discover. "Pyramids" was the premier issue. (See Magazines.)
Software:
Eye of Horus. Britannica Software, $39.95.

The Game of Great Composers
(Ages 10–Adult)
Aristoplay, $30.

With two levels of play, this game introduces kids and adults to the lives, times, and works of European classical composers. As well as a grounding in fine music, this challenging game offers a perspective on European history. The accompanying recordings were made by musicians at the University of Michigan School of Music. (See also Music Maestro II, p. 294.)

CONNECTIONS

Magazines:
Clavier's Piano Explorer. (See Magazines.)
Videos:
Bach and Broccoli. (See Videos.)

Audio:
(See Classics Come to Life, p. 233.)

Gone Birding
(Ages 7–Adult)
National Wildlife Federation, $49.94.

There are 10 different games within this set, which includes a playing board with a national map and a two-hour VHS video. On tape are scenes and songs featuring North America's finest avian residents and visitors. The game will sharpen birdwatching skills of young and old.

CONNECTIONS

Books:
Bird Talk by Roma Gans. 1971. HarperCollins, $12.95.
Bird Watch by Jane Yolen. (See Books.)
I Am Phoenix by Paul Fleischman. 1989. HarperCollins, paper, $3.95.
A Kid's First Book of Birdwatching by Scott Weidensaul. 1990. Running Press, $14.95, includes a songbird audiocassette.
State Birds by Arthur Singer and Alan Singer. 1986. Lodestar, paper, $5.95.
Magazines:
Owl (See Magazines.)
Ranger Rick. (See Magazines.)
Videos:
Birds of the Backyard: Winter into Spring. Eyelevel Video, $29.95.
Backyard Birds. National Geographic, $68.
C'mon Geese. (See Videos.)
Software:
Backyard Birds. (See Computer Software.)

Hail to the Chief: The Presidential Election Game
(Ages 10–Adult)
Aristoplay, $25.

You need to know more than clichés to get elected president in this game. Answering questions correctly about American history and the role of the chief executive, aided by lucky throws of the dice, will help you become a candidate. Once on the campaign trail, through all 50 states, players are faced with even more questions on history and geography. Elements of fate are added by the 36 campaign cards (as in real life, positive and negative events influence the outcome). Maybe the real candidates should be required to win this game before starting out!

CONNECTIONS

Books:
The Buck Stops Here by Alice Provensen. 1990. HarperCollins, $17.95.
Getting Elected: The Diary of a Campaign by Joan Hewett. 1989. Lodestar, $13.95.
Lincoln: A Photobiography by Russell Freedman. (See Books.)
How to Be President of the U.S.A. by Murray Suid. 1992. Monday Morning Books, paper, $9.95.
Videos:
American Portraits series. (See Videos.)
Software:
"*And If Re-elected . . .*". Focus Media, Inc. $89.

Indian Bead Loom
(Ages 8–Adult)
Eaglecrafts, Inc., $8, mass market.

A plastic beading loom that can accommodate beaded strips three inches wide and any length is the basic component of this kit. Beads, thread, needles, beeswax, graph paper, and thorough instructions are included. Once the basics of threading the loom are mastered, the beading is fairly simple—just a matter of threading beads on a needle and entwining them with the loom threads. New beads will soon be needed by any industrious crafts-person. Directions on selecting materials are given. Kids can make belts, ties, necklaces, earrings, headbands, and other adornments while participating in a traditional Native American craft.

Brio, creator of fantastic wooden trains, bridges, and so forth, also has a fabric weaving loom ($50). This elegant replica can transport children through history as they make cloth just as their ancestors did.

∞CONNECTIONS

Books:
Iktomi and the Buffalo Skull: A Plains Indian Story by Paul Goble. (See Books.)
Audio:
The Boy Who Lived with the Bears and Other Iroquois Stories. (See Audio.)
Cherokee Legends I. (See Audio.)

Lego Technic Sets
(Ages 8–Adult)
Lego Dacta (educational division of Lego; currently available only via catalog—see address under Toy Companies, below), $49–$170.

Besides the essential array of Lego rectangular construction blocks, these kits contain many gears, pulleys, wheels, pneumatic pumps, valves, switches, hoses, chain links, and motors. Step-by-step instructions are printed on activity cards that match photographs of real machines in action with the suggested models. The cranes, pulleys, cars, and robots that can be built with these components will introduce kids to the realities of technology.

Some Technic Legos are designed for link-up with a computer using the Lego TC LOGO program. The models built will operate when basic commands are typed into the computer (such as "look-for-line" or "waituntil"). The building experience demands that directions be followed precisely, as does the command writing. This visualization of programming can often spur the interest of casual computer users, especially those who have been interested only in word processing or playing games.

∞CONNECTIONS

Books:
1,2,3, My Computer and Me: A LOGO Funbook for Kids by Jim Muller. 1984. Reston, paper, $15.95.
Turtle Talk: A Beginner's Book of Logo by Seymour Simon. 1986. HarperCollins, paper, $4.50.
Videos:
Lego Dacta lends its 16-minute video introduction to Lego LOGO free to educators.
Software:
LOGO PLUS. (See Computer Software.)
Miner's Cave. MECC, $59.

NightStar
(Ages 10–Adult)
The Nightstar Company, $44.

This is a star map shaped like a bowl—as if the sky were inverted over the viewer. The map is actually a globe shape, deflated and set along a flexible ring that allows the user to turn the surface to duplicate a given night's sky. A latitude finder and time dial make accuracy easy. Once NightStar is held up to the skies and one constellation is located, the others can be readily sighted and identified with the markings on this curved map. There is also a planet finder on the map. No telescopes are necessary. According to inventor Bruce King, "NightStar is to the understanding of the night sky what the earth-globe is to the understanding of the earth."

CONNECTIONS

Books:
Look to the Night Sky: An Introduction to Star Watching by Seymour Simon. Illustrated by Jan Brett. 1979. Penguin, paper, $5.95.
Nebulae: The Birth & Death of Stars by Necia H. Apfel. (See Books.)
Magazines:
Odyssey. (See Magazines.)
Software:
Sky Lab. MECC, $59.

On Assignment with National Geographic
(Ages 10–Adult)
National Geographic Educational Services, $33.20.

The playing board is a colorful map of the world and the players represent *National Geographic* photographers. More than 800 questions about places and people around the globe test knowledge. Memory and observation are further challenged by 144 photo cards.

CONNECTIONS

Books:
National Geographic Picture Atlas of Our World. 1991. National Geographic Society, $21.95.
Magazines:
National Geographic World. (See Magazines.)
Videos:
Cameramen Who Dared. (See Videos.)
Software:
Nigel's World. (See Computer Software.)
Where in the World Is Carmen Sandiego? (See Computer Software.)
World GeoGraph. (See Computer Software.)

Poliopticon
(Ages 10–Adult)
D. F. Vasconcellos; dist., though not exclusively, by Edmund Scientific, $39.95.

The 25 pieces of this set of lenses and prisms come in bright yellow, sturdy plastic tubes and can be assembled to create binoculars, a microscope, telescope, magnifying glass, kaleidoscope, and five other instruments. Assembling the various viewing instruments teaches the concepts of magnified and telescopic viewing. For learning experience, it's far better than a simple "look in here" suggestion from a parent or teacher who has already set up the instrument.

CONNECTIONS

Books:
The Microscope by Maxine Kumin. Illustrations by Arnold Lobel. 1986. HarperCollins, paper, $2.95.

Small Worlds Close Up by Lisa Grillone and Joseph Gennaro. 1987. Crown, $12.95; paper, $4.95.
Hidden Worlds: Pictures of the Invisible by Seymour Simon. 1983. Morrow, $13.95.

Pollution Solution
(Ages 10–Adult)
Aristoplay, $20.

Subtitled *The Game of Environmental Impact,* this board game teaches environmental awareness, pollution prevention, and clean-up tactics in a challenging, stimulating fashion. It can be played by from one to six players.

⚮**CONNECTIONS**

Books:
50 Simple Things Kids Can Do to Save the Earth by John Javna. 1990. Andrews and McMeel, paper, $6.95.
Just a Dream by Chris Van Allsburg. 1990. Houghton Mifflin, $17.95.
Magazines:
P3. (See Magazines.)
Videos:
Help Save Planet Earth. (See Videos.)
The Man Who Planted Trees. (See Videos.)
Audio:
Hug the Earth by Tickle Tune Typhoon. Alcazar, $9.
Mother Earth by Tom Chapin. A & M Records, $9.
Piggyback Planet: Songs for a Whole Earth by Sally Rogers. (See Audio.)
Software:
Audubon Wildlife Adventures: Grizzly Bears. (See Computer Software.)
Galactic Zoo. (See Computer Software.)

Pottery Wheel
(Ages 9–14)
Tyco, $16.99, mass market.

Youngsters often witness pottery making in modern crafts shops or at historical parks, such as Williamsburg or the Cherokee Oconaluftee Indian Village (see Travel). This toy gives older children a chance to try their hand at an ancient art. The motorized potter's wheel comes with two pounds of air-drying clay, so no firing or oven-drying is necessary. Molding tools and paints for finishing touches are also supplied.

⚮**CONNECTIONS**

Books:
Potter's Wheel by Norma Johnston. 1988. Morrow, $12.95.
Clayworks: Colorful Crafts from Around the World by Virginie Fowler. 1986. Prentice Hall, $11.95.

60-in-1 Project Lab Kit
(Ages 10–14)
Radio Shack, $19.95.

Anyone who likes to tinker with wires, buzzers, and electronics will be delighted with this and other Radio Shack kits. With this single unit, it is possible to make a radio, metal detector, amplifier, burglar alarm, police light, memory circuit, and 54 other electronics, physics, and computer-related projects. The learning potential here is as great as the fun quotient. For school science fairs, these kits are a natural start. No soldering is required, and the young scientist/engineer works directly on a large board with many of the required elements already in place.

⌘CONNECTIONS

Books:

Dear Mr. Henshaw by Beverly Cleary. 1983. Morrow, $12.95; Dell, paper, $4.95.

The Way Things Work by David Macaulay. 1988. Houghton Mifflin, $29.95.

Build Your Own Radio by Jim Becker and Andy Mayer. 1991. Running Press, $19.95.

Videos:

Learning about Electricity. AIMS Media, $285.

Software:

Build a Circuit. 1991. Wings for Learning/Sunburst, $79.

Stampin'
(Ages 8–Adult)
Childcraft, $15.95.

An official guide to stamp collecting from the U.S. Postal Service is enclosed with this realistic board game, which teaches the how-tos and the pleasures of stamp collecting. As young collectors travel a circular path on the board, they must collect two sets of stamps, attend auctions, and beware of potential losses or hazards.

⌘CONNECTIONS

Books:

Stamp Collecting as a Hobby by Burton Hobson. 1986. Sterling, paper, $9.95.

Stamps! A Young Collector's Guide by Brenda Lewis. 1991. Lodestar, $14.95.

Start Collecting Stamps by Samuel Grossman. 1991. Running Press, $9.95.

Videos:

Tommy Tricker and the Stamp Travelers. (See Videos.)

Visible V-8 Engine
Visible Turbo Engine
(Ages 10–Adult)
Revell, $29, mass market.

The clear plastic engines are models of the real thing in 1/4 (V-8) and 1/3 (Turbo) scale. Moving pistons and belts, light-up spark plugs, oil dip sticks, and functional distributors are just some of the features. Building such an engine from a kit imparts an understanding of how it works and previews simple maintenance and repair for kids a few years away from real grease.

⌘CONNECTIONS

Books:

The Internal Combustion Engine by Ross R. Olney. Illustrated by Steven Lindblom. 1982. Lippincott. (o.p.)

Magazines:

Racing for Kids. (See Magazines.)

Weather Tracker's Kit
(Ages 10–Adult)
Running Press, $14.95.

The kit is a plastic unit consisting of a rain gauge, thermometer, wind-speed indicator, and wind-chill chart. It's designed to be fastened to a post or fence rail (screws and attaching metal arm are provided). The cloud chart expands upon the basic cumulus, cirrus, and stratus shapes, depicting 37 varieties. Best of all is the guide! Besides telling how to snap together the weather-tracking kit, it carries facts on the history of weather reporting, the meaning of pressure systems and acid rain, the hows and whys of wild weather, and advice on forecasting.

The WeatherCycler Slide Chart from The Weather School ($6.95) is a sliding card system that helps clarify weather forecasts by making sense of highs, lows, fronts, and weather-map symbols. This concise instructive guide lacks the fun of the Weather Tracker's Kit, but is fine for teens who want to forecast bright days for outdoor activities.

∞ CONNECTIONS

Books:
Simple Weather Experiments with Everyday Materials by Muriel Mandell. Illustrated by Frances Zweifel. 1990. Sterling, $12.95.
Weatherwatch by Valerie Wyatt. Illustrations by Pat Cupples. 1990. Addison-Wesley, $8.95.
Videos:
Water and Weather from the "Tell Me Why" series. Penguin Home Video; dist. by Prism, $19.95.
Software:
Five-Star Forecast. MECC, $59.

Where in the World?
(Ages 8–Adult)
Aristoplay, $35.

The best part of this game, besides its painless geography lesson, is its versatility. There are four games in one. A card game called Crazy Countries is played like Crazy Eights. Three board games, called Statesman, Diplomat, and Ambassador, teach world geography as well as an overview of the economic and cultural concerns of 174 countries. Challenge levels may be adjusted for each player, so that parents and kids play on equitable terms.

∞ CONNECTIONS

Books:
National Geographic Picture Atlas of Our World. 1991. National Geographic Society, $21.95.
Magazines:
National Geographic World. (See Magazines.)
Videos:
Where in the World series. (See Videos.)
Tommy Tricker and the Stamp Travelers. (See Videos.)
Software:
Nigel's World. (See Computer Software.)
Where in the World Is Carmen Sandiego? (See Computer Software.)
World GeoGraph. (See Computer Software.)

White Wings
(Ages 10–14)
Yasuaki Nimoniya; dist. by AG Industries; also available from Running Press, $15.95.

Here are paper airplanes way beyond those models made in study hall from notebook paper. The models in this kit feature six different designs. Built with balsa-wood bodies, weights, and fiber wings, the planes really fly after being launched from a catapult (included). Among the models is one for a McDonnell Douglas Phantom Racer. White Wings III, a new edition, has kits for a model CANARD and Stealth Bomber.

∽CONNECTIONS

Books:

Bored Nothing To Do by Peter Spier. 1978. Doubleday, $11.95; paper, $5.95.

Model Historical Aircraft by Barbara Curry. 1972. Watts, $10.40.

Software:

Paper Plane Pilot. 1991. MECC, $59.

Young Architects

(Ages 10–Adult)

Patail Enterprises, $70.

The blue plastic walls and clear corner blocks are the most eye-catching items in this toy, but the most important item is a pencil. Working on drafting paper set on a sturdy plastic work mat, walls can be sketched from 12 different templates. Furniture can be added using tracing guides. After the layout is composed, the blue walls are erected and a professional-looking layout of a home or office has been completed. This toy imparts a sense of perspective and fosters constructive creativity. The project can be realistic or out of this world—it's all up to the young architect.

∽CONNECTIONS

Books:

Model Buildings and How to Make Them by Harvey Weiss. 1979. HarperCollins, $13.95.

Software:

Design Your Own Home. (See Computer Software.)

TOY CATALOGS, COMPANIES, AND DISTRIBUTORS

CATALOGS

ALA Graphics Catalog
American Library Association
50 East Huron Street
Chicago, IL 60611
(800) 545-2433

Animal Town
P.O. Box 485
Healdsburg, CA 95448
(800) 445-8642

Aristoplay Ltd.
P.O. Box 7529
Ann Arbor, MI 48107
(800) 634-7738

Boston Museum of Fine Arts
Catalog Sales Department
P.O. Box 1044
Boston, MA 02120-0900
(800) 225-5592

Childcraft, Inc.
20 Kilmer Road
Edison, NJ 08818-3081
(800) 631-6100

Constructive Playthings
1227 East 119th Street
Grandview, MO 64030
(800) 832-0572

Discovery Toys
Local phone directory/
2530 Arnold Drive
Suite 400
Martinez, CA 94553
(800) 426-4777

Edmund Scientific
101 East Gloucester Pike
Barrington, NJ 08007
(609) 573-6250

Gessler Publishing Company
55 West 13th Street
New York, NY 10011
(800) 456-5825

Hearth Song
P.O. Box B
Sebastopol, CA 95473-0601
(800) 325-2502

Insect Lore
P.O. Box 1535
Shafter, CA 93263
(800) LIVE BUG

Lego Shop at Home Services
P.O. Box 1310
555 Taylor Road
Enfield, CT 06083
(800) 527-8339

Listening Library
BookMates Catalog
One Park Avenue
Old Greenwich, CT 06870-9978
(800) 243-4504

Metropolitan Museum of Art
Special Service Office
Middle Village, NY 11381-0001
(800) 468-7386

National Geographic Catalog
National Geographic Society
P.O. Box 2118
Washington, DC 20036
(800) 638-4077

National Wildlife Federation
1400 16th Street, NW
Washington, DC 20036-2266
(800) 432-6564

Nature Company
750 Hearst Avenue
Berkeley, CA 94710
(800) 227-1114

Pleasant Co.
8400 Fairway Place
Middleton, WI 53562-0998
(800) 845-0005

Rand McNally
P.O. Box 1697
Skokie, IL 60076
(800) 234-0679

Right Start Catalog
Right Start Plaza
5334 Sterling Center Drive
Westlake Village, CA 91361
(800) LITTLE 1

Sesame Street Catalog
2515 East 43rd Street
P.O. Box 182228
Chattanooga, TN 37422-7228
(800) 446-7527

Smithsonian Catalogue
Department 0006
Washington, DC 20073-0006
(703) 455-1700

Troll Learn & Play
100 Corporate Drive
Mahwah, NJ 07430
(800) 247-6106

U.S. Chess Federation
186 Route 9W
New Windsor, NY 12553
(800) 388-5464

Weston Woods
89 Newtown Turnpike
Weston, CT 06883
(800) 243-5020

TOY COMPANIES AND DISTRIBUTORS

Addresses for companies cited as *mass market* are not listed, for the most part, because their products and the information on them are readily available in most toy and department stores.

AG Industries
3832 148th Avenue, NE
Redmond, WA 98052
(206) 885-4599

Battat Games
Two Industrial Boulevard
West Circle
Plattsburgh, NY 12901
(800) 247-6144

Binney & Smith
1100 Church Lane
P.O. Box 431
Easton, PA 18044-0431
(800) CRAYOLA

Childswork/Childsplay
Center for Applied Psychology
441 North 5th Street
Philadelphia, PA 19123
(215) 592-1141

Creativity for Kids
Creative Arts Activities
1600 East 23rd Street
Cleveland, OH 44114
(216) 589-4800

Demco, Inc.
4810 Forest Run Avenue
P.O. Box 7488
Madison, WI 53707
(608) 241-1201

Duncan Toys
Flambeau Corporation
15981 Val-Plast Road
Middlefield, OH
(800) 356-8396

Educational Design
47 West 13th Street
New York, NY 10011
(800) 221-9372

Educational Insights
19560 South Rancho Way
Dominguez Hills, CA 90220
(800) 367-5713 (in Calif. 213-637-2131)

International Games, Inc.
1 Uno Circle
Joliet, IL 60435
(815) 741-4000

International Playthings
120 Riverdale Road
Riverdale, NJ 07457
(800) 631-1272

JTG of Nashville
1024-C 18th Avenue South
Nashville, TN 37212
(800) 222-2584

Klutz
2121 Staunton Court
Palo Alto, CA 94306
(415) 857-0888

Lego Dacta
Educational Division of Lego
555 Taylor Road
Enfield, CT 06082
(800) 527-8339

NightStar
1334 Brommer Street
Santa Cruz, CA 95062
(408) 462-1049

Pappa Geppetto's Toys
Victoria Ltd.
Box 81
Victoria, BC, Canada V8W 24M

Patail Enterprises
27324 Camino Capistrano
#129
Laguna Niguel, CA 92677
(714) 367-0530

Playmobil
11-E Nicholas Court
Dayton, NJ 08810
(908) 274-0101

Playskool
P.O. Box 200
Pawtucket, RI 02862-0200
(800) 327-8264

Playspaces
31 Union Avenue
Sudbury, MA 01776
(508) 443-7146

Radio Shack
500 One Tandy Center
Fort Worth, TX 76102
(817) 390-3011

Ravensburger (See International Playthings)

Reeves
107 Broadway
New York, NY 10010
(212) 929-5412

Revell/Skillcraft/Monogram Models
395 North 3rd Avenue
Des Plaines, IL 60016
(708) 390-8940

Running Press
125 South 22nd Street
Philadelphia, PA 19103
(215) 567-5080

Sanyei America Corporation
450 Harmon Meadow Boulevard
Secaucus, NJ 07094
(201) 864-4848

The Weather School
5075 Lake Road
Brockport, NY 14420-9750
(716) 637-5207

Wimmer-Fergusen Child Products
1073 South Pearl
P.O. Box 10427
Denver, CO 80210
(303) 733-0848

Workman Publishing
708 Broadway
New York, NY 10003
(212) 254-5900

RESOURCES

Buy Me! Buy Me!: The Bank Street Guide to Choosing Toys by Joanne Oppenheim. 1987. Pantheon, paper, $11.95.

The Gifted and Talented Catalogue by Susan Amerikaner and Sarina Simon. 1988. Price, Stern, & Sloan, paper, $10.95.

Lekotek, 2100 Ridge Avenue, Evanston, IL 60201. (708) 328-0001

Mudworks: Creative Clay, Dough, and Modeling Experiences by MaryAnn F. Kohl. 1989. Bright Ring Publishing (dist. by Gryphon House,

3706 Otis Street, P.O. Box 275, Mt. Rainier, MD 20712), paper, $14.95.

Oppenheim Toy Portfolio. Quarterly pamphlet. 40 East 9th Street, New York, NY 10003. $20 annually; $6 for a single issue. (800) 544-8697

Science Fare: An Illustrated Guide & Catalog of Toys, Books, and Activities for Kids by Wendy Saul with Alan R. Newman. 1986. Harper-Collins, paper, $14.95.

USA Toy Library Association. 2719 Broadway Avenue, Evanston, IL 60201. (708) 864-8240

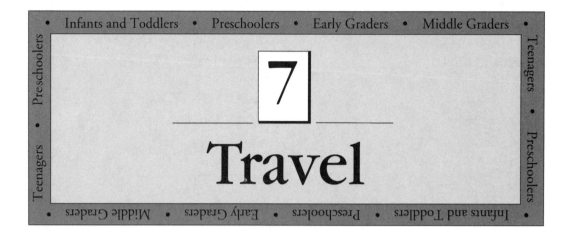

• Infants and Toddlers • Preschoolers • Early Graders • Middle Graders •

Preschoolers

Teenagers

Teenagers

Preschoolers

• Infants and Toddlers • Preschoolers • Early Graders • Middle Graders •

7
Travel

INTRODUCTION

The La Brea Tar Pits, Oregon Trail, Underground Railroad sites, and backstage at Disney World are just a few of the destinations suggested in this eclectic mix of travel experiences. Kids can journey by covered wagon, hot-air balloon, kayak, or paddle-wheel boat. They can excavate dinosaur bones, hobnob with major-league baseball players, or undergo astronaut training. The choices are staggering.

Travel can be more than whining workouts. Most of the travel suggestions here are for families; some, like Space Camp, are for kids on their own. We've selected the places, concepts, camps, and programs based on interviews with travel writers, the experiences of parents, and extensive research—in literary resources, of course.[*]

Recommended family travel guides are listed at the end of the chapter, and they provide plenty of travel advice. However, be sure to check out any claims that a hotel or resort offers children's programs and/or baby-sitting. Sometimes these programs are in effect only if a minimum number of children are present. Ask specifics about the qualifications of the program director and staff. Don't always expect a master's degree in early childhood education, but look for appropriate experience with and interest in children.

Write for information, ask for references, check published sources before committing to a vacation. The More Facts the More Fun, is our motto.

So pack some of the books, magazines, tapes (and even videos, if you have a traveling VCR!) suggested within this volume and set forth on an unforgettable journey.

---

[*]The appearance of a travel enterprise in this chapter does not constitute endorsement by the American Library Association itself, but reflects the advice of individual ALA members and others knowledgeable about travel activities for children.—*Ed.*

HOW TO USE THIS CHAPTER

Families are encouraged not only to visit the places described, but to use them as inspiration for local adventure. For example, a trip to the Exploratorium or Kennedy Space Center may not be feasible, but there are many local children's museums and space centers throughout the United States. You can find local travel guides at your library and check its "vertical file" of maps, pamphlets, and current travel information in file drawers. You will find that NASA and its astronauts have donated rockets, space gear, and other memorabilia to local colleges and historical centers. Hands-on museums for kids are being added to established science and natural history museums. Local wildlife centers can offer great tours and children's programs. So consider the suggestions below not only as target destinations, but as idea generators for family field trips or as stops along the way on lengthy journeys.

The operators of the covered wagon, hot-air balloon, and whitewater rafting expeditions that we've listed are not the only such enterprises; they were selected on the recommendations of reliable travel writers. We've cited those who responded positively when asked about family visits and who offered encouraging information about travel with children.

Travel experiences make for learning readiness, and learning enriches travel. We've suggested several connections with related books, magazines, videos, audio tapes, and computer software. Age levels are not cited for books, because when read aloud or shared by a family, picture books can work as well as nonfiction aimed at older readers. If the material is reviewed elsewhere in our guide, we've provided a *see* reference. Otherwise, we've given publisher, producer, and price. Use these titles to help plan, enliven, or relive your adventures.

1. ARIZONA SONORAN DESERT MUSEUM

2021 North Kinney Road
Tucson Mountain Park
Tucson, AZ 85743
(602) 883-2702

Genuine road runners, meerkats, and rare desert creatures are displayed in their natural habitats in this beautiful outdoor park. Full of winding trails, this site is more zoo than museum in the conventional sense. Beavers and river otters can be sighted above and below the surface of the water in a well-designed exhibit. In the Earth Sciences Center, within a limestone cave, our planet's evolution is explained in great detail.

For a genuinely natural tour of desert fauna and flora, the nearby Saguaro National Monument offers desert and mountainous regions open to hikers and auto-tourists.

The same trip might include a local dude ranch, such as Tanque Verde Guest Ranch, whose special programs for children ages 4 to 11 feature horseback riding instruction, tennis lessons, hikes, and nature programs. Good books for young dudes are *Cowboys* by Glen Rounds (1991, Holiday House, $14.95) and *On the Pampas* (see Multicultural Fare, p. 37).

◌⊃ CONNECTIONS

Books:
Desert Giant: The World of the Saguaro Cactus by Barbara Bash. 1989. Little, Brown/Sierra Club, paper, $5.95.

Deserts by Seymour Simon. 1990. Morrow, $13.95.

A Desert Year by Carol Lerner. 1991. Morrow, $13.95.

2. BASEBALL SPRING TRAINING
Arizona and Florida

Baseball fans who travel south to experience spring training will find "countless opportunities to see superstar baseball players in settings that are more informal and intimate," says Megan Stine in *Family Sports Adventures*. Stine suggests routes for a tour of the Florida camps, which are located in three areas (along the Atlantic Coast, the Gulf Coast, and central Florida). The teams that practice in Arizona are all in the Phoenix area, and visits between training parks are easily managed. Another helpful guide with more specifics on the teams, practice locations, ticket information, and autograph opportunities is *The Traveler's Guide to Baseball Spring Training* by John Garrity.

For in-season games, consult *Baseball Vacations: A Guide to Big League Teams, Towns, & Tickets* by Daniel P. George. An organization called Sports Tours, Inc. (Sports Tours, Inc., P.O. Box 84, Hatfield, MA 01038; (800) 722-7701) arranges "Ultimate Baseball Road Trips." Included are tickets to major-league games, transportation, and lodgings in the same hotels as the visiting teams.

∞CONNECTIONS

Books:
American Sports Poems selected and edited by R. R. Knudson and May Swenson. 1988. Orchard Books, $15.99.

Baseball, Football, Daddy, and Me by David Friend. Illustrated by Rick Brown. 1990. Viking, $12.95.

Matt's Mitt and Fleet-Footed Florence by Marilyn Sachs. Illustrated by Hilary Knight and Charles Robinson. 1989. Dutton, $11.95; paper, $2.95.

Magazines:
KidSports. (See Magazines.)
Sports Illustrated for Kids. (See Magazines.)

Videos:
Forever Baseball. (See Videos.)
Grand Slam. 1988. VidAmerica, $19.98.
The History of Great Black Baseball Players. 1990. Fries Home Video, $19.95.

3. CHEROKEE INDIAN RESERVATION
Cherokee, North Carolina

In the foothills of the Great Smoky Mountains (America's most-visited national park) sits the Cherokee Indian Reservation of western North Carolina. Visitors are educated and entertained with traditional ceremonies, arts and crafts demonstrations, museums, and a replica of a 1700s Cherokee village. A history of the Cherokee nation is reenacted in a moving outdoor drama, *Unto These Hills*, which runs from June through August. Hiking and horseback riding trails are available, as are streams for boating and fishing. Away from the educational center of town are bumper-boat rides, an amusement park, miniature golf, and shops galore. There's appeal for travelers of all interests and ages. For more information write Cherokee Tribal Travel and Promotion, P.O. Box 460, Cherokee, NC 28719.

This reservation is only one example of the

vast Native American culture to explore across the United States. *Indian America: A Traveler's Companion* by Eagle Walking Turtle is an introduction to Native American history and present-day visitor's centers. The author encourages use of the many fishing, hunting, camping, and resort facilities run by Indian tribes throughout the United States.

∞CONNECTIONS

Books:
Kanahena: A Cherokee Story by Susan L. Roth. (o.p.)
North American Legends edited by Virginia Haviland. Illustrated by Ann Strugnell. 1979. Putnam, $9.95.
Sequoyah, Cherokee Hero by Joanne Oppenheim. 1979. Troll, paper, $2.50.
Sequoyah, Father of the Cherokee Alphabet by David Peterson. 1991. Children's Press, $9.95.
Audio:
Cherokee Legends I by Kathi Smith. (See Audio.)

4. THE CHILDREN'S MUSEUM OF INDIANAPOLIS
P.O. Box 3000
Indianapolis, IN 46206

Five floors of exhibits keep visitors wishing for a time warp so they could play (and learn) forever. More than 4,000 exhibits involve children and parents directly in cultural, historical, and scientific activities. Whether riding an antique carousel, playing Dutch games, visualizing sound waves, or blasting through time to witness the history of the stars in the Spacequest Planetarium, the activities in this museum fascinate visitors of all ages. The balance of physical sciences with social sci-

ences and nature studies makes this an especially appealing place for many. In addition, the museum has restaurants with healthy options and a gift shop that is a wonderland for those looking for good books and unusual toys.

∞CONNECTIONS

Books:
Lost in the Museum by Miriam Cohen. Illustrated by Lillian Hoban. 1979. Greenwillow, paper, $2.95.
Prehistoric Pinkerton by Steven Kellogg. (See Books.)
Videos:
Don't Eat the Pictures: Sesame Street Video at the Metropolitan Museum of Art. Children's Television Workshop, $24.98.
Norman the Doorman. Children's Circle, $19.95.

5. CONSERVATION SUMMITS
National Wildlife Federation
1400 16th Street, NW
Washington, DC 20036-2266
(703) 790-4363

The National Wildlife Federation defines their summits as "a unique summer experience filled with outdoor adventure, nature study, environmental learning, and FUN." Three summits are held in settings such as the Adirondacks or Blue Ridge Mountains. Locations vary each season, and accommodations, ranging from deluxe inns to simpler rooms with bunks, are offered at universities, nature centers, or national parks. The summits are perfect for families because there are programs for preschoolers, junior naturalists (ages 5 to 12), teens, and adults as well as whole-family outings and social events. There is also a Wildlife Camp just for kids ages 9 to 13. At least 20 different classes and field trips are available at each summit, but none are compulsory. You can take a hike or listen to a lecture at your leisure. A special Educators' Summit not only offers a good variety of nature programs but demonstrates how to blend the experiences into a variety of teaching programs. With the range of planned activities, this is a good option for grandparent/grandchild travel.

CONNECTIONS

Magazines:
Chickadee. (See Magazines.)
OWL. (See Magazines.)
Ranger Rick. (See Magazines.)
Your Big Backyard. (See Magazines.)

6. COVERED WAGON TRIPS
Wyoming, Utah, and Kansas

If only our ancestors could see us climbing aboard wagon trains and calling it a vacation! Wagons West (Afton, WY 83110) offers comfortable wagon train rides through Utah Redrock Country and the Grand Teton National Forest in Wyoming. Travelers have the option of riding on horseback or sitting in the wagon. Children, older travelers, and camping novices are catered to. Pros handle the chuck wagon, campfire entertainment, and guided side trips into the hills. "European-style trekking," with nights spent in hotels and days on horseback, is another option.

Flint Hills Overland Wagon Trips (P.O. Box 1076, El Dorado, KS 67042) offers weekend-only adventures through the Flint Hills of Kansas. Modern-day pioneers get just a taste of the West since they stay only one night. (It's possible to go along just for the ride, at a reduced rate, and return to the point of embarkation Saturday evening after the campfire and before the braver souls retire to their sleeping bags for a night under the stars.)

Oregon Trail Wagon Train (Route 2, P.O. Box 502, Bayard, NE 69334; (308) 586-1850) hits the Nebraska prairies with treks lasting one, three, four, or six days. Travelers ride on scout horses or in the wagons or drive the teams. Pioneer and Indian artifact searches, square dances, muzzleloading and rifle demonstrations, and pioneer arts and crafts instruction are a few of the activities lined up for those who wish to retrace the historic Oregon Trail. One suggestion: Check the proposed routes, if possible, to be sure they do not run parallel to modern highways—there's a definite loss of ambience if you are trekking alongside an 18-wheeler.

CONNECTIONS

Books:
Aurora Means Dawn by Scott Russell. 1989. Bradbury, $12.95.
Beyond the Divide by Kathryn Lasky. 1981. Macmillan, paper, $3.25.
Black Heroes of the West by Ruth Pelz. 1990. Open Hand Publisher, dist. by Talman, $10.95; paper, $5.95.
The Josefina Story Quilt by Eleanor Coerr. (See Books.)
My Prairie Year: Based on the Diary of Elenore Plaisted by Brett Harvey. Illustrated by Deborah Kogan Ray. 1986. Holiday House, $12.95.
Wagon Wheels by Barbara Brenner. Illustrated by Don Bolognese. 1978. HarperCollins, paper, $3.25.

Software:
The Oregon Trail. (See Computer Software.)

7. EXPLORATORIUM

3601 Lyon Street
San Francisco, CA 94123
(415) 561-0360

Founded by Frank Oppenheimer in 1969, the Exploratorium is a hands-on museum that brings science down to earth—or lets it loose in giant bubbles or funneled sound waves. This haven of "playful discovery" (as it is called by artist-in-residence Peter Richards) is responsible for many spin-offs across the United States and the general restructuring of several older museums. "Explainers" on the floor help kids and parents interact—play— with nearly 700 exhibits, which have been carefully developed (and continue to develop) into "a carefully devised science curriculum."

For those who have wondered what *is* color, a sound wave, and so forth, here are the answers, presented via practical, entertaining experiments and exhibits. The hands-on fun appeals to kids of all ages.

∞CONNECTIONS

Books:
Bet You Can: Scientific Possibilities to Fool You by Vicki Cobb and Kathy Darling. 1983. Avon, paper, $2.95.
Bet You Can't: Scientific Impossibilities to Fool You by Vicki Cobb and Kathy Darling. 1980. Avon, paper, $2.95.
The Explorabook by John Cassidy and the Staff at the Exploratorium. 1991. Klutz Press, $16.95.

How to Make a Chemical Volcano and Other Mysterious Experiments by Alan Kramer. 1989. Watts, $11.95.
The Random House Book of 1001 Wonders of Science by Brian and Brenda Williams. 1990. Random House, $10.95.
Smithsonian Family Learning Project Science Activity Book. 1987. Galison, paper, $8.95. (Developed from the annual Smithsonian Family Learning Project Science Calendar.)
Magazines:
Exploratorium Quarterly. (Available from the museum.)

8. FOSSILS IN THE FIELD

Dinosaur National Monument
Mammoth Site of Hot Springs

Dinosaur National Monument (P.O. Box 210, Dinosaur, CO 81610), which straddles the borders of Utah and Colorado, has been a national park for three-quarters of a century. Since 1957, visitors have been able to view fossils from the Dinosaur Quarry building. Besides examining fossils of dinosaurs and other ancient creatures, visitors can hike, camp, fish, raft, and even snowmobile, with proper permits and due caution. Some areas of this desert park are inaccessible to conventional vehicles, and at certain times of the year some roads are closed.

At the Mammoth Site of Hot Springs (1910 Jennings Avenue, Hot Springs, SD 57747; (605) 745-6017), bones of 44 mammoths have been uncovered in a sinkhole, where they were buried for 26,000 years. In 1974, a housing developer ran across a pile of bones and launched the discovery of "the largest collection of Columbian Mammoth fossils in the

BEST OF THE BEST FOR CHILDREN

Western Hemisphere," according to a brief note in *National Geographic* (December 1988). An exhibition center has been built over the site and, in July, visitors can see paleontologists and Earthwatch volunteers at work collecting the fossils. The site remains open to visitors throughout the year.

CONNECTIONS

Books:
Dinosaur Dig by Kathryn Lasky. Illustrated by Christopher Knight. (See Books.)
Dinosaurs Walked Here: And Other Stories Fossils Tell by Patricia Lauber. 1987. Bradbury, $15.95.
If You Are a Hunter of Fossils by Byrd Baylor. Illustrated by Peter Parnall. 1984. Macmillan, $4.95.

Videos:
Dinosaurs: Lessons from Bones. American School Publishers, $129.
The Great Dinosaur Hunt. (See Videos.)
Will's Mammoth. SRA Group, $33.

Audio:
The Boy Who Loved Mammoths and Other Tales by Rafe Martin. Weston Woods, $9.98.

9. GEORGE C. PAGE MUSEUM
5801 Wilshire Boulevard
Los Angeles, CA 90036
(213) 931-5273

Prehistory goes downtown at the George C. Page Museum in Los Angeles, where visitors can see paleontologists at work uncovering finds in the La Brea Tar Pits. Here, some 100 tons of late Ice Age (Pleistocene) fossils have been discovered, more than anywhere else in the world. The discoveries are ongoing thanks to George Page, who established a museum to house and promote research on the fossils found in the sticky asphalt (not tar) that trapped many creatures fleeing from predators. Kids can see the skeletons of fully reconstructed saber-toothed cats, sloths, giant condors, and mammoths, as well as the actual pits. The sheer quantity of plant and animal fossils, plus the high level of preservation provided by their setting, has enabled scientists to develop a very clear picture of this postdinosaur world. The laboratory's glass walls allow visitors to observe the cleaning and classification of bones.

CONNECTIONS

Books:
Fossils Tell of Long Ago by Aliki. Harper/Trophy, paper, $4.50.
Trapped in Tar: Fossils from the Ice Age by Caroline Arnold. Photographs by Richard Hewett. 1990. Clarion, paper, $5.95.

10. GRANDTRAVEL
6900 Wisconsin Avenue
Suite 706
Chevy Chase, MD 20815
(800) 247-7651

Excursions designed just for grandparents and their grandchildren are available through Grandtravel, formed by travel adviser Helena Koenig in 1985 when she became a grandmother. A typical list of annual tours may offer an Alaskan wilderness adventure, a journey to the Galapagos Islands, a Kenya adventure safari, a patriotic panorama of the nation's capital, and a tour of Native American country in the Southwest. While on the tour, older adults and kids pursue both separate activities and many unforgettable shared ones. Of course, grandparents and kids can cook up their own plans for a special vacation, using some of the other ideas suggested in this chapter and the books listed at its conclusion.

11. HENRY FORD MUSEUM AND GREENFIELD VILLAGE

20900 Oakwood Boulevard
Dearborn, MI 48121-1970
(313) 271-1976

Henry Ford founded this museum in part to memorialize the work of his good friend Thomas Edison. However, considerable evidence of Ford's own career can be found within the walls of the museum and on the grounds of Greenfield Village. The village contains the Menlo Park laboratory of Thomas Edison, the workshop of the Wright brothers, Noah Webster's 1830s home, George Washington Carver's home, the nineteenth-century Firestone Farm, a Cotswold cottage, a coal-powered paddle-wheeler, and much more. The exhibits aim to mark the transformation of America over the past three centuries from a rural to industry-based society. It is a celebration laced with nostalgia, and an unbeatable tour through popular American history. (One young observer noted when he saw a pot-bellied stove: "Look, Mom, an antique microwave.")

The museum houses steam engines, early model cars (and futuristic versions), household furnishings, an authentic diner, and other life-size examples of Americana. There are plenty of hands-on opportunities as well

as a special activities center designed to stimulate youthful minds.

☌ CONNECTIONS

Videos:
Henry Ford Museum and Greenfield Village. (See *Old Sturbridge Village* in Videos.)
Sturbridge Village: Growing Up in New England. (See *Old Sturbridge Village* in Videos.)

12. HOT-AIR BALLOONING

It's not for everyone, but an hour or more in a hot-air balloon drifting in the skies is a heavenly experience. What a way to commemorate a birthday or highlight a special vacation! The sense of motion is ethereal. "You can hardly tell you're moving," said one experienced balloonist, "yet you're soaring high above the land." You can find ballooning companies by looking in the phone book, but make serious inquiries about experience, licensing, and sites. Pilots must be licensed by the FAA.

Most companies recommend a minimum age of seven or eight (although some companies do allow infants and toddlers aboard) because young children are often frightened by the noise from the burner that creates the hot air. Depending on the size of the gondola, four to eight persons can travel together, but the charge is per person (often $100 or more—some may find it prohibitive for so brief a journey). Families may prefer to attend balloon rallies or call ahead to a local operator and ask if they can witness the liftoff or descent up close.

Here are a few companies that responded favorably to our request about family balloon trips:

Aspen Balloon Adventure
P.O. Box 4995
Aspen, CO 81612
(303) 925-5749

Balloon Aviation of Napa Valley
2299 Third Street
P.O. Box 3298
Napa, CA 94558
(800) FOR-NAPA

Festival Flights, Inc.
Lamington Road
Bedminister, NJ 07921
(800) HOT-AIR4

Sky Rides, Inc.
17306 South Delia
Plainfield, IL 60544
(708) 904-4600

CONNECTIONS

Books:
Balloon Ride by Evelyn Clarke Mott.
1991. Walker, $12.95.
The Big Balloon Race by Eleanor Coerr.
1981. HarperCollins, paper, $3.50.
Hot Air Henry by Mary Calhoun. 1981.
Morrow, $12.95; paper, $4.95.
Videos:
Terrific Trips: A Trip to the Aquarium
and *A Trip to the Hot Air Balloon
Festival.* Fisher-Price; Lancit Media
Productions, $14.95.

13. LEWIS AND CLARK TRAIL

Gerald Olmsted, author of *Fielding's Lewis &
Clark Trail* (see Resources), followed the trail
of the famous explorers Meriwether Lewis and
William Clark from St. Louis to the Pacific
Ocean. Olmsted's guide directs today's
families from St. Louis to Portland along
routes parallel to those tracked by Lewis and
Clark. The explorers, under orders from
Thomas Jefferson, scoped out the territory
purchased from Spain. Segments of these
routes can be followed easily by travelers who
haven't the time to pursue the entire route.
Olmsted interlaces quotes from the explorers'
diaries with directions and notes on contemporary monuments relating to the journey.
Olmsted says, "I hope this book will be read
aloud—a passenger reading to a driver about
the things they are seeing along the way." Even
more fascinating for kids will be reading about
Sacagawea, the Shoshone Indian woman who
guided Lewis and Clark.

CONNECTIONS

Books:
*The Incredible Journey of Lewis and
Clark* by Rhoda Blumberg. 1987.
Lothrop, $17.95.
*Streams to the River, River to the Sea: A
Novel of Sacagawea* by Scott O'Dell.
1986. Houghton Mifflin, $14.95.
Videos:
Sacajawea. FilmFair Communications,
$385.
Software:
Lewis and Clark Stayed Home. MECC,
$59.
The Oregon Trail. (See Computer
Software.)

14. MISSISSIPPI CRUISING

As a boy, Samuel Langhorne Clemens fan-
tasized about piloting a river boat along the
Mississippi. His pen name, Mark Twain, was
derived from the system used by pilots to

measure the river's depth. The dreams that he passed on in his fiction, travel lore, and memoirs can be realized today by families who rent houseboats along the Wisconsin, Idaho, and Minnesota shores of the Mississippi. A few rental companies are:

Boatels
McGregor, Iowa 52157
(319) 873-3718

Great River Cruises
400 Winona Street
LaCrosse, WI 54601
(608) 783-3879

Northport Marine, Inc.
Alma Marina
Alma, WI 54610
(608) 685-3333

Even more in keeping with Twain's era is traveling on the *Mississippi Queen*. Modeled on the old paddle-wheelers, it has the luxuries of a modern cruise ship—three- and four-bed cabins, pool, sauna, gym, and movie theater. The ship offers three-day to eleven-day trips along the Mississippi, Ohio, Tennessee, and Cumberland rivers, sailing from Pittsburgh to New Orleans to St. Paul (with stops in several other cities, such as Chattanooga, Cincinnati, and Memphis). Information and reservations are available from Delta Queen Steamboat Company, 30 Robin Street Wharf, New Orleans, LA 70130; (800) 543-1949.

⌒◯CONNECTIONS

Videos:
The Unsinkable Delta Queen.
Sentimental Productions. P.O. Box 4005, Cincinnati, OH 45024, $29.95.

15. MYSTIC SEAPORT

P.O. Box 6000
Mystic, CT 06355-0990
(203) 572-0711

The East boasts several wonderful re-creations of American history that should be high on the travel agenda. Besides Mystic Seaport, there is Plimouth Plantation, Jamestown, Old Sturbridge Village, and, probably the most famous, Williamsburg. In many, the guides dress in period costumes and actually maintain the lifestyle of their forebears.

The "Save the Whales" campaign should not diminish the historic value of Mystic Seaport, for wonderful it is. This small nineteenth-century whaling village has 60 buildings that illuminate the days of the whale hunts, shipbuilders, markets, smithies, and other crucial aspects of the era. Several old ships are on view: the *Charles R. Morgan* can be boarded. To walk stoop-shouldered through this old whaling ship provides some understanding of the sailor's hard life. Well-informed guides in period attire perform activities of the time and readily answer visitors' questions. In the children's museum, kids can try out the swaying bunks of a ship and play with toys of the era. A contemporary mariner training program for older kids, ages 12 to 17, offers a course in boat safety, sailing, rowing, and weather prediction.

⌒◯CONNECTIONS

Books:
The Adventures of Obadiah by Brinton Turkle. 1972. Viking, $13.95.
Island Boy by Barbara Cooney. (See Books.)

The Story of the New England Whalers by Conrad Stein. 1982. Children's Press, paper, $3.95.

Videos:

Cavaliers & Craftsmen: Colonial Williamsburg and Jamestown. Atlas Video, $19.95.

Mystic Seaport. (See *Old Sturbridge Village* in Videos.)

Old Sturbridge Village. (See Videos.)

Plimouth Plantation. (See *Old Sturbridge Village* in Videos.)

16. SMITHSONIAN MUSEUMS
Washington, DC 20560
(202) 357-2700

The Smithsonian has been called the "nation's attic." Within its nine museums is something for every interest, and admission is usually free (a nominal fee is charged for special films and the planetarium show).

Miniatures, art treasures, airplanes, trains, and historic memorabilia fill the museums of art, aviation, natural history, arts and industry, and American history. The National Museum of African Art and the Sackler Gallery, with more than 1,000 pieces of Asian art and sculpture, are among newer additions to the complex. The National Air and Space Museum, the largest and perhaps most popular museum in the world, celebrates the history of air travel from the original Wright Flyer to a life-size Skylab model. In keeping with the lofty atmosphere, there's even a five-story-high screen showing films about flight. According to *The Air & Space Catalog,* those who want to see even more of the collection can arrange (by calling the Air and Space Museum) to visit the

Smithsonian's Paul Garber Preservation, Restoration, and Storage Facility in Sutland, Maryland, where planes and artifacts not on exhibit can be viewed.

CONNECTIONS

Books:

Auks, Rocks, & the Odd Dinosaur: Inside Stories from the Smithsonian Museum of Natural History by Peggy Thomson. 1985. Crowell, $13.89.

17. SPACE VACATIONS

U.S. SPACE CAMP
One Tranquility Base
Huntsville, AL 35807
and
NASA Parkway
Titusville, FL 32780
(205) 837-3400

U.S. Space Camp is an out-of-this-world experience that teaches children the ins and outs of space travel and survival. There are two locations, with programs for kids in grades 4–12 and a great variety of three-day and five-day programs suited to various age groups, including a parent/child weekender. Besides learning the basics of space travel, kids get the genuine feel of being an astronaut by trying out the microgravity trainer, eating freeze-dried food, and participating in other activities that simulate space flight.

Additional programs throughout the United States are described in *The Air and Space Catalog: The Complete Sourcebook for Everything in the Universe.* For space cadets at the Titusville site, a tour of the Kennedy Space Center is often part of the package.

THE KENNEDY SPACE CENTER
Spaceport U.S.A.
Mail Code TWRS
Kennedy Space Center, FL 32899
(407) 452-2121

The Kennedy Space Center is a must-see for families. Set within a 140,000-acre wildlife preserve, only 46 miles from Disney World, the center offers access to a lunar rover, the massive crawler transporter, actual rockets, and a space shuttle replica. A two-hour bus tour includes the actual launch site (if no launching is scheduled, of course). Seeing the rockets, shuttles, and space mementos is a mind-stretching experience and an exciting opportunity, especially for fans of *Odyssey* magazine.

∞CONNECTIONS

Books:
Space Camp: The Great Adventure for NASA Hopefuls by Anne Baird. 1992. Morrow, $13.95.
Space Songs by Myra Cohn Livingston. 1988. Holiday House, $14.95.
To Space and Back by Sally Ride and Susan Okie. (See Books.)
Your Future in Space: The U.S. Space Camp Training Program by Flip Schulke and others. 1987. Crown, paper, $14.95.
Magazines:
Odyssey. (See Magazines.)

Software:
Space Station Freedom. (See Computer Software.)

18. UNDERGROUND RAILROAD

A secret network of routes and hiding places was developed by abolitionists before and during the Civil War to assist slaves escaping to freedom. This network came to be known as the Underground Railroad. Families with a penchant for learning vacations can visit historical sites that were once used as part of the Underground Railroad. It is possible, to a limited degree, to follow the routes that escaping slaves took as they fled the South. Glennette Turner's *Underground Railroad in DuPage County, Illinois* (Newman Educational Publishers, 1986) suggests that children try to "take a walk in their shoes"; that is, reenact the experiences of these fugitives. "Imagine the danger of trying to escape and keep your family intact."

Documentation of the routes or safehouses is of course very difficult owing to the secrecy that was required and the time that has passed. Fortunately, some records do exist, and the U.S. government is seeking more thorough identification. On a Congressional advisory committee for that purpose is Charles Blockson, author of *The Underground Railroad* (1987, Berkley, paper, $4.95). His book is an excellent resource, as is his article in *National Geographic* (May 1984). In an interview for this guide, Blockson cautioned that some lands and surviving structures are private property and should not be trespassed upon. He also states that some local histories may blend documented facts with legend, which can misdirect travelers. A surer route would be to visit such designated historical sites as the Harriet Tubman home in Auburn, New York, or the Levi Coffin House in Fountain City, Indiana. Blockson also suggests that visitors consult guides, such as George Cantor's *Historic Landmarks of Black America*.

Watch for more travel guides once the government gathers its data and decides on the best method for commemorating the Underground Railroad.

∞CONNECTIONS

Books:
The Drinking Gourd by F. N. Monjo. 1969. HarperCollins, $11.89.
Escape From Slavery: Five Journeys to Freedom by Doreen Rappaport. 1991. HarperCollins, $12.95.
Magazines:
Cobblestone. (See Magazines.)
Videos:
Follow the Drinking Gourd. (See Videos.)
Audio:
Underground Railroad: Escape to Freedom. (See Audio.)

19. WASHBURN-NORLANDS LIVING HISTORY CENTER
R.D. 2 Box 3395
Livermore Falls, ME 04254
(207) 897-2236

Historic villages and towns are sometimes too passive for young visitors. At the Norlands Living History Center, a family can time-travel back to the 1800s. For one or two nights, children over age 8 and their parents can relive the past, complete with outhouses and cornhusk mattresses. The involvement is total. You

don't simply view spinning, weaving, and nineteenth-century farming; you do it. Ice-cutting, quilt-making, haying, and storytelling are some of the other activities. Much of the center's schedule is taken up by single-day programs for students, children's groups, teachers, and adults interested in history. (The adults-only programs have the lure of college and teacher recertification credits.) As a result, there are few family weekends available, so early reservations are essential.

20. WHALE WATCHING AT SEA AND ON LAND

"The waters off North America are rich with whales, and the shores are lined with whale-watch tour operators," states Patricia Corrigan, author of *Where the Whales Are: Your Guide to Whale Watching Trips in North America.* Some participants can even swim with the whales—spend several days in their company and get to know them. Less expensive possibilities include one-hour tours or expeditions by kayak or rubber raft. The sites range from Alaska all along the West Coast to Mexico. Hawaii and the New England coastline also have plenty of whale-watch possibilities. Corrigan's book is rich in suggestions. Here are just a few sources for activities:

American Cetacean Society
P.O. Box 2639
San Pedro, CA 90731
(213) 548-6279

Baja Expeditions
2625 Garnet Avenue
San Diego, CA 92109
(619) 581-3311

Earthwatch
680 Auburn Street
P.O. Box 403
Watertown, MA 02272
(617) 926-8200

Nature Expeditions International
474 Willamette
P.O. Box 11496
Eugene, OR 97440
(503) 484-6529

JOHN G. SHEDD AQUARIUM
1200 South Lake Shore Drive
Chicago, IL 60605
(312) 939-2438

Midwesterners need not miss out on whale-watching. They can sight the creatures at the Shedd Aquarium's outstanding Oceanarium in Chicago. Within a scientifically designed model of the coastline of the Pacific Northwest reside whales, dolphins, penguins, seals, and otters. Exhibits geared to children allow them to touch a penguin feather and reach into tide pools filled with sea anemones, crabs, and starfish. Outside the aquarium is a terrific city filled with parks, museums, beaches, art, music, and historical adventures for kids of all ages.

∞CONNECTIONS

Books:
The Aquarium Book by George Ancona. 1991. Clarion, $15.95.
How the Whale Got His Throat by Rudyard Kipling. Illustrated by Jonathon Langley. 1988. Philomel, $5.95.

I Wonder If I'll See a Whale by Frances Ward Weller. 1991. Philomel, $14.95.
Whales by Gilda Berger. Illustrated by Lisa Bonforte. 1987. Doubleday, $10.95.
Whales by Joyce Milton. Illustrated by Alton Langford. 1989. Random House, paper, $2.95.
Videos:
"Burt Dow: Deep Water Man" on *The Robert McCloskey Library*. (See Videos.)
Gift of the Whales. Miramar; dist. by Music for Little People, $19.98.
Terrific Trips: A Trip to the Aquarium. Fisher-Price; Lancit Media Productions, $14.95.
Software:
The Voyage of the Mimi. (See Computer Software.)

21. WHITEWATER AND RIVER RAFTING

Many families drive to the rim of the Grand Canyon and peer into its depths. More adventurous travelers visit it from below, riding along the Colorado River in kayaks or rafts. The National Park Service will send a list of river trip operators on request (Grand Canyon National Park, P.O. Box 129, Grand Canyon, AZ 86023-0129). The age minimum for most of these whitewater raft trips is 10 or 12.

Families with smaller children can try Big Bend River Tours (P.O. Box 317, Lajitas, TX 79852; (800) 545-4240), whose owners state, "We can take children as young as two. We do not have big, dangerous whitewater." They travel along the Rio Grande River in Big Bend National Park, offering half-day to seven-day tours that are suitable for novices. A father-son trip is one of the many specialty trips offered.

Farther north is Hughes River Expeditions, Inc. (P.O. Box 217, Cambridge, ID 83610; (208) 257-3477), which has a variety of boating expeditions geared to families. Their Salmon River Canyon is "the best trip for little kids . . . with warm water, huge sand bar camps and plenty of fun big wave rapids." Their supply pontoon carries kids' food (PBJ, hot dogs, and cereal) as well as the fixings for elegant riverside dining (fish, steaks, Dutch-oven biscuits, and fresh fruit). They put up the tents while the families play.

Natahala Outdoor Center (NOC Adventure Travel, 41 U.S. Highway 19 West, Bryson City, NC 28713; (704) 488-2175) offers whitewater rafting and kayak trips throughout the world. The company strictly enforces the U.S. Forest Service regulation of minimum weight (60 pounds), so the age limit is usually 7 and over. Headquartered in North Carolina, on the edge of the Great Smoky Mountains, the center's guided whitewater trips will lure the novice into Carolina rivers and, possibly, into a lifetime of whitewater adventures.

✑CONNECTIONS

Videos:
Wilderness Rivers. Camera One Productions, $60.

22. WONDERS OF WALT DISNEY WORLD: WALT DISNEY WORLD LEARNING PROGRAMS
P.O. Box 10100
Lake Buena Vista, FL 32830-1000
(407) 345-5860

Backstage at Disney World is magical. It's also educational and accessible to those who register for special tours and classes. There are natural, technical, and artistic adventures awaiting kids ages 10 to 15. "Exploring Nature" involves visiting a cypress swamp, meeting alligators, and exploring Epcot's "Living Seas" pavilion behind the scenes. Disney animators take part in the course, "Art Magic: Bringing Illusion to Life." The class also looks into costuming, set design, landscaping, and architecture. "Show Biz Magic" gives kids a chance to participate in staging, lighting, costumes, and, possibly, performing. Classroom materials and lunch are included in the fee for the six-hour programs that run for three or four days. Parents who are feeling left out can sign up for backstage tours of Epcot. Classes are small, so register well in advance.

FAMILY REUNION

Start a tradition if you don't have one; liven it up if you do. Plan a summer picnic or a winter rendezvous at a resort. What could be better than helping your children know their family? Meeting second, third, fourth, or even tenth cousins and swapping tall tales could be the ultimate family vacation. Even if it's just a weekend with your immediate family, plan it as a reunion (regular holiday celebrations don't count).

✑CONNECTIONS

Books:
Do People Grow on Family Trees? Genealogy for Kids and Other Beginners by Ira Wolfman. 1991. Workman, paper, $9.95.

Videos:

Make a Family Video Album. Produced by Christopher Stanton for Edgewater Productions, $19.95.

Audio:

Family Tree by Tom Chapin. (See Audio.)

RESOURCES

The Air and Space Catalog: The Complete Sourcebook for Everything in the Universe edited by Joel Makower. 1989. Random House, $27.50; paper, $16.95.

Baseball Vacations: A Guide to Big League Teams, Towns, & Tickets by Daniel P. George. 1991. Bon A Tirer Publishing (P.O. Box 3480, Shawnee, KN 66203), $12.95.

Family Sports Adventures: Exciting Vacations for Parents and Kids to Share by Megan Stine. 1991. A Sports Illustrated for Kids Book from The Time, Inc. Co., $9.95.

The Family Travel Times. A newsletter published by TWYCH (Travel with Your Children), 80 Eighth Avenue, New York, NY 10011.

Fielding's Lewis & Clark Trail by Gerald Olmsted. 1986. Fielding Travel Books, paper, $12.95.

Floating Vacations: River, Lake, and Ocean Adven- tures by Michael White. 1990. John Muir, $17.95.

Great Vacations with Your Kids by Dorothy Jordan and Marjorie Cohen. 1990. Penguin, $12.95.

Historic Landmarks of Black America by George Cantor. 1991. Gale, $29.95.

Indian America: A Traveler's Companion by Eagle Walking Turtle. 1989. John Muir, $16.95.

Recommended Family Resorts by Jane Wilford with Janet Tice. 1990. Globe Pequot Press, $12.95.

Super Family Vacations: Resort and Adventure Guide by Martha Shirk and Nancy Klepper. 1989. HarperCollins, $12.95.

The Traveler's Guide to Baseball Spring Training by John Garrity. 1991. Andrews and McMeel, $9.95.

INDEX

Pages numbers in **boldface** refer to main entries in respective sections for books, magazines, audiotapes, videotapes, software, toys, and travel ideas.

A

Brackets follow all titles of children's materials as follows: [A] = audio, [B] = book, [M] = magazine, [S] = software, [To] = toy, [Tr] = travel, [V] = video.

Brackets follow all titles of children's materials as follows: [A] = audio, [B] = book, [M] = magazine, [S] = software, [To] = toy, [Tr] = travel, [V] = video.

Brackets follow all titles of children's materials as follows: [A] = audio, [B] = book, [M] = magazine, [S] = software, [To] = toy, [Tr] = travel, [V] = video.

Brackets follow all titles of children's materials as follows: [A] = audio, [B] = book, [M] = magazine, [S] = software, [To] = toy, [Tr] = travel, [V] = video.

Brackets follow all titles of children's materials as follows: [A] = audio, [B] = book, [M] = magazine, [S] = software, [To] = toy, [Tr] = travel, [V] = video.

Brackets follow all titles of children's materials as follows: [A] = audio, [B] = book, [M] = magazine, [S] = software, [To] = toy, [Tr] = travel, [V] = video.

E

Brackets follow all titles of children's materials as follows: [A] = audio, [B] = book, [M] = magazine, [S] = software, [To] = toy, [Tr] = travel, [V] = video.

F

Brackets follow all titles of children's materials as follows: [A] = audio, [B] = book, [M] = magazine, [S] = software, [To] = toy, [Tr] = travel, [V] = video.

G

Brackets follow all titles of children's materials as follows: [A] = audio, [B] = book, [M] = magazine, [S] = software, [To] = toy, [Tr] = travel, [V] = video.

Brackets follow all titles of children's materials as follows: [A] = audio, [B] = book, [M] = magazine, [S] = software, [To] = toy, [Tr] = travel, [V] = video.

Brackets follow all titles of children's materials as follows: [A] = audio, [B] = book, [M] = magazine, [S] = software, [To] = toy, [Tr] = travel, [V] = video.

Brackets follow all titles of children's materials as follows: [A] = audio, [B] = book, [M] = magazine, [S] = software, [To] = toy, [Tr] = travel, [V] = video.

L

Brackets follow all titles of children's materials as follows: [A] = audio, [B] = book, [M] = magazine, [S] = software, [To] = toy, [Tr] = travel, [V] = video.

M

Brackets follow all titles of children's materials as follows: [A] = audio, [B] = book, [M] = magazine, [S] = software, [To] = toy, [Tr] = travel, [V] = video.

Brackets follow all titles of children's materials as follows: [A] = audio, [B] = book, [M] = magazine, [S] = software, [To] = toy, [Tr] = travel, [V] = video.

Brackets follow all titles of children's materials as follows: [A] = audio, [B] = book, [M] = magazine, [S] = software, [To] = toy, [Tr] = travel, [V] = video.

N

O

Brackets follow all titles of children's materials as follows: [A] = audio, [B] = book, [M] = magazine, [S] = software, [To] = toy, [Tr] = travel, [V] = video.

Brackets follow all titles of children's materials as follows: [A] = audio, [B] = book, [M] = magazine, [S] = software, [To] = toy, [Tr] = travel, [V] = video.

Q

R

Brackets follow all titles of children's materials as follows: [A] = audio, [B] = book, [M] = magazine, [S] = software, [To] = toy, [Tr] = travel, [V] = video.

S

Brackets follow all titles of children's materials as follows: [A] = audio, [B] = book, [M] = magazine, [S] = software, [To] = toy, [Tr] = travel, [V] = video.

Brackets follow all titles of children's materials as follows: [A] = audio, [B] = book, [M] = magazine, [S] = software, [To] = toy, [Tr] = travel, [V] = video.

Brackets follow all titles of children's materials as follows: [A] = audio, [B] = book, [M] = magazine, [S] = software, [To] = toy, [Tr] = travel, [V] = video.

Brackets follow all titles of children's materials as follows: [A] = audio, [B] = book, [M] = magazine, [S] = software, [To] = toy, [Tr] = travel, [V] = video.

BEST OF THE BEST FOR CHILDREN

Brackets follow all titles of children's materials as follows: [A] = audio, [B] = book, [M] = magazine, [S] = software, [To] = toy, [Tr] = travel, [V] = video.

Brackets follow all titles of children's materials as follows: [A] = audio, [B] = book, [M] = magazine, [S] = software, [To] = toy, [Tr] = travel, [V] = video.

Y

Z